The Guide of the Perplexed of Maimonides, Volume 1

You are holding a reproduction of an original work that is in the public domain in the United States of America, and possibly other countries. You may freely copy and distribute this work as no entity (individual or corporate) has a copyright on the body of the work. This book may contain prior copyright references, and library stamps (as most of these works were scanned from library copies). These have been scanned and retained as part of the historical artifact.

This book may have occasional imperfections such as missing or blurred pages, poor pictures, errant marks, etc. that were either part of the original artifact, or were introduced by the scanning process. We believe this work is culturally important, and despite the imperfections, have elected to bring it back into print as part of our continuing commitment to the preservation of printed works worldwide. We appreciate your understanding of the imperfections in the preservation process, and hope you enjoy this valuable book.

THE ENGLISH AND FOREIGN PHILOSOPHICAL LIBRARY.

Vol. IX.]   Post 8vo, pp. xviii.—198, cloth, 7s. 6d.

A CANDID EXAMINATION OF THEISM.

By PHYSICUS.

"An essay of marked ability that does not belie its title."—*Mind.*

"On the whole a candid, acute, and honest attempt to work out a problem which is of vast and perpetual interest."—*Scotsman.*

"It is impossible to go through this work without forming a very high opinion of his speculative and argumentative power, and a sincere respect for his temperance of statement and his diligent endeavour to make out the best case he can for the views he rejects."—*Academy.*

"This is a telling contribution to the question of questions. The author has pushed a step further than any one before him the bearing of modern science on the doctrine of Theism."—*Examiner.*

Vol. X.]   Post 8vo, pp. xii.—282, cloth, 10s. 6d.

THE COLOUR SENSE: Its Origin and Development.

AN ESSAY IN COMPARATIVE PSYCHOLOGY.

By GRANT ALLEN, B.A., Author of "Physiological Æsthetics."

"The book is attractive throughout, for its object is pursued with an earnestness and singleness of purpose which never fail to maintain the interest of the reader."—*Saturday Review.*

"A work of genuine research and bold originality."—*Westminster Review.*

"All these subjects are treated in a very thorough manner, with a wealth of illustration, a clearness of style, and a cogency of reasoning, which make up a most attractive volume."—*Nature.*

Vol. XI.]   Post 8vo, pp. xx.—316, cloth, 10s. 6d.

THE PHILOSOPHY OF MUSIC.

BEING THE SUBSTANCE OF

A COURSE OF LECTURES

DELIVERED AT THE ROYAL INSTITUTION OF GREAT BRITAIN, IN FEBRUARY AND MARCH 1877.

By WILLIAM POLE, Mus. Doc. Oxon.

Fellow of the Royal Societies of London and Edinburgh; one of the Examiners in Music to the University of London.

"We may recommend it as an extremely useful compendium of modern research into the scientific basis of music. There is no want of completeness."—*Pall Mall Gazette.*

"The book must be interesting to all musical students, and to candidates for the musical degrees at London University (where the author is an examiner) it will be indispensable."—*Tonic-Sol-fa Reporter.*

"The 'Philosophy of Music' will be read with eagerness by a large class of readers who might turn over with a certain impatience the laboriously reasoned pages of Helmholtz."—*Musical Times.*

THE ENGLISH AND FOREIGN PHILOSOPHICAL LIBRARY.

Vol. XII.]   Post 8vo, pp. 168, cloth, 6s.

CONTRIBUTIONS TO THE HISTORY OF THE DEVELOPMENT OF THE HUMAN RACE.

LECTURES AND DISSERTATIONS

By LAZARUS GEIGER,

Author of "Origin and Evolution of Human Speech and Reason."

Translated from the Second German Edition by DAVID ASHER, Ph.D.,
Corresponding Member of the Berlin Society for the Study
of Modern Languages and Literature.

"The papers translated in this volume deal with various aspects of a very fascinating study. Herr Geiger had secured a place in the foremost ranks of German philologers, but he seems to have valued his philological researches chiefly as a means of throwing light on the early condition of mankind. He prosecuted his inquiries in a thoroughly philosophical spirit, and he never offered a theory, however paradoxical it might seem at first sight, for which he did not advance solid arguments. Unlike the majority of German scholars, he took pleasure in working out his doctrines in a manner that was likely to make them interesting to the general public; and his capacity for clear and attractive exposition was hardly inferior to that of Mr. Max Müller himself."—*St. James's Gazette.*

Vol. XIII.]   Post 8vo, pp. 350, with a Portrait, cloth, 10s. 6d.

DR. APPLETON: His Life and Literary Relics.

By JOHN H. APPLETON, M.A.,

Late Vicar of St. Mark's, Staplefield, Sussex;

AND

A. H. SAYCE, M.A.,

Fellow of Queen's College, and Deputy Professor of Comparative Philology, Oxford.

"Although the life of Dr. Appleton was uneventful, it is valuable as illustrating the manner in which the speculative and the practical can be combined. His biographers talk of his geniality, his tolerance, his kindliness, and these characteristics, combined with his fine intellectual gifts, his searching analysis, his independence, his ceaseless energy and ardour, render his life specially interesting."—*Nonconformist.*

Vol. XIV.]   Post 8vo, pp. xxvi.—370, with Portrait, Illustrations, and an Autograph Letter, cloth, 12s. 6d.

EDGAR QUINET:

HIS EARLY LIFE AND WRITINGS.

By RICHARD HEATH.

"La plante est visible dans son germe. Et qui ne voudrait, s'il le pouvait, voir un monde dans l'embryon."—*Histoire de mes Idées.*

"Without attaching the immense value to Edgar Quinet's writings which Mr. Heath considers their due, we are quite ready to own that they possess solid merits which, perhaps, have not attracted sufficient attention in this country. To a truly reverent spirit, Edgar Quinet joined the deepest love for humanity in general. Mr. Heath . . . deserves credit for the completeness and finish of the portraiture to which he set his hand. It has evidently been a labour of love, for the text is marked throughout by infinite painstaking, both in style and matter."—*Globe.*

THE ENGLISH AND FOREIGN PHILOSOPHICAL LIBRARY.

VOL. XV.] Second Edition, post 8vo, cloth, 7s. 6d.

THE ESSENCE OF CHRISTIANITY.

By LUDWIG FEUERBACH.

Translated from the Second German Edition by MARIAN EVANS, Translator of Strauss's "Life of Jesus."

"I confess that to Feuerbach I owe a debt of inestimable gratitude. Feeling about in uncertainty for the ground, and finding everywhere shifting sands, Feuerbach cast a sudden blaze into the darkness, and disclosed to me the way."
—*From S. Baring-Gould's "The Origin and Development of Religious Belief," Part II., Preface, page* xii.

VOL. XVI.] Third Edition, revised, post 8vo, pp. 200, cloth, 3s. 6d.

AUGUSTE COMTE AND POSITIVISM.

By the late JOHN STUART MILL, M.P.

VOL. XVII.] Post 8vo, pp. xliv.—216, cloth, 7s. 6d.

ESSAYS AND DIALOGUES OF GIACOMO LEOPARDI.

Translated from the Italian, with Biographical Sketch, by CHARLES EDWARDES.

"He was one of the most extraordinary men whom this century has produced, both in his powers, and likewise in his performances."—*Quarterly Review.*
"This is a good piece of work to have done, and Mr. Edwardes deserves praise both for intention and execution."—*Athenæum.*
"Gratitude is due to Mr. Edwardes for an able portraiture of one of the saddest figures in literary history, and an able translation of his less inviting and less known works."—*Academy.*
SCHOPENHAUER writes:—"No one has treated the subject (The Misery of Life) so thoroughly and exhaustively as Leopardi in our own days. He is wholly filled and fermented with it; everywhere the mockery and misery of this existence are his theme; on every page of his works he represents them, but with such diversity of form and expression, with such wealth of illustration, that he never wearies, but rather entertains and stimulates us throughout."

VOL. XVIII.] Post 8vo, pp. xii.—178, cloth, 6s.

RELIGION AND PHILOSOPHY IN GERMANY:

A FRAGMENT.

By HEINRICH HEINE.

Translated by JOHN SNODGRASS,
Translator of " Wit, Wisdom, and Pathos from the Prose of Heinrich Heine."

"Nowhere is the singular charm of this writer more marked than in the vivid pages of this work. . . . Irrespective of subject, there is a charm about whatever Heine wrote that captivates the reader and wins his sympathies before criticism steps in. But there can be none who would fail to admit the power as well as the beauty of the wide-ranging pictures of the intellectual development of the country of deep thinkers. Beneath his grace the writer holds a mighty grip of fact, stripped of all disguise and made patent over all confusing surroundings."—*Bookseller.*
"No better selection could have been made from the prose writings of an author who, though until lately known in this country only, or at least chiefly, as a song-writer, produced as much German prose as fills nearly a score of volumes."—*North British Daily Mail.*

THE ENGLISH AND FOREIGN PHILOSOPHICAL LIBRARY.

VOL. XIX.] Post 8vo, pp. xviii.—310, with Portrait, cloth, 10s. 6d.

EMERSON AT HOME AND ABROAD.

By MONCURE D. CONWAY.
Author of "The Sacred Anthology," "The Wandering Jew," "Thomas Carlyle," &c.

This book reviews the personal and general history of the so-called "Transcendental" movement in America; and it contains various letters by Emerson not before published, as well as personal recollections of his lectures and conversations.

". . . The loftiest, purest, and most penetrating spirit that had ever shone in American literature."—*Professor Tyndall.*

"Almost all Americans appear to be agreed that Emerson holds the foremost place in the history of their national literature. . . . For more than thirty years Mr. Conway was intimately acquainted with Emerson, from whom, in truth, he received much kindness; and he has been able to record in a clear and attractive style his recollections of his friend's character and modes of thought as they revealed themselves at different periods in daily intercourse. Mr. Conway has not, however, confined himself to personal reminiscences; he brings together all the important facts of Emerson's life, and presents a full account of his governing ideas—indicating their mutual relations, and tracing the processes by which Emerson gradually arrived at them in their mature form."—*St. James's Gazette.*

VOL. XX.] Fifteenth Edition. Post 8vo, pp. xx.—314, cloth, 10s. 6d.

ENIGMAS OF LIFE.

By W. R. GREG.

Contents:—Realisable Ideals — Malthus Notwithstanding — Non-Survival of the Fittest—Limits and Directions of Human Development—The Significance of Life—De Profundis—Elsewhere—Appendix.

"What is to be the future of the human race? What are the great obstacles in the way of progress? What are the best means of surmounting these obstacles? Such, in rough statement, are some of the problems which are more or less present to Mr. Greg's mind; and although he does not pretend to discuss them fully, he makes a great many observations about them, always expressed in a graceful style, frequently eloquent, and occasionally putting old subjects in a new light, and recording a large amount of reading and study."—*Saturday Review.*

VOL. XXI.] Post 8vo, pp. 328, cloth, 10s. 6d.

ETHIC

DEMONSTRATED IN GEOMETRICAL ORDER AND DIVIDED INTO FIVE PARTS,

WHICH TREAT

    I. OF GOD.
   II. OF THE NATURE AND ORIGIN OF THE MIND.
  III. OF THE ORIGIN AND NATURE OF THE AFFECTS.
  IV. OF HUMAN BONDAGE, OR OF THE STRENGTH OF THE AFFECTS.
   V. OF THE POWER OF THE INTELLECT, OR OF HUMAN LIBERTY.

By BENEDICT DE SPINOZA.

Translated from the Latin by WILLIAM HALE WHITE.

"Mr. White's translation, though it is not, perhaps, so polished in some parts as it might have been, is faithful, clear, and effective. . . . We can only express the hope that the book may meet with the acceptance it deserves."—*British Quarterly Review.*

"Mr. White only lays claim to accuracy, the Euclidian form of the work giving but small scope for literary finish. We have carefully examined a number of passages with the original, and have in every case found the sense correctly given in fairly readable English. For the purposes of study it may in most cases replace the original; more Mr. White could not claim or desire."—*Athenæum.*

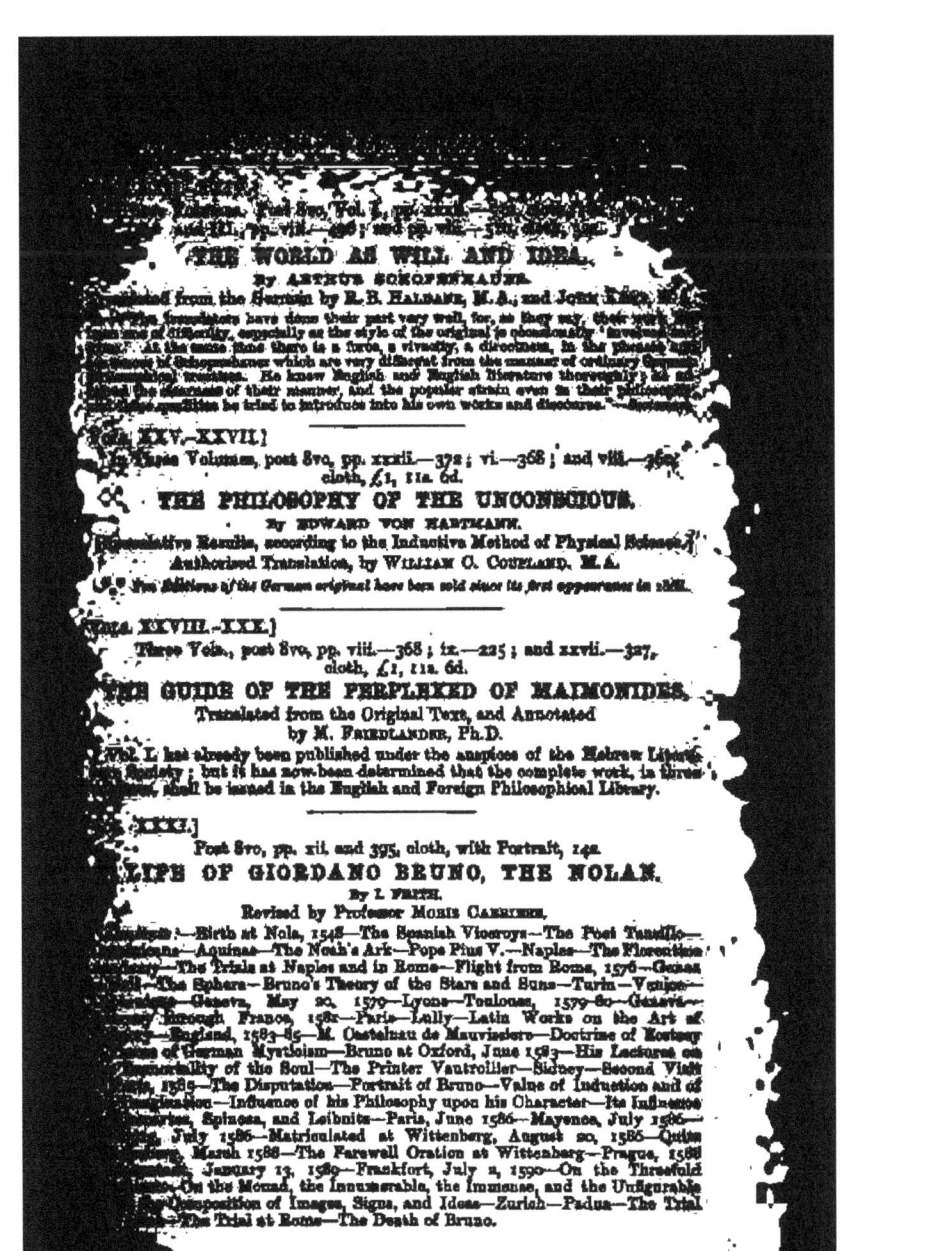

Volumes, Post 8vo, Vol. I., pp. xxxii—372; Vol. II., pp. vi—368; and Vol. III., pp. viii—360, cloth, £1, 11s. 6d.

THE WORLD AS WILL AND IDEA.

By ARTHUR SCHOPENHAUER.

Translated from the German by R. B. HALDANE, M.A., and JOHN KEMP, M.A.

"The translators have done their part very well, for, as they say, their work has been one of difficulty, especially as the style of the original is occasionally involved and loose. At the same time there is a force, a vivacity, a directness, in the phrases and sentences of Schopenhauer which are very different from the manner of ordinary German (philosophical) treatises. He knew English and English literature thoroughly; he admired the clearness of their manner, and the popular strain even in their philosophical writers; qualities he tried to introduce into his own works and discourse."—*Scotsman.*

[Vols. XXV.-XXVII.]

Three Volumes, post 8vo, pp. xxxii—372; vi.—368; and viii.—360, cloth, £1, 11s. 6d.

THE PHILOSOPHY OF THE UNCONSCIOUS.

By EDWARD VON HARTMANN.

Speculative Results, according to the Inductive Method of Physical Science. Authorised Translation, by WILLIAM C. COUPLAND, M.A.

*** Nine Editions of the German original have been sold since its first appearance in 1868.

[Vols. XXVIII.-XXX.]

Three Vols., post 8vo, pp. viii.—368; ix.—225; and xxvii.—327, cloth, £1, 11s. 6d.

THE GUIDE OF THE PERPLEXED OF MAIMONIDES.

Translated from the Original Text, and Annotated by M. FRIEDLANDER, Ph.D.

Vol. I. has already been published under the auspices of the Hebrew Literary Society; but it has now been determined that the complete work, in three volumes, shall be issued in the English and Foreign Philosophical Library.

[XXXI.]

Post 8vo, pp. xii. and 395, cloth, with Portrait, 14s.

LIFE OF GIORDANO BRUNO, THE NOLAN.

By I. FRITH.

Revised by Professor MORIZ CARRIERE.

Contents:—Birth at Nola, 1548—The Spanish Viceroys—The Poet Tansillo—Dominicans—Aquinas—The Noah's Ark—Pope Pius V.—Naples—The Florentine Academy—The Trials at Naples and in Rome—Flight from Rome, 1576—Genoa—Noli—The Sphere—Bruno's Theory of the Stars and Suns—Turin—Venice—Padua—Geneva, May 20, 1579—Lyons—Toulouse, 1579-80—Geneva—Journey through France, 1581—Paris—Lully—Latin Works on the Art of Memory—England, 1583-85—M. Castelnau de Mauvissière—Doctrine of Ecstasy—Source of German Mysticism—Bruno at Oxford, June 1583—His Lectures on the Immortality of the Soul—The Printer Vautrollier—Sidney—Second Visit to Paris, 1585—The Disputation—Portrait of Bruno—Value of Induction and of Imagination—Influence of his Philosophy upon his Character—Its Influence on Descartes, Spinoza, and Leibnitz—Paris, June 1586—Mayence, July 1586—Wittenberg, July 1586—Matriculated at Wittenberg, August 20, 1586—Quits Wittenberg, March 1588—The Farewell Oration at Wittenberg—Prague, 1588—Helmstadt, January 13, 1589—Frankfort, July 2, 1590—On the Threshold of Death—On the Monad, the Innumerable, the Immense, and the Unfigurable—The Composition of Images, Signs, and Ideas—Zurich—Padua—The Trial at Venice—The Trial at Rome—The Death of Bruno.

THE ENGLISH AND FOREIGN PHILOSOPHICAL LIBRARY.

EXTRA SERIES.

Two Volumes, post 8vo, pp. xxii.—328 and xvi.—358, with Portrait, cloth, 21s.

LESSING: His Life and Writings.
By JAMES SIME, M.A.
Second Edition.

"It is to Lessing that an Englishman would turn with readiest affection. We cannot but wonder that more of this man is not known amongst us."—THOMAS CARLYLE.

"But to Mr. James Sime has been reserved the honour of presenting to the English public a full-length portrait of Lessing, in which no portion of the canvas is uncovered, and in which there is hardly a touch but tells. We can say that a clearer or more compact piece of biographic criticism has not been produced in England for many a day."—*Westminster Review.*

"An account of Lessing's life and work on the scale which he deserves is now for the first time offered to English readers. Mr. Sime has performed his task with industry, knowledge, and sympathy; qualities which must concur to make a successful biographer."—*Pall Mall Gazette.*

"This is an admirable book. It lacks no quality that a biography ought to have. Its method is excellent, its theme is profoundly interesting: its tone is the happiest mixture of sympathy and discrimination: its style is clear, masculine, free from effort or affectation, yet eloquent by its very sincerity."—*Standard.*

"He has given a life of Lessing clear, interesting, and full, while he has given a study of his writings which bears distinct marks of an intimate acquaintance with his subject, and of a solid and appreciative judgment."—*Scotsman.*

In Three Volumes, post 8vo. Vol. I. pp. xvi.—248, cloth, 7s. 6d.; Vol. II. pp. viii.—400, cloth, 10s. 6d.; Vol. III. pp. xii.—292, cloth, 9s.

AN ACCOUNT OF THE POLYNESIAN RACE:
ITS ORIGIN AND MIGRATIONS,
AND THE ANCIENT HISTORY OF THE HAWAIIAN PEOPLE TO THE TIMES OF KAMEHAMEHA I.

By ABRAHAM FORNANDER, Circuit Judge of the Island of Maui, H.I.

"Mr. Fornander has evidently enjoyed excellent opportunities for promoting the study which has produced this work. Unlike most foreign residents in Polynesia, he has acquired a good knowledge of the language spoken by the people among whom he dwelt. This has enabled him, during his thirty-four years' residence in the Hawaiian Islands, to collect material which could be obtained only by a person possessing such an advantage. It is so seldom that a private settler in the Polynesian Islands takes an intelligent interest in local ethnology and archæology, and makes use of the advantage he possesses, that we feel especially thankful to Mr. Fornander for his labours in this comparatively little-known field of research."—*Academy.*

"Offers almost portentous evidence of the acquaintance of the author with the Polynesian customs and languages, and of his industry and erudite care in the analysis and comparison of the tongues spoken in the Pacific Archipelagoes."—*Scotsman.*

In Two Volumes, post 8vo, pp. viii.—408; viii.—402, cloth, 21s.

ORIENTAL RELIGIONS,
AND THEIR RELATION TO UNIVERSAL RELIGION.
By SAMUEL JOHNSON.
I.—INDIA.

LONDON: TRUBNER & CO., LUDGATE HILL.

PRINTED BY BALLANTYNE, HANSON AND CO.
EDINBURGH AND LONDON.

THE
ENGLISH AND FOREIGN
PHILOSOPHICAL LIBRARY.

VOLUME XXVIII.

מורה נבוכים שא שלומי עם שלום
כל יודעי דעת ופי סכלות בלום ׃
מכיר בערכו שור בטורי יהלם ׃
סורר ומורה סור ואל תקרב תלום:
[Brit. Mus. MSS. Add. 27,038.]

THE
GUIDE OF THE PERPLEXED

OF

MAIMONIDES,

TRANSLATED FROM THE ORIGINAL AND ANNOTATED

BY

M. FRIEDLÄNDER, Ph.D.

VOL. I.

LONDON:
TRÜBNER & CO., LUDGATE HILL.
1885.
[*All rights reserved.*]

PREFACE.

In compliance with a desire repeatedly expressed by the Committee of the Hebrew Literature Society, I have undertaken to translate Maimonides' *Dalalât al-Hairin*, better known by the Hebrew title *Moreh Nebhuchim*, and I offer the first instalment of my labours in the present volume. This contains—(1.) A short Life of Maimonides, in which special attention is given to his alleged apostasy. (2.) An analysis of the whole of the Moreh Nebhuchim. (3.) A translation of the First Part of this work from the Arabic, with explanatory and critical notes.

Parts of the Translation have been contributed by Mr. Joseph Abrahams, B.A., Ph. D., and Rev. H. Gollancz—the Introduction by the former, and the first twenty-five chapters by the latter.

In conclusion, I beg to tender my thanks to Rev. A. Loewy, Editor of the Publications of the Hebrew Literature Society, for his careful revision of my manuscript and proofs, and to Mr. A. Neubauer, M.A., for his kindness in supplying me with such information as I required.

M. FRIEDLÄNDER.

Jews' College, June, 1881.

CONTENTS.

	PAGE
Life of Maimonides...	ix
Note on Maimonides' Alleged Apostasy ...	xxxiii
Analysis of the Guide of the Perplexed—	
Introduction ...	xli
Part I. ...	1
„ II. ...	lx
„ III. ...	lxxii

THE GUIDE OF THE PERPLEXED.

Introduction—

Dedicatory Letter	1
The Object of the Guide ...	4
On Similes ...	10
Directions for the Study of this Work	20
Introductory Remarks	23

CHAPTER

I.—On תואר and דמות, צלם	28
II.—On Genesis iii. 5	33
III.—On תמונה and תבנית	39
IV.—On ראה, הבים, חזה	41
V.—On Exod. xxiv. 10	44
VI.—On איש and אשה, אח and אחות	47
VII.—On ילד	48
VIII.—On מקום	50
IX.—On כסא	53
X.—On ירד and עלה	54
XI.—On ישב	58
XII.—On קום	60
XIII.—On עמד	62
XIV.—On אדם	63

CHAPTER		PAGE
XV.—On נצב and יצב	...	64
XVI.—On צור	...	66
XVII.—On Mishnah Chagigah ii. 1	...	68
XVIII.—On נגע, קרב and נגש	...	69
XIX.—On מלא	...	73
XX.—On רם and נשא	...	74
XXI.—On עבר	...	76
XXII.—On בא	...	82
XXIII.—On יצא and שוב	...	84
XXIV.—On הלך	...	86
XXV.—On שכן	...	88
XXVI.—On דברי תורה כלשון בני אדם	...	89
XXVII.—On Targum of Gen. xlvi. 4	...	92
XXVIII.—On רגל	...	96
XXIX.—On עצב	...	102
XXX.—On אכל	...	103
XXXI., XXXII.—On the Limit of Man's Intellect	...	106
XXXIII. to XXXVI.—On the Study and Teaching of Metaphysics	...	114
XXXVII.—On פנים	...	135
XXXVIII.—On אחר	...	138
XXXIX.—On לב	...	139
XL.—On רוח	...	141
XLI.—On נפש	...	143
XLII.—On חיים and מות	...	145
XLIII.—On כנף	...	147
XLIV.—On עין	...	149
XLV.—On שמע	...	150
XLVI., XLVII.—On the attribution of Senses and Sensations to God	...	151
XLVIII.—The Targum of שמע and ראה	...	164
XLIX.—Figurative Expressions applied to Angels	...	167
L.—On Faith	...	171
LI.—LX.—On Attributes—		
LI.—On the Necessity of Proving the Inadmissibility of Attributes in Reference to God	...	172
LII.—Classification of Attributes	...	178
LIII.—The Arguments of the Attributists	...	185

CONTENTS.

CHAPTER	PAGE
LIV.—On Exod. xxxiii. 13 ; xxxiv. 7	191
LV.—On Attributes Implying Corporeality, Emotion, Non-existence and Comparison ...	199
LVI.—On Attributes denoting Existence, Life, Power, Wisdom, and Will	201
LVII.—On the Identity of the Essence of God and His Attributes	203
LVIII.—On the Negative Sense of the True Attributes of God	207
LIX.—On the Character of the Knowledge of God Consisting of Negations	213
LX.—On the Difference between Positive and Negative Attributes	220
LXI.—On the Names of God	226
LXII.—On the Divine Names composed of Four, Twelve and Forty-two Letters	231
LXIII.—On Ehyeh, Yah and Shaddai	236
LXIV.—On "The Name of the Lord," and "The Glory of God"	241
LXV.—On the phrase "God spake"	243
LXVI.—On Exod. xxxii. 16	247
LXVII.—On שבת and נוח	249
LXVIII.—On the Terms : The Intellectus, the Intelligens and the Intelligibile	252
LXIX.—On the Primal Cause	259
LXX.—On רכב בערבות	265
LXXI.—The Origin of the *Kalām*	272
LXXII.—A Parallel between the Universe and Man	288
LXXIII.—Twelve Propositions of the *Kalām* ...	309
LXXIV.—Proofs of the *Kalām* for *the creatio ex nihilo*	343
LXXV.—Proofs of the *Kalām* for the Unity of God	355
LXXVI.—Proofs of the *Kalām* for the Incorporeality of God	362
Addenda and Corrigenda	369

THE LIFE OF MOSES MAIMONIDES.[1]

"Before the sun of Eli had set the sun of Samuel had risen."[2] Before the voice of the prophets had ceased to guide the people, the Interpreters of the Law, the Doctors of the Talmud, had commenced their labours, and before the Academies of Sura and of Pumbaditha were closed, centres of Jewish thought and learning were already flourishing in the far West. The circumstances which led to the transference of the head-quarters of Jewish learning from the East to the West in the tenth century are thus narrated in the *Sefer ha-kabbalah*[3] of Rabbi Abraham ben David:

"After the death of Hezekiah, the head of the Academy and Prince of the Exile,[4] the academies were closed and no new Geonim were appointed. But long before that time Heaven had willed that there should be a discontinuance

---

[1] Comp. Peter Beer, "Leben und Wirken des Maimonides," Prague, 1834; Geiger, "Zeitschrift," I., pp. 97 *sqq*., 210 *sqq*., 414 *sqq*.; II., 127 *sqq*., 564 *sqq*.; Geiger, Moses ben Maimon, Breslau, 1850; Jost, "Annalen," 1839, 308 *sqq*. 1840, 32 *sqq*.; Orient, L. Bl., 1846, pp. 338, 350, 355, 375, 377; Jost, Geschichte der Israeliten, VI., ch. 6, page 166 *sqq*.; Geschichte des Judenthums, II., 430 *sqq*.; Munk, Notice sur Joseph b. Jehouda, 1842; Archives Israelites, 1851, pag. 319; Grätz, Geschichte der Juden, VI., ch. x., pag. 310 *sqq*.; A. Benisch, Two Lectures on the Life and Writings of Maimonides; Steinschneider, Cat. Bodl. *sub voce*; Weiss, Beth Talmud, I., No. 6 *sqq*., page 161 *sqq*.

[2] Babyl. Talmud, Yoma 38a.

[3] "The Book of the Tradition," ed. Basel, 1580, page 69a. The author wrote this book (1160) in order to show, in opposition to the Karaites, that there was a continuous chain of tradition from the Prophets to the author's time. He died as a martyr, 1180.

[4] Resh-galutha, or, in Hebrew, Rosh ha-golah. The Resh-galutha was recognised by the Persian king as the chief of the Jews in the Persian dominions; he collected the taxes, appointed officers and judges, but rarely interfered with the proceedings in the schools. According to *Seder olam sutta*, the Princes of the Exile were descendants of the kings of Judah.

of the pecuniary gifts which used to be sent from Palestine, North Africa and Europe. Heaven had also decreed that a ship sailing from Bari should be captured by Ibn Romahis, commander of the naval forces of Abd-er-rahmanal-nasr. Four distinguished Rabbis were thus made prisoners—Rabbi Chushiel, father of Rabbi Chananel, Rabbi Moses, father of Rabbi Chanoch, Rabbi Shemarjahu, son of Rabbi Elchanan, and a fourth whose name has not been recorded. They were engaged in a mission to collect subsidies in aid of the Academy in Sura.[1] The captor sold them as slaves; Rabbi Chushiel was carried to Kairuan, R. Shemarjahu was left in Alexandria, and R. Moses was brought to Cordova. These slaves were ransomed by their brethren and were soon placed in important positions. When Rabbi Moses was brought to Cordova, it was supposed that he was uneducated. In that city there was a synagogue known at that time by the name of *Keneseth ha-midrash*,[2] and Rabbi Nathan, renowned for his great piety, was the head[3] of the congregation. The members of the community used to hold meetings at which the Talmud was read and discussed. One day when Rabbi Nathan was expounding the Talmud and was unable to give a satisfactory explanation of the passage under discussion, Rabbi Moses promptly removed the difficulty and at the same time answered several questions which were submitted to him. Thereupon R. Nathan thus addressed the assembly :—' I am no longer your leader; that stranger in sackcloth shall henceforth be my teacher, and you shall appoint him to be your chief.' The admiral on hearing of the high attainments of his

[1] The Hebrew text has *hachnasath-kallah*; the original meaning of the term is, "assisting a bride in the preparation for her wedding"; but as *kalla* was the designation for the meetings of the scholars in the months of Adar and Ellul, and *reshe-challe* were the heads or presidents of these meetings, the author employed the term hachnasath-kallah in the above sense.

[2] "Assembly for study."

[3] Lit., "Judge." The office of a rabbi included that of a judge. The court was usually formed of three scholars; the president was probably the dayyan, or judge; the other two were called chabherim (colleagues).

prisoner, desired to revoke the sale, but the king would not permit this retraction, being pleased to learn that his Jewish subjects were no longer dependent for their religious instruction on the schools in the East."

Henceforth the schools in the West asserted their independence, and even surpassed the parent institutions. The Caliphs, mostly opulent, gave every encouragement to philosophy and poetry; and, being generally liberal in sentiment, they entertained kindly feelings towards their Jewish subjects. These were allowed to compete for the acquisition of wealth and honour on equal terms with their Mahometan fellow-citizens. Philosophy and poetry were consequently cultivated by the Jews with the same zest as by the Arabs. Ibn Gabirol, Ibn Chasdai, Juda ha-levi, Chananel, Alfasi, the Ibn Ezras and others who flourished in that period were the ornaments of their age, and became the pride of their brethren. The same favourable condition was maintained during the reign of the Omeyades[1]; but when the Moravides[2] and the Almohades[3] came into power, the horizon darkened once more, and misfortunes threatened to destroy the fruit of several centuries. Amidst this gloom there appeared a brilliant luminary which sent forth rays of life and comfort: this was Maimonides.

Moses, the son of Maimon,[4] was born at Cordova, on

[1] Abd-er-rahman, a grandson of the Calif Hisham, escaped into Spain after the defeat of the Omeyades by the Abassides, and founded there the Califat of Cordova, 756. His descendants reigned till 1086.

[2] The Moravides who had established themselves in Africa, and had founded there Morocco, 1070, were invited by the Omeyades to come over to Spain, and to fight as their allies against the Christians; but they took possession of the country for themselves, and kept it till they were displaced by the Almohades, 1148.

[3] The Almohades ("Confessors of the Unity" of God) were a Mahometan sect founded by Ibn Tamurt, the Mahadi, 1120. Their power was increased and established in Maghreb and Spain by Abd-el-mumen (1130-1163), the successor of Ibn Tamurt.

[4] Maimonides is also called Rabbi Mosheh ha-sefardi, Mosheh b. Obed Elohim ha-cordovi ha-yisreeli, Abu Amran Musa ben Maimun al-Cordovi al-Israëli, Abd-allah, and by other names. See Steinschneider, Bodl. Catal., *sub voce*.

the 14th of Nisan, 4895 (30th March, 1135).[1] Although the date of his birth has been recorded with the utmost accuracy, no trustworthy notice has been preserved concerning the early period of his life. But his entire career is a proof that he did not pass his youth in idleness; his education must have been in harmony with the hope of his parents,[2] that one day he would, like his father and forefathers,[3] hold the honourable office of *Dayyan*[4] or *Rabbi*, and distinguish himself in theological learning. It is probable that the Bible and the Talmud formed the chief subjects of his study; but he unquestionably made the best use of the opportunities which Mahometan Spain, and especially Cordova, afforded him for the acquisition of general knowledge. It is not mentioned in any of his writings who were his teachers; his father, as it seems, was his principal guide and instructor in many branches of knowledge. David Conforte, in his historical work, *Kore ha-doroth*, states that Maimonides was the pupil of two eminent men, namely, Rabbi Joseph ibn Migash[5]

[1] This date is given by Rabbi David, a grandson of Maimonides, in a postscript to Maimonides' Commentary on the Babyl. Talmud, Rosh ha-shanah. From a note appended to the Commentary on the Mishnah it might be inferred that he was born in 1138; for, according to that note, the Commentary was completed in the author's thirtieth year, = 1479 Sel. = 4928 M. = 1168. In order to reconcile these two statements it has been suggested that a copyist wrote שלשים (30) instead of שלשים ושש (33) in the second statement. Other dates mentioned in Yuchasin, in *maamar al seder ha-doroth* by Saadiah ibn Danan (Edelman, Chemdah genuzah, pag. 30), and in other works may therefore be disregarded. See Geiger, Zeitschrift I., pag. 106-107.

[2] According to Shalsheleth ha-kabbalah of R. Gedaliah b. Yachyah, Maimonides in his youth appeared dull and disinclined to study.

[3] In the postscript to the Comm. on the Mishnah the author gives the following pedigree: Moses, the son of Maimon, dayyan, son of the learned R. Joseph, son of R. Isaac, dayyan, son of R. Joseph, dayyan, son of R. Obadiah, dayyan, son of R. Shelomoh, son of R. Obadiah. According to Azulai in his biographical work, *Shem ha-gedolim*, Maimonides was a descendant of Rabbi Jehudah ha-nasi. [4] See pag. x., note 2.

[5] Joseph Ibn Migash was born 1077; he died 1141. When 26 years old he was elected Rabbi of the Congregation in Lucena. He is the author of Chiddushim (notes) on various treatises of the Talmud. His Responses have partly been collected and published (Azulai *sub voce*). Maimonides, in quoting

and Ibn Roshd (Averroes)[1]; that by the former he was instructed in the Talmud, and by the latter in philosophy. This statement seems to be erroneous, as Maimonides was only a child at the time when Rabbi Joseph died, and already far advanced in years[2] when he became acquainted with the writings of Ibn Roshd. The origin of this mistake, as regards Rabbi Joseph, can easily be traced. Maimonides, in his Mishne thorah, employs, in reference to R. Isaac Alfasi and R. Joseph, the expression "my teachers" (*rabbothai*), and this expression, by which he merely describes his indebtedness to their writings, has been taken in its literal meaning.

Whoever his teachers may have been, it is evident that he was well prepared by them for his future mission. At the age of twenty-three he entered upon his literary career with a treatise on the Jewish Calendar.[3] It is unknown where this work was composed, whether in Spain or in Africa. At the beginning of this treatise the author states that he wrote it at the request of a friend, whom he leaves unnamed. The subject was generally considered to

---

his decisions, employs the formula, וכן הורו רבתי, "and thus my teachers (*i.e.*, R. Joseph and his teacher Alfasi) decided."

[1] One of the greatest Arabic philosophers. He was born at Cordova, 1126; he died at Morocco, 1198. For his philosophy and works see Munk, Mélanges, etc. (418 *sqq*.); Rénan, "Averroes"; and Hercz, "Averroes, drei Abhandlungen" (Berlin, 1869).

[2] Comp. Letter addressed to his disciple, Ibn Aknin, ed. Goldberg in Birchath Abraham, Lyck, 1859. It is dated Rosh-chodesh Marcheshvan, 1503, Sel. = 1191.

[3] *Sefer* (or *maamar*, or *cheshbon*) *haïbbur*. The treatise consists of two parts: 1, On the *Molad* (conjunction of the moon); 2, On the *Tekufoth* (seasons of the year). In the first part the author shows how to calculate the *molad* of each month from certain data, viz., the first *molad* (בהר״ד, 2 days 6,$\frac{384}{1080}$ hours), and the space between two consecutive conjunctions: 29 d. 12,$\frac{793}{1080}$ h.; how to find what place a certain year occupies in the *machzor* (cycle of 19 years), and how to determine thereby the character of the year. In the second part the author shows how to find the beginning of a certain season (tekufah) of the year, assuming, according to the *tekufoth Shemuel*, each season to consist of 91¼ days. It is contained in Dibhre Chachamim of Eliezer of Tunis; also in Kobets teshubhoth Rambam, Leipzig, 1859, II., p. 17.

be very abstruse, and to involve a thorough knowledge of mathematics. Maimonides must, therefore, even at this early period, have been regarded as a profound scholar by those who knew him. It must, however, be owned that this treatise is of an elementary character.—It was probably about the same time that he wrote an explanation of Logical terms,[1] known by the Hebrew name of "Milloth higgayon."

The earlier period of his life does not seem to have been marked by any incident worth noticing. It may, however, be easily conceived that the later period of his life, which was replete with interesting incidents, engaged the exclusive attention of his biographers. So much is certain, that his youth was beset with trouble and anxiety; the peaceful development of science and philosophy was disturbed by wars raging between Mahometans and Christians, and also between the several Mahometan sects. The Moravides, who had succeeded the Omeyades, were opposed to liberality and toleration; but they were surpassed in cruelty and fanaticism by their successors. Cordova was taken by the Almohades in the year 1148, when Maimonides was about thirteen years old. The victories of the Almohades, first under the leadership of the Mahadi Ibn Tamurt, and then under Abd-al-mumen, were, according to all testimonies, attended by acts of excessive intolerance. Abd-al-mumen would not suffer in his dominions any other faith but the one which he himself confessed. Jews and Christians had the choice between Islam, emigration, or a martyr's death. The Sefer ha-kabbalah[2] contains the following description of one of the persecutions which then occurred:—

"After the death of R. Joseph ha-levi the study of the Torah was interrupted, although he left a son and a nephew, both of whom had under his tuition become profound scholars. 'The righteous man (R. Joseph) was taken

---

[1] The Arabic is מקאלת פי צנאעת אלמנטק; in Hebrew, מלות ההגיון. Moses Ibn Tibbon translated it into Hebrew. It has also been translated into Latin and German.   [2] Page 77a.

away on account of the approaching evils.' After the death of R. Joseph there came for the Jews a time of oppression and distress. They quitted their homes, 'Such as were for death, to death, and such as were for the sword, to the sword; and such as were for the famine, to the famine, and such as were for the captivity, to the captivity;' and—it might be added to the words of Jeremiah (xv. 2)—'such as were for apostasy, to apostasy.' All this happened through the sword of Ibn Tamurt, who, in 4902 (1142), determined to blot out the name of Israel, and actually left no trace of the Jews in any part of his empire."

Ibn Verga in his work on Jewish martyrdom, in Shebhet Jehudah,[1] gives the following account of events then happening:—"In the year 4902 the armies of Ibn Tamurt made their appearance. A proclamation was issued that any one who refused to adopt Islam would be put to death, and his property would be confiscated. Thereupon the Jews assembled at the gate of the royal palace and implored the king for mercy. He answered—'It is because I have compassion on you, that I command you to become Muslemim; for I desire to save you from eternal punishment.' The Jews replied—'Our salvation depends on our observance of the Divine Law; you are the master of our bodies and of our property, but our souls will be judged by the King who gave them to us, and to whom they will return; whatever be our future fate, you, O king, will not be held responsible for it.' 'I do not desire to argue with you,' said the king; 'for I know you will argue according to your own religion. It is my absolute will that you either adopt my religion or be put to death.' The Jews then proposed to emigrate, but the king would not allow his subjects to serve another king. In vain did the Jews implore the nobles to

[1] "The Rod of Judah," *ha-shemad ha-rebhii*, (fourth persecution), ed. Wiener, pag. 3. The book contains an account of the persecutions of the Jews. It was begun by Judah ibn Verga, and continued by his son Solomon, and by his grandson Joseph, Rabbi of Adrianople (1554). It has been translated into Jewish German (1591, 1648, 1700), into Spanish (1640), into Latin (1651), and into German (1856).

intercede in their behalf; the king remained inexorable. Thus many congregations forsook their religion; but within a month the king came to a sudden death; the son, believing that his father had met with an untimely end as a punishment for his cruelty to the Jews, assured the involuntary converts that it would be indifferent to him what religion they professed. Hence many Jews returned to the religion of their fathers, while others hesitated for some time, from fear that the king meant to entrap the apparent converts."

From such records it appears that during these calamities some of the Jews fled to foreign countries, some died as martyrs, and many others submitted for a time to outward conversion. What course was followed by the family of Maimon? Did they sacrifice personal comfort and safety to their religious conviction, or did they, on the contrary, for the sake of mere worldly considerations dissemble their faith and pretend that they completely submitted to the dictates of the tyrant? An answer to this question presents itself in the following note which Maimonides has appended to his commentary on the Mishnah: "I have now finished this work in accordance with my promise, and I fervently beseech the Almighty to save us from error. If there be one who shall discover an inaccuracy in this Commentary or shall have a better explanation to offer, let my attention be directed unto it; and let me be exonerated by the fact that I have worked with far greater application than any one who writes for the sake of pay and profit, and that I have worked under the most trying circumstances. For Heaven had ordained that we be exiled, and we were therefore driven about from place to place; I was thus compelled to work at the Commentary while travelling by land, or crossing the sea. It might have sufficed to mention that during that time I, in addition, was engaged in other studies, but I preferred to give the above explanation in order to encourage those who wish to criticise or annotate the Commentary, and at the same time to account for the slow progress of this work. I, Moses, the son of Maimon, commenced it when I was twenty-three years old, and finished it in Egypt, at the age of thirty [-three][1] years, in the year 1479 Sel. (1168)."

The Sefer Charedim[2] of R. Eleazar Askari of Safed contains the following statement of Maimonides: "On Sabbath evening, the 4th of Iyyar, 4925 (1165), I went on board; on the following Sabbath the waves threatened to destroy our lives.... On the 3rd of Sivan, I arrived safely at Acco, *and was thus rescued from apostasy*.... On Tuesday, the 4th of Marcheshvan, 4926, I left Acco, arrived at Jerusalem after a journey beset with difficulties and with dangers, and prayed on the spot of the great and holy house on the 4th, 5th, and 6th of Marcheshvan. On Sunday, the 9th of that month, I left Jerusalem and visited the cave of Machpelah, in Hebron."

From these two statements it may be inferred that in times of persecution Maimonides and his family did not seek to protect their lives and property by dissimulation. They submitted to the troubles of exile in order that they might remain faithful to their religion. Carmoly,[3] Geiger,[4] Munk,[5] and others are of opinion that the treatise of Maimonides on involuntary apostasy,[6] as well as the accounts of some Mahometan authors, contain strong evidence to show that there was a time when the family of Maimon[7] pub-

---

[1] See pag. xii., note 1.
[2] The *Sefer Charedim* treats of the 613 precepts, and pays especial attention to those which are still practised. It was written in 1588.
[3] Jost, Annalen, 1839, pag. 325 *sqq.*
[4] Moses b. Maimon, by A. Geiger, ed. S. Breslauer, Breslau, 1850.
[5] Notice sur Joseph b. Jehouda, Paris, 1842, and Archives Israelites, 1851, pag. 319 *sqq.*
[6] *Iggereth ha-shemad;* it is also called *Maamar kiddush ha-shem.* Ed. A. Geiger, Breslau, 1850; Edelman, Chemdah Genuzah, pag. 6.
[7] The same assertion has been made in reference to Joseph Ibn Aknin, the pupil of Maimonides. (See Munk, l.c.) Lebrecht (Magazin für die Lit. des Auslandes, 1844, n. 62) rejects the apostasy of Maimonides, but admits that of Ibn Aknin. In support of the theory that Ibn Aknin was for some time an apostate, the following lines of Charizi (50) are adduced:— חרש זמן אחרי־ בלותו · ורחץ במים טהורים · ופשט את בנדיו ולבש בגדים אחרים · וביום טהרתו לקח לו שני תורים · תור התורה ותור המשרה: In the change of

licly professed their belief in Mahomet. A critical examination[1] of these documents compels us to reject their evidence as inadmissible.—After a long period of trouble and anxiety, the family of Maimon arrived at Fostat,[2] in Egypt, and settled there. David, the brother of Moses Maimonides,[3] carried on a trade in precious stones, while Moses occupied himself with his studies and interested himself in the communal affairs of the Jews.[4]

It appears that for some time Moses was supported by his brother, and when this brother died, he earned a living by practising as a physician; but he never sought or derived any benefit from his services to his community, or from his correspondence or from the works he wrote for the instruction of his brethren;[5] the satisfaction of being of service to his fellow-creatures was for him a sufficient reward.

The first public act in which Maimonides appears to have taken a leading part was a decree promulgated by the Rabbinical authorities in Cairo in the year 1167.[6] The decree begins as follows:—" In times gone by, when storms and tempests threatened us, we used to wander about from place to place; but by the mercy of the Almighty we have now been enabled to find here a resting-place. On our arrival, we noticed to our great dismay that the learned were dis-

---

garments an allusion has been found to the change of religion. But it is far more probable that Charizi alludes here to the change of Ibn Aknin's occupation, to his retirement from mercantile speculations in order to devote himself entirely to instructing and guiding his fellow-men. Comp. Steinschneider, in Frankel's Monatsschrift, 1845.

[1] This examination is given in a note appended to this sketch (pag. xxxiii. and *sqq*.).

[2] In Hebrew *Mitsraim*, *Misr* in Arabic. Comp. The Travels of Benjamin of Tudela, ed. Asher, vol. II. pag. 197.

[3] Comp. Letter of Maimonides to R. Yepheth, Kobbets, etc. Part II. pag. 37. According to Alkifti Maimonides himself was engaged in this trade. This is refuted by Lebrecht, Magazin für die Literatur des Auslandes, 1845, No. 45.

[4] See Kobhets teshubhoth, etc., Part I. pag. 30a.

[5] Comp. Postscriptum to Comm. on the Mishnah.

[6] Kobhets theshubhoth, etc. Part I. pag. 30a.

united; that none of them turned his attention to what was going on in the congregation. We therefore felt it our duty to undertake the task of guiding the holy flock, of inquiring into the condition of the community, of reconciling the hearts of the fathers to their children, and of correcting their corrupt ways. The injuries are great, but we may succeed in effecting a cure, and—in accordance with the words of the prophet—'I will seek the lost one, and that which has been cast out I will bring back, and the broken one I will cure' (Micah iv. 6). When we therefore resolved to take the management of the communal affairs into our hands, we discovered the existence of a serious evil in the midst of the community," etc.

It was probably about that time that Maimon died. Letters of condolence were sent to his son Moses from all sides, both from Mahometan and from Christian countries; in some instances the letters were several months on their way before they reached their destination.[1]

The interest which Maimonides now took in communal affairs did not prevent him from completing the great and arduous work, the Commentary on the Mishnah,[2] which he had begun in Spain and continued during his wanderings in Africa. In this Commentary he proposed to give the quintessence of the Gemara, to expound the meaning of each dictum in the Mishnah, and to state which of the several opinions had received the sanction of the Talmudical authorities. His object in writing this work was to enable those who are not disposed to study the Gemara to understand the Mishnah, and to facilitate the study of the Gemara for those who are willing to engage in it. The commentator generally adheres to the explanations given in the Gemara, and it is only in cases where the *halachah*, or practical law, is not affected, that he ventures to dissent.[3]

---

[1] Letter to R. Yepheth, Kobheta, etc., Part II., pag. 37b.

[2] The original title is Kitab al-sirag', in Hebrew: Sefer ha-maor, "the luminary." It was finished 1168.

[3] See Z. Frankel, Hodegetica in Mishnam, pag. 320.

He acknowledges the benefit he derived from such works of his predecessors as the Halachoth of Alfasi, and the writings of the Geonim,[1] but afterwards he asserted that errors which were discovered in his works arose from his implicit reliance on those authorities.[2] His originality is conspicuous in the Introduction and in the treatment of general principles, which in some instances precedes the exposition of an entire section or chapter,[3] in others that of a single rule.[4] The commentator is generally concise, except when occasion is afforded to treat of ethical and theological principles,[5] or of a scientific subject, such as weights and measures, or mathematical and astronomical problems.[6] Although exhortations to virtue and warnings against vice are found in all parts of his work, they are especially abundant in the Commentary on Abhoth, which is prefaced by a separate psychological treatise, called "The Eight Chapters."[7] The dictum "He who speaketh much commits a sin," elicited a lesson on the economy of speech; the explanation of *olam ha-ba* in the treatise Sanhedrin (xi. 1) led him to discuss the principles of faith, and to lay down the thirteen articles of the Jewish creed. The Commentary was written in Arabic,[8] and was subsequently translated into

---

[1] Introduction to the Comm. on the Mishnah.

[2] *E.g.* The Megillath Setharim of R. Nissim and the Sefer ha-mitsvoth of R. Chefets. Letter addressed to his pupil Ibn Aknin, Kobhets, etc., Part II., pag. 31.

[3] *E.g.*, Introd. to Abhoth; Sanhedrin xi. (Chelek), Berachoth vii. ; Demai, i. ; Shebhiith, viii. ; Shabbath i., etc.

[4] *E.g.*, Shabbath x. 6; xi. 1; xix. 6, etc.; Baba-bathra v. 9; viii. 2; Sanhedrin viii. 6. These principles are generally introduced by the phrase והעקר אצלנו.

[5] *E.g.*, Berachoth ix. 5 and 7; Peah i. 1; it is remarkable that the author is exceedingly profuse on Abhoth i. 15, on the rule " speak little."

[6] *E.g.*, Berachoth, i. 1; Kilaïm iii. 1, 6; v. 5; Chullin, iii.; Rosh-hashanah, ii. 4, 7.

[7] שמונה פרקים להרמב״ם; translated into Hebrew from the Arabic original, and provided with an introduction by Samuel Ibn Tibbon. The original has been edited and translated into German by Dr. M. Wolf, Leipzig, 1863. The Hebrew translation has several times been translated into German and Latin.

[8] The introductions to the several parts were edited in the original, with a

Hebrew[1] and into other languages.[2] The estimation in which the Commentary was held may be inferred from the following fact: When the Jews in Italy became acquainted with its method and spirit, through a Hebrew translation of one of its parts, they sent to Spain in search of a complete Hebrew version of the Commentary.[3] R. Simcha, who had been entrusted with the mission, found no copy extant, but he succeeded, through the influence of Rabbi Shelomoh ben Adereth, in causing a Hebrew translation of this important work to be prepared.—In the Introduction, the author states that he has written a Commentary on the Babylonian Talmud treatise Chullin and on nearly three entire sections, viz., *Moëd, Nashim,* and *Nezikin.* Of all these Commentaries only the one on Rosh ha-shanah is known.[4]

In the year 1172 [5] Maimonides wrote the *Iggereth Teman,* or *Pethach-tikvah* ("Letter to the Jews in Yemen," or "Opening of hope") in response to a letter addressed to him by Rabbi Jacob al-Fayumi on the critical condition of the Jews in Yemen. Some of these Jews had been forced into apostasy; others were made to believe that certain passages in the

---

Latin translation and notes by E. Pococke, under the title Porta Mosis, Oxoniæ, 1655.

[1] The Hebrew translation was executed by several scholars, viz., the treatises Berachoth, Peah, Demai, Shebhiith, by Judah Charizi; the remainder of Seder Zeraïm and Seder Moëd by Joseph b. Isaak Ibn Alfual; Soder Nashim by Jacob ben Mose of Huesca; Seder Nezikin—with the exception of Abboth, which Samuel Ibn Tibbon translated—by Salomo ben Jacob of Saragossa; Seder Kodashim by Nathaniel b. Joseph of Saragossa; Seder Taharoth by an anonymous scholar.

[2] Into Latin by Surenhusius, and Spanish by Ruben ben Nachman, Abi Saglo.

[3] See Translator's Preface to Seder Moëd.

[4] Edited by T. Brill in the Hebrew Periodical Ha-lebhanon, Vol. VIII., page 199, *sqq.*

[5] The date is not given by Maimonides in this letter, but in a letter addressed to the Wise men of the Marseille congregation, which bears the date 11th Tishri, 1506 Sel. = October, 1194 (Geiger, Moses b. Maimon, note 47, pag. 66), the author says, twenty-two years ago I wrote to Yemen about the Messiah. Comp. The Travels of Benjamin of Tudela, ed. Asher, II. pag. 162.

Bible alluded to the mission of Mahomet;[1] others again had been misled by an impostor who pretended to be the Messiah.[2] The character and style of Maimonides' reply appear to have been adapted to the intellectual condition of the Jews in Yemen, for whom it was written.[3] These probably read the Bible with Midrashic commentaries, and preferred the easy and attractive *Agadah* to the more earnest study of the *Halachah*. It is therefore not surprising that the letter contains remarks and interpretations which cannot be reconciled with the philosophical and logical method by which all the other works of Maimonides are distinguished. After a few complimentary words, in which the author modestly disputes the justice of the praises lavished upon him, he attempts to prove that the present sufferings of the Jews, together with the numerous instances of apostasy, were foretold by the prophets, especially by Daniel,[4] and must not perplex the faithful. It must be borne in mind, he continues, that the attempts made in past times to do away with the Jewish religion, had invariably failed; the same would be the fate of the present attempts; for "religious persecutions are of but short duration."[5] The arguments which profess to demonstrate that in certain Biblical passages allusion is made to Mahomet, are based on interpretations which are totally opposed to common sense. He urges that the Jews, faithfully adhering to their religion, should impress their children with the greatness of the Revelation on Mount Sinai, and of the miracles

[1] Gen. xvii. 20, במאד מאד ("exceedingly") bimod meod=be-Mahomet; Deut. xviii. 15, "A prophet from the midst of thee of thy brethren;" and similar passages.

[2] Maimonides in referring to earlier impostors, mentions one that made his appearance twenty years before, probably alluding to David Alroy. See Benjamin of Tudela, etc., II. pag. 162.

[3] Comp. the Midrashic explanation of Deut. xxx. 12; and the allegorical interpretation of Song of Solomon, iv. 1.

[4] Dan. xi. 36; xii. 10. Maimonides explains also such passages as Numbers xxiv. 23; Amos vii. 5; Is. xi. 4, as referring to these persecutions, and describing the approach of the Messianic period.

[5] שמדא עביד דבטיל.

wrought through Moses; they also should remain firm in the belief that God will send the Messiah to deliver their nation, but they must abandon futile calculations of the Messianic period, and beware of impostors. Although there be signs which indicate the approach of the promised deliverance, and the times seem to be the period of the last and most cruel persecution mentioned in the visions of Daniel (xi. and xii.), the person in Yemen who pretends to be the Messiah is an impostor, and if care be not taken, he is sure to do mischief. Similar impostors in Cordova, France, and Africa, have deceived the multitude, and brought great troubles upon the Jews.—Yet, inconsistently with this sound advice the author gives a positive date of the Messianic time,[1] on the basis of an old tradition; the] inconsistency is so obvious that it is impossible to attribute this passage to Maimonides himself. It is probably spurious, and has, perhaps, been added by the translator. With the exception of the rhymed introduction, the letter was written in Arabic, "in order that all should be able to read and understand it;" for that purpose the author desires that copies should be made of it, and circulated among the Jews. R. Nachum, of the Maghreb, translated the letter into Hebrew.

The success in the first great undertaking of explaining the Mishnah encouraged Maimonides to propose to himself another task of a still more ambitious character. In the Commentary on the Mishnah, it was his object that those who were unable to read the Gemara should be made acquainted with the results obtained by the Amoraim in the course of their discussions on the Mishnah. But the Mishnah, with the Commentary, was not such a code of laws as might easily be consulted in cases of emergency; only the initiated would be able to find the section, the chapter, and

[1] 4976 A.M. = 1216; the date is derived from a mystic interpretation of Num. xxiii. 23, כעת יאמר ליעקב וגו׳, "After the lapse of the same period, Jacob and Israel shall again be told," etc., i.e., prophets will again declare the word of God, and the return of prophecy will be the forerunner of the Messianic period. According to the author 2,488 years had passed from the creation up to the time of Balaam; 4,976 (=2488×2) is therefore the year of the Messiah.

the paragraph in which the desired information could be found. The *halachah* had, besides, been further developed since the time when the Talmud was compiled. The changed state of things had suggested new questions; these were discussed and settled by the Geonim, whose decisions, being contained in special letters or treatises, were not generally accessible. Maimonides therefore undertook to compile a complete code, which would contain, in the language and style of the Mishnah, and without discussion, the whole of the Written and the Oral Law, all the precepts recorded in the Talmud, Sifra, Sifri and Tosefta, and the decisions of the Geonim. According to the plan of the author, this work was to present a solution of every question touching the religious, moral, or social duties of the Jews. It was not in any way his object to discourage the study of the Talmud and the Midrash; he only sought to diffuse a knowledge of the Law amongst those who, through incapacity or other circumstances, were precluded from that study. In order to ensure the completeness of the code,[1] the author drew up a list of the six hundred and thirteen precepts of the Pentateuch, divided them into fourteen groups, these again he subdivided, and thus showed how many positive and negative precepts were contained in each section of the Mishneh thorah. The principles by which he was guided in this arrangement were laid down in a separate treatise, called *Sefer ha-mitsvoth*. Works of a similar kind, written by his predecessors, as the *Halachoth gedoloth* of R. Shimon Kahira,[2] and the several *Asharoth*[3] were, according to Maimonides, full of errors, because their authors had not adopted any method or system. But an examination of the rules laid down by Maimonides and of their application leads to the

[1] See Introduction to Sefer ha-mitsvoth.

[2] In the Introduction to *Sefer ha-mitsvoth*, Maimonides appears to consider the Halachoth Gedoloth as full of errors, while in a letter addressed to R. Pinchas, of Alexandria (Kobhets, etc., I. 27a), he speaks of the mistakes found in all such enumerations, except in his own and in the *halachoth gedoloth*.

[3] See L. Dukes, Zur Kenntniss der neuhebräischen religiösen Poesie, Frankfort o/M., 1842.

THE LIFE OF MOSES MAIMONIDES.

conclusion that his results were not less arbitrary ; as has, in fact, been shown by the criticisms of Nachmanides.[1] The *Sefer ha-mitsvoth* was written in Arabic, and thrice translated into Hebrew, namely, by Rabbi Abraham ben Chisdai, Rabbi Shelomoh ben Joseph ben Job, and Rabbi Moses ibn Tibbon. Maimonides himself desired to translate the book into Hebrew, but to his disappointment he found no time.[2]

This *Sefer ha-mitsvoth* was executed as a preparation for his principal work, the *Mishneh thorah*, or *Yad ha-chazakah*, which consists of an Introduction and of fourteen[3] Books. In the Introduction the author first describes the chain of tradition from Moses to the close of the Talmud, and then he explains his method in compiling the work. He distinguishes between the dicta found in the Talmud, Sifri, Sifra, or Tosefta, on the one hand, and the dicta of the Geonim on the other; the former were binding on all Jews, the latter only as far as their necessity and their utility or the authority of their propounders was recognised. Having once for all, stated the sources from which he compiled his work, he did not deem it necessary to name in each case the authority for his opinion or the particular passage from which he derived his dictum. Any addition of references to each paragraph he probably considered useless to the uninformed and superfluous to the learned. At a later time he discovered his error,[4] he being himself unable to find again the sources of some of his decisions. Rabbi Joseph Caro, in his commentary on the Mishneh

---

[1] The principal aim of Nachmanides' criticisms appears to have been to defend the *halachoth gedoloth*; his criticisms were examined by Isaac di Leon, in *Megillath-aster*. The latter sides with Maimonides.

[2] See Letter addressed to Mar Joseph b. Gabar, of Bagdad (Kobhets, etc., II. pag. 15b), and Letter addressed to the Congregation of Lunel (*Ibid.*, pag. 44a).

[3] The number is alluded to in the title, יד החזקה ; the numerical value of יד being 14. Maimonides, when referring to it in his writings, calls it חבור, or חבורנו, or חבורנו הגדול.

[4] See Letter addressed to R. Pinchas, of Alexandria (Kobhets, etc., I. pag. 25a).

thorah, termed Keseph Mishneh,[1] remedied this deficiency. The Introduction is followed by the enumeration of the six hundred and thirteen precepts and a description of the plan of the work, its division into fourteen books, and the division of the latter into sections, chapters, and paragraphs.

According to the author, the *Mishneh thorah* is a mere compendium of the Talmud; but he found sufficient opportunities to display his real genius, his philosophical mind, and his ethical doctrines. For in stating what the traditional Law enjoined he had to exercise his own judgment, and to decide whether a certain dictum was meant to be taken literally or figuratively; whether it was the final decision of a majority or the rejected opinion of a minority; whether it was part of the Oral Law or a precept founded on the scientific views of a particular author; and whether it was of universal application or was only intended for a special period or a special locality. The first Book, *Sefer ha-madda*, is the embodiment of his own ethical and theological theories, although he frequently refers to the Sayings of the Sages, and employs the phraseology of the Talmud. Similarly, the section on the Jewish Calendar, *Hilchoth ha-ibbur*, may be considered as his original work. In each group of the *halachoth*, its source, a certain passage of the Pentateuch, is first quoted, with its traditional interpretation, and then the detailed rules follow in systematic order. The *Mishneh thorah* was written by the author in pure Hebrew; when subsequently a friend asked him to translate it into Arabic, he said he would prefer to have his Arabic writings translated into Hebrew instead of the reverse. The style is an imitation of the Mishnah; he did not choose, the author says, the philosophical style, because that would be un-

[1] The same task had been undertaken by Don Vidal, of Tolosa, in Catalonia, in the Comm. on the Mishneh thorah called *Maggid mishneh;* but as only a few parts of this Comm. were extant, R. Joseph Caro wrote a complete Commentary, and at the same time he proposed to himself to refute the criticisms of R. Abraham b. David (Rabad) and the author of the *Hasagoth maimonijoth*. (See Introd. to *Keseph mishneh*.)

intelligible to the common reader; nor did he select the prophetic style, because that would not harmonise with the subject.[1]

Ten years[2] of hard work by day and by night were spent in the compilation of this code, which had originally been undertaken for "his own benefit, to save him in his advanced age the trouble and the necessity of consulting the Talmud on every occasion."[3] Maimonides knew very well that his work would meet with the opposition of those whose ignorance it would betray, also of those who were incapable of comprehending it, and of those who were inclined to condemn every deviation from their own preconceived notions. But he had the satisfaction to learn that it was well received in most of the congregations of Israel, and that there was a general desire to possess and study it. This success confirmed him in his hope that at a later time, when all cause for jealousy would have disappeared, the *Mishneh thorah* would be received by all Jews as an authoritative code.[4] This hope has not been realised. The genius, earnestness, and zeal of Maimonides are generally recognised; but there is no absolute acceptance of his dicta. The more he insisted on his infallibility, the more did the Rabbinical authorities examine his words and point out errors wherever they believed that they could discover any. It was not always from base motives, as contended by Maimonides and his followers, that his opinions were criticised and rejected. The language used by Rabbi Abraham ben David in his notes *(hasagoth)*[5] on the *Mishneh thorah* appears harsh and disrespectful, if read together with the text of

[1] See Introd. to *Sefer ha-mitsvoth*.
[2] Letter addressed to R. Jonathan, of Lunel; Kobhets teshubhoth, etc., I., pag. 12*b*.
[3] Letter addressed to Ibn Aknin (*Ibid*. II., pag. 30 *b*).
[4] Letter addressed by Maimonides to his pupil Ibn Aknin (*Ibid*., II. pag. 30*b*). When he discovered that his hope was not fulfilled, he consoled himself with the fact that even the books of the Prophets did not obtain universal recognition (*Ibid*.).
[5] The critic was guided in his strictures by the idea that the simple authority of Maimonides was not sufficient reason why the decisions, which he gave with-

the criticised passage, but it seems tame and mild if compared with expressions used now and then by Maimonides about men who happened to hold opinions differing from his own.

Maimonides received many complimentary letters, congratulating him upon his success; but likewise letters with criticisms and questions respecting individual *halachoth*.[1] In most cases he had no difficulty in defending his position. From the replies[2] it must, however, be inferred that Maimonides made some corrections and additions, which were subsequently embodied in his work. The letters addressed to him on the *Mishneh thorah* and on other subjects were so numerous that he frequently complained of the time he had to spend in their perusal, and of the annoyance they caused him; but "he bore all this patiently, as he had learned in his youth to bear the yoke."[3] He was not surprised that many misunderstood his words, for even the simple words of the Pentateuch, "the Lord is one," had met with the same fate. Some inferred from the fact that he treated fully of *Olam ha-ba*, "the future state of the soul," and neglected to expatiate on the resurrection of the dead, that he altogether rejected that principle of faith. They therefore asked Rabbi Samuel ha-levi of Bagdad to state his opinion; the Rabbi accordingly discussed the subject, but, according to Maimonides, he attempted to solve the problem in a very unsatisfactory manner. The latter thereupon likewise wrote a treatise "On the Resurrection of the Dead," in which he protested his adherence to

---

out proof or reference, should be accepted without demur, especially when he differed from his predecessors. See his last note on Maimonides' Introduction to the *Mishneh thorah*.

[1] Comp. Letter of R. Jonathan of Lunel, and series of questions included in it. (Introd. to *Sefer ha-mitsvoth*, I., pag. 6a.)

[2] See Kobhets, etc., I., pag. 10 a., No. 38; 11 a, No. 44; 11 b, No. 47. Comp. Letter addressed to Ibn Aknin (*Ibid.* II., pag. 31 a.)

[3] Letter addressed to Ibn Aknin (*Ibid.*) Some of the letters were collected and translated into Hebrew by R. Mordecai Tamah, and edited under the title of Peer ha-dor (Amsterdam, 1765).

this article of faith. He repeated the opinion he had stated in the Commentary on the Mishnah and in the *Mishneh thorah*, but "in more words; the same idea being reiterated in various forms, as the treatise was only intended for women and for the common multitude."

These theological studies engrossed his attention to a great extent, but did not occupy it exclusively. In a letter addressed to R. Jonathan, of Lunel, he says: "Although from my birth the Torah was betrothed to me, and continues to be loved by me as the wife of my youth in whose love I find a constant delight, strange women whom I at first took into my house as her handmaids have become her rivals and absorb a portion of my time."[1] He devoted himself especially to the study of medicine, in which he distinguished himself to such a degree that, according to Alkifti, "the King of the Franks in Ascalon"[2] wanted to appoint him as his physician. Maimonides declined the honour. Alfadhel, the Vizier of Saladin king of Egypt, admired the genius of Maimonides, and bestowed upon him many distinctions. The name of Maimonides was entered on the roll of physicians, he received a pension, and was introduced to the court of Saladin. The method adopted in his professional practice he describes in a letter to his pupil, Ibn Aknin, as follows: "You know how difficult this profession is for a conscientious and exact person who only states what he can support by argument or authority."[3] This method is more fully described in a treatise on hygiene, composed for Alfadhel, son of Saladin, who was suffering from a severe illness and had applied to Maimonides for advice.[4] In a letter to Rabbi Samuel ibn Tibbon he alludes to the amount of time spent in his medical practice, and says:[5] "I reside in Egypt (or Fostat); the king

---

[1] Letter addressed to R. Jonathan of Lunel (*Ibid.* I., pag. 12 *b*).

[2] According to Grätz, Geschichte, etc., VI., pag. 358, note 1, King Richard I. of England (Cœur de Lion) is meant.

[3] Munk, Archives Israélites, 1851, p. 319.   [4] See Kerem chemed III.

[5] Kobhets, etc., II., pag. 28 *b*; Miscellany of Hebrew Literature, First Series, page 224.

resides in Cairo, which lies about two Sabbath-day journeys from the first-named place. My duties to the king are very heavy. I am obliged to visit him every day, early in the morning; and when he or any of his children or the inmates of his harem are indisposed, I dare not quit Cairo, but must stay during the greater part of the day in the palace. It also frequently happens that one or two of the royal officers fall sick, and then I have to attend them. As a rule, I go to Cairo very early in the day, and even if nothing unusual happens I do not return before the afternoon, when I am almost dying with hunger; but I find the antechambers filled with Jews and Gentiles, with nobles and common people, awaiting my return," etc.

Notwithstanding these heavy professional duties of court physician, Maimonides continued his theological studies. After having compiled a religious guide—Mishneh thorah.—based on Revelation and Tradition, he found it necessary to prove that the principles there set forth were confirmed by philosophy. This task he accomplished in his *Dalalat al-haïrin* "The Guide of the Perplexed,"[1] of which an analysis will be given below. It was composed in Arabic, and written in Hebrew characters.[2] Subsequently it was translated into Hebrew by Rabbi Samuel Ibn Tibbon, in the lifetime of Maimonides, who was consulted by the translator on all difficult passages. The congregation in Lunel, ignorant of Ibn Tibbon's undertaking, or desirous to possess the most correct translation of the Guide, addressed a very flattering letter to Maimonides, requesting him to translate the work into Hebrew. Maimonides replied that he could not do so, as he had not sufficient leisure for even more pressing work,

---

[1] In Hebrew *Moreh nebhuchim*.—Instead of Dalalat al-haïrin there occurs also the form Delil al-haïrin.—Brit. Mus. MS. Or. 2,213.

[2] Abdellatif reports that it was the wish of Maimonides that his work should only be copied in Hebrew characters, with a view to prevent the Mahometans from reading it. This, however, is not the case; Ibn Tibbon in his letter to Maimonides, suggests that his copy of the Guide was made from an original written in Arabic characters, and Maimonides in his answer does not deny it. The copies known at present are all in Hebrew characters.

and that a translation was being prepared by the ablest and fittest man, Rabbi Samuel Ibn Tibbon.[1] A second translation was made later on by Jehudah Alcharizi.[2]—The Guide delighted many, but it also met with much adverse criticism on account of the peculiar views held by Maimonides concerning angels, prophecy, and miracles, especially on account of his assertion that if the Aristotelian proof for the Eternity of the Universe had satisfied him, he would have found no difficulty in reconciling the Biblical account of the Creation with that doctrine.[3] The controversy on the Guide continued long after the death of Maimonides to divide the community, and it is difficult to say how far the author's hope to effect a reconciliation between reason and revelation was realised. His disciple, Joseph Ibn Aknin, to whom the work was dedicated, and who was expected to derive from it the greatest benefit, appears to have been disappointed. His inability to reconcile the two antagonistic elements of faith and science, he describes allegorically in the form of a letter addressed to Maimonides,[4] in which the following passage occurs: "Speak, for I desire that you be justified; if you can, answer me. Some time ago your beloved daughter, the beautiful and charming Kimah, obtained grace and favour in my sight, and I betrothed her unto me in faithfulness, and married her in accordance with the Law, in the presence of two trustworthy witnesses, viz., our master, Abd-allah[5] and Ibn Roshd. But she soon became faithless to me; she could not have found fault with me, yet she left me and departed from my tent. She does no longer let me behold her pleasant countenance or hear her melodious voice. You have not rebuked or punished her, and perhaps you are the cause of

[1] See Kobhets, etc., II., page 44 a.
[2] The first part of this Version was edited with notes by Scheyer (London, 1851), the second and third parts by Schlossberg (London, 1876, and Vienna, 1879).
[3] See Guide II., ch. xxv.
[4] Kobhets, etc., II., 29 a; comp. Rénan, Averroes, page 180.
[5] I.e., Maimonides.

this misconduct. Now, 'send the wife back to the man, for he is'—or might become—'a prophet; he will pray for you that you may live,' and also for her that she may be firm and steadfast. If, however, you do not send her back, the Lord will punish you. Therefore seek peace and pursue it; listen to what our sages said: 'Blessed be he who restores to the owner his lost property;' for this blessing applies in a higher degree to him who restores to a man his virtuous wife, the crown of her husband." Maimonides replied in the same strain, and reproached his "son-in-law" that he falsely accused his wife of faithlessness after he had neglected her; but he restored him his wife with the advice to be more cautious in future. In another letter Maimonides exhorts Ibn Aknin to study his works, adding, "apply yourself to the study of the Law of Moses; do not neglect it, but on the contrary, devote to it the best and the most of your time, and if you tell me that you do so, I am satisfied that you are on the right way to eternal bliss."

Of the letters written after the completion of the "Guide," one addressed to the wise men of Marseilles (1194)[1] is especially noteworthy. Maimonides was asked to give his opinion on astrology. He regretted in his reply that they were not yet in possession of his *Mishneh thorah*; they would have found in it the answer to their question. According to his opinion, man should only believe what he can grasp with his intellectual faculties, or perceive by his senses, or what he can accept on trustworthy authority. Beyond this nothing should be believed. Astrological statements, not being founded on any of these three sources of knowledge, must be rejected. He had himself studied astrology, and was convinced that it was no science at all. If some dicta be found in the Talmud which appear to represent Astrology as a true source of knowledge, these may either be referred to the rejected opinion of a small minority, or may have an allegorical meaning, but they

[1] Comp. note 5, page xxi.

are by no means forcible enough to set aside principles based on logical proof.[1]

The debility of which Maimonides so frequently complained in his correspondence, gradually increased, and he died, in his seventieth year, on the 20th Tebeth, 4964 (1204).[2] His death was the cause of great mourning to all Jews. In Fostat a mourning of three days was kept; in Jerusalem a fast was appointed; a portion of the *tochachah* (Lev. xxvi. or Deut. xxix.) was read, and also the history of the capture of the Ark by the Philistines (1 Sam. iv.). His remains were brought to Tiberias.[3] The general regard in which Maimonides was held, both by his contemporaries and by succeeding generations, has been expressed in the popular saying: "From Moses to Moses there was none like Moses."[4]

NOTE.—*Examination of the proofs adduced for the alleged apostasy of Maimonides* (pag. xviii.).

First of all, we have to examine the treatise on involuntary apostasy. A certain Rabbi being asked to state his opinion on the relation of forced converts to Judaism replied that if a Jew publicly professes his belief in Mahomet and joins the Moslems in their worship, his prayer would not be acceptable before the Lord, his observance of the divine precepts had no merit whatever, and he could no longer be considered a Jew. The Rabbi exhorted his brethren to be firm, and prefer death to apostasy, as he put no faith in the clandestine observance of religious precepts. In the treatise attributed to Maimonides this reply is criticised, and pronounced to be

---

[1] Comp. Friedländer, "Essays on Ibn Ezra," pag. 96 *sqq*.

[2] According to R. Saadiah b. Maimon ibn Danan: Monday the 18th of Kislev 4965. (Chemdah genuzah by Edelman, Königsberg, 1856.) Comp. Rappoport in Geiger's Zeitschrift, etc., II. 127 *sqq*.

[3] Comp. Carmoly, Itiner., pages 186, 385, 446.

[4] ממשה עד משה לא קם כמוהו. The phrase has its origin in Deut. xxxiv. 10.

the product of ignorance and folly. In the first place, the author holds that the Law only demanded martyrdom when men are compelled to worship idols, but that Islam is not idolatry. Life need not be sacrificed, since the Mahometans do not compel the Jews to transgress any divine precept; they only ask them to make a profession of their belief in Mahomet. Secondly, a compulsory transgression of the Law does not render the transgressor liable to punishment, nor does it deprive him of his privileges as a Jew. He admits that those who prefer to die the death of a martyr do "what is right in the sight of the Lord;" but at the same time he declares that those who save their lives by pretended conversion, act in strict accordance with the Law,[1] provided that they seek the earliest opportunity to quit the country, and do not hesitate to abandon, if necessary, their property, and even their families. In the course of this treatise the author seems to describe himself as belonging to the involuntary converts; for he says: "In this *our* involuntary conversion *we* do not simulate idolatry, but merely a belief in Islam; the Mahometans know that in reality *we* do not believe in the truth of what *we* profess, and that *we* deceive the king."[2] "What I consider the best thing to do for *myself*, my friends, and for all who would follow my advice, is this—to quit the country, without the least regard to property, friends or family."[3]

If Maimonides were the author of this treatise, his apostasy would seem to be established; but at the same time also his great inconsistency. Contrary to the advice re-

---

[1] Babyl. Talm. Sanhedrin 74a, נמנו ונגמרו בעליית בית נתזא בלוד כל עבירות שבתורה אם אומרים לו לאדם עבור ואל תהרג יעברו ואל יהרג חוץ מגלוי עריות שפיכות דמים וע״ז.—Comp. Maim., Yad ha-chazakah, Hilchoth Yesode ha-torah, v.

[2] והשמד הזה אשר אנחנו בו אין אנו מראים בו שאנו עובדים ע״ז אלא שנאמין מה שהם אומרים בלבד וכבר נתאמת אצלם שאין אנו מאמינים זה בשום פנים:

[3] והדעת שאני רוצה בה לי ולאוהבי ולכל מבקש ממני עצה וגו׳

corded here, and still more forcibly in a letter to the Jews in Yemen,[1] he remained, according to most of his biographers,[2] more than ten years in Mahometan countries in which the Jewish religion was not tolerated. It is, however, by no means certain that Maimonides is the author of this treatise; there is, on the contrary, sufficient reason to doubt the genuineness of the introductory phrase, "Moses, the son of Maimon, said." The following are the arguments against its authenticity:—

1. Maimonides never quotes this treatise, though he was in the habit of referring to his own works; such reference might be expected in the letter to the Jews in Teman (Yemen),[3] in which he advised them how to conduct themselves in times of religious persecution, or in the letters which he wrote to a proselyte in Palestine.[4]

2. No mention of this treatise is noticed in any of the works of the thirteenth and the fourteenth centuries.[5]

3. Although it was but natural that the Jews should hail with joy the open return of involuntary converts, and abstain from reminding them of their past trials, it is nevertheless remarkable that, in the heat of the controversy between Maimonists and anti-Maimonists, at a time when harsh and insulting words were exchanged on both sides, no

[1] "They must flee into deserts and solitary places; they must not regret the separation from friends, or the loss of property, for this is trifling when compared with the service of God."

[2] Grätz (Gesch. vi., pag. 316) suggests that the family of Maimon did not profess Islam in Spain, where they remained till 1159-60; but when at Fez, they were, like the other Jews, obliged to comply with the command of the king.

[3] *Iggereth Teman.* See p. xxii. Comp. also Letter to the Marseilles Congregation:— ואם שמעתם שהגיע כתבי לפאס שמא אותן הדברים ששלחתי בארץ תימן הועתקו והגיעו לפאס. If the *Iggereth ha-shemad* had been composed by Maimonides, he would surely have mentioned the *possibility* that it was that same *Iggereth* of which the Jews in Marseilles had heard.

[4] Kobets Teshubhoth Rambam, Nos. 158–160., ed. Lichtenberg, Leipzig, 5619 (1859).

[5] Resp. of Isaac b. Shesheth, No. 11, and of Shimon b. Tsemach Duran, No. 63, appear to contain the earliest mention of this treatise; both were written in the fifteenth century.

reference is made to the views expressed by the author of this treatise or to Maimonides' alleged lapse into Islam.

4. In an important point the opinion expressed by Maimonides in his Mishneh-thorah differs from that adduced in the Iggereth ha-shemad. In the latter praise is bestowed upon those who would sacrifice their lives *in gloriam Dei* on occasions when the Law did not demand such a sacrifice; according to the Mishneh-thorah,[1] such martyrs are sinners, and almost guilty of suicide.

5. The first part of the treatise, which in style and contents widely differs from the second part, and in which the author appears to have had no other object than to revile his opponent, is wholly unworthy of Maimonides. The invectives here employed are not dictated by an indignant apprehension of the evils resulting from a false theory; they are simply the weapons of casuistry, and serve to display the author's superiority.[2]

6. The treatise contains inconsistencies which cannot be conceived to be the product of Maimonides' logical genius. *E.g.*: In one paragraph the opponent is called a sinner and transgressor, because he recommends martyrdom where the Law does not enjoin it, and in the next paragraph he assures such martyrs that their reward will be great because the Lord is pleased with such a sacrifice. Again, the Introduction begins with a eulogy of speech as the sublimest gift of man,[3] which would even be defiled if it were employed to

---

[1] Hilchoth Yesode ha-torah, v. 1.

[2] The author admits that his opponent had a good intention (חשב לעשות טובה אחת), nevertheless he calls him קל מקלי עולם. He also is shocked at the wish expressed by the opponent, that the religious earnestness of the Karaites and the Christians should be imitated, and calls it הוללות רעה, forgetting that the prophet Jeremiah expressed himself in the same sense when he exclaimed ההמיר גוי אלהים (Jer. ii. 11). It is absurd to ascribe such views to one of the greatest men in Israel. For the same reason the authenticity of the letter addressed to his son Abraham (מוסר נאה מאד מהרמ״בם ז״ל להרב החכם אברהם בנו) appears doubtful. The letter contains base invectives and calumnies.

[3] Comp. Maimon., Comm. on Mishnah, Abhoth, i. 15.

refute baseless and absurd assertions; but the author appears to attribute little value to speech when he bases his principal argument on the fact that the tyrant demands of the Jews *nothing but the mere* utterance of a few words.

7. It is remarkable that, contrary to the usual practice[1] of Maimonides, neither the person to whom the letter was addressed nor the person against whom it was directed is mentioned by name. Again, if Maimonides were the author, he would probably have written in Arabic; the name of the translator is not stated.

8. It is improbable that Maimonides took upon himself the responsibility of deciding a question of such importance without making an allusion to his father, who, in his authority as *dayyan*, had addressed his brethren in Fez, and exhorted them to remain faithful to their religion.

These considerations lead to the conclusion that Maimonides was not the author of this treatise, at least not in its present form.

The next witnesses to be examined as to the alleged apostasy of Maimon and his family are some Arabic authors. The most important of these are Ibn Ali Osaiba and Alkifti;[2] for they were almost contemporaries of Maimonides, and stood in such relation to him as would enable them to ascertain whether the rumoured conversion of Maimonides was true or not. Osaiba was a fellow-physician of Rabbi Abraham, the son of Maimonides, in the great hospital at Cairo; Alkifti was an intimate friend of Ibn Aknin, the faithful pupil of Maimonides. Writers of a later period, as, *e.g.*, Abulfaragius,[2] who establish their assertions on the evidence of these witnesses, may be ignored altogether.

Osaiba, in his history of the Physicians, gives the following account: "*It is said* that Maimonides became a

---

[1] See Treatises on Resurrection, on Astrology (Letter to Marseilles congregation), the Yemen letter, Guide, etc.

[2] Comp. I. Chwolson, Materialien zu Biographieen jüdischer Gelehrten die unter den Arabern gelebt, aus arabischen Schriftstellern gesammelt. Orient, 1846, pag. 337 *sqq*.

Mahometan in the Maghreb; that he learnt the Koran by heart, and devoted himself to the study of the Mahometan Law; but when he came to Egypt and settled in Fostat, he was accused of apostasy."[1] It would certainly be absurd to accept as an established fact a statement founded on a mere *on dit*, perhaps on the charge of apostasy which was brought against Maimonides at Cairo, but of which he was acquitted. Alkifti speaks with greater certainty: "Abdulmumen ben Ali Alkuni, the Jezedite, ruler of the Maghreb, commanded that all Jews and Christians residing in his territory should become Moslems or emigrate before a certain date; the converts would in every respect enjoy the same privileges as their Mahometan fellow-citizens; but if, after the fixed date, any Jews or Christians remained in the country without changing their religion, their property would be confiscated, and they would be put to death. Thereupon Maimonides, in order to save his property, professed outwardly the Mahometan religion, but after some time he fled with his family to Egypt, where he found a refuge amongst the Jews in Fostat, and where he again openly professed Judaism." "In his old age a serious danger threatened him; for when the Spanish lawyer Abu'l-arab ben Moisha came to Egypt, he recognised Maimonides, and brought the charge of apostasy against him. Abd-er-rahem al-fadhel ruled that a forced conversion was illegal, and acquitted Maimonides." According to Dzehebi it was in the house of this Abu'l-arab that Maimonides when outlawed, and in imminent danger of his life, found protection and hospitality in Spain. The protector, however, was in consequence of this humane act subjected to persecution.[2]

Although Alkifti, as an intimate friend of Joseph Ibn Aknin, might be expected to have had the most accurate information on the subject, his account does not appear to be trustworthy. The imputation that Maimonides was through covetousness induced to renounce his religion,

[1] Comp. Orient, l.c., pag. 349, note 14.
[2] See Munk, Archives Israelites, 1851, pag. 329.

suffices to prove that Maimonides' enthusiastic disciple was not Alkifti's informant. It is more likely that Alkifti also founded his account of that conversion on the charges of apostasy which were brought against Maimonides in Cairo. Osaiba, who lived in that city, introduces his narrative as a mere rumour; when the report reached Alkifti, who was far away from Cairo, it had already assumed the form of an established fact. But on what grounds did Abu'l-arab and others rest their charges of apostasy against Maimonides? That charges of this kind were made cannot be denied. Maimonides, in a letter addressed to R. Yefeth, mentions the fact among other causes of his troubles.[1] If it were true that he pretended to be a convert to Mahometanism, he would have enjoyed, according to Alkifti, the same protection of the law as all other Moslems, and would not have been outlawed or compelled to wander as a fugitive from place to place. On the contrary, Maimon, with his family, far from simulating conversion, preferred danger and anxiety, if ease and security were to be purchased at the expense of religion. They made, perhaps, no display of their faith, and might therefore a long time have been able to reside where they were without being recognised as Jews. We may explain these difficulties by the following assumption: Maimonides, like many other Jews, had friends amongst the Mahometans; his scientific career brought him into close contact with teachers and fellow-students, and in his treatises on medical matters he frequently mentions what he had noticed and experienced amongst the Mahometans in the West.[2] Many of these friends probably believed him to be a Moslem, whilst others altogether ignored the king's decree against the Jews. Besides, the decree may perhaps not have been executed with the same rigour in all parts of the kingdom, or against all Jews; and Maimonides had in such cases an opportunity of noticing the religious practices and customs of the Jews

[1] Kobhets teshubhoth ha-rambam, Part II. pag. 37.
[2] Comp. Munk, Archives Israelites, 1851, pag. 326.

in the Maghreb.[1] As soon, however, as an enforcement of the king's decree was feared, or actually took place, so that Maimonides was outlawed, he sought safety in flight. It may have been on such an occasion that Maimonides was protected by Abu'l-arab, the latter not knowing the true cause of his *protégé's* danger. Abu'l-arab, like many other Mahometans, had no reason to suspect that Maimonides was a follower of the Jewish faith. Hence might have arisen the charges of apostasy when it was discovered in Egypt that his *protégé* was a Jew.

[1] Comment. on the Mishnah, Nedarim x. 8; Kelim ii. 1; x. 1; Okzin ii. 5. Kobhets, etc., Part I. p. 4a; 7b.

ANALYSIS OF THE GUIDE OF THE PERPLEXED.
INTRODUCTION.

It is the object of this work "to afford a guide for the perplexed," *i.e.*, "to thinkers whose studies have brought them into collision with religion" (p. 21), "who have studied philosophy and have acquired sound knowledge, and who, while firm in religious matters, are perplexed and bewildered on account of the ambiguous and figurative expressions employed in the holy writings" (p. 13). Joseph, the son of Jehudah ibn Aknin, a disciple of Maimonides, is addressed by his teacher as an example of this kind of students. It was "for him and for those like him" that the treatise was composed, and to him this work is inscribed in the dedicatory letter with which the Introduction begins. Maimonides, having discovered that his disciple was sufficiently advanced for an exposition of the esoteric ideas in the books of the Prophets, commenced to give him such expositions "by way of hints." His disciple then begged him to give him further explanations, to treat of metaphysical themes, and to expound the system and the method of the Kalām, or Mahometan Theology.[1] In compliance with this request, Maimonides composed the Guide of the Perplexed. The reader has, therefore, to expect that the subjects mentioned in the disciple's request indicate the design and arrangement of the present work, and that the Guide consists of the following parts:—1. An exposition of the esoteric ideas (*sodoth*) in the books of the Prophets. 2. A treatment of certain metaphysical problems. 3. An examination of the system and the method of the Kalām. This, in fact, is a correct account of the contents of the book; but in the second part of the Introduction, in which the theme of this work is defined, the author mentions only the first-named subject. He observes: "My primary object is to explain

[1] See *infra*, page 4, note 1.

certain words occurring in the prophetic books. Of these some are homonymous, some figurative, and some hybrid terms" (p. 4). "This work has also a second object. It is designed to explain certain obscure figures which occur in the Prophets, and are not distinctly characterised as being figures" (p. 6). Yet from this observation it must not be inferred that Maimonides abandoned his original purpose; for he examines the Kalām in the last chapters of the First Part (ch. lxx.-lxxvi.), and treats of certain metaphysical themes in the beginning of the Second Part (Introd. and ch. i.-xxv.). But in the passage quoted above he confines himself to a delineation of the *main* object of this treatise, and advisedly leaves unmentioned the other two subjects, which, however important they may be, are here of subordinate interest. Nor did he consider it necessary to expatiate on these subjects; he only wrote for the student, for whom a mere reference to works on philosophy and science was sufficient. We therefore frequently meet with such phrases as the following: "This is fully discussed in works on metaphysics." By references of this kind the author may have intended to create a taste for the study of philosophical works. But our observation only holds good with regard to the Aristotelian philosophy. The writings of the Mutakallemim are never commended by him; he states their opinions, and tells his disciple that he would *not* find any additional argument, even if he were to read all of their voluminous works (p. 343). Maimonides was a zealous disciple of Aristotle, although the theory of the Kalām might seem to have been more congenial to Jewish thought and belief. The Kalām upheld the theory of God's Existence, Incorporeality, and Unity, together with the *creatio ex nihilo*. Maimonides nevertheless opposed the Kalām, and, anticipating the question, why preference should be given to the system of Aristotle, which included the theory of the Eternity of the Universe, a theory contrary to the fundamental teaching of the Scriptures, he exposed the weakness of the Kalām and its fallacies.

ANALYSIS OF THE GUIDE OF THE PERPLEXED. xliii

The exposition of Scriptural texts is divided by the author into two parts; the first part treats of homonymous, figurative, and hybrid terms,[1] employed in reference to God; the second part relates to Biblical figures and allegories. These two parts do not closely follow each other; they are separated by the examination of the Kalām, and the discussion of metaphysical problems. It seems that the author adopted this arrangement for the following reason: first of all, he intended to establish the fact that the Biblical anthropomorphisms do not imply corporeality, and that the divine Being of whom the Bible speaks could therefore be regarded as identical with the Primal Cause of the philosophers. Having established this principle, he discusses from a purely metaphysical point of view the properties of the Primal Cause and its relation to the universe. A solid foundation is thus established for the esoteric exposition of Scriptural passages. Before discussing metaphysical problems, which he treats in accordance with Aristotelian philosophy, he disposes of the Kalām, and demonstrates that its arguments are illogical and illusory.

The "Guide of the Perplexed" contains, therefore, an Introduction and the following four parts:—1. On homonymous, figurative, and hybrid terms. 2. On the Supreme Being and His relation to the universe, according to the Kalām. 3. On the Primal Cause and its relation to the universe, according to the philosophers. 4. Esoteric exposition of some portions of the Bible (*sodoth*): *a, Maaseh bereshith*, or the history of the Creation (Genesis, ch. i.-iv.): *b*, on Prophecy; *c, Maaseh mercabhah*, or the description of the divine chariot (Ezekiel, ch. i.).

According to this plan, the work ends with the seventh chapter of the Third Part. The chapters which follow may be considered as an appendix; they treat of the following theological themes: the Existence of Evil, Omniscience and Providence, Temptations, Design in Nature, in the Law, and in the Biblical Narratives, and finally the true Worship of God.

[1] See *infra*, page 5, note 4.

In the Introduction to the "Guide," Maimonides (1) describes the object of the work and the method he has followed; (2) treats of similes; (3) gives "directions for the study of the work;" and (4) discusses the most usual causes of inconsistencies in authors.

1 (pag. 4-10). Inquiring into the root of the evil which this work was intended to remove, namely, the conflict between science and religion, the author perceived that in most cases it originated in a misinterpretation of the anthropomorphisms in Holy Writ. The main difficulty is found in the ambiguity of the words employed to describe the mode of action of the Divine Being; the question arises whether they are applied to the Deity and to other things in one and the same sense or equivocally; in the latter case the author distinguishes between homonyms pure and simple, figures, and hybrid terms. In order to show that the Biblical anthropomorphisms do not imply the corporeality of the Deity, he seeks in each instance to demonstrate that the expression under examination is a perfect homonym denoting things which are totally distinct from each other, and whenever such a demonstration is impossible, he assumes that the expression is a hybrid term, that is, being employed in one instance figuratively and in another homonymously. His explanation of "form" (צלם) may serve as an illustration. According to his opinion, it invariably denotes "form" in the philosophical acceptation of the term, viz., the complex of the essential properties of a thing. But to obviate objections he proposes an alternative view, and takes צלם as either a homonym, and denoting as such two different things—"form" in the philosophical sense of the word, and "external shape," or as a hybrid term, i.e., that the several objects which it describes may be equally considered as belonging to the same class and to different classes. Maimonides seems to have refrained from explaining anthropomorphisms as figurative expressions, lest by such interpretation he might implicitly admit the existence of a certain relation and comparison between the Creator and His creatures.

Maimonides appears to be the first who distinguished in the interpretation of Biblical anthropomorphisms between perfect homonyms, *i.e.*, terms which denote two or more absolutely different things, and imperfect homonyms or hybrid terms. It is true that some of his predecessors had enunciated and demonstrated the Unity and the Incorporeality of the Divine Being, and they had interpreted Scriptural metaphors on the principle that "the Law speaks in the language of man"; but our author adopted a new and altogether original method. The Commentators, when treating of anthropomorphisms, generally contented themselves with the statement that the term under consideration must not be taken in a literal sense, or they paraphrased the passage in expressions which implied a lesser degree of materiality. The Talmud, the Midrashim, and the Targumim abound in paraphrases of this kind. The Jewish philosophers anterior to Maimonides, as Saadiah in "*Emunoth ve-deoth*," Bachya in his "*Chobhoth ha-lebhabhoth*," and Jehudah ha-levi in the "*Cusari*," insist on the necessity and the appropriateness of such interpretations. Saadiah enumerates ten terms which primarily denote organs of the human body, and are figuratively employed with reference to God. To establish this point of view he cites numerous instances in which the terms in question are used in a figurative sense without being applied to God. Saadiah further shows that the Divine attributes are either qualifications of such of God's actions as are perceived by man, or they imply a negation. The correctness of this method was held to be so obvious that some authors found it necessary to apologise to the reader for introducing such well-known subjects. From R. Abraham ben David's strictures on the Yad ha-chazakah it is, however, evident that in the days of Maimonides persons were not wanting who defended the literal interpretation of certain anthropomorphisms. Maimonides, therefore, did not content himself with the vague and general rule, "The Law speaks in the language of man," but sought carefully to define the meaning of each term when applied to God, and to identify it with some transcendental and metaphysical term. In pursuing this course he is sometimes forced to venture upon interpretations which are much too far-fetched to commend themselves even to the supposed philosophical reader. In such instances he generally adds a simple and plain explanation, and leaves it to the option of the reader to choose the one which may appear preferable. The enumeration of the different meanings of a word is often, from a philological point of view, incomplete; he introduces only such significations as serve his object. When treating of an imperfect homonym, the several significations of which are derived from one primary signification, he apparently follows a certain system which he does not employ in the interpretation of perfect homonyms. The homonymity of the term is not proved; the author confines himself to the remark, "It is employed homonymously," even when the various meanings of a word might easily be traced to a common source.

2 (pag. 10-20). In addition to the explanation of homonyms Maimonides undertakes to interpret similes and allegories. At first it had been his intention to write two distinct works—*Sefer ha-nebhuah*, "A Book on Prophecy," and "*Sefer ha-shevaah*, "A Book of Reconciliation." In the former work he had intended to explain difficult passages of the Bible, and in the latter to expound such passages in the Midrash and the Talmud as seemed to be in conflict with common sense. With respect to the "Book of Reconciliation," he abandoned his plan, because he apprehended that neither the learned nor the unlearned would profit by it: the one would find it superfluous, the other tedious. The subject of the "Book on Prophecy" is treated in the present work, in which he explains difficulties in the Scripture, and occasionally such as occur in the Talmud and the Midrash.

The treatment of the simile must vary according as the simile is compound or simple. In the first case, each part represents a separate idea and demands a separate interpretation; in the other case, only one idea is represented, and it is not necessary to assign to each part a separate metaphorical meaning. This division the author illustrates by citing the dream of Jacob (Gen. xxviii. 12 *sqq.*), and the description of the adulteress (Prov. vii. 6 *sqq.*). He gives no rule by which it might be ascertained to which of the two categories a simile belongs, and, like other Commentators, he seems to treat as essential those details of a simile for which he can offer an adequate interpretation. As a general principle, he warns against the confusion and the errors which arise when an attempt is made to expound every single detail of a simile. His own explanations are not intended to be exhaustive; on the contrary, they are to consist of brief allusions to the idea represented by the simile, of mere suggestions, which the reader is expected to develop and to complete. The author thus aspires to follow in the wake of the Creator, whose works can only be understood after a long and persevering study. Yet it is possible that he derived his preference for a reserved and mysterious style from the example of ancient philosophers, who discussed metaphysical problems in figurative and enigmatic language. Like Ibn Ezra, who frequently concludes his exposition of a Biblical passage with the phrase, "Here a profound idea (*sod*) is hidden," Maimonides somewhat mysteriously remarks at the end of different chapters, "Note this," "Consider it well." In such phrases some Commentators fancied that they found references to metaphysical theories which the author was not willing fully to discuss. Whether this was the case or not, in having recourse to that method he was not, as some have suggested, actuated by fear of being charged with heresy. He expresses his opinion on the principal theological questions without reserve, and does not dread the searching inquiries of opponents; for he boldly announces that their displeasure would not deter him from teaching the truth and guiding those who are able and willing to follow him, however few these might be.[1] When, however, we

[1] He stated his view frankly and fully, and he therefore entrusted the work

examine the work itself, we are at a loss to discover to which parts the professed enigmatic method was applied. His theories concerning the deity, the divine attributes, angels, *creatio ex nihilo*, prophecy, and other subjects, are treated as fully as might be expected. It is true that a cloud of mysterious phrases enshrouds the interpretation of *Maaseh bereshith* (Gen. i.-iii.), and *Maaseh mercabhah* (Ez. i.). But the significant words occurring in these portions are explained in the First Part of this work, and a full exposition is found in the Second and Third Parts. Nevertheless the statement that the exposition was never intended to be explicit occurs over and over again. The treatment of the first three chapters of Genesis concludes thus: "These remarks, together with what we have already observed on the subject, and what we may have to add, must suffice both for the object and for the reader we have in view" (II. xxx.). In like manner, he declares, after the explanation of the first chapter of Ezekiel: "I have given you here as many suggestions as may be of service to you, if you will give them a further development. . . . Do not expect to hear from me anything more on this subject, for I have, though with some hesitation, gone as far in my explanation as I possibly could go" (III. vii.).

3 (pag. 20-23). In the next paragraph, headed, "Directions for the Study of this Work," he implores the reader not to be hasty with his criticism, and to bear in mind that every sentence, indeed each word, had been fully considered before it was written down. Yet it might easily happen that the reader could not reconcile his own view with that of the author, and in such a case he is asked to ignore the disapproved chapter or section altogether. Such disapproval Maimonides attributes to a mere misconception on the part of the reader, a fate which awaits every work composed in a mystical style. In adopting this peculiar style, he intended to reduce to a

---

only to trustworthy persons, lest he might be accused by the Mahometans that he was spreading heretical views. See Letter of Maimonides to Ibn Aknin ed. Goldberg in Birchath Abraham, Lyck, 1859.

minimum the violation of the rule laid down in the Mishnah (Chagigah ii. 1), that metaphysics should not be taught publicly. The violation of this rule he justifies by citing the following two Mishnaic maxims: "It is time to do something in honour of the Lord" (Berachoth ix. 5), and "Let all thy acts be guided by pure intentions" (Aboth ii. 17). Maimonides increased the mysteriousness of the treatise, by expressing his wish that the reader should abstain from expounding the work, lest he might spread in the name of the author opinions which the latter never held. But it does not occur to him that the views he enunciates might in themselves be erroneous. He is positive that his own theory is unexceptionably correct, that his esoteric interpretations of Scriptural texts are sound, and that those who differed from him—viz., the Mutakallemin on the one hand, and the unphilosophical Rabbis on the other—are indefensibly wrong. In this respect other Jewish philosophers—*e. g.*, Saadiah and Bahya—were far less positive; they were conscious of their own fallibility, and invited the reader to make such corrections as might appear needful. Owing to this strong self-reliance of Maimonides, it is not to be expected that opponents would receive a fair and impartial judgment at his hands.

4 (pag. 23-27). The same self-reliance is noticeable in the next and concluding paragraph of the Introduction. Here he treats of the contradictions which are to be found in every literary work, and he divides them with regard to their origin into seven classes. The first four classes comprise the apparent contradictions, which can be traced back to the employment of elliptical speech; the other three classes comprise the real contradictions, and are due to carelessness and oversight, or they are intended to serve some special purpose. The Scriptures, the Talmud, and the Midrash abound in instances of apparent contradictions; later works contain real contradictions, which escaped the notice of the writers. In the present treatise, however, there occur only such contradictions as are the result of intention and design.

PART I.

The homonymous expressions which are discussed in the First Part include—(1) nouns and verbs used in reference to God, ch. i. to ch. xlix.; (2) attributes of the Deity, ch. l. to lx.; (3) expressions commonly regarded as names of God, ch. lxi. to lxx. In the first section the following groups can be distinguished—(a) expressions which denote form and figure, ch. i. to ch. vi.; (b) space or relations of space, ch. viii. to ch. xxv.; (c) parts of the animal body and their functions, ch. xxviii. to ch. xlix. Each of these groups includes chapters not connected with the main subjects, but which serve as a help for the better understanding of previous or succeeding interpretations. Every word selected for discussion bears upon some Scriptural text which, according to the opinion of the author, has been misinterpreted. But such phrases as "the mouth of the Lord," and "the hand of the Lord" are not introduced, because their figurative meaning is too obvious to be misunderstood.

The lengthy digressions which are here and there interposed appear like outbursts of feeling and passion which the author could not repress. Yet they are "words fitly spoken in the right place;" for they gradually unfold the author's theory, and acquaint the reader with those general principles on which he founds the interpretations in the succeeding chapters. Moral reflections are of frequent occurrence, and demonstrate the intimate connection between a virtuous life and the attainment of higher knowledge, in accordance with the maxim current long before Maimonides, and expressed in the Biblical words, "The fear of the Lord is the beginning of wisdom" (Ps. cxi. 10). No opportunity is lost to inculcate this lesson, be it in a passing remark or in an elaborate essay.

The discussion of the term "*tselem*" (ch. i.) afforded the first occasion for reflections of this kind. Man, "the image of God," is defined as a living and rational being, as though the moral faculties of man were not an essential element of his existence, and his power to discern between good and evil were the result of the first sin. According to Maimonides, the moral faculty would, in fact, not have been required, if man had remained a purely rational being. It is only through the senses that "the knowledge of good and evil" has become indispensable. The narrative of Adam's fall is, according to Maimonides, an allegory representing the relation which exists between sensation, moral faculty, and intellect. In this early part (ch. ii.), however, the author does not yet mention this theory; on the contrary, every allusion to it is for the present studiously avoided, its full exposition being reserved for the Second Part.

The treatment of ראה, "to behold" (ch. vi.), is followed by the advice that the student should not approach metaphysics otherwise than after a sound and thorough preparation, because a rash attempt to solve abstruse problems brings nothing but injury upon the inexperienced investigator. The author points to the "nobles of the children of Israel" (Exod. xxiv. 11), who, according to his interpretation, fell into this error, and received their deserved punishment. He gives additional force to these exhortations by citing a dictum of Aristotle to the same effect. In a like way he refers to the allegorical use of certain terms by Plato (ch. xvii.) in support of his interpretation of "*tsur*" (*lit.*, "rock") as denoting "Primal Cause."

The theory that nothing but a sound moral and intellectual training would entitle a student to engage in metaphysical speculations is again discussed in the digression which precedes the third group of homonyms (xxxi.—xxxvi.). Man's intellectual faculties, he argues, have this in common with his physical forces, that their sphere of action is limited, and they become inefficient whenever they are overstrained. This happens when a student approaches metaphysics without due preparation. He goes on to argue that the non-success of metaphysical studies is attributable to the following causes: the transcendental character of this discipline, the imperfect state of the student's knowledge, the persistent efforts which have to be made even in the preliminary studies, and finally the waste of energy and time owing to the physical condition of man. For these reasons the majority of persons are debarred from pursuing the study of metaphysics. Nevertheless, there are certain metaphysical truths which have to be communicated to all men, *e.g.*, that God is One, and that He is incorporeal; for to assume that God is corporeal, or that He has any properties, or to ascribe to Him any attributes, is a sin bordering on idolatry.

Another digression occurs as an appendix to the second group of homonyms (ch. xxvi.—xxvii.). Maimonides found that only a limited number of terms are applied to God in a figurative sense; and again, that in the "Targum" of Onkelos some of the figures are paraphrased, while other figures received a literal rendering. He therefore seeks to discover the principle which was applied both in the Sacred text and in the translation, and he found it in the Talmudical dictum, "The Law speaketh the language of man." For this reason all figures are eschewed which, in their literal sense, would appear to the multitude as implying debasement or a blemish. Onkelos, who rigorously guards himself against using any term that might suggest corporification, gives a literal rendering of figurative terms when there is no cause for entertaining such an apprehension. Maimonides illustrates this rule by the mode in which Onkelos renders "*yarad*" ("to go down,"), when used in reference to God. It is generally paraphrased, but in one exceptional instance, occurring in Jacob's "visions of the night" (Gen. xlvi. 4), it is translated literally; in this instance the literal rendering does not lead to corporification; because visions and dreams were generally regarded as mental operations, devoid of objective reality. Simple and clear as this explanation may be, we do not consider that it really explains the method of

ANALYSIS OF THE GUIDE OF THE PERPLEXED.

Onkelos. On the contrary, the translator paraphrased anthropomorphic terms, even when he found them in passages relating to dreams or visions; and indeed it is doubtful whether Maimonides could produce a single instance in favour of his view. He was equally unsuccessful in his explanation of "*chasah*," "to see" (ch. xlviii.). He says that when the object of vision was derogatory, it was not brought into direct relation with the deity; in such instances the verb is paraphrased, while in other instances the rendering is literal. Although Maimonides grants that the force of this observation is weakened by three exceptions, he does not doubt its correctness.

The next Section (ch. l. to ch. lix.) "On the Divine Attributes" begins with the explanation that "faith" consists in thought, not in mere utterance; in conviction, not in mere profession. This explanation forms the basis for the subsequent discussion. The several arguments advanced by Maimonides against the employment of attributes show that those who assume the real existence of divine attributes may possibly utter with their lips the creed of the Unity and the Incorporeality of God, but they cannot truly believe it. A demonstration of this fact would be needless, if the Attributists had not put forth their false theses and defended them with the utmost tenacity, although with the most absurd arguments.

After this explanation the author proceeds to discuss the impropriety of assigning attributes to God. The Attributists admit that God is the Primal Cause, One, incorporeal, free from emotion and privation, and that He is not comparable to any of His creatures. Maimonides therefore contends that any attributes which, either directly or indirectly, are in contradiction to this creed should not be applied to God. By this rule he rejects four classes of attributes: namely, those which include a definition, a partial definition, a quality, or a relation.

The definition of a thing includes its efficient cause; and since God is the Primal Cause, He cannot be defined, or described by a partial definition. A quality, whether psychical, physical, emotional, or quantitative, is always regarded as something distinct from its substratum; a thing which possesses any quality, consists, therefore, of that quality and of a substratum, and should not be called *one*. All relations of time and space imply corporeality; all relations between two objects are, to a certain degree, a comparison between these two objects. To employ any of these attributes in reference to God would be as much as to declare that God is not the Primal Cause, that He is not One, that He is corporeal, or that He is comparable to His creatures.

There is only one class of attributes to which Maimonides makes no objection, namely, such as describe actions, and to this class belong all the Divine attributes which occur in the Scriptures. The "Thirteen Attributes" (*shelosh esreh middoth*, Ex. xxxiv. 6-7) serve as an illustration. They were communicated to Moses when he, as the chief of the Israelites, wished to know the way in which God governs the universe, in order that he himself in ruling the nation might follow it, and thereby promote their real well-being.

On the whole, the opponents of Maimonides admit the correctness of this theory. Only a small number of attributes are the subject of dispute. The Scriptures unquestionably ascribe to God Existence, Life, Power, Wisdom, Unity, Eternity, and Will. The Attributists regard these as properties distinct from, but co-existing with, the Essence of God. With great acumen, and with equally great acerbity, Maimonides shows that their theory is irreconcilable with their belief in the Unity and the Incorporeality of God. He points out three different ways of interpreting these attributes:—1. They may be regarded as descriptive of the works of God, and as declaring that these possess such properties as, in works of man, would appear to be the result of the will, the power, and the wisdom of a living being. 2. The terms "existing," "one," "wise," etc., are applied to God and to His creatures homonymously; as attributes of God they coincide with His Essence; as attributes of anything beside God they are distinct from the essence of the thing. 3. These terms do not describe a positive quality, but express a negation of its opposite. This third interpretation appears to have been preferred by the author; he discusses it more fully than the two others. He observes that the knowledge of the incomprehensible Being is solely of a negative character, and he shows by simple and appropriate examples that an approximate knowledge of a thing can be attained by mere negations, that such knowledge increases with the number of these negations, and that an error in positive assertions is more injurious than an error in negative assertions. In describing the evils which arise from the application of positive attributes to God, he unsparingly censures the *paytanim*, because he found them profuse in attributing positive epithets to the Deity. On the basis of his own theory, he could easily have interpreted these epithets in the same way as he explains the Scriptural attributes of God. His severity may, however, be accounted for by the fact that the frequent recurrence of positive attributes in the literary compositions of the Jews was the cause that the Mahometans charged the Jews with entertaining false notions of the Deity.

The inquiry into the attributes is followed by a treatment of the names of God. It seems to have been beyond the design of the author to elucidate the etymology of each name, or to establish methodically its signification; for he does not support his explanations by any proof. His sole aim is to show that the Scriptural names of God in their true meaning strictly harmonise with the philosophical conception of the Primal Cause. There are two things which have to be distinguished in the treatment of the Primal Cause: the Primal Cause *per se*, and its relation to the Universe. The first is expressed by the tetragrammaton and its cognates, the second by the several attributes, especially by *rochebh baarabhoth*, "He who rideth on the arabhoth" (Ps. lxviii. 4).

The tetragrammaton exclusively expresses the essence of God, and therefore is employed as a *nomen proprium*. In the mystery of this name, and others mentioned in the Talmud, as consisting of twelve and of forty-two letters, Maimonides finds no other secret than the solution of some metaphysical problems. The subject of these problems is not actually known, but the author supposes that it referred to the "absolute existence of the Deity." He discovers the same idea in *ehyeh* (Ex. iii. 14), in accordance with the explanation added in the Sacred Text: *asher ehyeh*, "that is, I am." In the course of this discussion he exposes the folly or sinfulness of those who pretend to work miracles by the aid of these and similar names.

With a view of preparing the way for his peculiar interpretation of *rochebh baarabhoth*, he explains a variety of Scriptural passages, and treats of several philosophical terms relative to the Supreme Being. Such expressions as "the word of God," "the work of God," "the work of His fingers," "He made," "He spake," must be taken in a figurative sense; they merely represent God as the cause that some work has been produced, and that some person has acquired a certain knowledge. The passage, "And he rested (וינח) on the seventh day" (Ex. xx. 11) is interpreted as follows: On the seventh Day the forces and laws were complete, which during the previous six days had been established for the preservation of the Universe. They were not to be increased or modified.

It seems that Maimonides introduced this figurative explanation with a view of showing that the Scriptural "God" does not differ from the "Primal Cause" or "Ever-active Intellect" of the philosophers. On the other hand, the latter do not reject the Unity of God, although they assume that the Primal Cause comprises the *causa efficiens*, the *agens*, and the *causa finalis* (or, the cause, the means, and the end); and that the Ever-active Intellect comprises the *intelligens*, the *intellectus*, and the *intellectum* (or, the thinking subject, the act of thought, and the object thought of); because in this

ANALYSIS OF THE GUIDE OF THE PERPLEXED. lvii

case these apparently different elements are, in fact, identical. The Biblical term corresponding to "Primal Cause" is *rochebh baarabhoth*, "riding on *araboth*." Maimonides is at pains to prove that *araboth* denotes "the highest sphere," which causes the motion of all other spheres, and which thus brings about the natural course of production and destruction. By "the highest sphere" he does not understand a material sphere, but the immaterial world of intelligences and angels, "the seat of justice and judgment, treasures of life, peace, and blessings, the seat of the souls of the righteous," etc. *Rochebh baarabhoth*, therefore, means: He presides over the immaterial beings, He is the source of their powers, by which they move the spheres and regulate the course of nature. This theory is more fully developed in the Second Part.

The next section (ch. lxxi.-lxxvi.) treats of the Kalām. According to the author, the method of the Kalām is copied from the Christian Fathers, who applied it in the defence of their religious doctrines. The latter examined in their writings the views of the philosophers, ostensibly in search of truth, in reality, however, with the object of supporting their own dogmas. Subsequently Mahometan theologians found in these works arguments which seemed to confirm the truth of their own religion; they blindly adopted these arguments, and made no enquiry whence these had been derived. Maimonides rejects à priori the theories of the Mutakallemim, because they explain the phenomena in the Universe in conformity with preconceived notions, instead of following the scientific method of the philosophers. Among the Jews, especially in the East and in Africa, there were also some who adopted the method of the Kalām; in doing so they followed the Mutazilah (dissenting Mahometans), not because they found it more correct than the Kalām of the Ashariyah (orthodox Mahometans), but because at the time when the Jews became acquainted with the Kalām it was only cultivated by the Mutazilah. The Jews in Spain, however, remained faithful to the Aristotelian philosophy.

The four principal dogmas upheld by the dominant

religions were the *creatio ex nihilo*, the Existence of God, His Incorporeality, and His Unity. By the philosophers the *creatio ex nihilo* was rejected, but the Mutakallemim defended it, and founded upon it their proofs in favour of the other three dogmas. Maimonides adopts the philosophical proofs for the Existence, Incorporeality, and Unity of God, because they must be admitted even by those who deny the *creatio ex nihilo*, the proofs being independent of this dogma. In order to show that the Mutakallemim are mistaken in ignoring the organisation of the existing order of things, the author gives a minute description of the analogy between the Universe, or Kosmos, and man, the mikrokosmos (ch. lxxii.). This analogy is merely asserted, and the reader is advised either to find the proof by his own studies, or to accept the fact on the authority of the learned. The *Kalām* does not admit the existence of law, organization, and unity in the universe. Its adherents have, accordingly, no trustworthy criterion to determine whether a thing is possible or impossible. Everything that is conceivable by imagination is by them held as possible. The several parts of the universe are in no relation to each other; they all consist of equal elements; they are not composed of substance and properties, but of atoms and accidents; the law of causality is ignored; man's actions are not the result of will and design, but are mere accidents. Maimonides in enumerating and discussing the twelve fundamental propositions of the *Kalam* (ch. lxiii.), which embody these theories, had apparently no intention to give a complete and impartial account of the *Kalām*; he solely aimed at exposing the weakness of a system which he regarded as founded not on a sound basis of positive facts, but on mere fiction; not on the evidences of the senses and of reason, but on the illusions of imagination.

After having shown that the twelve fundamental propositions of the *Kalām* are utterly untenable, Maimonides finds no difficulty in demonstrating the insufficiency of the proofs advanced by the Mutakallemim in support of the above-named dogmas. Seven arguments are cited which the Mutakallemim employ in support of the *creatio ex nihilo*.[1] The first argument is based on the atomic theory, viz., that the universe consists of equal atoms without inherent properties: all variety and change observed in nature must therefore be attributed to an external force. Three arguments are supplied by the proposition that finite things of an infinite number cannot exist (Propos. xi.). Three other arguments derive their support from the following proposition (x.): Everything that can be imagined can have an actual existence. The present order of things is only one out of the many forms which are possible, and exist through the *fiat* of a determining power.

The Unity of God is demonstrated by the Mutakallemim as follows: Two Gods would have been unable to produce the world; one would have impeded the work of the other. Maimonides points out that this might have been avoided by a suitable division of labour. Another argument is as follows: The two Beings would have one element in common, and would differ in another; each would thus consist of two elements, and would not be God. Maimonides might have suggested that the argument moves in a circle, the unity of God being proved by assuming His unity. The following argument is altogether unintelligible: Both Gods are moved to action by will; the will, being without a substratum, could not act simultaneously in two separate beings. The fallacy of the following argument is clear: The exis-

[1] Saadiah proves the existence of the Creator in the following way:—1. The Universe is limited, and therefore cannot possess an unlimited force. 2. All things are compounds; the composition must be owing to some external cause. 3. Changes observed in all beings are effected by some external cause. 4. If time were infinite, it would be impossible to conceive the progress of time from the present moments to the future, or from the past to the present moment. (Emunoth vedeoth, ch. i.).—Bahya founds his arguments on three propositions:—1. A thing cannot be its own maker. 2. The series of successive causes is finite. 3. Compounds owe their existence to an external force. His arguments are:—1. The Universe, even the elements, are compounds consisting of substance and form. 2. In the Universe plan and unity is discernible. (Chobhoth ha-lebhabhoth, ch. i.)

tence of *one* God is proved; the existence of a second God is not proved, it would be possible; and as possibility is inapplicable to God, there does not exist a second God. The possibility of ascertaining the existence of God is here confounded with potentiality of existence. Again, if *one* God suffices, the second God is superfluous; if *one* God is not sufficient, he is not perfect, and cannot be a deity. Maimonides objects that it would not be an imperfection in either deity to act exclusively within their respective provinces. As in the criticism of the first argument, Maimonides seems here to forget that the existence of separate provinces would require a superior determining Power, and the two Beings would not properly be called Gods.

The weakest of all arguments are, according to Maimonides, those by which the Mutakallemim sought to support the doctrine of God's Incorporeality. If God were corporeal, He would consist of atoms, and would not be *one*; or He would be comparable to other beings; but a comparison implies the existence of similar and of dissimilar elements, and God would thus not be *one*. A corporeal God would be finite, and an external power would be required to define those limits.

PART II.

The Second Part includes the following sections:—1. Introduction; 2. Philosophical Proof of the Existence of One Incorporeal Primal Cause (ch. i.); 3. On the Spheres and the Intelligences (ii.-xii.); 4. On the theory of the Eternity of the Universe (xiii.-xxix.); 5. Exposition of Gen. i.-iv. (xxx., xxxi.); 6. On Prophecy (xxxii.-xlviii.).

The enumeration of twenty-six propositions, by the aid of which the philosophers prove the Existence, the Unity, and the Incorporeality of the Primal Cause, forms the introduction to the Second Part of this work. The propositions treat of the properties of the finite and the infinite (i.-iii., x.-xii., xvi.), of change and motion (iv.-ix., xiii.-xviii.)

and of the possible and the absolute or necessary (xx.-xxv.); they are simply enumerated, but are not demonstrated. Whatever the value of these Propositions may be, they were inadequate for their purpose, and the author is compelled to introduce auxiliary propositions to prove the existence of an infinite, incorporeal, and uncompounded Primal Cause. (Arguments 1. and III.)

The first and the fourth arguments may be termed cosmological proofs. They are based on the hypothesis that the series of causes for every change is finite, and terminates in the Primal Cause. There is no essential difference in the two arguments: in the first are discussed the causes of the motion of a moving object ; the fourth treats of the causes which bring about the transition of a thing from potentiality to reality. To prove that neither the spheres nor a force residing in them constitute the Primal Cause, the philosophers employed two propositions, of which the one asserts that the revolutions of the spheres are infinite, and the other denies the possibility that an infinite force should reside in a finite object. The distinction between the finite in space and the finite in time appears to have been ignored ; for it is not shown why a force infinite in time could not reside in a body finite in space. Moreover, those who, like Maimonides, reject the eternity of the universe, necessarily reject this proof, while those who hold that the universe is eternal do not admit that the spheres have ever been only potential, and passed from potentiality to actuality. The second argument is supported by the following supplementary proposition: If two elements coexist in a state of combination, and one of these elements is to be found at the same time separate, in a free state, it is certain that the second element is likewise to be found by itself. Now, since things exist which combine in themselves motive power and mass moved by that power, and since mass is found by itself, motive power must also be found by itself independent of mass.

The third argument has a logical character: The universe is either eternal or temporal, or partly eternal and partly temporal. It cannot be eternal in all its parts, as many parts undergo destruction; it is not altogether temporal, because, if so, the universe could not be reproduced after being destroyed. The continued existence of the universe leads, therefore, to the conclusion that there is an immortal force, the Primal Cause, besides the transient world.

These arguments have this in common, that while proving the existence of a Primal Cause, they at the same time demonstrate the Unity, the Incorporeality, and the Eternity of that Cause. Special proofs are nevertheless superadded for each of these postulates, and on the whole they differ very little from those advanced by the Mahometan Theologians.

This philosophical theory of the Primal Cause was adapted by Jewish scholars to the Biblical theory of the Creator. The universe is a living, organised being, of which the earth is the centre. Any changes on this earth are due to the revolutions of the spheres; the lowest or innermost sphere, namely, the one nearest to the centre, is the sphere of the moon; the outermost or uppermost is "the all-encompassing sphere." Numerous spheres are interposed; but Maimonides divides all the spheres into four groups, corresponding to the moon, the sun, the planets, and the fixed stars. This division is claimed by the author as his own discovery; he believes that it stands in relation to the four causes of their motions, the four elements of the sublunary world, and the four classes of beings, viz., the mineral, the vegetable, the animal, and the rational. The spheres have souls, and are endowed with intellect; their souls enable them to move freely, and the impulse to the motion is given by the intellect in conceiving the idea of the Absolute Intellect. Each sphere has an intellect peculiar to itself; the intellect attached to the sphere of the moon is called "the active intellect" (*Sechel ha-poël*). In support of this theory numerous passages are cited both from Holy Writ and from post-Biblical Jewish literature. The angels (*elohim, malachim*) mentioned in the Bible are assumed to be identical with the intellects of the spheres; they are free agents, and their volition invariably tends to that which is good and noble; they emanate from the Primal Cause, and form a descending series of beings, ending with the active intellect. The transmission of power from one element to the other is called "emanation" (*shepha'*). This transmission is performed without the utterance of a sound; if any voice is supposed to be heard, it is only an illusion, originating in the human imagination, which is the source of all evils (ch. xii.).

In accordance with this doctrine, Maimonides explains that the three men who appeared to Abraham, the angels whom Jacob saw ascend and descend the ladder, and all other angels seen by man, are nothing but the intellects of the spheres, four in number, which emanate from the Primal Cause (ch. x.). In his description of the spheres he, as usual, follows Aristotle. The spheres do not contain any of the four elements of the sublunary world, but consist of the quintessence, an entirely different element. Whilst things on this earth are transient, the beings which inhabit the spheres above are eternal. According to Aristotle, these spheres, as well as their intellects, coexist with the Primal Cause. Maimonides, faithful to the teaching of the Scriptures, here departs from his master, and holds that the spheres and the intellects had a beginning, and were brought into existence by the will of the Creator. He does not attempt to give a positive proof of his doctrine; all he contends is that the theory of the *creatio ex nihilo* is, from a philosophical point of view, not inferior to the doctrine which asserts the eternity of the universe, and that he can refute all objections advanced against his theory (ch. xiii.-xxviii.).

He next enumerates and criticises the various theories respecting the origin of the Universe, viz.: A. God created the Universe out of nothing. B. God formed the Universe from an eternal substance. C. The Universe originating in the eternal Primal Cause is co-eternal.—It is not held necessary by the author to discuss the view of those who do not assume a Primal Cause, since the existence of such a cause has already been proved (ch. xiii.).

The objections raised to a *creatio ex nihilo* by its opponents are founded partly on the properties of Nature, and partly on those of the Primal Cause. They infer from the properties of Nature the following arguments: (1.) The first moving force is eternal; for if it had a beginning, another motion must have produced it, and then it would not be the First moving force. (2.) If the *formless* matter be not eternal, it must have been produced out of another substance; it would then have a certain form by which it might be distinguished from the primary substance, and then it would not be *formless*. (3.) The circular motion of the spheres does not involve the necessity of termination; and anything that is without an end, must be without a beginning. (4.) Anything brought to existence existed previously *in potentia*; something must therefore have pre-existed of which potential existence could be predicated. Some support for the theory of the eternity of the heavens has been derived from the general belief in the eternity of the heavens.—The properties of the Primal Cause furnished the following arguments:—If it were assumed that the Universe was created from nothing, it would imply that the First Cause had changed from the condition of a potential Creator to that of an actual Creator, or that His will had undergone a change, or that He must be imperfect, because He produced a perishable work, or that He had been inactive during a certain period. All these contingencies would be contrary to a true conception of the First Cause (ch. xiv.).

Maimonides is of opinion that the arguments based on the properties of things in Nature are inadmissible, because the laws by which the Universe is regulated need not have been in force before the Universe was in existence. This refutation is styled by our author "a strong wall built round the Law, able to resist all attacks" (ch. xvii.). In a similar manner the author proceeds against the objections founded on the properties of the First Cause. Purely intellectual beings, he says, are not subject to the same laws as material bodies; that which necessitates a change in the latter or in the will of man need not produce a change in immaterial beings. As to the belief that the heavens are inhabited by angels and deities, it has not its origin in the real existence of these supernatural beings; it was suggested to man by meditation on the apparent grandeur of heavenly phenomena (ch. xviii.).

Maimonides next proceeds to explain how, independently of the authority of Scripture, he has been led to adopt the belief in the *creatio ex nihilo*. Admitting that the great variety of the things in the sublunary world can be traced to those immutable laws which regulate the influence of the spheres on the beings below—the variety in the spheres can only be explained as the result of God's free will. According to Aristotle — the principal authority for the eternity of the Universe — it is impossible that a simple being should, according to the laws of nature, be the cause of various and compound beings. Another reason for the rejection of the Eternity of the Universe may be found in the fact that the astronomer Ptolemy has proved the incorrectness of the view which Aristotle had of celestial spheres, although the system of that astronomer is likewise far from being perfect and final (ch. xxiv.). It is impossible to obtain a correct notion of the properties of the heavenly spheres; "the heaven, even the heavens, are the Lord's, but the earth hath he given to the children of man." (Ps. cxv. 16.) The author, observing that the arguments against the *creatio ex nihilo* are untenable, adheres to his theory, which was taught by such prophets as Abraham and Moses. Although each Scriptural quotation could, by a figurative interpretation be made to agree with the opposite theory, Maimonides declines to ignore the literal sense of a term, unless it be in opposition to well-established truths, as is the case with anthropomorphic expressions; for the latter, if taken literally, would be contrary to the demonstrated truth of God's incorporeality (ch. xxv.). He is therefore surprised that the author of Pirke-di-Rabbi Eliezer ventured to assume the eternity of matter, and he thinks it possible that Rabbi Eliezer carried the license of figurative speech too far. (Ch. xxvi.)

The theory of the *creatio ex nihilo* does not involve the belief that the Universe will at a future time be destroyed ; the Bible distinctly teaches the creation, but not the destruction of the world except in passages which are undoubtedly conceived in a metaphorical sense. On the contrary, respecting certain parts of the Universe it is clearly stated "He established them for ever." (Ps. cxlviii. 5.) The destruction of the Universe would be, as the creation has been, a direct act of the Divine will, and not the result of those immutable laws which govern the Universe. The Divine will would in that case set aside those laws, both in the initial and the final stages of the Universe. Within this interval, however, the laws remain undisturbed (ch. xxvii.). Apparent exceptions, the miracles, originate in these laws, although man is unable to perceive the causal relation. The biblical account of the creation concludes with the statement that God rested on the seventh day, that is to say, He declared that the work was complete; no new act of creation was to take place, and no new law was to be introduced. It is true that the second and the third chapters of Genesis appear to describe a new creation, that of Eve, and a new law, namely, that of man's mortality, but these chapters are explained as containing an allegorical representation of man's psychical and intellectual faculties, or a supplemental detail of the contents of the first chapter. Maimonides seems to prefer the allegorical explanation which, as it seems, he had in view without expressly stating it, in his treatment of Adam's sin and punishment. (Part I. ch. ii.) It is certainly inconsistent on the one hand to admit that at the pleasure of the Almighty the laws of nature may become inoperative, and that the whole Universe may become annihilated, and on the other hand to deny, that during the existence of the Universe, any of the natural laws ever have been or ever will be suspended. It seems that Maimonides could not conceive the idea that the work of the All-wise should be, as the Mutakallemim taught—without plan and system, or that the laws once laid down should not be sufficient for all emergencies.

The account of the Creation given in the book of Genesis is explained by the author according to the following two rules: First its language is allegorical; and Secondly, the terms employed are homonyms. The words *erets, mayim, ruach,* and *choshech* in the second verse (ch. i.), are homonyms and denote the four elements: earth, water, air, and fire; in other instances *erets* is the terrestrial globe of the earth, *mayim* is water or vapour, *ruach* denotes wind, and *choshech* darkness. According to Maimonides, a summary of the first chapter may be given thus: God created the Universe by producing first the *reshith* the "beginning" (Gen. i. 1), or *hathchalah, i.e.,* the intellects which give to the spheres both existence and motion, and thus become the source of the existence of the entire Universe. At first this Universe consisted of a chaos of elements, but its form was successively developed by the influence of the spheres, and more directly by the action of light and darkness, the properties of which were fixed on the first day of the Creation. In the subsequent five days minerals, plants, animals, and the intellectual beings came into existence. The seventh day, on which the Universe was for the first time ruled by the same natural laws which continue in operation, was distinguished as a day blessed and sanctified by the Creator, who designed it to proclaim the *creatio ex nihilo* (Exod. xx. 11). The Israelites were moreover commanded to keep this Sabbath in commemoration of their departure from Egypt (Deut. v. 15), because during the period of the Egyptian bondage, they had not been permitted to rest on that day. In the history of the first sin of man, Adam, Eve, and the serpent represent the intellect, the body, and the imagination. In order to complete the imagery, *Samael* or *Satan,* mentioned in the Midrash in connection with this account, is added as representing man's appetitive faculties. Imagination, the source of error, is directly aided by the appetitive faculty, and the two are intimately connected with the body, to which man generally gives paramount attention, and for the sake of which he indulges in sins; in the end, however, they subdue the intellect and weaken its power. Instead of obtaining pure and real knowledge, man forms false conceptions; in consequence, the body is subject to suffering, whilst the imagination, instead of being guided by the intellect and attaining a higher development becomes debased and depraved. In the three sons of Adam, Kain, Abel, and Seth, Maimonides finds an allusion to the three elements in man: the vegetable, the animal, and the intellectual. First, the animal element (Abel) becomes extinct; then the vegetable elements (Kain) are dissolved; only the third element, the intellect (Seth), survives, and forms the basis of mankind (ch. xxx., xxxi.).

Maimonides having so far stated his opinion in explicit terms, it is difficult to understand what he had in view by the avowal that he could not disclose everything. It is unquestionably no easy matter to adapt each verse in the first chapters of Genesis to the foregoing allegory; but such an adaptation is, according to the author's own view (Part I., Introd., p. 19), not only unnecessary, but actually objectionable.

In the next section (xxxii.-xlviii.) Maimonides treats of Prophecy. He mentions the following three opinions:—
1. Any person, irrespective of his physical or moral qualifications, may be summoned by the Almighty to the mission of a prophet. 2. Prophecy is the highest degree of mental development, and can only be attained by training and study. 3. The gift of prophecy depends on physical, moral, and mental training, combined with inspiration. The author adopts the last-mentioned opinion. He defines prophecy as an emanation (*shepha'*), which through the will of the Almighty descends from the Active Intellect to the intellect

and the imagination of thoroughly qualified persons. The prophet is thus distinguished both from wise men whose intellect alone received the necessary impulse from the Active Intellect, and from diviners or dreamers, whose imagination alone has been influenced by the Active Intellect. Although it is assumed that the attainment of this prophetic faculty depends on God's will, this dependence is nothing else but the relation which all things bear to the Primal Cause; for the Active Intellect acts in conformity with the laws established by the will of God; it gives an impulse to the intellect of man, and, bringing to light those mental powers which lay dormant, it merely turns potential faculty into real action. These faculties can be perfected to such a degree as to enable man to apprehend the highest truths intuitively, without passing through all the stages of research required by ordinary persons. The same fact is noticed with respect to imagination; man sometimes forms faithful images of objects and events which cannot be traced to the ordinary channel of information, namely, impressions made on the senses. Since prophecy is the result of a natural process, it may appear surprising that, of the numerous men excelling in wisdom, so few became prophets. Maimonides accounts for this fact by assuming that the moral faculties of such men had not been duly trained. None of them had, in the author's opinion, gone through the moral discipline indispensable for the vocation of a prophet. Besides this, everything which obstructs mental improvement, misdirects the imagination or impairs the physical strength, and precludes man from attaining to the rank of prophets. Hence no prophecy was vouchsafed to Jacob during the period of his anxieties on account of his separation from Joseph. Nor did Moses receive a divine message during the years which the Israelites, under divine punishment, spent in the desert. On the other hand, music and song awakened the prophetic power (comp. 2 Kings iii. 15), and "The spirit of prophecy alights only on him who is wise, strong, and rich" (Babyl. Talm. Shabbath, 92a). Although the preparation for a prophetic mission, the pursuit of earnest and persevering study, as also the execution of the divine dictates, required physical strength, yet in the moment when the prophecy was received the functions of the bodily organs were suspended. The intellect then acquired true knowledge, which presented itself to the prophet's imagination in forms peculiar to that faculty. Pure ideals are almost incomprehensible; man must translate them into language which he is accustomed to use, and he must adapt them to his own mode of thinking. In receiving prophecies and communicating them to others the exercise of the prophet's imagination was therefore as essential as that of his intellect, and Maimonides seems to apply to this imagination the term "angel," which is so frequently mentioned in the Bible as the medium of communication between the Supreme Being and the prophet.

Only Moses held his bodily functions under such control that even without their temporary suspension he was able to receive prophetic inspiration; the interposition of the imagination was in his case not needed: "God spoke to him mouth to mouth." (Numb. xii. 8.) Moses differed so completely from other prophets that the term "prophet" could only have been applied to him and other men by way of homonymy.

The impulses descending from the Active Intellect to man's intellect and imagination produce various effects, according to his physical, moral, and intellectual condition. Some men are thus endowed with extraordinary courage and with an ambition to perform great deeds, or they feel themselves impelled to appeal mightily to their fellowmen by means of exalted and pure language. Such men are filled with "the spirit of the Lord," or, "with the spirit of holiness." To this distinguished class belonged Jephthah, Samson, David, Solomon, and the authors of the Hagiographa. Though above the standard of ordinary men, they were not included in the rank of prophets. Maimonides divides the prophets into two groups, namely, those who

receive inspiration in a dream and those who receive it in a vision. The first group includes the following five classes:—
1. Those who see symbolic figures; 2. Those who hear a voice addressing them without perceiving the speaker; 3. Those who see a man and hear him addressing them; 4. Those who see an angel addressing them; 5. Those who see God and hear His voice. The other group is divided in a similar manner, but contains only the first four classes, for Maimonides considered it impossible that a prophet should see God in a vision. This classification is based on the various expressions employed in the Scriptures to describe the several prophecies.

When the Israelites received the Law at Mount Sinai, they distinctly heard the first two commandments, which include the doctrines of the Existence and the Unity of God; of the other eight commandments, which enunciate moral, not metaphysical truths, they heard the mere " sound of words"; and it was through the mouth of Moses that the divine instruction was revealed to them. Maimonides defends this opinion by quotations from the Talmud and the Midrashim.

The theory that imagination was an essential element in prophecy is supported by the fact that figurative speech predominates in the prophetical writings, which abound in figures, hyperbolical expressions and allegories. The symbolical acts which are described in connection with the visions of the prophets, such as the translation of Ezekiel from Babylon to Jerusalem (Ez. viii. 3), Isaiah's walking about naked and barefoot (Is. xx. 2), Jacob's wrestling with the angel (Gen. xxxii. 27 *sqq.*), and the speaking of Balaam's ass (Num. xxii. 28), had no positive reality. The prophets, employing an elliptical style, frequently omitted to state that a certain event related by them was part of a vision or a dream. In consequence of such elliptical speech events are described in the Bible as coming directly from God, although they simply are the effect of the ordinary laws of nature, and as such depend on the will of God. Such passages cannot be misunderstood when it is borne in mind that every event and every natural phenomenon can for its origin be traced to the Primal Cause. In this sense the prophets employ such phrases as the following: "And *I* will command the clouds that they rain no rain upon it" (Is. v. 6); " I have also called my mighty men" (*ibid.* xi. 3).

PART III.

This part contains the following six sections:—1. Exposition of the *maaseh mercabhah* (Ez. i.), ch. i.-vii.; 2. On the nature and the origin of evil, ch. viii.-xii.; 3. On the object of the creation, ch. xiii.-xv.; 4. On Providence and Omniscience, ch. xvi.-xxv.; 5. On the object of the Divine precepts (*taame ha-mitsvoth*) and the historical portions of the Bible, ch. xxv.-xl.; 6. A guide to the proper worship of God.

With great caution Maimonides approaches the explanation of the *maaseh mercabhah*, the chariot which Ezekiel beheld in a vision (Ez. i.). The mysteries included in the description of the divine chariot had been orally transmitted from generation to generation, but in consequence of the dispersion of the Jews the chain of tradition was broken, and the knowledge of these mysteries had vanished. Whatever he knew of those mysteries he owed exclusively to his own inventive faculties; he therefore could not reconcile himself to the idea that his knowledge should die with him. He committed his exposition of the *maaseh mercabhah* and the *maaseh bereshith* to writing, but did not divest it of its original mysterious character; so that the explanation was fully intelligible to the initiated—that is to say, to the philosopher—but to the ordinary reader it was a mere paraphrase of the biblical text.—(Introduction.)

The first seven chapters are devoted to the exposition of the divine chariot. According to Maimonides three distinct parts are to be noticed, each of which begins with the phrase "And I saw." These parts correspond to the three parts of the Universe, the sublunary world, the spheres and the intelligences. First of all the prophet is made to behold the material world which consists of the earth and the spheres, and of these the spheres as the more important, are noticed first. In the Second Part, in which the nature of the spheres is discussed, the author dwells with pride on his discovery that they can be divided into four groups. This discovery he now employs to show that the four "chayyoth" (animals) represent the four divisions of the spheres. He points out that the terms which the prophet uses in the description of the *chayyoth* are identical with terms applied to the properties of the spheres. For the four *chayyoth*, or "angels," or *cherubim*, (1) have human form; (2) have human faces; (3) possess characteristics of other animals; (4) have human hands; (5) their feet are straight and round (cylindrical); (6) their bodies are closely joined to each other; (7) only their faces and their wings are separate; (8) their substance is transparent and refulgent; (9) they move uniformly; (10) each moves in its own direction; (11) they run; (12) swift as lightning they return towards their starting point; and (13) they move in consequence of an extraneous impulse (*ruach*). In a similar manner the spheres are described:—(1) they possess the characteristics of man, viz., life and intellect; (2) they consist like man of body and soul; (3) they are strong, mighty and swift, like the ox, the lion, and the eagle; (4) they perform all manner of work as though they had hands; (5) they are round, and are not divided into parts; (6) no vacuum intervenes between one sphere and the other; (7) they may be considered as one being, but in respect to the intellects, which are the causes of their existence and motion, they appear as four different beings; (8) they are transparent and refulgent; (9) each sphere moves uniformly, (10) and according to its special laws; (11) they revolve with great velocity; (12) each point returns again to its previous position; (13) they are self-moving, yet the impulse emanates from an external power.

In the second part of the vision the prophet saw the *ofannim*. These represent the four elements of the sublunary world. For the *ofannim* (1) are connected with the *chayyoth* and with the earth; (2) they have four faces, and are four separate beings, but interpenetrate each other "as though it were a wheel in the midst of a wheel" (Ez. i. 16); (3) they are covered with eyes; (4) they are not self-moving; (5) they are set in motion by the *chayyoth;* (6) their motion is not circular but rectilinear. The same may almost be said of the four elements:—(1) they are in close contact with the spheres, being encompassed by the sphere of the moon; earth occupies the centre, water surrounds earth, air has its position between water and fire; (2) this order is not invariably maintained; the respective portions change and they become intermixed and combined with each other; (3) though they are only four elements they form an infinite number of things; (4) not being animated they do not move of their own accord; (5) they are set in motion by the action of the spheres; (6) when a portion is displaced it returns in a straight line to its original position.

In the third vision Ezekiel saw a human form above the *chayyoth*. The figure was divided in the middle; in the upper portion the prophet only noticed that it was *chashmal*, (mysterious); from the loins downwards there was " the vision of the likeness of the Divine Glory," and "the likeness of the throne." The world of Intelligences was represented by the figure; these can only be perceived in as far as they influence the spheres, but their relation to the Creator is beyond human comprehension. The Creator himself is not represented in this vision.

The key to the whole vision Maimonides finds in the introductory words, "And the heavens were opened," and in the minute description of the place and the time of the revelation. When pondering on the grandeur of the spheres and their influences, which vary according to time and place, man begins to think of the existence of the Creator. At the conclusion of this exposition Maimonides declares that he will, in the subsequent chapters, refrain from giving further explanation of the *maaseh mercabhah*. The foregoing summary, however, shows that the opinion of the author on this subject is fully stated, and it is indeed difficult to conceive what additional disclosures he could still have made.

The task which the author has proposed to himself in the Preface he now regarded as accomplished. He has discussed the method of the Kalām, the system of the philosophers, and his own theory concerning the relation between the Primal Cause and the Universe; he has explained the Biblical account of the creation, the nature of prophecy, and the mysteries in Ezekiel's vision. In the remaining portion of the work the author attempts to solve certain theological problems, as though he wished to obviate the following objections, which might be raised to his theory that there is a design throughout the creation, and that the entire Universe is subject to the law of causation :—What is the purpose of the evils which attend human life? For what purpose was the world created? In how far does Providence interfere with the natural course of events? Does God know and foresee man's actions? To what end was the Divine Law revealed? These problems are treated seriatim.

All evils, Maimonides holds, originate in the material element of man's existence. Those who are able to emancipate themselves from the tyranny of the body, and unconditionally to submit to the dictates of reason, are protected from many evils. Man should disregard the cravings of the body, avoid them as topics of conversation, and keep his thoughts far away from them; convivial and erotic songs debase man's noblest gifts—thought and speech. Matter is the partition separating man from the pure Intellects; it is "the thickness of the cloud" which true knowledge has to traverse before it reaches man. In reality, evil is the mere negative of good: "God saw *all* that he had made, and behold it was very good" (Gen. i. 31). Evil does not exist at all. When evils are mentioned in the Scriptures as the work of God, the scriptural expressions must not be taken in their literal sense.

There are three kinds of evils :—1. Evils necessitated by those laws of production and destruction by which the species are perpetuated. 2. Evils which men inflict on each other; they are comparatively few, especially among civilised men. 3. Evils which man brings upon himself, and which comprise the majority of existing evils. The consideration of these three classes of evils leads to the conclusion that " the Lord is good to all, and His tender mercies are over all His works " (Ps. cxlv. 9).

The question, What is the object of the creation? must be left unanswered. The creation is the result of the will of God. Also those who believe that the Universe is eternal must admit that they are unable to discover the purpose of the Universe. It would, however, not be illogical to assume that the spheres have been created for the sake of man, notwithstanding the great dimensions of the former and the smallness of the latter. Still it must be conceded that, even if mankind were the main and central object of creation there is no absolute interdependence between them; for it is a matter of course that, under altered conditions, man could exist without the spheres. All teleological theories must therefore be confined within the limits of the Universe as it now exists. They are only admissible in the relation in which the several parts of the Universe stand to each other; but the purpose of the Universe as a whole cannot be accounted for. It is simply an emanation from the will of God.

Regarding the belief in Providence, Maimonides enumerates the following five opinions :—1. There is no Providence; *everything* is subject to chance ; 2. Only a part of the Universe is governed by Providence, viz., the spheres, the species, and such individual beings as possess the power of perpetuating their species (*e.g.*, the stars)—the rest, that is, the sublunary world is left to mere chance; 3. Everything is predetermined; according to this theory, revealed Law is inconceivable; 4. Providence assigns its blessings to *all* creatures, according to their merits; accordingly, all beings, even the lowest animals, if innocently injured or killed receive compensation in a future life. 5. According to the Jewish belief, all living beings are endowed with free-will; God is just, and the destiny of man depends on his merits. Maimonides denies the existence of trials inflicted by Divine love (יסורין של אהבה), as mentioned in the Talmud, *i.e.* afflictions which befall man, not as punishments of sin, but as means to procure for him a reward in times to come. Maimonides also rejects the notion that God ordains special temptation. The Biblical account, according to which God tempts men, "to know what is in their hearts," must not be taken in its literal sense; it merely states that God made the virtues of certain people known to their fellowmen in order that their good example should be followed. Of all creatures man alone enjoys the especial care of Providence; because the acts of Providence are identical with certain influences (*shefa'*) which the Active Intellect brings to bear upon the human intellect; their effect upon man varies according to his physical, moral, and intellectual condition; irrational beings, however, cannot be affected by these influences. If we cannot in each individual case see how these principles are applied, it must be borne in mind that God's wisdom is far above that of man. The author seems to have felt that his theory has its weak points, for he introduces it as follows:—"My theory is not established by demonstrative proof; it is based on the authority of the Bible, and it is less subject to refutation than any of the theories previously mentioned."

Providence implies omniscience, and men who deny this, *eo ipso*, have no belief in Providence. Some are unable to reconcile the fate of man with Divine Justice, and are therefore of opinion that God takes no notice whatever of the events which occur on earth. Others believe that God, being an absolute Unity, cannot possess a knowledge of a multitude of things, or of things that do not yet exist, or the number of which is infinite. These objections, which are based on the nature of man's perception, are illogical; for God's knowledge cannot be compared to that of man; it is identical with His essence. Even the Attributists, who assume that God's knowledge is different from His essence, hold that it is distinguished from man's knowledge in the following five points:—1. It is *one*, although it embraces a plurality. 2. It includes even such things as do not yet exist. 3. It includes things which are infinite in number. 4. It does not change when new objects of perception present themselves. 5. It does not determine the course of events. —However difficult this theory may appear to human comprehension, it is in accordance with the words of Isaiah (lv. 8): "Your thoughts are not my thoughts, and your ways are not my ways." According to Maimonides, the difficulty is to be explained by the fact that God is the Creator of all things, and His knowledge of the things is not dependent on their existence; but, on the other hand, the knowledge of man is solely dependent on the objects which come under his cognition.

According to Maimonides, the book of Job illustrates the several views which have been mentioned above. Satan, that is, the material element in human existence, is described as the cause of Job's sufferings. Job at first believed that man's happiness depends on riches, health, and children; being deprived of these sources of happiness, he conceived the notion that Providence is indifferent to the fate of mortal beings. After a careful study of natural phenomena, he rejected this opinion. Eliphaz held that *all* misfortunes of man serve as punishments of past sins. Bildad, the second friend of Job, admitted the existence of those afflictions which Divine love decrees in order that the patient sufferer may be fitted to receive a bountiful reward. Zophar, the third friend of Job, declared that the ways of God are beyond human comprehension; there is but one explanation assignable to all Divine acts, namely: Such is His Will. Elihu gives a fuller development to this idea; he says that such evils as befell Job may be remedied once or twice, but the course of nature is not altogether reversed. It is true that by prophecy a clearer insight into the ways of God can be obtained, but there are only few who arrive at that exalted intellectual degree, whilst the majority of men must content themselves with acquiring a knowledge of God through the study of nature. Such a study leads man to the conviction that his understanding is unable to fathom the secrets of nature and the wisdom of Divine Providence.

The concluding section of the Third Part treats of the purpose of the Divine precepts. In the Pentateuch they are described as the means of acquiring wisdom, enduring happiness, and also bodily comfort (ch. xxxi.). Generally a distinction is made between "*chukkim*" ("statutes") and *mishpatim* ("judgments"). The object of the latter is, on the whole, known, but the *chukkim* are considered as tests of man's obedience; no reason is given why they have been enacted. Maimonides rejects this distinction; he states that all precepts are the result of wisdom and design, that all contribute to the welfare of mankind, although with regard to the *chukkim* this is less obvious. The author draws another line of distinction between the general principles and the details of rules. For the selection and the introduction of the latter there is but one reason, namely: "Such is the will of God."

The laws are intended to promote man's perfection; they improve both his mental and his bodily condition; the former in so far as they lead him to the acquisition of true knowledge, the latter through the training of his moral and social faculties. Each law thus imparts knowledge, improves the moral condition of man, or conduces to the well-being of society. Many revealed laws help to enlighten man, and to correct false opinions. This object is not always clearly announced. God in His wisdom sometimes withheld from the knowledge of man the purpose of commandments and actions. There are other precepts which tend to restrain man's passions and desires. If the same end is occasionally attainable by other means, it must be remembered that the Divine laws are adapted to the ordinary mental and emotional state of man, and not to exceptional circumstances. In this work, as in the *Yad ha-chazakah*, Maimonides divides the laws of the Pentateuch into fourteen groups, and in each group he discusses the principal and the special object of the laws.

In addition to the legislative contents, the Bible includes historical information; and Maimonides, in briefly reviewing the Biblical narratives, shows that these are likewise intended to improve man's physical, moral, and intellectual condition. "It is not a vain thing for you" (Deut. xxxii. 47), and when it proves vain to anyone, it is his own fault.

In the final chapters the author describes the several degrees of human perfection, from the sinners who have turned away from the right path to the best of men, who in all their thoughts and acts cling to the Most Perfect Being, who aspire after the greatest possible knowledge of God, and strive to serve their Maker in the practice of "loving-kindness, righteousness, and justice." This degree of human perfection can only be attained by those who never forget the presence of the Almighty, and remain firm in their fear and love of God. These servants of the Most High inherit the choicest of human blessings; they are endowed with wisdom: they are godlike beings.

My theory aims at pointing out a straight way, at casting up a high-road. Ye who have gone astray in the field of the holy Law, come hither and follow the path which I have prepared. The unclean and the fool shall not pass over it. It shall be called the way of Holiness.

INTRODUCTION.

[*Letter of the Author to his Pupil, R. Joseph Ibn Aknim.*[1]]

In the name of GOD, Lord of the Universe.

To R. Joseph (may God protect him!), son of R. Jehudah (may his repose be in Paradise![2]):—

"My dear pupil, ever since you resolved to come to me[3] from a distant country,[4] and to study under my direction, I thought highly of your thirst for knowledge,[5] and your fond-

[1] Munk, in his "Notice sur Joseph Ben-Jehoudah ou Aboul Hadjadj Yousouf Ben-Yahja al Sabti al Maghrebi" (Paris, 1842), described the life of this pupil of Maimonides. The following are the principal facts:—Joseph b. Jehudah was born in Maghreb about the middle of the twelfth century. Although his father was forced to conform to the religious practices of the Mahomedans, Joseph was taught Hebrew and trained in the study of Hebrew literature. He left his native country about 1185, and went to Egypt, where he continued his scientific pursuits under the tuition of Maimonides, who instructed him in mathematics, astronomy, philosophy, and theology. Afterwards (1187) he resided at Aleppo, and married Sarah, the daughter of Abu'l Ala. After a successful journey to India, he devoted himself chiefly to science, and delivered lectures on various subjects to numerous audiences. He practised as physician to the Emir Faris ad-din Maimun al-Karsi, and to the king Ed-Dhahir Ghazi, son of Saladin. The Vizier Djemal ad-din el-Kofti was his intimate friend. When Charizi (1217) came to Aleppo, he found Joseph in the zenith of his career. He says of him (Tachkemoni, xlvi.):—

חכמתו כקוהלת , ושכלו כנחלת , ולשונו אש אוכלת
גביר ישאג בכל חכמה כאריה   ויטרוף לב מתי שכל כלביא
וים חכמות לפיו נקרע ונבקע   בעת יאמר לצולתו חרבי
ומפיו ילמדו חכמה חכמים   ואם הם כאלישע הוא כתשבי
יחיד הדור אבל הוליד ילדים   אשר הם בזמן לפאר ולצבי
ולמדו עניני מוסר בטרם   אשר ידעו קרא אמי ואבי
ובא ממערב לשכון במזרח   וצבאות כל יקר אסף והצביא
ולו הדור יהי דור הנבואה   משחו אל בישראל לנביא
ולו קדם יהי נמצא בציון   נתנהו כמו נר מערבי :

His poetical talents are praised by Charizi, in the eighteenth chapter of Tachkemoni, and in the fiftieth chapter his unparalleled generosity is mentioned. Of his poetical productions, one poem beginning נאום טוביה בן

ness for speculative pursuits, which found expression in your poems. I refer to the time when I received your writings in prose and verse[1] from Alexandria. I was then not yet able to test your powers of apprehension, and I thought that your desire might possibly exceed your capacity. But when you had gone with me through a course of astro-

---

צדקיה is named by Charizi (xviii.), and others are referred to by Maimonides in the present work. A Bodleian MS. (Uri, 341) contains a work on the Medicine of the Soul (טב הנפש or מרפא אלנפוש). It is written in Arabic, and Joseph b. Yehudah Albarceloni Ibn Aknin is named as its author. Munk (Arch. Isr., 1851, p. 327), Neubauer (Monatsschrift, 1870, p. 448), and Grätz (Introd. to מבוא התלמוד לר׳ יוסף בן עקנין), are of opinion that there were two authors of the same name, both living about the same time and following the same course of studies, the one being described as Almaghrebi, the other as Ibn Aknin Albarceloni. Steinschneider, however (Hammaskir, 1873, p. 38 ff.), thinks that there is not sufficient proof for the co-existence of the two scholars with the same name, but that in a Münetian MS. he has discovered a passage in which the Joseph b. Yehudah referred to in the More Nebuchim was likewise called Ibn Aknin Albarceloni. Besides the טב אלנפוש, Ibn Aknin wrote a commentary on Shir hashshirim and מאמר על המדות, a treatise on the measures mentioned in the Talmud, part of which is מבוא התלמוד (edited by the teachers of the Rabbinical Seminary at Breslau, 1871).

[2] The original has the *Hebrew* formulæ שצ״ו = שמרהו צורו "May his Rock be his guardian;" נ״ע = נוחו עדן "May Paradise be his repose." (Charizi has אלהים יחנך, Gen. xliii. 29).

[3] The original—מאן באת אלי; Ibn Tibbon למה מתלת ענדי וקצדת; Char. מאן עמדת לפני ובאת; Munk, Lorsque tu te représentas chez moi, etant venu. In the marginal notes of the Br. Mus. MS. Or. 1423 the verb מתל is explained by רנב "to wish," "to resolve."

[4] Lit. "From the remotest of the countries (or cities)." The North-west of Africa was called by the Arabs Al-Aghreb al-Aksa, "the extreme occident." Munk.

[5] Arabic, אלאמור אלנטריה; Hebrew, דברים עיוניים. עיון (derivative from עין "eye,") to look, to speculate; עיון, study, speculation; עיוני, speculative, requiring to be studied; דברים העיוניים, problems for speculation, philosophical or scientific matter.

[1] Arab. רשאיל, Hebr. כתביך; letter, a short treatise. חרוז, pearls joined together (comp. Shir ha-shirim, i. 10); a rhymed composition; rhyme משקל, metre). The original מקאמה is rendered by Charizi מחברת, "séance," a narrative in rhymed prose, interwoven with metric verses. (Munk.) In his Tachkemoni (xviii.), Charizi mentions one מחברת of Joseph b. Jehuda. (See p. 1, Note 1.)

nomy, after having completed the [other] elementary studies[1] which are indispensable for the understanding of that science, I was still more gratified by the acuteness and the quickness of your apprehension. Observing your great fondness for mathematics,[1] I let you study them more deeply, for I felt sure of your ultimate success.[2] Afterwards, when I took you through a course of logic,[3] I found that my great expectations of you were confirmed, and I considered you fit to receive from me an exposition of the esoteric ideas contained in the prophetic books, that you might understand them as they are understood by other men of culture. When I commenced by way of hints, I noticed that you desired additional explanation, urging me to treat of metaphysical themes; to teach you the system of the

[1] Arabic, תעאלם; Hebrew, חכמות למודיות; elementary discipline, subjects of direct instruction and training, in contradistinction to physics and metaphysics, that require deeper thought and study. This principally refers to mathematics (חכמות המספר והתשבורת Efodi, des sciences mathématiques, Munk) as preliminaries to the study of astronomy; (עלם אלהיאה, Hebr., חכמת התכונה, signifies both astronomy and geometry; literally, the science of the form, scil., the form of things in general—geometry, or of the universe—astronomy). In the fourteenth chapter of Milloth Higgayon, the speculative (עיונית) philosophy is divided into (1) למודית or שמושית, elementary or auxiliary science; (2) טבעית, physics; (3) אלהית, metaphysics. The למודית includes the quadrivium: arithmetic, geometry, astronomy, and music. Astronomy being one of the תעאלים, the word "other" has been added in the translation. The grammatical analysis of this complicated sentence is rather difficult, especially as regards the pronoun להא in the original (absent in the British Museum MS., Or. 1423), and להם in Ibn Tibbon's version, evidently referring to עלם אלהיאה and חכמת התכונה respectively. Charizi translates as follows: ומה שקדם לך מחכמת הלמודים שאי אפשר זולתם כדי להיות הצעה לחכמת התכונה.

[2] The original is במאלך or כמאלך; Ibn Tibbon appears to have had the former reading, and rendered it מה אחריתך; Charizi had the second reading, and translated it שכלך השלם. (Munk.)

[3] Arabic, אלמנטק. The Hebrew הגיון is a derivative of הגה ("to utter," "to think"), and signifies both "speech" and "thought." מלאכת ההגיון is the term used for "logic." (See Milloth Higgayon xiv.) Maimonides appears here to have taken the quadrivium, the lesser arts, before the trivium (grammar, rhetoric and logic), although in ch. xxxiv. he insists on logic being studied before any other science.

4   GUIDE OF THE PERPLEXED.

Mutakallemim ;[1] to tell you whether their arguments were based on logical proof; and if not, what was their method. I perceived that you had acquired some knowledge in those matters from others, and that you were perplexed and bewildered; yet you sought to find out a solution to your difficulty.[2] I urged you to desist from this pursuit, and enjoined you to continue your studies systematically; for my object was that the truth should present itself in connected order, and that you should not hit upon it by mere chance. Whilst you studied with me I never refused to explain difficult verses in the Bible or phrases in rabbinical literature which we happened to meet. When, by the will of God, we parted, and you went your way, our discussions aroused in me a resolution which had long been dormant. Your absence has prompted me to compose this treatise for you and for those who are like you, however few they may be. I have divided it into chapters, each of which shall be sent to you as soon as it is completed. Farewell!"

[*Prefatory Remarks.*]

"Cause me to know the way wherein I should walk, for I lift up my soul unto Thee." (Psalm cxliii. 8.)

"Unto you, O men, I call, and my voice is to the sons of men." (Prov. viii. 4.)

"Bow down thine ear and hear the word of the wise, and apply thine heart unto my knowledge." (Prov. xxii. 17.)[3]

My primary object in this work is to explain certain

[1] אלמתכלמין in Arabic and המדברים in Hebrew are Mahomedan theologians who discussed "the word" or "the principle" (כלאם דבר), of the Koran, and wished to establish its truth by philosophical argumentation. (Compare i. 69, 71, 73, *sqq.*) "Some of the teachers mixed up the method of the philosophers with that of the Kalām, and thus established a special discipline which they called Kalām, either because the principal subject of discussion was the Kalām (word of God), or because they wanted to imitate the way of the philosophers who called one of their disciplines 'Mantik' (*i.e.*, logic). Kalām and Mantik are synonyms" (Shahrastani's "Religionsparteien," etc., translated from the Arabic into German, by D. Theodor Haarbrücker, i., p. 26).

[2] Lit., "to find out acceptable words," Eccl. xii. 10.

[3] These three verses are probably intended to be an allusion to the three factors that must be combined to produce the good fruit expected from the work: 1. The divine support and guidance obtained by the author; 2. The work of the author; and 3. Attention and application on the part of the reader.

words[1] occurring in the prophetic books. Of these some are homonyms,[2] and of their several meanings the ignorant choose the wrong ones;[3] other terms which are employed in a figurative sense are erroneously taken by such persons in their primary signification. There are also hybrid terms, denoting things which are the same[4] from one

[1] The term اسم in Arabic, שם in Hebrew, generally signifying "noun" or "name," is here employed by Maimonides in the wider sense of "expression," or "term," including verbs. It is possible that the author assumed that a verbal noun was implied in every verb.

[2] Maimonides divides those words which are used in more than one sense into three classes (in Milloth Higgayon xiii., into six) viz., 1. שמות משתתפים "homonyms" (lit., "names joined in partnership;") words which accidentally coincide, but are totally different in meaning and derivation. (Comp. c. 56, note 5). 2. שמות מושאלים "metaphors" (lit., "names borrowed.") The two meanings, the primary and the figurative, have either a real or an imaginary *tertium comparationis*. 3. שמות מסופקים "hybrids or amphibious (lit. doubtful) nouns," words whose several significations can be explained as either homonymous, or as being derived from one common source. (See note 4 infra.) This division, apparently the basis for the first part of the Moreh, is in itself correct, but it can hardly be applied to the terms discussed by Maimonides in this work. According to our notions they are all metaphors (מושאלים). Maimonides probably preferred to explain צלם and similar expressions as homonyms (משתתפים), because he thought that to explain anthropomorphistic phrases as figures would imply the admission that God could be compared to material beings, an admission which our philosopher would by no means make.

[3] Lit., "and the ignorant take them according to some of the significations of that homonym."

[4] Arabic, אנהא תקאל בתואטו; Heb., שהם יאמרו בהסכמה, lit. "which are said (of the several things) by agreement," that is, by the agreement of the things in certain properties. Munk: qu'ils sont employés comme noms appellatifs. Things, to which the same term is applied, either agree in the essential properties contained in that term, or in some non-essential properties, or agree in neither of them. In the first case the term is employed as a class noun or appellative (נאמר בהסכמה, קיל בתואטו), in the third as a homonym (משותף), in the second as a hybrid, namely, as a class noun in reference to the non-essential properties, as a homonym in reference to the essential properties of the things. The word "man" is given by Maimonides in Milloth Higgayon xiii., as an instance of a hybrid term, for the word is applied to a living person, to a dead person, to a statue or likeness; as regards the essential properties of man (living, thinking חי מדבר), these are totally different things and the term is applied to them by homonymity: as regards the non-essential properties, figure and appearance, these things are alike, and the term may be said to be applied to them as a class noun.

point of view and different from another. It is not here intended to explain all these expressions to the unlettered or to mere tyros, a previous knowledge of Logic and Natural Philosophy being indispensable, or to those who confine their attention to the study of our holy Law, I mean the study of the canonical law alone; for the true knowledge of the Torah is the special aim of this and of similar works.[1]

The object of this treatise is to enlighten a religious man who has been trained to believe in the truth of our holy Law, who conscientiously fulfils his moral and religious duties, and at the same time has been successful in his philosophical studies. Human reason has impelled him to abide within its sphere; and, on the other hand, he is disturbed by the literal interpretation of the Law, and by ideas formed by himself or received from others, in connection with those homonymous, metaphorical, or hybrid expressions. Hence he is lost in perplexity and anxiety. If he be guided solely by reason, and renounce his previous views which are based on those expressions, he would consider that he had rejected the fundamental principles of the Law; and even if he retain the opinions which were derived from those expressions, and if, instead of following his reason, he abandon its guidance altogether, he would still feel that his religious convictions had suffered loss and injury.[2] He would then be left with those errors which give rise to fear and anxiety, constant grief and great perplexity.

This work has also a second object in view. It seeks to explain certain obscure figures which occur in the Prophets, and are not distinctly characterised as being figures. Ignorant and superficial readers take them in a literal, not in a figurative sense. Even well-informed persons are bewildered

---

[1] Maimonides distinguishes two kinds of חכמת התורה (עלם אלשעריה‎): 1. The knowledge of the laws contained in the Torah and explained by tradition (פקה‎ in Arabic, תלמוד‎ in Hebrew); 2. The science of the principles of faith as a subject for speculation (חכמת התורה על האמת‎).

[2] Arabic, אלאעתקאדאת אלביאליה‎; Tibbon, המחשבות הדמיונות‎; Charizi, מחשבות המבהלות‎.

if they treat these passages in their literal signification, but they are entirely relieved of their perplexity when we explain the figure, or merely suggest that the terms are figurative. For this reason I have called this book "Guide of the Perplexed" (Dalālat al-haïrin, MOREH NEBUCHIM).[1]

I do not pretend that this treatise settles every doubt in the minds of those who understand it, but I maintain that it settles the greater part of their difficulties. No intelligent man will require and expect that on introducing any subject I shall completely exhaust it; or that on commencing the exposition of a figure I shall fully explain all its parts. Such a course could not be followed by a teacher in a *vivâ voce* exposition, much less by an author in writing a book, without becoming a target for every foolish conceited person to discharge the arrows of folly at him. Some general principles bearing upon this point have been fully discussed in our works on the Talmud,[2] and we have there called the attention of the reader to many themes of this kind. We also stated that the expression "Ma'aseh Bereshith" signified "Natural Science," and "Ma'aseh Mercabah" Metaphysics, and we explained the force of the Rabbinical dictum,[3] "The

---

[1] Some read Nebochim (part. Niph. of בוך ; comp. Esther iii. 15) ; others Nebuchim (like Exod. xiv. 3).

[2] Mishnah Torah, especially Book I., Sefer ha-madda', and Commentary on the Mishnah; the Eight Chapters, introductory to Treatise Aboth.

[3] The vision, described in the first chapter of the prophecies of Ezekiel, is called "the work of the chariot" (מעשה המרכבה), because the Divine glory and its relation to the earth is shown to the prophet allegorically represented in the figure of a wonderfully constructed chariot. This chapter was held to include the principles of Theology and Metaphysics, which are too difficult for the comprehension of the ordinary reader, and if imperfectly apprehended, would lead to the gravest errors. For this reason the rule was laid down, that that chapter should not be expounded in the presence of more than one person, and even then only on condition that the person be able thoroughly to understand the expounder's words. The account of the Creation (מעשה בראשית), contained in the first chapter of the Book of Genesis, included the principles of Physics. Only one person at a time was allowed to listen to the exposition of that chapter; the admission to the secrets of Ma'aseh Bereshith was less restricted than to those of the Ma'aseh Mercabah. Mishnah Torah, i. 2, §§ 11, 12; and i. 4, §§ 10—13. Commentary on Mishnah Chagigah, ii. 1.

Ma'aseh Mercabah, must not be fully expounded even in the presence of a single student, unless he be wise and able to reason for himself, and even then you should merely acquaint him with the heads of the different sections of the subject. (Chagigah, fol. 11 b.) You must, therefore, not expect from me more than such heads. And even these have not been methodically and systematically arranged in this work, but have been, on the contrary, scattered, and are interspersed with other topics which we shall have occasion to explain. My object in adopting this arrangement is that the truths should be at one time apparent, and at another time concealed. Thus we shall not be in opposition to the Divine Will (from which it is wrong to differ) for it has withheld from the multitude the truths required for the knowledge of God, according to the words, "The secret of the Lord is with them that fear Him." (Ps. xxv. 14.)

Even with regard to Natural Science, it should be observed that there are some principles which are not to be explained *in extenso*. For our Sages have said, "The Ma'aseh Bereshith must not be expounded in the presence of two." If an author were to explain these principles in writing, it would be equal to expounding them unto thousands of men. For this reason the prophets treat these subjects in figures, and our Sages, imitating the method of Scripture, speak of them in metaphors and allegories; for there is a close affinity between these subjects and metaphysics, and indeed they form part of its mysteries. Do not imagine that these most difficult problems can be thoroughly understood by any one of us. This is not the case. At times the truth shines so brilliantly that we perceive it as clear as day. Nature and habit then draw a veil over our perception, and we return to a darkness almost as dense as before. We are like those who, though beholding frequent [1] flashes of lightning, still find

---

[1] (פעם אחר פעם) מרה בעד מרה is here quite superfluous, and is probably an erroneous repetition of the אלמרה בעד אלמרה of the next sentence.

themselves in the thickest darkness of the night. On some the lightning flashes in rapid succession, and they seem to be in perpetual light, and their night is as clear as the day. This was the degree of prophetic excellence attained by (Moses) the greatest of prophets, to whom God said, "But as for thee, stand thou here by Me." (Deut. v. 31), and of whom it is written "the skin of his face shone," etc. (Exod. xxxiv. 29.) [Some[1] perceive the prophetic flash at long intervals; this is the degree of most prophets.] By others only once during the whole night is a flash of lightning perceived. This is the case with those of whom we are informed, "They prophesied, and did not prophesy again." (Num. xi. 25.) There are some to whom the flash of lightning appears though with varying intensity;[2] others are in the condition of men, whose darkness is illumined not by lightning, but by some kind of crystal or similar stone, and other things that possess the property of

[1] In the Arabic text this sentence is absent; also in Charizi's version. Munk is of opinion that it is superfluous because it is nearly the same as the sentence which follows the words, "They prophesied and did not prophesy again." In truth, however, the two sentences referred to are not identical, as may be seen already from the additional וקלילה ("and less"). The different classes enumerated by Maimonides are the following five:—1. Those who enjoy an almost perpetual light; 2. Those who are favoured with moments of enlightenment after long intervals of darkness; 3. Those who, in their whole life, had only one moment of light; 4. Those whose light cannot be compared to a bright flash of lightning, but to an imperfect one, with more or less intensity; 5. Those whose illumination cannot be compared at all to the flash of lightning, but to the shining of some luminous substance. It is also possible that two different readings were fused into one, a fact which, in the course of these remarks, will be noticed several times. According to the one reading only two classes were enumerated, viz., 1. Prophets who perceived frequent flashes of light with more or less intensity; 2. Those who never perceived any flashes of light, but only the reflex of light as if coming through some transparent substance. The other reading contained the first three classes, mentioned above, arranged from another point of view, and illustrated by examples taken from the Pentateuch.

[2] הפרשים רבים או מעטים admits of two renderings, 1. "Long and short intervals;" 2. Great and small differences as regards the intensity. The context is here in favour of the second meaning, and the sentence must be interpreted as follows:—Others received a flash of lightning, but with an intensity which was greater in one case, and smaller in the other.

shining during the night;[1] and to them even this small amount of light is not continuous, but now it shines and now it vanishes, as if it were "the flame of the rotating sword."[2]

The degrees in the perfection of men[3] vary according to these distinctions. Concerning those who never beheld the light even for one day, but walk in continual darkness, it is written, "They know not, neither will they understand; they walk on in darkness." (Ps. lxxxii. 5.) Truth, in spite of all its powerful manifestations, is completely withheld from them, and the following words of Scripture may be applied to them, "And now men see not the light which is bright in the skies." (Job xxxvii. 21.) They are the multitude of ordinary men; there is no need to notice them in this treatise.

You must know that if a person, whatever degree of perfection he has attained, wishes to impart to others, either orally or in writing, any portion of the knowledge which he has acquired of these subjects, he is utterly unable to be as systematic and explicit as he could be in a science of which the method is well known. The same difficulties which he encountered when investigating the subject for himself will attend him when endeavouring to instruct others; viz., at one time the explanation will appear lucid, at another time, obscure; this property of the subject appears to remain the same both to the advanced scholar and to the beginner. For this reason, great theological scholars[4] gave instruction in all such matters only by means of metaphors and allegories. They frequently employed them in forms varying more or less[5] essentially. In most

---

[1] Most probably we have here a fusion of two readings—נשם טהור זך מן האבנים וזולתם, and נשם טהור זך וכיוצא בו מן האבנים.

[2] Taken from Gen. iii. 24.

[3] אלכאמלין, Hebrew השלמים, lit., "the perfect," generally opp. to the ignorant and uneducated, appears here to be distinguished from the various degrees of "prophets" enumerated before.

[4] According to Munk the terms רבני and אלהי are synonyms and signify theologians or metaphysicians, רבני being the Arabic רבאני, "relating to God," derived from רב "master," "God." See note 1, p. 13.

[5] אלנוע, Hebrew סוג, "kind" or "class" is a larger division than אלגנס (מין) "species." Comp. Maim. Milloth Higg. x. "A term including

cases they placed the lesson to be illustrated at the beginning, or in the middle, or at the end of the simile. When they could find no simile which from beginning to end corresponded to the idea which was to be illustrated,[1] they divided the subject of the lesson, although in itself one whole, into different parts, and expressed each by a separate figure. Still more obscure are those instances in which one simile is employed to illustrate many subjects, the beginning of the simile representing one thing, the end another. Sometimes the whole metaphor may refer to two cognate subjects in the same branch of knowledge.

If we were to teach in these disciplines, without the use of parables and figures, we should be compelled to resort to expressions both profound and transcendental, and by no means more intelligible than metaphors and similes; as though the wise and learned were drawn into this course by the Divine Will, in the same way as they are compelled to follow the laws of nature in matters relating to the body. You should observe that the Almighty, desiring to lead us to perfection and to improve our state of society, has revealed to us laws which are to regulate our actions. These laws, however, pre-suppose an advanced state of intellectual culture. We must first form a conception of the Existence of the Creator according to our capacities; that is, we must have a knowledge of Metaphysics,[2] which can only be acquired after the study of Physics; for the science of Physics is closely connected with Metaphysics,[3] and must even

---

several individuals is called מִין; several species form a סוּג." In our passage the two terms are not used in their strictly philosophical signification, but in the general sense "more" or "less."

[1] Munk joining this sentence with the preceding, begins here a new sentence, and supplies "quelque fois." There is no reason why the lesson should be placed in the beginning, the middle or the end of the simile, in the case when it is not complete, more than in any other case. But there is sufficient reason to express one idea through several similes, if there cannot be found one simile that could express it adequately.

[2] Lit., "theology," "the science of God;" it is the same as metaphysics.

[3] Arabic, מתאכם; Tibbon, מצרנית; lit. "bordering"; Charizi, אחרון, a translation of the Arabic מתאכר, a reading found in two Leyden MSS. (Munk), and in a MS. of Brit. Mus. Or. 1423.

precede it in the course of our studies, as is clear to all who are familiar with these questions. Therefore the Almighty commenced Holy Writ with the description of the Creation, that is, with Physical Science; the subject on the one hand being most weighty and important, and on the other hand our means of fully comprehending those great problems being limited, He described those profound truths, which His Divine Wisdom found it necessary to communicate to us, in allegorical, figurative, and metaphorical language. Our Sages have said, "It is impossible to give a full account of the Creation to man. Therefore Scripture simply tells us, In the beginning God created the heavens and the earth (Gen. i. 1)." Thus they have suggested that this subject is a deep mystery, and in the words of Solomon, "Far off and exceedingly deep, who can find it out?" (Eccles. vii. 24). It has been treated in metaphors in order that the uneducated may comprehend it according to the measure of their faculties and the feebleness of their apprehension, while educated persons may take it in a different sense. In the commentary on the Mishnah [1] we stated our intention to explain difficult problems in the Sepher ha-nebuah (Book of Prophecy), and in the Sepher ha-shevaah (Book of Harmony.) In the latter we intended to examine all the passages in the Midrash which, if taken literally, appear to be inconsistent with truth and common sense, and must therefore be taken figuratively. Many years have elapsed since I first commenced those works. I had proceeded but a short way when I became dissatisfied with my original plan. For I observed that by expounding these passages by means of allegorical and mystical terms, we do not explain anything, but merely substitute one thing for another of the same nature, whilst in explaining them fully our efforts displease the generality of men; and my sole object in writing those books was to make the contents of Midrashim and the exoteric lessons of the prophecies intelligible to everybody. We have further noticed that when an

[1] Comp. Maim. Comm. on Mishnah Sanhedrin, x. 1.

ill-informed rabbi[1] reads these Midrashim, he will find no
difficulty; for possessing no knowledge of the properties of
things, he will not reject statements which involve impossibilities. When, however, a person who is both religious and well
educated reads them, he cannot escape the following dilemma:
either he takes them literally, and questions the abilities of
the author and the soundness of his mind—doing thereby
nothing which is opposed to the principles of our faith—or
he will acquiesce in assuming that the passages in question
have some secret meaning, and he will continue to hold the
author in high estimation whether he understood the allegory
or not. As regards prophecy with its various degrees and
the different metaphors used in the prophetic books, we
shall give in the present work an explanation, according to
another method.[2] Guided by these considerations I have
refrained from writing those two books as I previously intended. In my larger work, the Mishnah Torah, I have
contented[3] myself with briefly stating the principles of
our faith and its fundamental truths, together with such
hints as approach a clear exposition. In this work, however, I address those who have studied philosophy and have
acquired sound knowledge, and who while firm in religious
matters are perplexed and bewildered on account of the ambiguous and figurative expressions[4] employed in the holy
writings. Some chapters may be found in this work which
contain no reference whatever to homonyms. These chapters
will serve as an introduction to others; contain some refe-

[1] סכל מהמון רבנים seems to have been used here as distinguished from
חכם נדול אלהי רבני, mentioned above. This supports the translation of
רבני by "Rabbanite."

[2] Some of the editions of Ibn Tibbon's Version have בדרך אחד instead
of בדרך אחר; Arabic אכֿר, another; different from the two mentioned;
" being explicit on one part, reserved on the other " (מגלה טפח ומכסה טפח).
Efodi.

[3] Charizi: ושמתי כוונתי "and I directed my attention." Arabic,
ואקתצרנא; Charizi perhaps read ואקצדנא. (Scheyer, Charizi's Version of
the More Nebuchim, page 6, note 19.)

[4] והמושאלים in both the Hebrew translations is a corruption of והמשלים.
Arabic אמתֿאל "similes." Munk.

rence to the signification of a homonym which I do not wish to mention in that place; explain some figure; point out that a certain expression is a figure; treat of difficult passages generally misunderstood in consequence of the homonymy they include, or because the simile they contain is taken in place of that which it represents, and *vice versâ*.

Having spoken of similes, I proceed to make the following remark:[1]—The key to the understanding and to the full comprehension of all that the Prophets have said, consists in the knowledge of the figures, their general ideas, and the meaning of each word they contain. You know the verse—"I have also spoken in similes by the Prophets" (Hosea xii. 10); and also the verse, "Put forth a riddle and speak a parable" (Ezek. xvii. 2). And because the Prophets continually employ figures, Ezekiel said, "Does He not speak parables?" (xxi. 5.) Again, Solomon begins his book of Proverbs with the words, "To understand a proverb and the interpretation; the words of the wise and their dark sayings" (Prov. i. 6); and we read in the Midrash,[2] "To what were the words of the Law to be compared before the time of Solomon? To a well the waters of which are at a great depth, and though cool and fresh, yet no man could drink of them. A clever man joined cord with cord, and rope with rope, and drew up and drank. So Solomon[3] went from figure to figure, and from subject to subject, till he obtained the true sense of the Law." So far go the words of our Sages. I do not believe that any intelligent man thinks that "the words of the Law" mentioned here as requiring the application of figures in order to be understood, can refer to the rules for building tabernacles, or for the Lulab, or for the four kinds of trus-

---

[1] Arabic, מקדמה פלנקדם; Hebrew, ונקדים הקדמה; Munk "énoncer une proposition." As that which follows has not the character of a scientific מקדמה "proposition" (comp. lxxiii.), it is more probable that the word has here the meaning "prefatory remark" or simply "remark."

[2] Shirha-shirim, Rabba i. 1.

[3] Supply בא or הולך. In the Midrash we read כך מדבר לדבר וממשל למשל עמד שלמה וגו'.

tees.¹ What is really meant is the apprehension of profound and difficult subjects, concerning which our Sages said, "If a man loses in his house a sela,² or a pearl, he can find it by lighting a taper worth only one issar.² Thus the parables in themselves are of no great value,³ but through them the words of the holy Law are rendered intelligible." These likewise are the words of our Sages;⁴ consider well their statement, that the deeper sense of the words of the holy Law are pearls, and the literal acceptation of a figure is of no value in itself. They compare the hidden meaning included in the literal sense of the simile to a pearl lost in a dark room, which is full of furniture. It is certain that the pearl is in the room, but the man can neither see it nor know where it lies. It is just as if the pearl were no longer in his possession, for, as has been stated, it affords him no benefit whatever until he kindles a light. The same is the case with the comprehension of that which the simile represents. The wise king said, "A word fitly spoken is like apples of gold in pictures of silver" (Prov. xi. 25). Hear the explanation of what he said:—The word משכיות means "filigree network"—i.e., things in which there are very small aper-

---

¹ The rules concerning the tabernacles in which the Israelites were commanded (Levit. xxiii. 42) to dwell seven days in the seventh month (from the 15th to the 21st), are mentioned and discussed in the Talmud, Treatise Sukkah, i.-ii., and by Maimonides, Mishnah Torah, in the third book (זמנים), vi. 4—6. The details concerning the Lulab, one of the four kinds of plants to be used on the Feast of Tabernacles (Lev. xxiii. 40) are given in the Talmud, Sukkah, iii.—iv., and Mishnah Torah, ibid. 7—8. The law concerning the four classes of Trustees, based on Exodus xxii. 6—14, is discussed in the Talmud, Baba Metsia, iv., vi., viii.; Mishnah Torah, thirteenth book (משפטים), ii. The four classes are—שומר חנם, who keeps the property of his neighbour without receiving a reward for it; שומר שכר, who receives payment for keeping his neighbour's property; השואל, who borrows something without paying for its use; השכיר, who hires something.

² The sela (originally a Tyrian weight), was a silver coin, equal to 4 denar or 96 issar (Roman as). The proportion of a sela to an issar was approximately as 81:1.

³ The words המשל הזה אינו כלום are not found in Midrash Shir ha-shirim.

⁴ This phrase appears to correspond to the formula עד כאן (abbrev. ע״כ) generally found at the end of a quotation.

tures, such as are frequently wrought by silversmiths. They are called in Hebrew משכיות, "*transpicuous*" (derived from שכה, "to look:" Onkelos renders the Hebrew וישקף, "and he looked," by the word ואסתכי, Gen. xxvi. 8), because the eye penetrates through them. Thus Solomon meant to say, "Just as apples of gold in silver filigree with small apertures, so is a word fitly spoken."

See [how beautifully the conditions of a good simile are described in this figure! It shows that in every word which has a double sense, a literal and a figurative meaning, the plain meaning must be as valuable as silver, and the hidden meaning still more precious; so that the figurative meaning bears the same relation to the literal one as gold to silver. It is further necessary that the plain sense of the phrase shall give to those who consider it some notion of that which the figure represents. Just as a golden apple overlaid with a net-work of silver, when seen at a distance, or looked at superficially, is mistaken for a silver apple; but when a keen-sighted person looks at the object well, he will find what is within, and see that the apple is gold. The same is the case with the figures employed by prophets. Taken literally, such expressions contain wisdom useful for many purposes, among others, for the amelioration of the condition of society; *e.g.*, the Proverbs (of Solomon),[1] and similar sayings in their literal sense. Their hidden meaning, however, is profound wisdom, conducive to the recognition of real truth.

Know that the figures employed by prophets are of two kinds: first, where every word which occurs in the simile represents a certain idea; and, secondly, where the simile, as a whole, represents a general archetype, but has a great many points which have no reference whatever to that typical idea; they are simply required to give to the simile its proper form and order, or better to conceal the archetype; and the simile is continued as far as necessary, according to its literal sense. Consider this well.

[1] In the editions of Tibbon's version we read משליהם instead of משלי.

An example of the first class of prophetic figures is to be found in Genesis:—"And, behold, a ladder set up on the earth, and the top of it reached to heaven; and, behold, the angels of God ascending and descending on it." (Gen. xxviii. 12.) The word "ladder" refers to one idea; "set up on the earth" to another; "and the top of it reached to heaven" to a third; "angels of God" to a fourth; "ascending" to a fifth; "descending" to a sixth; "the Lord stood above it" (ver. 13) to a seventh. Every word in this figure introduces a fresh idea into the archetype.

An example of the second class of prophetic figures is found in Proverbs (vii. 6—26):—"For at the window of my house I looked through my casement, and beheld among the simple ones; I discerned among the youths a young man void of understanding, passing through the street near her corner: and he went the way to her house, in the twilight, in the evening, in the black and dark night: and, behold, there met him a woman with the attire of a harlot, and subtil of heart. (She is loud and stubborn; her feet abide not in her house: now is she without, now in the streets, and lieth in wait in every corner.) So she caught him, and kissed him, and with an impudent face said unto him, I have peace offerings with me; this day have I paid my vows. Therefore came I forth to meet thee, diligently to seek thy face, and I have found thee. I have decked my bed with coverings of tapestry, with carved works, with fine linen of Egypt. I have perfumed my bed with myrrh, aloes, and cinnamon. Come, let us take our fill of love until the morning: let us solace ourselves with loves. For the goodman is not at home, he is gone a long journey: he hath taken a bag of money with him, and will come home at the day appointed. With her much fair speech she caused him to yield, with the flattering of her lips she forced him. He goeth after her straightway, as an ox goeth to the slaughter, or as a fool to the correction of the stocks: till a dart strike through his liver; as a bird hasteth to the snare, and knoweth not that it is for his life. Hearken unto me now therefore, O ye children, and attend to the words of my mouth. Let not thine heart decline to her ways, go not astray in her paths. For she hath cast down many wounded: yea, many strong men have been slain by her."

The general principle expounded in all these verses is to abstain from excessive indulgence in bodily pleasures. The author compares the body, which is the source of all sensual pleasures, to a married woman who at the same time is a harlot. And this figure he has taken as the basis of his entire book. We shall hereafter show the wisdom of Solomon in comparing sensual pleasures to an adulterous harlot. We shall explain how he concludes that work with the praises of a faithful wife who devotes herself to the welfare of her husband and of her household. All obstacles which prevent man from attaining his highest aim in life, all the deficiencies in the character of man, all his evil propensities, are to be traced to the body alone. This will be explained later on. The predominant idea running throughout the figure is, that man shall not be entirely guided by his animal, *i.e.*, his material nature; for the material substance of man is identical with that of the brute creation.[1] An adequate explanation of the figure having been given, and its meaning having been shown,

---

[1] Lit., "The substance that is near," next to us. The difference between the near and the remote substance of a thing is illustrated in Milloth Higgayon IX. as follows: "The near substance (החומר הקרוב) of, *e.g.*, Reuben, is formed by the limbs of the body; the remote substance consists in the humour and the four elements of which the limbs are formed; the ὕλη, which is common to all the elements, is the first substance." The "near substance" of man is identical with that of animals, since the formation of the limbs and the nature of the body are the same in both. From another point of view their identity as regards the "near substance" is explained thus (comp. Shemtob): Life is the substance (*genus*) of man as well as of all animals; the form (specific difference) of man (defined as חי מדבר, "a living being gifted with speech"), differs from that of other animals. (Comp. Mill. Higg., IX.) If, instead of defining man as a living being with the capacity of thinking, we said, "Man is a created being," etc., the term "created being" would be more comprehensive than "living being." The former is called by Maimonides the remote substance; the latter, the near substance, because it approaches nearer the individuality of man.

do not imagine that you will find[1] in its application a corresponding element for each part; you must not ask what is meant by "I have peace offerings with me," (ver. 14); by "I have decked my bed with coverings of tapestry," (ver. 16); or what is added to the force of the figure by the observation "for the goodman is not at home," (ver. 19), and so on to the end of the chapter. For all this is merely to complete the illustration of the metaphor in its literal meaning. The circumstances described here are such as are common to adulterers. Such conversations take place between all adulterous persons. You must well understand what I have said, for it is a principle of the utmost importance with respect to those things which I intend to expound. If you observe in one of the chapters that I explained the meaning of a certain figure, and pointed out to you its general scope, do not trouble yourself further in order to find an interpretation of each separate portion, for that would lead you to one of the two following erroneous courses; either you will miss the sense included in the metaphor, or you will be induced to explain certain things which require no explanation, and which are not introduced for that purpose. Through this unnecessary trouble you may fall into the great error which besets most modern sects in their foolish writings and discussions; they all endeavour to find some hidden meaning in expressions which were never uttered by the author in that sense. Your object should be to discover in most of the figures the general idea which the author wishes to express. In some instances it will be sufficient if you understand from my remarks that a certain expression contains a figure, although I may offer no further comment. For when you know that it is not to be taken literally, you will understand at once to what subject it refers. My statement that it is a figurative expression will, as it were, remove the screen from between the object and the observer.

[1] למצא כל עניני המשל בנמשל. The Arabic for this phrase is not found in any MS. It is omitted in Charizi's translation. (Munk.)

Directions for the Study of this Work.[1]

If you desire to grasp all that is contained in this book so that nothing shall escape your notice, consider the chapters in connected order. In studying each chapter, do not content yourself with comprehending its principal subject, but attend to every term mentioned therein, although it may seem to have no connection with the principal subject. For what I have written in this work was not the suggestion of the moment; it is the result of deep study and great application. Care has been taken that nothing that appeared doubtful should be left unexplained. Whenever a thing is mentioned apparently out of place, it will still be found to illustrate the subject-matter of the respective chapter. Do not read superficially, lest you do me an injury, and derive no benefit for yourself. You must study thoroughly and read continually; for you will then find the solution of those important problems of religion, which are a source of anxiety to all intelligent men. I conjure[2] any reader of my book, in the name of the Most High, not to add any explanation even to a single word; nor to explain to another any portion of it except such passages as have been fully treated of by previous theological authorities; he must not teach others anything that he has learnt from my work alone, and that has not been hitherto discussed by any of

---

[1] Charizi adds here, זאת אות הברית, "This is the sign of the covenant," taken from Gen. ix. 12.

[2] This request of the author has been entirely ignored, as the numerous Commentaries on the Moreh Nebhuchim clearly show. The authors of those Commentaries can point to the same plea on which Maimonides himself relied when he composed his work notwithstanding the prohibition of the Mishnah (Chagigah ii. 1); the excuse being, "It is time to do something in honour of the Lord: for they have made void Thy law." (Psalm cxix. 126.) Joseph Ibn Caspi, in the Preface to his Commentary on the Moreh, says: "If any person should blame me for explaining this book contrary to the wish of the author, I answer that I gladly incur this blame because I prefer to serve and to benefit every one that will read it. If I have assisted the reader in understanding what might otherwise have remained a *terra incognita*, 'let thy curse come upon me' (Gen. xxvii. 13), and let the reader accept my blessing."

our authorities. The reader must, moreover, beware of raising objections to any of my statements,[1] because it is very probable that he may understand my words to mean the exact opposite to what I intended to say. He will injure me, while I endeavoured to benefit him. " He will requite me evil for good." Let the reader make a careful study of this work; and if his doubt be removed on even one point, let him praise his Maker and rest contented with the knowledge he has acquired. But if he derive from it no benefit whatever, he may consider that no such book was ever composed. Should he notice any opinions with which he does not agree, let him endeavour to find a suitable explanation, even if it seem far-fetched, "in order that he may judge me charitably."[2] Such a duty we owe to everyone. We owe it especially to our scholars and theologians, who endeavour to teach us what is the truth according to the best of their ability. I feel assured that those of my readers who have not studied philosophy, will still derive profit from many chapters. But the thinker whose studies have brought him into collision with religion, will, as I have already mentioned, derive much benefit from every chapter. How greatly will he rejoice! How agreeably will my words strike his ears! Those, however, whose minds are confused with false notions and perverse methods, who regard their misleading studies as sciences, and imagine themselves philosophers, though they have no knowledge which may truly be termed science, will object to many chapters, and will find in them many insuperable difficulties, because they do not understand their meaning, and also because I expose the absurdity of their perverse notions, which constitute their riches and peculiar treasure, "stored up for

---

[1] The translation given by Ibn Tibbon ולא יהרוס ויקפוץ עצמו להשיב על דברי, was suggested by Maimonides himself. Comp. Bodl. MS., Poc. 74. (Munk.)

[2] The expression ידין אותו לכף זכות refers to the rule והוי דן את כל אדם לכף זכות. Mishnah Abhoth, i. 6. לכף זכות, means literally, "according to the scale of merit." The figure is taken from a balance in which the merits and faults are weighed against each other.

their ruin."[1] God knows that I hesitated very much before writing on the subjects contained in this work, since they are profound mysteries; they are topics which, since the time of our captivity[2] have not been treated by any of our scholars as far as we possess their writings;[3] how then shall I now make a beginning and discuss them? But I rely on two precedents: first, to similar cases our Sages applied the verse, "It is time to do something in honour of the Lord: for they have made void thy law" (Ps. cxix. 126).[4] Secondly, they have said, "Let all thy acts be guided by pure intentions." On these two principles I relied while composing some parts of this work. Lastly, when I have a difficult subject before me—when I find the road narrow, and can see no other way of teaching a well-established truth except by pleasing one intelligent man and displeasing ten thousand fools—I prefer to address myself to the one man, and to take no notice whatever of the condemnation of the multitude; I prefer to extricate that intelligent man from his embarrassment and show him the cause of his perplexity, so that he may attain perfection and be at peace.

[1] According to Munk, Maimonides alluded here to the Mutakallemim; but the censure "whose minds are confused," etc., is far too severe, if compared with the account of the Mutakallemim given by Maimonides below in ch. lxxi. It is more probable that he means the המון הרבנים who have not received a proper training in general knowledge, who confine all their energy to the study of the Talmud, and take the allegorical sayings in the Talmud and the Midrashim in their literal sense. The theories based on such sayings are overthrown by the present work of Maimonides, which on that account was considered as heretical.

[2] The writings of Saadiah, Gabirol, Bachjah, etc., are entirely ignored. In ch. lxxi. he states that the philosophical works of Jewish writers are based on the writings of Mahomedan authors, and are few in comparison with the latter.

[3] אלתי ערנא מא אלף פיה, lit.: "The writings concerning which things we possess." This phrase is absent in both Hebrew versions, and appears indeed superfluous after the words "which have not been treated by any, etc."

[4] Comp. Talmud Babl. Berachoth, fol. 63, where two interpretations are given, both applicable in this instance; (1), "It is now time to act in honour of God, for they (i.e., the people) have broken Thy law;" (2), "They (i.e. the authorities) have set aside Thy law, because it was time to do so in honour of God.'

Introductory Remarks.
[On Method.]

There are seven causes of inconsistencies and contradictions to be met with in a literary work.[1] The first cause arises from the fact that the author collects the opinions of various men, each differing from the other, but he neglects to mention the name of the author of any particular opinion. In such a work contradictions or inconsistencies must occur, since each statement is the opinion of a different man. Second cause: The author holds at first one opinion which he subsequently rejects; in his work, however, both his original and altered views are retained. Third cause: The passages in question are not all to be taken literally; some only are to be understood in their literal sense, while in others figurative language is employed, including another meaning[2] besides the literal one: or, in the apparently inconsistent passages, figures are used which, if taken literally, would seem to be contradictories or contraries. Fourth cause: The premises are not identical in both, but for certain reasons are not fully stated in one of the passages; or two propositions having different subjects (but the same predicate) occur in two passages, and the subject is distinctly mentioned only in one of them, and is omitted in the other. The contradiction is therefore only apparent. The fifth cause is traceable to use of the method which is adopted in teaching and expounding certain things. For, a difficult and obscure theorem must sometimes be mentioned and assumed as known, for the illustration of some elementary

---

[1] *E.g.* I. lxx., Maimonides says that God moves the highest sphere; II. iv., that it is moved by intelligences (שכלים). An instance of the seventh cause is afforded in I. lxxi., where he says that, without entering into a discussion on the eternity of the universe (קדמות העולם), the existence of God, His unity, and His incorporeality can be proved; while in other places he most vehemently attacks the theory of the eternity of the universe. (Munk.)

[2] Arabic באטן, Hebrew תוך, "an inner part." The simile (משל) is compared to the husk (קלימה), its application to the fruit which is within the husk (תוך).

and intelligible subject which must be taught beforehand,[1] the commencement being always made with the easier thing. The teacher must therefore facilitate, in any manner which he can devise, the explanation of those theorems, which have to be assumed as known, and he must content himself with giving a general notion on the subject, though this may deviate from the exact meaning. It will, for the present, be explained according to the capacity of the students, that they may comprehend it as far as they are required to understand the subject. Later on, the same subject is thoroughly treated and fully developed in its right place. Sixth cause: The contradiction is not apparent, and only becomes evident through a series of premises. The larger the number of premises necessary to prove the contradiction between the two conclusions, the greater the chance that it will escape detection, and that the author will not perceive his own inconsistency. Only when from each conclusion, by means of suitable premises, an inference is made, and from the enunciation thus inferred, by means of proper arguments, other conclusions are formed, and after that process has been repeated many times, then it becomes clear that the original conclusions are contradictories or contraries. Even able writers are liable to overlook such inconsistencies. If, however, the contradiction between the original statements can at once be discovered, and the author, while writing the second, does not think of the first, he evinces a great deficiency, and his words deserve no notice whatever. Seventh cause: It is sometimes necessary to introduce such metaphysical matter as may partly be disclosed, but must partly be concealed; while, therefore, on one occasion the object which the author has in view may demand that the metaphysical problem be treated as solved in one way, it may be convenient on another occasion to treat it as solved in the opposite

---

[1] Lit., "before that first," Arabic אלאול, Hebrew הראשון, "the first;" the difficult theorem is called "the first," because it forms the basis for the knowledge of the other, easier subjects.

way. The author must endeavour, by concealing the fact as much as possible, to prevent the uneducated reader from perceiving the contradiction.

Inconsistencies occurring in the Mishnah and Boraithoth [1] are traceable to the first cause. You meet frequently in the Gemara with passages like the following [2]:—"Does not the beginning of the passage contradict the end? No; the beginning is the dictum of a certain Rabbi; the end that of another;" or "Rabbi (Jehudah ha-Nasi) approved of the opinion of a certain rabbi in one case and gave it therefore anonymously, and having accepted that of another rabbi in the other case he introduced it without naming the authority;" or "Who is the author of this anonymous dictum? Rabbi A." "Who is the author of that paragraph in the Mishnah? Rabbi B." Instances of this kind are innumerable.

Apparent contradictions or differences occurring in the Talmud may be traced to the first cause and to the second, as e.g., "In this particular case he agrees with this rabbi;" or "He agrees with him in one point, but differs from him in another;" or "These two dicta are the opinions of two Amoraim,[3] who differ as regards the statement of a certain rabbi." These are examples of contradictions traceable to the first cause. The following are instances which may be traced to the second cause. "Rabba altered his opinion on that point;" it then becomes necessary to consider which

---

[1] The Oral Law as handed down from generation to generation, and discussed in the early schools of the Tanaim, is contained in Mishnah and Boraitha; the former is the authorised collection; the Boraitha is the portion which was excluded from the canon: the greater authority rested therefore with the Mishnah. In the Gemara, the Mishnah is introduced with the formula תנן "we have learnt," the Boraitha, with תניא "it has been learnt."

[2] Namely, when two Rabbis differ on a certain question, and in a Mishnah in which this question is treated, partly the opinion of one and partly that of the other is given (anonymously), so that the Mishnah agrees with neither authority.

[3] Amoraïm (from אמר, to say, to explain), the authorities mentioned in the Gemara, as explaining the Mishnah; the authorities of the Mishnah are called Tanaïm (from תנא = שנה, to learn by heart, "who transmitted the Oral Law"), and their names are generally preceded by the title Rabbi; while the names of the Amoraïm are preceded by the title Rab.

of the two opinions came second. Again, "In the first recension of the Talmud by Rabbi Ashi, he made one assertion, and in the second a different one."

The inconsistencies and contradictions met with in some passages of the prophetic books if taken literally, are all traceable to the third or fourth cause, and it is exclusively in reference to this subject that I wrote the present introduction. You know that the following expression frequently occurs, "One verse says this, another that," showing the contradiction, and explaining that either some premise is wanting or the subject is altered. Comp. "Solomon, it is not sufficient that thy words contradict thy father; they are themselves inconsistent, etc."[1] Many similar instances occur in the writings of our Sages. The passages in the prophetical books which our Sages have explained, mostly refer to religious or moral precepts.[2] Our desire, however, is to discuss such passages as contain apparent contradictions in regard to the principles of our faith.[3] I shall explain some of them in various chapters of the present work; for this subject also belongs to the secrets of the Torah.[3]

Contradictions traceable to the seventh cause occurring in the prophetical works require special investigation; and no one should express his opinions on that matter by reasoning and arguing without weighing the matter well[4] in his mind.

Inconsistencies in the writings of true philosophers are traceable to the fifth cause. Contradictions occurring in most other works, and in any commentaries not previously

---

[1] Talm. Babyl. Shabbath, 30 a.

[2] אחכאם, Hebrew דינים, laws (civil, political, and religious); אדאב, Hebrew מוסר דרך ארץ, ethics; ארא ואעתקאדאת, Hebrew דעות ואמונות, matters relating to knowledge and faith.

[3] That is, and deserve to be as closely investigated as matters relating to religious precepts and to ethics.

[4] אזון וחקור (from Koheleth xii. 9) weighing and searching is here opposed to שקול הדעת and סברא, superficial argument and judgment. The Arabic has simply אן לא ינזף מי דלך ינזרו לבל וצריך, and Charizi's translation עליו כפי מה שיזדמן.

mentioned are due to the sixth cause. Many examples of this class of contradictions are found in the Midrash and the Agada; hence the saying, "We must not raise questions concerning the contradictions in the Agada." You may also notice in them contradictions due to the seventh cause. Any inconsistency discovered in the present work will be found to arise in consequence of the fifth cause or the seventh. Notice this, consider its truth, and remember it well, lest you misunderstand some of the chapters in this book.

Having concluded these introductory remarks I proceed to examine those expressions, to the true meaning of which, as apparent from the context, it is necessary to direct your attention. This book will then be a key admitting to places the gates of which would otherwise be closed. When the gates are opened and men enter, their souls will enjoy repose, their eyes will be gratified, and even their bodies, after all toil and labour, will be refreshed.

" Open ye the gates, that the righteous nation which keepeth the truth may enter in."—(Is. xxvi. 2.)

PART I.

CHAPTER I.

צלם, *Form.* דמות, *Likeness.* תואר, *Shape.*[1]

SOME have been of opinion that by צלם in Hebrew, the shape and figure of a thing is to be understood, and this explanation led men to believe in the corporeality [of the Divine Being] : for they thought that the words נעשה אדם בצלמנו, "Let us make man in our form" (Gen. i. 26), implied that God had the form of a human being, *i.e.*, that He had figure and shape, and that, consequently, He was corporeal.[2] They adhered faithfully to this view, and thought that if they were to relinquish it they would *eo ipso* reject the

---

[1] The author begins the homonymous expressions explained in this part of the work with צלם, because it is both the first and the most striking instance of anthropomorphism occurring in the Bible. According to Narboni (*ad locum*), Maimonides here confirms the rule, that " the end of the work is the beginning in thought " תכלית המעשה תחלת המחשבה. The aim of man's life, *viz.*, the highest development of his intellectual faculties (שכל הפועל), is treated in the last chapter of this work ; these intellectual faculties of man are also discussed in the present chapter.

[2] Comp. Annotations of R. Abraham, son of David (השנת רא״בד) on Maimonides' Mishnah Torah, Book I. (ספר המדע), on Teshubhah iii. 7. "Why does Maimonides call him (who says that God is corporeal, endowed with a certain form) a heretic (מין) ? Many men, even greater and better than Maimonides, believed it, they being apparently supported by some passages in the Bible, and particularly by Agadic writings, which frequently lead the reader astray." Comp. I. xxvi. *sqq*.

truth of the Bible: and further, if they did not conceive God as having a body possessed of face and limbs, similar to their own in appearance, they would have to deny even the existence of God. The sole difference which they admitted, was that He excelled in greatness and splendour, and that His substance was not flesh and blood. Thus far went their conception of the greatness and glory of God. The incorporeality of the Divine Being, and His unity, in the true sense of the word—for there is no real unity without incorporeality—will be fully proved in the course of the present treatise. (Part II., ch. i.) In this chapter it is our sole intention to explain the meaning of the words צלם and דמות.[1] I hold that the Hebrew equivalent of "form" in the ordinary acceptation of the word,[2] viz., the figure and shape of a thing, is תאר. Thus we find יפה תאר ויפה מראה "(And Joseph was) beautiful in form and beautiful in appearance" (Gen. xxxix. 6): מה תארו, "What form is he of?" (1 Sam. xxviii. 14) : כתאר בני מלך, "As the form of the children of a king" (Judges viii. 18). It is also applied to form produced by human labour, as יתארהו בשרד and ובמחוגה יתארהו, "He marketh its form with a line," "and he marketh its form with the compass" (Is. xliv. 13). This term is not at all applicable to God. The term צלם, on the other hand, signifies the specific form,[3] viz., that which

[1] The object of this chapter is to prove that the expression צלם, "form," and דמות "likeness," which have been applied to the Deity, do not denote any material property. In all other instances of anthropomorphic phrases, Maimonides contents himself with showing that the term in question has, in addition to the common signification, another meaning, which has no relation to corporeal properties. In the instance of צלם, however, he attempts—but in vain—to prove that צלם in the Bible is employed exclusively in that latter sense (See p. 31, note 2.)

[2] It appears that Maimonides had no adequate term for this class of forms, viz., the natural forms of things as distinguished from their artificial forms (צורה המלאכיית). הצורה הטבעית if translated literally, would express "natural forms," but is employed by our author in the sense of "specific characteristic." In Milloth Higgayon IX., this class is called צורה בלתי מלאכיית, "non-artificial form."

[3] From צורה in the sense of "outlines," "lineaments" of a thing, Mai-

constitutes the essence of a thing, whereby the thing is what it is; the reality of a thing in so far as it is that particular being. In man the "form" is that constituent which gives him human perception: and on account of this intellectual perception[1] the term צלם is employed in the phrase בצלם אלחים ברא אותו, "In the form of God He created him" (Gen. i. 27). It is therefore rightly said, צלמם תבזח, "Thou despisest their form" (Ps. lxxiii. 20); the "contempt" can only concern the soul—the specific form[2] of man, not the bodily properties and shape.[3] I am

---

monides distinguishes the philosophical term צורה "form," which corresponds to the Aristotelian εἶδος, and signifies the cause of the essential properties of things (τὸ τί ἦν εἶναι). Form in the latter sense is called in Hebrew צורה טבעית, "physical form," i.e., that which gives to the things their nature (φύσις), the sum of their essential properties. (See III., viii., and the Eight Chapters, I.) The formless substance is the thing potentially (δυνάμει), the form gives the real existence (אמתתו, ἐν ἐντελεχείᾳ).—Aaron b. Elijah in his Etz Chayyim (Tree of Life ed. by M. Steinschneider and F. Delitzsch, Leipzig, 1841), ch. xxii., explains the word צלם as follows: שם מוסכם לכל צורה הסקימת דבר בין בתכונה בין במציאות והצורה המסיקמת הדבר בתכונה בין היותה טבעית בין היותה מלאכותית. "Tselem is the name given to the constituent element of a thing in reference to both its geometrical form and its entire existence. As to the former the term expresses both the natural form and the artificial." Aaron b. Elijah has evidently seen the work of Maimonides, and adopted the second explanation of צלם suggested in this chapter for those who could not be satisfied with the first.

[1] השגה שכלית (Char. שכל אנושי) and השגה אנושית in the version of Ibn Tibbon appear to be identical, and to denote the essential characteristic of man, viz., his intellectual faculties. Ibn Caspi in Ammude Khesef (edited by S. Verblumer, Francf. a M., 1848) remarks, that while generally man is defined as חי מדבר, "speaking, living being," the property which is common to the whole race, Maimonides defines man as possessing intellectual comprehension, because he has in view man's highest degree of perfection, the full development of his intellectual faculties.

[2] Tibbon renders the original אלצורת אלנועית by צורה מינית; Charizi has instead צורה פרטית, and both may perhaps mean one and the same thing. מינית "specific" is the literal translation of the Arabic, and is also correct in so far as it refers to the soul of man; but as the contempt is limited to the soul of some individuals, and does not extend to the soul of all men, Charizi is not incorrect in substituting צורה פרטית.

[3] Some commentators explain the words of Maimonides as follows: In *this*

PART I.—CHAPTER I. 31

also of opinion that the reason why "idols" are called צלמים, may be found in the circumstance that they are worshipped on account of some idea conveyed by them,[1] not on account of their figure and shape. In the same way is used the expression צלמי טחוריכם, "the forms of your emerods" (1 Sam. vi. 5), for the chief object was the removal of the injury caused by the emerods, not a change of their shape. If, however, it must be assumed that the images of the emerods and the idols are called צלמים on account of their external shape, the term צלם would be either a real or an apparent homonym, and would denote both the specific form and the artificial shape,[2] or similar properties relating to the dimensions and the figure of material bodies; and in the phrase נעשה אדם בצלמנו, "Let us make man in our form" (Gen. i. 26), the term צלם would then

---

passage, viz., צלמם תבזה, the object of תבזה cannot be the outer appearance of the persons referred to in that Psalm; for God looks only to the heart of man, not to his outer appearance. Comp. Etz Chayyim, ch. xxii., אמנם מה שאמר צלמם תבזה אינו רוצה לתכונת האברים רק לנפשם שהיא מקיטת אותם במציאותם ומנהגת אותם כי הבזיון לא יפול רק על החלק המעולה שנמצא בעצמו. "But when he says (צלמם תבזה) 'thou wilt despise their form,' he does not mean by 'form' (צלם) the shape of the limbs, but their soul, the constituent and leading element in their existence; for the contempt can only apply to the nobler part in man's essence."

[1] Lit., "that which is sought in them, the idea which they represent" (Arab., מאנאהא; Tibbon, ענינם, Ch. (כוחם an abstract conception, not their external form, etc. The Arabic אלמטנן בהא is rendered by T. הנחשב, by Ch. העולה על לב. Munk (page 35, note 2), leur sens (l'idée) qu'on s'imaginait, c'est à dire, la fausse idée qu'on se formait d'elles ou la vertu qu'on leur attribuait par erreur.

[2] Here Maimonides abandons his proposition that צלם in the Bible denotes *exclusively* "form" in the philosophical sense of the word. He admits, that in צלמים "idols" and in צלמי טחוריכם "the images of your emerods," the word may perhaps refer to external likeness. The only proof maintained by our author in all circumstances is the phrase צלמם תבזה. Comp. Etz Chayyim xxii.; ונאמר צלמי טחוריכם רוצה בהם צורתם המלאכותית, ולתכונה 'צלמי טחוריכם In". הטבעית רוצה באטרו וצלם אנפוהי אשתנו 'the images of your emerods' the word refers to their artificial form; it refers to the natural form in the following passage, 'and the form of his visage was changed'" (Dan. iii. 19).

signify "the specific form,"[1] *viz.*, intellectual preception, not "figure" or "shape." Thus we have shown the difference between צלם and תאר, and explained the meaning of צלם.

דמות is derived from the verb דמה, "to be similar." This term likewise denotes agreement with regard to some abstract relation: Comp. דמיתי לקאת מדבר, "I am like a pelican of the wilderness" (Ps. cii. 7); the author does not compare himself to the pelican in point of wings and feathers, but in point of sadness. כל עץ בגן אלהים לא דמה אליו ביפיו, "nor any tree in the garden of God was like unto him in beauty" (Ez. xxxi. 8); the comparison refers to the idea of beauty. חמת למו כדמות חמת נחש, "Their poison is like the poison of a serpent" (Ps. lviii. 5); דמיונו כאריה, "He is like unto a lion" (Ps. xvii. 12); the resemblance indicated in these passages does not refer to the figure and shape, but to some abstract idea. In the same manner is used דמות הכסא, "the likeness of the throne" (Ez. i. 26); the comparison is made with regard to greatness and glory, not, as many believe, with regard to its square form, its breadth, or the length of its legs: this explanation applies also to the phrase דמות החיות, "the likeness of the living creatures" (Ez. i. 13).

As man's distinction consists in a property which no other creature on earth[2] possesses, *viz.*, intellectual perception, in the exercise of which he does not employ his senses, nor move his hand or his foot,[3] it has been compared—though only apparently, not in truth—to the Divine excellency, which requires no instrument whatever. On this account, *i.e.*, on account of the Divine intellect with which

[1] See note 2, p. 30, and note 3, p. 29.
[2] Lit., "under the sphere of the moon," "sublunary beings."
[3] Arabic: נאנחה ולא נארחה פיה חאסה תתצרף לא; Tibb. has the additional phrase ולא מעשה גוף, which originally was perhaps intended as an emendation of חוש, or as the explanation of the two expressions which follow. נארחה and נאנחה denote parts of the body in general, and also special parts, as "hand" and "side" or "wing;" hence rendered by Tib. יד, אבר, נתח by Char. רגל.

man has been endowed,[1] he is said to have been made in the form and likeness of the Almighty, but far from it be the notion that the Supreme Being is corporeal, having a material form.

CHAPTER II.

וחייתם כאלהים ידעי טוב ורע "*And ye shall be like* ELOHIM *knowing good and evil.*"[2] (Gen. iii. 5.)

SOME years ago[3] a learned man asked me a question of great importance; the problem and the solution which we gave in our reply deserve the closest attention. Before, however, entering upon this problem and its solution I must premise that every Hebrew knew[4] that the term "Elohim" was a homonym, and denoted God, angels,[5] judges, and the rulers of countries, and that Onkelos the prose-

---

[1] Munk: qui se joint à l'homme. According to this writer's opinion, Maimonides here alludes to the union of the passive intellect (שכל הנקנה) with the active intellect (שכל הפועל). It is, however, more probable that Maimonides simply refers to man's soul, as having its temporary abode in his body, without any reference to philosophical theories.

[2] Having shown in the first chapter that the *tselem elohim* in which man was created consisted in his intellectual perception, the author distinguishes in this chapter that intellectual perception from man's moral feelings. He appears to be of opinion that the latter originated in some kind of disturbance in the action of the former. The faculty of distinguishing between good and evil is therefore considered by Maimonides as the result of man's degeneration.

[3] Arab. מנד סנין; Ibn Tibbon: זה לו שנים, lit. "it has years;" the more usual phrase in Hebrew is that employed by Charizi, זה שנים רבות or זה כמה שנים.

[4] Munk: Tout Hebreu sait. Ibn Tibbon and Charizi more correctly כי כבר ידע; for Maimonides evidently refers to the ancient Hebrews, who spoke the language and understood how to apply the term *elohim* in its various significations.

[5] It is noteworthy that *elohim* in this passage is not employed to mean "angels." According to Maimonides the angels are purely intellectual beings, ideals (שכלים נפרדים), and the attribute "knowing good and evil" is not applicable to them. Maimonides was on this account accused of heresy; it

D

34   GUIDE OF THE PERPLEXED.

lyte[1] explained it in the true and correct manner by taking the words והייתם כאלהים (*lit.*, "ye shall be as gods," Gen. iii. 5) in the last-mentioned meaning, and rendering them ותהון כרברביא "and ye shall be like rulers." Having pointed out the homonymity of the term "*Elohim*" we return to the question under consideration. "It would at first sight," said the objector, "appear from Scripture that man was originally intended to be perfectly equal to the rest of the animal creation, which is not endowed with intellect, reason, or power of distinguishing between good and evil: but that Adam's disobedience to the command of God procured him that great perfection which is the peculiarity of man, *viz.*: the power of distinguishing between good and evil—the noblest of all the faculties of our nature, the essential characteristic of the human race. It thus appears strange that the punishment for rebelliousness should be the means of elevating man to a pinnacle of perfection to which he had not attained previously. This is equivalent to saying that a certain man was rebellious and extremely wicked, his nature was therefore changed for the better,[2] and he was made to shine as a star in the heavens.[3]" Such was the purport and subject of the question, though not in the exact words of the inquirer. Now mark our reply,

---

was argued as follows:—If angels do not possess the faculty of distinguishing between good and evil because they are intellectual beings, then, *à fortiori* this faculty must be denied to God, who is intellectual in the highest degree; consequently, the laws concerning good and evil could not be divine. Abarbanel, in his Commentary on the Moreh, refutes these insinuations.

[1] See Babyl. Talmud, Gittin, 56 b. Onkelos, in his version of the Pentateuch, avoids, as far as possible, all anthropomorphic expressions. (See ch. xxvii. Comp. Introd. to Nethinah lagger, Comm. on the Targum of Onkelos, by Dr. N. Adler, Chief Rabbi, and Deutsch, "Literary Remains," etc., pp. 319, *sqq.*) He renders אלהים in this passage by רברביא "great men." The so-called Targum Jonathan has מלאכין רברבין, probably a combination of two different readings.

[2] Arabic פמסך, "and he changed," Shem-tob Palquera, in Moreh ha-moreh שנו בריתו לרע; Ibn Tibbon, שנו בריתו למוב; the former is more correct.

[3] This probably alludes to the constellation of Nimrod or Gabbar, which, in the mythology of the Arabs, has the same origin as the hunter Orion in the mythology of the Greeks.

PART I.—CHAPTER II. 35

which was as follows:—"You appear to have studied the matter superficially, and nevertheless you imagine that you can understand a book which has been the guide of past and present generations, when you for a moment withdraw from your lusts and appetites, and glance over its contents as if you were reading a historical work or some poetical composition.[1] Collect your thoughts and examine the matter carefully, for it is not to be understood as you at first sight thought, but as you will find after due deliberation; namely, the intellect which was granted to man as the highest endowment, was bestowed on him before his disobedience. With reference to this gift the Bible states that "man was created in the form and likeness of God." On account of this gift of intellect man was addressed by God, and received His commandments, as it is said: "And the Lord God commanded Adam" (Gen. ii. 16)— for no commandments are given to the brute creation[2] or to those who are devoid of understanding. Through the intellect man distinguishes between the true and the false. This faculty Adam possessed perfectly and completely. The right and the wrong are terms employed in the science of apparent truths[3] (morals), not in that of necessary

---

[1] History and poetry did not stand in high estimation with the philosophers of those days. Comp. Yesod Mora of Ibn Ezra, ch. i, and Ibn Ezra Literature by M. Friedländer, Vol. IV., page 60.

[2] ולא תאבה למה שאמר האפודי שרמז הרב לאמרו ולא היתה הצוואה לבהמות לויאמר יי לדג כי הרב לא כיוון בזה ולא עלתה על לבו. "Do not listen to the words of the Efodi that Maimonides in his remark 'the command could not be given to beasts' implied a criticism on the passage 'and the Lord spake unto the fish' (Jonah ii. 10), for Maimonides did not mean that, and did not think of it."—(Abarbanel.)

[3] מפורסם has the same two significations as the Greek ἔνδοξον and the English "apparent," viz., 1, clear, well-known; 2 (opposed to positively true), probable, generally believed to be true. That which is universally known is better known by direct perception than by proof. Maimonides in his Milloth Higgayon, c. viii., enumerates four kinds of assertions which are accepted without requiring further proof:—1. Such as are based on perception by the senses (המוחשים); 2. Axioms or innate ideas (המושכלות הראשונות); 3. Those assertions which are generally accepted (המפורסמות), public opinion;

D 2

truths, as, *e.g.*, it is not correct to say, in reference to the proposition "the heavens are spherical," it is "right" or to declare the assertion that "the earth is flat" to be "wrong"; but we say of one it is true, of the other it is false. Similarly our language expresses the idea of true and false by the terms אמת and שקר, of the right and the wrong, by טוב and רע. Thus it is the function of the intellect to discriminate between the true and the false—a distinction which is applicable to all objects of intellectual perception. When Adam was yet in a state of innocence, and was guided solely by reflection and reason—on account of which it is said: "Thou hast made him (man) little lower than the angels" (Ps. viii. 6)—he was not at all able to follow or to understand those principles of apparent truths; the most manifest impropriety, *viz.*, to appear in a state of nudity, was nothing unbecoming according to his idea: he could not comprehend why it should be so. After man's disobedience, however, when he began to give way to desires which had their source in his imagination and in the gratification of his bodily appetites, as it is said "that the tree was good for food and delightful to the eyes" (Gen. iii. 6), he was punished by the loss of part of this intellectual faculty. He therefore transgressed a command with which he had been charged on the score of his reason; and having obtained a knowledge of the apparent truths, he was wholly absorbed in the study of the beautiful and its opposite. Then he fully understood the magnitude of the loss he had sustained, what he had forfeited, and in what situation he was thereby placed.[1] Hence we read, "And ye shall be like

---

4. Those which are made on good authority (המקבלות).—The assertions of the third class (המפורסמות) are explained by two instances, גלוי הערוה מגונה, and חסד המטיב ביותר נכבד.

[1] The theory of Maimonides appears to be the following: If Adam had remained in the full possession of his intellectual power, so that his bodily desires and appetites had been completely under the control of his intellect and reason, the moral principles mostly tending to restrain those desires and to prevent their consequences, would not have been necessary, and therefore not known to man. In the biblical account of the first man's state of innocence,

Elohim, knowing good and evil," and not "knowing" or "discerning the true and the false:" while in necessary[1] truths we can only apply the words "true and false," not "good and evil." Further observe the passage, "And the eyes of both were opened, and they knew they were naked." (Gen. iii. 7): it is not said, "And the eyes of both were opened, and they *saw*"; for what the man had seen previously and what he saw after this circumstance was precisely the same; there had been no blindness which was now removed, but he received a new faculty whereby he found things wrong which previously he had not regarded as wrong. Besides, you must know that the word פקח is exclusively used in the sense of receiving new sources of knowledge, not in that of regaining the sense of sight. Comp., "God opened her eyes," (Gen. xxi. 19). "Then shall the eyes of the blind be opened," (Isaiah xxxviii. 8). "Open ears, he heareth not," (*ibid.* xlii. 20), similar in sense to the verse, "Which have eyes to see, and see not," (Ezek. xii. 2). When, however, Scripture says of Adam, משנה פניו ותשלחהו (*lit.*, "He changes his face and thou sendest him forth," Job xiv. 20), it must be understood in the following way: On account of the change of his

---

this is, according to Maimonides, figuratively expressed in the commandment, "But of the tree of the knowledge of good and evil thou shalt not eat of it" (Gen. ii. 17). Adam disobeyed the Divine command, he then saw the necessity of rules for restraining the desires; he had then to investigate and to learn the difference between good and evil, between that which is right and that which is wrong.

[1] The term הכרחי "necessary," is the opposite of מפורסמות "generally believed." The assertions based on logical operations are called מושכלות, and because they alone can be established by scientific proof which conveys the conviction that it must necessarily be so and cannot be otherwise, they are also known by the term "necessary truths" (הכרחי). In reference to the assertion of Maimonides, "in necessary truth we can only apply the words 'true' and 'false,' not 'right' and 'wrong,'" Ibn Caspi remarks: וכל זה בפירוש פילוסופיא דק מאוד לא ראיתי ולא שמעתי מי שעמד על אמונת זה לפי דעתי אבל חלקו עליו גדולים ממנו ויודע יי את אשר לו" all this is very ingenious in a philosophical argument, but I never heard of or met with any person who defended and proved this assertion, but many great men differ from him, and 'the Lord will show who is His.'"

original aim he was sent away.[1]—For the term פנים signifies "face," "aim," derived from פנה, "to turn," as man generally turns his face towards the thing he desires.—In accordance with this interpretation, our text suggests that Adam, as he altered his intention and directed his thoughts to the acquisition of what he was forbidden, he was banished from Paradise: this was his punishment; it was measure for measure. At first he had the privilege of tasting pleasure and happiness, and of enjoying repose and security; but as his appetites grew stronger, and he followed his desires and impulses, (as we have already stated above), and partook of the food he was forbidden to taste, he was deprived of everything, was doomed to subsist on the meanest kind of food, such as he never tasted before, and this even only after exertion and labour, as it is said, "Thorns and thistles shall grow up for thee" (Gen. iii. 18), "By the sweat of thy brow," etc., and in explanation of this the text continues, "And the Lord God drove him from the Garden of Eden, to till the ground whence he was taken." He was now with respect to food and many other requirements, brought to the level of the lower animals; comp., "Thou shalt eat the grass of the field" (Gen. iii. 18). Reflecting on his condition, the Psalmist says, "Adam (man) unable to dwell in dignity, was brought to the level of the dumb beast" (Ps. xlix. 13).[2]

[1] It is generally supposed that the subject to the verb משנה is God; as to ותשלחהו, Maimonides thinks that it refers to Adam, to whom also the pronoun פניו is referred. Comp. Bereshith Rabba, ch. xxi.

[2] This verse is generally understood as referring not to Adam but to mankind. "A man who is without understanding is like the rest of the animal world." Maimonides considers it as especially applying to the fate of Adam; otherwise he would have said כמבאר (כמבינא). The punishment ואכלת את עשב השדה, "and thou shalt eat the herb of the field" (Gen. iii. 18), is taken in contradistinction to the first blessing, by which Adam was allowed to eat the fruit of the trees (ib. i. 28), called by our author לחם ערבים, "pleasant food." Comp. Bereshith Rabba xxi. It is noteworthy that R. Levi—in opposition to Rabbi Jitschak, who thinks that the first sentence "thou shalt eat the herb of the field" was rather mitigated by the second "in the sweat of thy face thou shalt eat bread"—exclaims, Would that the first sentence had remained in force! (men would have had less trouble and care).

"May the Almighty[1] be praised, whose design and wisdom cannot be fathomed.[2]

CHAPTER III.

תבנית *Construction.* תמונה, 1, *Shape.* 2, *Image.* 3, *Idea.*

It might be thought that תמונה and תבנית in Hebrew have one and the same meaning, but it is not the case. תבנית, on the one hand, is derived from the verb בנה (to build), and signifies the build and construction of a thing—that is to say, its figure, whether square, round, triangular, or of any other shape. Comp.[3] את תבנית המשכן ואת תבנית כל כליו

---

[1] Lit., "the master of the will," that is, He who alone has the power to do what he wills. Ibn Tibbon בעל הרצון, literally; Char. בעל היכלת, according to the sense.

[2] After having described the sin of Adam, and his punishment, and having explained the apparent difficulties of the Biblical account, Maimonides strangely exclaims, "Praised be the Lord, whose plan and wisdom cannot be fully comprehended," as if some difficult problem had been still left without satisfactory solution. He probably alludes in these words to the question, Why was Adam endowed with the power of leaving the higher sphere of pure intellect, and falling into the lower grade of animal life? He therefore names the Creator, Master of the will (בעל הרצון), and declares that it is impossible to penetrate into the depth of His wisdom.

[3] While giving the several significations of *temunah* under three heads, material form, imaginary form, and intellectual form, Maimonides does not think it necessary to assign to *tabhnith* more than one meaning, although the instances given include the forms perceived by our senses and also those originated in the imagination or seen in a vision, namely תבנית המשכן ואת תבנית (Ex. xxv. 9); כחבניתם (*Ib.* xxv. 40); תבנית יד (Ezek. viii. 3; and x. 8). Not having found any instance of תבנית denoting a purely immaterial form, he probably did not consider it necessary to divide the instances quoted into two classes, especially since the forms of the second class originating in the imagination (ברמיון) are abstracted from material bodies, and are therefore in some cases treated as material, in others as immaterial. Ibn Caspi suggests another solution, material forms presenting themselves to a prophet in a vision, are in the account of such a vision treated as material, and even Onkelos would not hesitate to retain in his version anthropomorphic phrases of this kind. Comp. ch. xxvii.

"the pattern of the Tabernacle and the pattern of all its vessels" (Exod. xxv. 9); כתבניתם אשר אתה מראה בהר; "according to the pattern which thou wast shown upon the mount" (Exod. xxv. 40); תבנית כל צפור, "the form of any bird" (Deut. iv. 17); תבנית יד, "the form of a hand" (Ezek. viii. 3); תבנית האולם, "the pattern of the porch" (1 Chron. xxviii. 11). In all these quotations it is the shape which is referred to; consequently the Hebrew language never employs the word תבנית in speaking of the qualities of God Almighty.

The term תמונה, on the other hand, is used in the Bible in three different senses. It signifies, first, the outlines of things which are perceived by our bodily senses, i.e., their shape and form;[1] as, e.g., ועשיתם פסל תמונת כל סמל, "And ye make an image the form of some likeness" (Deut. iv. 16); כי לא ראיתם כל תמונה, "for ye saw no likeness" (Deut. iv. 15). Secondly, the forms of our imagination, i.e., the impressions retained in imagination when the objects have ceased to affect our senses.[2] In this sense it is used in the passage which begins "In thoughts from the visions of the night" (Job iv. 13), and which concludes "it remained but I could not recognise its sight, only an image (תמונה) was before my eyes," i.e., an image which presented itself to my sight during sleep. Thirdly, the true form of an object, which is perceived only by the intellect: and it is in this third signification that the term is applied to God. The words ותמונת ה' יביט (Numb. xii. 8) therefore mean "he comprehended the true essence of the Lord."[3]

[1] Ibn Tibbon has only תאר, Charizi תבניתו וצורתו.

[2] The words אחר העלמו מן החושים taken literally imply that the object has for some time been in contact with our senses, but after this contact has ceased, an image of the object is still perceived in our imagination. Visions of the night, and dreams, brought under this category, are explained by Maimonides to be nothing but impressions previously received from real objects. As, however, נעלם also means "hidden," "absent," the meaning of the words אחר העלמו מן החושים may also be this: images of objects which have not been in contact with the senses.

[3] This is not in contradiction to the assertion made by our author (ch. xxxvii.)

CHAPTER IV.

ראה, חביט, חזה 1, *To see.* 2, *To comprehend.*[1]

The three words ראה, חביט, חזה, which denote "to perceive with the eye," are also used figuratively in the sense of intellectual perception. As regards ראה, this is well known, *e.g.*, וירא והנה באר בשדה, "And he looked, and beheld a well in the field" (Gen. xxix. 2): here ראה signifies ocular perception; ולבי ראה הרבה חכמה ודעת, "yea, my heart has seen much of wisdom and of knowledge" (Eccles. i. 16); in this passage ראה refers to the intellectual perception.

In this figurative sense[2] the expression ראה is to be understood, when applied to God[3]; *e.g.*, ראיתי את ח׳, "I saw the Lord" (1 Kings xxii. 19); וירא אליו ח׳, "And the Lord

---

"that no man can have a conception of the real existence of God," for a distinction must be made between ואמתת ח׳ ישיג, "he comprehends the true idea of the Lord," *scil.*, as far as man is able to comprehend it, and אמתת מציאותו כפי מה שהוא לא תושג, "His existence as it is in reality, cannot be apprehended." Some commentators find here a contradiction, and explain it to be an instance of the seventh cause of apparent contradictions, described by Maimonides in the introduction to this work. Comp. Albo Ikkarim, Introd. to Book II.—Crescas justly notices that the only instance adduced by Maimonides in support of the third signification of the word, is one that requires to be proved. The word "temunah" is here applied to God, and the object of these chapters is to show that such expressions, used in reference to God, are not to be taken in their common signification.

[1] The last-mentioned instance of תמונה containing the verb 'to see' in reference to God, suggested probably to the author the appropriateness of giving here the explanation of these three verbs.

[2] By this term (in Hebrew ולפי זאת השאלה), Maimonides indicates that these words are not really homonymous (משתתפים), but are used both in a literal sense and in a figurative. According to Shem-tob this formula indicates that in the instances which follow the word is employed in a similar meaning, but not in exactly the same as that mentioned before. The rule does not hold good in all cases. The phrase generally occurs before instances to which the author desires to call our special attention.

[3] That is, both in instances in which God is described as seeing, and in which He is described as being seen.

appeared unto him" (Gen. xviii. 1); וירא אלהים כי טוב
"And God saw that it was good" (Gen. i. 10); הראני נא
את כבודך, "I beseech Thee, show me Thy glory" (Exod.
xxxiii. 18); ויראו את אלהי ישראל, "And they saw the God
of Israel" (Exod. xxiv. 10). All these instances refer to perception by the intellect, and by no means to perception with the eye as in its literal meaning: for, on the one hand, the eye can only perceive a corporeal object, and even this only from one point of view,[1] and in connection with it certain accidents, as colour, shape, etc.; and, on the other hand, God does not make use of any means in perceiving a thing, as will be explained.[2]

In the same manner הביט signifies "to view" with the eye; comp. אל תביט אחריך, "Look not behind thee" (Gen. xix. 17); ותבט אשתו מאחריו, "But his wife looked back from him" (Gen. xix. 26); ונבט לארץ, "And if one look into the land" (Isaiah v. 30); and figuratively, "to view and observe" with the intellect, "to contemplate" a thing till it be understood. In this sense הביט is used in passages like the following: לא הביט און ביעקב, "He[3] hath not beheld iniquity in Jacob" (Num. xxiii. 21); for "iniquity" cannot be seen with the eye. The words והביטו אחרי משה, "And they looked after Moses" (Exod. xxxiii. 8)—in addition to the literal understanding of the phrase—were explained by our Sages in a figurative sense. According to them, these words mean that the Israelites examined and criticised the actions

[1] In Arabic וּמִן נָהָה (in Hebrew ובצד), "and only in a side," or "and only the surface" (like פנים = ונה), only the exterior of a body being exposed to our eye. Charizi has ובמקום, "and in a certain place," that is, not all the sides of the object at the same time. Some MSS. of the editions of Tibbon's version have ובצד וקצת, others ובצדו קצת "and in connection with it some." Although the first reading agrees with the Arabic, the second reading gives evidently a better sense.

[2] See ch. liv.

[3] Maimonides appears to hold that the subject to the verb הביט is either the indefinite "one," or "Balaam." Comp. Onkelos אסתכלית לית פלחי גלולין, "I considered, there are no idolaters," etc.; Targ. Jon. אמר בלעם רשיעא לית אנא מסתכל, "The wicked Balaam said, I see no," etc. Others explain "God does not see," etc.

PART I.—CHAPTER IV. 43

and sayings of Moses.[1] Compare also הבט נא השמימה "Contemplate, I pray thee, the heaven" (Gen. xv. 5); for this took place in a prophetic vision.[2] The term הביט, when applied to God, is employed in this figurative sense; e. g., מהביט אל האלהים, "to look upon God" (Exod. iii. 6); ותמונת ה' יביט, "And the similitude of the Lord shall he behold" (Num. xii. 8); והביט אל עמל לא תוכל, "And thou canst not look on iniquity" (Habak. i. 13).

The same explanation applies to חזה. It denotes to view with the eye, as: ותחז בציון עינינו, "And let our eye look upon Zion" (Micah iv. 11); and also figuratively, to perceive mentally: אשר חזה על יהודה וירושלים, "which he saw concerning Judah and Jerusalem" (Isaiah i. 1); היה דבר ה' אל אברם במחזה, "The word of the Lord came unto Abram in a vision" (Gen. xv. 1); in this sense חזה is used in the phrase ויחזו את האלהים, "Also they saw God" (Exod. xxiv. 11). Note this well![3]

---

[1] Comp. Shemoth Rabba xli., and the Commentary of Rashi on Exod. xxxiii. 8.

[2] According to the literal meaning Abraham was told, although in a vision, to go out of his tent and to look up to the heavens. In the Midrash the words ויוצא אתו החוצה are interpreted צא מאצטגנינות שלך, "renounce thy knowledge of the influence of the stars," and in accordance with this interpretation Maimonides appears to understand the verb הבט in the sense of "to reflect." The words "for this took place in a prophetic vision," do not refer to the phrase "in a vision" (במחזה), by which the biblical account is introduced; for in a vision Abraham may have looked at the heavens, and according to Maimonides (ch. xxvii.), the account of a vision is given as it really took place. These words are merely an explanation of הבט that Abraham was told to reflect in a prophetic vision on the heavens.

[3] The author invites the reader to notice this explanation of חזה in the last-mentioned instance, as his interpretation of that passage, which will be given *in extenso* in ch. v. is founded on the fact that חזה there signifies "to perceive mentally."

CHAPTER V.

ויחזו את האלהים "*Also they saw God.*"[1]

WHEN the chief of Philosophers[2] [Aristotle] was about to inquire into some very profound subjects, and to establish his theory by proofs, he commenced his treatise with an apology, and requested the reader to attribute the author's inquiries not to presumption, vanity, egotism, or arrogance, as though he were interfering with things of which he had no knowledge, but rather to zeal and desire to discover and establish true doctrines, as far as lay in human power. We take the same position, and think that a man, when he commences to speculate, ought not to embark at once on a subject so vast and important; he should previously adapt himself to the study of the several branches of science and knowledge,[3] should most thoroughly refine his moral character and subdue his passions and desires,[4] the offspring of his imagi-

[1] Maimonides, fond of moral reflections, introduces them in all his works wherever opportunity is given. The last-mentioned words of the Pentateuch, taken according to his interpretation, afford an opportunity for such a digression, and he therefore devotes a whole chapter to the explanation of that passage.

[2] The Greek philosopher Aristotle is meant, who was regarded as the greatest authority in all questions relating to philosophy. He was called the philosopher κατ' ἐξοχήν, and his works were the text-books, which were read, studied, and expounded in the schools of the Mahomedans, not from their original, but from Arabic translations. As to the apology referred to, comp. Arist. De cœlo, ii. 12.

[3] Munk: "sans s'être exercé dans les sciences et les connaissances." It would be strange that the curriculum of a Theological student should begin with exercise in science and knowledge, a step certainly not the first in the course of any student, or that other disciplines—which do not require a knowledge of Logic—must for a long time have engaged the attention of the scholar before he *prepared* himself for Theology. Both kinds of advice would be equally absurd. Most probably Maimonides meant by ירוץ (Hebr. ירגיל עצמו) that he should adapt himself to the requirements of the life of a Theological scholar by learning to bear with equanimity every kind of privation, exertion, and hard work for the sake of truth. This general advice is developed in the words which follow.

[4] Both Shem-tob and Efodi find these conditions indicated in the Commandments וכבסו שמלותם, and אל תגשו אל אשה (Exod. xix. 14-15), given to the Israelites when preparing for the Revelation on Mount Sinai. Comp. Plat.

nation; when, in addition, he has obtained a knowledge of the true fundamental propositions, a comprehension of the several methods of inference and proof (logic), and the capacity of guarding against fallacies, then he may approach the investigation of this subject. He must, however, not decide any question by the first idea that suggests itself to his mind, or at once direct his thoughts to command a knowledge of the Creator, but he must wait modestly and patiently, and advance step by step.

In this sense we must understand the words "And Moses hid his face, for he was afraid to look upon God" (Exod. iii. 6), retaining at the same time the literal meaning of the passage, that Moses was afraid to gaze at the light which appeared to his eye; but it must on no account be assumed that the Being which is exalted far above every imperfection can be perceived by the eye. This act of Moses was highly commended by God, who bestowed on him a well-deserved portion of His goodness, as it is said: "And the similitude of the Lord shall he behold." (Num. xii. 8.) This, say our Sages, was the reward for having previously hidden his face, lest he should gaze at the Eternal.[1]

"The nobles of the Children of Israel," on the other hand, were impetuous, and allowed their thoughts to go unrestrained: what they perceived was but imperfect. Therefore it is said of them, "And they saw the God of Israel, and there was under his feet," etc. (Exod. xxiv. 10); and not merely, "and they saw the God of Israel:" the purpose of the whole passage is to criticise their act of seeing and not to describe it. They are blamed for the nature of

---

Phaed. 9. καὶ ἐν ᾧ ἂν ζῶμεν, οὕτως, ὡς ἔοικεν, ἐγγυτάτω ἐσόμεθα τοῦ εἰδέναι, ἐὰν ὅτι μάλιστα μηδὲν ὁμιλῶμεν τῷ σώματι, μηδὲ κοινωνῶμεν ὅ,τι μὴ πᾶσα ἀνάγκη, μηδὲ ἀναπιμπλώμεθα τῆς τούτου φύσεως, ἀλλὰ καθαρεύωμεν ἀπ' αὐτοῦ, ἕως ἂν ὁ θεὸς αὐτὸς ἀπολύσῃ ἡμᾶς: "while we live, we shall probably be nearest to knowledge when we most ignore the body, and only take notice of it when absolutely necessary; when we do not allow ourselves to be entirely occupied with the wants of the body, but try to make ourselves independent of it till God Himself deliver us entirely from it." (Comp. Part II., chap. xxxvii.)

[1] Talmud Babli Berachoth, 7 a.

their perception, which was to a certain extent corporeal—a result which necessarily followed, from the fact that they ventured too far before being perfectly prepared. They deserved to perish, but at the intercession of Moses this fate was averted by God for the time. They were afterwards burnt at Taberah, except Nadab and Abihu, who were burnt in the Tabernacle of the congregation, according to what is stated by authentic tradition.[1]

If such was the case with them, how much more is it incumbent on us who are inferior, and those still lower than we, to persevere in perfecting our knowledge of the elements, and in rightly understanding the preliminaries which purify the mind from the defilement of error; then we may enter the holy and divine camp in order to gaze: as the Bible says, "And let the priests also, which come near to the Lord, sanctify themselves, lest the Lord break forth upon them." (Exod. xix. 22.) Solomon, also, has cautioned all who endeavour to attain this high degree of knowledge in the following figurative terms, "Keep thy foot when thou goest to the house of God." (Eccles. iv. 17.)

I will now return to complete what I commenced to explain. The nobles of the Children of Israel, besides erring in their perception were, through this cause, also misled in their actions; for, in consequence of their confused perception, they gave way to bodily cravings. This is meant by the words, "Also they saw God and did eat and drink." (Exod. xxiv. 11.) The principal part[2] of that passage, viz., "And there was under his feet as it were a paved work of a sapphire stone" (Exod. xxiv. 10), will be further explained in the course of the present treatise. (ch. xxviii.) All we here intend to say is, that wherever in a similar passage the word ראה, חזה, or הביט occurs, it has reference to intellectual

---

[1] In the Midrashim the words ואל אצילי בני ישראל לא שלח ידו (Exod. xxiv. 11) are interpreted as follows:—God did not punish the nobles of the Israelites (Nadab, Abihu, and the seventy Elders) on that occasion, but subsequently they did receive their punishment: the sons of Aaron on the eighth day of Dedication (Lev. x. 2), and the elders at Taberah (Num. xi. 1-3). Comp. Midrash Rabba et Tanchumah ad locum.

[2] Arab. תמאם; סוף in the Hebrew versions is incorrect.

perception, not to the sensation of sight by the eye; for God is not a being to be perceived by the eye.

It will do no harm,[1] however, if those who are unable to comprehend what we here endeavour to explain[2] should refer all the words in question to sensuous perception, such as lights created [for the purpose], angels, or similar beings.

CHAPTER VI.[3]

איש 1, *Man.* 2, *Male.* 3, *One* (—*the other*).

אשה 1, *Woman.* 2, *Female.* 3, *One* (—*the other*).

אח 1, *Brother.* 2, (*one*—) *the other.*

אחות 1, *Sister.* 2, (*one*—) *the other.*

THE two nouns איש and אשה were originally employed to designate the "male and female" of human beings, but were afterwards applied to the "male and female" of the other species of the animal creation. For instance, we read, "Of every clean beast thou shalt take to thee by sevens," איש ואשתו (Gen. vii. 2), which is identical in meaning with זכר ונקבה, "male and female." The term אשה[4] was afterwards applied to anything designed and prepared for union with another object. Thus we read, "The five curtains

---

[1] That is to say, The interpretation which follows does not contradict the principle laid down by Maimonides, that the terms ראה, חזה, הביט, when applied to God, denote intellectual perception, nor does such a view necessarily include the corporification of God.

[2] Lit., "those who fall short of attaining that degree towards which we endeavour to go up with him."

[3] It appears that Maimonides intends to return to the words *Tzelem* and *Demuth*, and to show that the significations mentioned above apply also to them in the phrase ויולד בדמותו ובצלמו, "and he begat in his likeness and in his image." For that reason probably the explanation of איש ואשה and ילד are introduced here.

[4] Although only אשה is mentioned here by Maimonides, the explanation must be understood to apply likewise to איש. It would otherwise be strange that Maimonides should have ignored the circumstance that in the instance quoted by him, the feminine אשה is used on account of the feminine form of the noun יריעה.

shall be coupled together אשה אל אחותה, one to the other" (Exod. xxvi. 3).

It will easily be seen that the terms אח and אחות, "brother and sister," are likewise treated as homonyms, and used, in a figurative sense, like איש and אשה.[1]

CHAPTER VII.

ילד 1, To bear. 2, To create. 3, To produce. 4, To cause to happen. 5, To infer. 6, To teach.

It is well known that the term ילד means, "to bear," וילדו לו בנים, "they have born him children" (Deut. xxi. 15). The word was next used in a figurative sense with reference to objects in nature, meaning, "to create," as in בטרם הרים ילדו, "before the mountains were created" (Ps. xc. 2); also, "to produce," in reference to that which the earth causes to come forth as if by birth, e.g., והולידה והצמיחה "He will cause her to bear and bring forth" (Isa. lv. 10). The term ילד further denotes, "to bring forth," scil. changes in the process of time, as though they were things which were born, e.g., כי לא תדע מה ילד יום, "for thou knowest not what a day may bring forth" (Prov. xxvii. 1). Another figurative use of the word is its application to the formation of thoughts and of ideas, and opinions resulting from them; comp. וילד שקר "and brought forth falsehood" (Ps. vii. 14); also, ובילדי נכרים ישפיקו, "and they please themselves in the children of strangers" (Isa. ii. 6), i.e., "they delight in their opinions." Jonathan ben Uzziël paraphrases the passage, ובנימוסי עממיא אזלין, "they walk in the customs of the Gentiles."

[1] It deserves notice how very little Maimonides has to say on אח and אחות, leaving it entirely to the reader to find the gradations between the primitive and the figurative meanings of the words from the analogous איש and אשה; and to explain accordingly the phrases איש אל אחיו (Exod. xxv. 20) and אשה אל אחותה (Ez. i. 9). The explanation of these words is here introduced, probably because they occur in a figurative sense in the first chapter of Ezekiel.

PART I.—CHAPTER VII. 49

A man who has instructed another in any subject, and has improved his knowledge, may in like manner be regarded as the parent of the person taught, because he is the author of that knowledge; and thus the pupils of the prophets are called "sons" of the prophets, as I shall explain when treating of the homonymity of בן "son."[1] In this figurative sense, the word ילד is employed when it is said of Adam, "And Adam lived an hundred and thirty years, and begat a son in his own likeness, in his form" (Gen. v. 3). As regards the phrase, "form of Adam, and his likeness," we have already stated[2] what it means. Those sons of Adam who were born before that time were not human in the true sense of the word, they had not "the form of man." With reference to Seth who had been instructed, enlightened and brought to human perfection, it could rightly be said, " he (Adam) begat *a son* in his likeness, in his form." It is acknowledged that a man who does not possess this "form" (the nature of which has just been explained) is not human, but a mere animal in human shape and form. Yet such a creature has the power of causing harm and injury: a power which does not belong to other creatures. For those gifts of intelligence and judgment with which he has been endowed for the purpose of acquiring perfection, but which he has failed to apply to their proper aim, are used by him for wicked and mischievous ends; he begets evil beings, as though he merely resembled man, or simulated[3] his outward appearance. Such was the condition of those sons of Adam

[1] The chapter on בן, promised here, is not contained in the present treatise. According to the opinion of Efodi, Maimonides referred here to the explanation of ויולד בדמותו, given in the second part of this chapter, and which implies the explanation of ותלד בן (Gen. iv. 25).   [2] Ch. i., p. 29, *seq.*

[3] The Arabic יחאכיה או אלאנסאן ישבה שי פכאנה, which Munk renders "il est donc, pour ainsi dire, quelque chose qui ressemble à l'homme ou qui le contrefait," is rendered by Charizi, who paraphrases rather than translates the passage, ובאלו הוא חיה מן החיות דומה לבני אדם ואינו מהם; by Tibbon, יזיקהו או לאדם ידמה דבר הוא כאלו. יזיקהו has perhaps its origin in reading יחאקיה for יחאכיה.

E

who preceded Seth. In reference to this subject the Midrash says: "During the 130 years when Adam was under rebuke (נזוף),[1] he begat spirits," *i.e.*, demons;[2] when, however, he was again restored to divine favour "he begat in his likeness, in his form." This is the sense of the passage, "Adam lived one hundred and thirty years, and he begat in his likeness, in his form" (Gen. v. 3).

CHAPTER VIII.

מקום 1, *Space.* 2, *Place.* 3, *Position (fig.)*.[3]

ORIGINALLY the term מקום applied both to a particular spot and to space in general; subsequently it received a

---

[1] נזף denotes originally "to rebuke;" comp. Targ. Onkel., Gen. xxxvii. 10, where וינער is rendered ונזף; נזיפה is used also as a synonym of נדוי and חרם, and signifies a certain kind of excommunication. Comp. Moëd Katon, 16a: אין נדוי פחות מל' יום ואין נזיפה פחות' מז' יום. The term is figuratively applied to a similar relation between God and man; by misdeed the latter makes himself unworthy, as it were, of communing with God. This was, *e.g.*, according to Midrash, the case with Adam from his expulsion from Paradise to the birth of Seth (Comp. Bereshith Rabba *ad locum*).

[2] שדים is given by Maimonides as the explanation of רוחות of the Midrash; whilst רוחות does not exclusively denote evil spirits, the word שדים is always used in that sense in the Talmud and the Midrash. Some of the Kabbalists understand by שדים the several forces of nature.

[3] The next group of anthropomorphic expressions to be interpreted (ch. viii.—xxvii.) consists of those which refer to space and motion. Having shown that the terms figure, likeness, etc., cannot be applied to God in their ordinary sense, Maimonides now proceeds to explain that the expressions which imply the idea of space in reference to God cannot be taken literally. It is possible that this order was suggested to our author by the passage, "And Cain went out from the presence of the Lord" (Gen. iv. 16); or, "And Enoch walked with God, and he was not, for God took him" (*ib.* v. 24); for these are the most striking instances of anthropomorphism in the beginning of Genesis after the phrase "in our form and likeness." Ibn Caspi, Efodi, and others are of opinion that this chapter is intended to explain the word *there* in the passage "and there he put the man" (*ib.* ii. 8). The order of the chapters from viii. to xxvii. is as follows:—God occupies no space (מקום); the throne (כסא), שמים, heavens) which He is said to occupy, is not to be considered a material throne.—He does not ascend (עלה), descend (ירד), sit (ישב), stand (עמר, קום, יצב), approach (קרוב), or fill a place (מלא). He is not above a place (רום), does not pass by (עבר), come in (בא), go out (יצא), return (הלך), walk (הלך), or rest (שכן).

PART I.—CHAPTER VIII.

wider signification and denoted "position," or "degree," as regards the perfection of man in certain points. We say, e.g., this man occupies a certain place in such and such a subject. In this sense this term, as is well known, is frequently used by orators,[1] e.g., ממלא מקום אבותיו בחכמה וביראה, " He fills his ancestors' place in point of wisdom and piety ; " עדין מחלוקת במקומה עומדת, " the dispute still remains in its place," i.e., in statu quo [ante]. In the verse ברוך כבוד ה' ממקומו, " Blessed be the glory of the Lord from His place " (Ezek. iii. 12), ממקומו has this figurative meaning, viz., "according to the exalted nature of His existence,"[2] and wherever מקום is applied to God, it expresses the same idea, namely, the degree of His existence, to which nothing is equal or comparable, as will be shewn below (ch. lvi.).

It should be observed that when we treat in this work of any homonym, we do not desire you to confine yourself to that which is stated in that particular chapter; but we open for you a portal and direct your attention to those significations of the word which are suited to our purpose,[3] though

---

[1] Arabic اهل أللغة ; אהל אללגה ; Munk translates: "dans notre langue"; for " notre " there is no equivalent in the original. Both Charizi and Tibbon render the phrase literally by בעלי הלשון. The phrase in Hebrew as well as in Arabic admits of two meanings: 1, those who master the language by compiling and explaining all its words—i.e., lexicographers ; 2, those who master it in speech and writing—speakers, orators, and authors. As there is no reason why philologists or lexicographers should use the phrase more than any one else, it may be assumed that Maimonides meant authors and orators, who have occasion to speak of other men and of their merits. It is different from אהל אללסאן (בעלי הלשון) mentioned below. (See Note 3.)

[2] Lit., "To His degree and His great share in the existence." This phrase shows how impossible it is to avoid anthropomorphisms and incorrect terms in speaking of God. Maimonides does not mean that the Supreme has the largest portion of existence; the expression is a mere figure resulting from the comparison of His existence with that of other beings ; each of the latter having its portion of existence, the same expression has naturally been applied to God, in so far as a comparison between the Creator and His creatures is admissible. Munk is of opinion that חֹם of the original does not mean "portion," but "dignity," כבוד ; but even this meaning can only be found in חֹם in the sense of " the best portion."

[3] I.e., To explain anthropomorphic phrases occurring in the prophetical

they may not be complete from a philological point of view.[1] You should examine the prophetical books and other works composed by men of science, notice the meaning of every word which occurs in them, and take homonyms in that sense which is in harmony with the context. What I say in a particular passage is a key for the comprehension of all similar passages.[2] For example, we have explained here *makom* in the phrase ברוך כבוד יי ממקומו; but you must understand that the word *makom* has the same signification in הנה מקום אתי ("behold, a place is with me," Exod. xxxiii. 26), *viz.*, a certain degree of contemplation and intellectual intuition (not an ocular inspection), in addition to its literal meaning "a place," *viz.*, the mountain which was pointed out to Moses for seclusion and for the attainment of perfection.

---

books; to substitute a metaphorical meaning for the primary significations of the words.

[1] The original לא בחסב אנראיץ מן יתכלם פי לגה אהל לסאן מא Munk, et non pas par rapport au but de ceux qui parlent au langage vulgaire quelconque. Charizi, ולא לפי כוונת מי שידבר בלשון שום אנשי אומה. The word אנשי, the equivalent of אהל, spoils the sense of the passage, or it must be transposed, בלשון אנשי שום אומה. The rendering of Tibbon is certainly more correct: אהל לסאן — ולא לפי ענין שפת בעלי לשון מן הלשונות admits of two meanings: 1, the people who speak a certain language; 2, those who treat of a language, by writing down its vocabulary and the meanings of the words—"lexicographers." This is meant in Hebrew by בעלי לשון. Maimonides says that he does not pretend to enumerate all possible meanings of a word, but to establish certain significations, required for the proof of those principles which form the basis of his work. Comp. "This is no philological treatise" (chap. x., page 55).

[2] פהדא אלכלאם מנא הו מפתאח הדא אלמקאלה וגירהא Munk: "Ce qui nous venons de dire est la clef de ce traité et d'autres (de nos écrits)." From the instance which follows we may infer that הדא אלמקאלה does not refer to the treatise of Maimonides, but to the Biblical passage which is being explained. The explanation given of one passage, implies that of other passages, and if the same rendering is not applicable to all instances, the student must find the proper rendering in each case according to the principle illustrated by the one example.

CHAPTER IX.

כסא 1, *Throne.* 2, *Emblem of royalty.* 3, *Greatness.*

THE original meaning of the word כסא, "throne," requires no comment. Since men of greatness and authority, as, *e.g.*, kings, use the throne as a seat, and כסא, "the throne," thus [1] relates to the rank, dignity, and position of the person for whom it was made, the Sanctuary has been styled כסא, inasmuch as it likewise refers to the superiority of Him who manifested Himself, and caused His light and glory to dwell therein. Comp. "A glorious high throne from the beginning is the place of our sanctuary" (Jer. xvii. 12). For the same reason the heavens are called כסא, for to the mind of him who observes them with intelligence they suggest the Omnipotence of the Being which has called them into existence, regulates their motions, and governs the sublunary world by their beneficial influence: as we read, "Thus saith the Lord, The heavens are my throne, and the earth my footstool" (Isaiah lxvi. 1); *i.e.*, they testify to my Existence, my Essence, and my Omnipotence, as the throne testifies to the greatness of him who is worthy to occupy it.

This is the idea which true believers should entertain; not, however, that the Omnipotent, Supreme God is supported by any material object; for God is incorporeal, as we shall prove further on; how, then, can He be said to occupy any space, or rest on a body? The fact to which we call the reader's attention is this: every place distinguished by the Almighty, and chosen to receive His light and splendour, as, for instance, the Sanctuary or the Heavens, is termed כסא, "throne;" and, taken in a wider sense,[2] as in כי יד על

---

[1] Lit., "a thing found," that is, being in existence. מונורא (Hebrew נמצא) has been rendered by Munk "visible," although neither the Arabic מונורא, nor the Hebrew נמצא denotes exclusively a thing which is visible; even the Supreme Being is called נמצא.

[2] Three figurative meanings of כסא are given by Maimonides. The third, "greatness," is introduced by the phrase הרחיב בו הלשון, "the use of the

כס יה, "For my hand upon the throne of God" (Exod. xvii. 16), כסא denotes the Greatness and Power of God. These, however, need not be considered as something separate[1] from the existence of God or as part of the Creation, so that God would appear to have existed both without the throne, and with the throne; such a belief would be undoubtedly heretical. It is distinctly stated, "Thou, O Lord, remainest for ever; Thy throne from generation to generation" (Lament. v. 19). By "Thy throne" we must, therefore, understand something inseparable from God. On that account, both here and in all similar passages, the word כסא denotes God's Greatness and Omnipotence, which are identical with His essence.

Our opinion will be further elucidated in the course of this Treatise.[2]

CHAPTER X.

עלה 1, *To go up*. 2, *To rise*. 3, *To act in reference to superior beings*. ירד. 1, *To go down*. 2, *To fall*. 3, *To act in reference to inferior beings*.

WE have already remarked[3] that when we treat in this work of homonyms, we have not the intention to exhaust the meanings of a word (for this is not a philological treatise);

---

word has been amplified," whereby he indicated that it is an extraordinary application of the word. It appears that it has been suggested solely by the phrase quoted and explained, *viz.*, בי יד על כס יה. The reason why Maimonides could not apply the second signification of the word כסא, is given by Ibn Caspi as follows:—These are either the words of Moses or of God. In the first case Moses could only swear by the name of God; to swear by "the heavens" or anything else would appear to be a sin. (Comp. Ex. xxiii. 13.) In the other case we cannot imagine that God would swear by anything else than by Himself, because he who confirms a declaration by an oath must name something superior to himself, at least nothing inferior.

[1] Maimonides adds, that although he takes כס in this passage as an attribute of God, the phrase "the throne of God" does not necessarily imply that this attribute is something separable from God, as though we were able to imagine God with that attribute, and also without it. According to the author it is tantamount to heresy to assume that God possesses attributes of this kind.

[2] See *infra*, ch. li. *et seq*.   [3] See p. 52, Notes 1 and 2.

we shall mention no other significations but those which bear on our subject. We shall thus proceed in our treatment of the terms עלה and ירד.

These two words עלה and ירד are Hebrew terms used in the sense of ascending and descending.[1] When a body moves from a higher to a lower place, the verb, ירד " to go down " is used : when it moves from a lower to a higher place, the word עלה " to go up " is applied. These two verbs were afterwards employed with regard to greatness and power. When a man falls from his high position, we say ירד, " he has come down," and when he rises in station, עלה, " he has risen." Thus the Almighty says, "The stranger that is within thee shall get up (יעלה) above thee very high, and thou shalt come down (תרד) very low." (Deut. xxviii. 43). Again, " the Lord thy God will set thee on high (עליון) above all nations of the earth " (Deut. xxviii. 1) : " And the Lord magnified Solomon exceedingly " (למעלה) (1 Chron. xxix. 25). The Sages often employ these expressions, as :—מעלין בקודש ואין מורידין " In holy matters men must ascend and not descend."[2] The expression עלה and ירד are also applied to intellectual processes, namely, when we reflect on something beneath ourselves we are said to go down (ירד), and when our attention is raised to a subject above us we are said to rise (עלה).

[1] Ibn Tibbon, הירידה והעלייה שני שמות סונחים בלשון העברי וענינם ידוע, " The two terms ירד and עלה are frequently employed in Hebrew texts, and their meaning is well known." Having no other terms to express the sense of ירידה and עלייה than the same verbs ירד and עלה, he omitted the translation of סונחים and ללהבוט, and wrote instead of it וענינם ידוע, leaving סונחים, which word gives no sense. Instead of וענינם ידוע, we expect לענין ידוע. Charizi, העלייה והירידה שמות כנויים לזה הענין.

[2] In the Talmud and in the Midrashim we find various applications of this rule ; e.g., when R. Eleazar b. Azariah had been elected Nasi in the place of R. Gamaliel, who had been deposed, he was allowed to remain in office, after R. Gamaliel had been reinstated in his former dignity, on the following plea נעבריה ? גמירי מעלין בקודש ואין מורידין, " Shall we depose him (R. Eleazar) ? We have the tradition, that we are allowed to raise a person to a post of honour, but if once he is raised, we must not (without cause) depose him " (Talm. Babl. Berachoth 28a). Comp. Shekalim, vi. 4 ; Megillah, iii. 1, etc.

Now, we occupy a lowly position, both in space and rank in comparison with the heavenly sphere,[1] and the Almighty is Most High not in space, but with respect to absolute existence, greatness and power. When it pleased the Almighty to grant to a human being a certain degree of wisdom or prophetic inspiration, the divine communication thus made to the prophet and the entrance of the Divine Presence into a certain place is termed ירידה "descending," while the termination of the prophetic communication or the departure of the divine glory from a place is called עליה "ascending."

The expressions עלה and ירד when used in reference to God, must be interpreted in this sense.[2] Again, when, in accordance with the divine will, some misfortune befalls a nation or a region of the earth,[3] and when the biblical account of that misfortune is preceded by the statement that the Almighty visited the actions of the people, and that he punished them accordingly, then the prophetic author employs the term ירד (descend): for man is so low and insignificant that his actions would not be visited nor bring

---

[1] Lit., that which surrounds us, i.e., the heavenly spheres; according to Munk this means the highest sphere, which moves all the rest.

[2] הדא אלמעני, in Hebrew זה הענין, "this idea" does not refer to the last-named signification, "prophetic inspiration," but relates to the general idea contained in it, viz., an act of the Supreme Being in relation to man as one of the inferior creatures. Efodi takes this passage to mean that ירד and עלה, whenever used in relation to God, have reference to Divine inspiration and revelation or their discontinuance; he was therefore obliged to add "with a few exceptions mentioned below."

[3] The expression "according to his previous will" led many to the erroneous supposition that Maimonides held the heretical opinion that the punishment inflicted on the victims of the Deluge, on Sodom, etc., was the inevitable result of the Divine scheme (משיתה אלקדימה ירצונו הקדום) manifested in the Creation, and that the prophetic writers only represented the Divine will as in connection with certain events which had been determined since the beginning of the world. (See Ibn Caspi, Narboni, and the replies of Abarbanel.) In fact, Maimonides does not use here קדימה in the sense of "eternal;" it means simply "previous," "preceding," scil., the event. There is nothing in this sentence to justify the inference of Ibn Caspi, Narboni, and others, that according to Maimonides the prophets described events which had been determined upon since the Creation as a punishment for sins arising from man's free will.

punishment on him, were it not for the divine will :[1] as is clearly stated in the Bible, with regard to this idea, "What is man that thou shouldst remember him, and the son of man that thou shouldst visit him" (Ps. viii. 5).

The design of the Deity to punish man is, therefore, introduced in the word ירד; comp. הבה נרדה ונבלה, "Go to, let us go down and there confound their language" (Gen. xi. 7); וירד ח' לראת, "And the Lord came down to see" (Gen. xi. 5); ארדה נא ואראה, "I will go down now and see" (Gen. xviii. 21). All these instances convey the idea that man here below has to incur punishment.

More numerous, however, are the instances of the first case,[2] *viz.*, in which ירד is used in connection with the revelation of the word and of the glory of God, *e.g.*, "And I will come down and talk with thee there" (Num. xi. 17); "And the Lord came down upon Mount Sinai" (Exod. xix. 20); "The Lord will come down in the sight of all the people" (Exod. xix. 11); "And God went up from him" (Gen. xxxv. 13); "And God went up from Abraham" (Gen. xvii. 22). When, on the other hand, it says, "And Moses went up unto God" (Exod. xix. 3), it must be taken in the third[3] signification of the verb עלה, in addition to its literal meaning that Moses also ascended to the top of the mount, upon which a certain material light[4] (the manifestation of God's glory) was visible; but we must not imagine that the

---

[1] These words, simple and clear as they are, have still produced long and obscure notes on the Divine will, as the medium between God and the universe. (See Munk, p. 57, note 2.) Maimonides here simply says, that man is too unimportant to be noticed by the Supreme Being, but it is nevertheless the will of the latter to take notice of His creatures.

[2] When applied to God, the third meaning of עלה and ירד, "to act in reference to superior and in reference to inferior beings" is subdivided as follows:— (*a*), to reveal Himself to a man or in a certain place; (*b*), to punish or reward. "The first," mentioned here, refers to the first of this subdivision.

[3] "The third," does not refer to the foregoing "first," but to the number of principal significations of the terms, as enumerated in this chapter, *viz.*, 1, literally, to go up, to go down; 2, to rise, to fall in dignity and power; 3, to act in reference to superior or inferior beings.

[4] Lit., "the light which has been created." The phrase admits of two mean-

Supreme Being, who is far beyond the imagination of the ignorant, occupies a place to which we can ascend, or from which we can descend.

CHAPTER XI.

ישב 1, *To sit.* 2, *To remain.*

THE primary meaning of the word ישיבה, in Hebrew, denotes "being seated," as, ועלי הכהן ישב על הכסא, "Now Eli the priest sat upon a seat" (1 Sam. i. 9); but, since a person can best remain motionless[1] and at rest when sitting, the term ישב was applied to everything that is permanent and unchanging; thus, in the promise that Jerusalem should remain constantly and permanently in an exalted condition, it is stated, "She will rise and sit (וישבה) in her place" (Zech. xiv. 10); further, "He maketh the woman who was childless to sit (מושיבי) as a joyful mother of children" (Ps. cxiii. 9); *i.e.*, He makes her condition to be permanent and enduring.

When applied to God, ישב is to be taken in that latter sense: "Thou, O Lord, remainest (תשב) for ever" (Lam. v. 19); "O thou who sittest (היושבי) in the heavens" (Psalm cxxiii. 1); "He who sitteth (יושב) in the heavens" (ii. 4), *i.e.*, He who is everlasting, constant, and in no way subject to change; immutable in His Essence, and as He consists of nought but His Essence, He is mutable in no way whatever[2]; not mutable in His relation to other things; for

---

ings, either natural light as distinguished from purely spiritual light, which, not having been created, is eternal; or the light which has been expressly created for the purpose of representing the Divine presence (שכינה). Comp. chap. lxiv.

[1] The apparent contradiction in the Hebrew of Tibbon ומאשר היה האדם היושב נח עומד does not occur in the original, or in the translation of Charizi; for עמד in the version of Tibbon corresponds to the Arabic קער, which Charizi renders by שקט, "to be still."

[2] That is to say, change cannot be applied to God as regards any attribute of Him, because, according to Maimonides, no attributes can be predicated of God. See chap. li. *seqq.*

there is no relation whatever existing between Him and any other being, as will be explained below,[1] and therefore no change as regards such relations can take place in Him. Hence He is immutable in every respect, as He expressly declares, אני ה׳ לא שניתי, "I, the Lord, do not change" (Mal. iii. 6); *i. e.*, in Me there is not any change. The term ישב must be taken in this sense when referring to God.

The verb ישב when employed of God is frequently complemented by the noun שמים (Heavens), inasmuch as the heavens are without change or mutation, that is to say, they do not individually change,[2] as the individual beings on earth, by transition from existence into non-existence.

The term ישב is also used in descriptions of God's relation (the term relation is here employed as a homonym) to existing *species* of evanescent things; for those species are as constant, well-organised, and unvarying as the individuals of the heavenly hosts. Thus we find חישב על חוג הארץ (lit., "Who sitteth over the circle of the earth," Isaiah xl. 22), "Who presides constantly and unremittingly over the circuit of the earth"; that is to say, over its revolution; the prophet refers in this term to those things on earth which are in a perpetual revolution.[3]

---

[1] Chap. lvi. Two things connected by a certain relationship must, according to our author, have some common properties, otherwise the idea of relationship cannot be applied. Between God and His creatures, such a relationship cannot exist, as he has no property in common with them.

[2] See I. lxxii.; II. iv. The stars are all unchangeable according to Maimonides, the fixed stars as well as the planets; they move constantly with the same velocity and in the same sphere (*gilgal*), their substance remaining always the same. Munk (note *ad locum*) refers this remark of Maimonides only to the fixed stars, but there is no reason why the planets should be excluded.

[3] It is clear, that Maimonides finds in the term חוג הארץ, a reference to the species. In order to demonstrate this he substitutes for חוג, אאתמה, — the Arabic for the Biblical חוג (סבוב, Tibbon; הקפת הגלגל Charizi), "circle,"—the term דורהא, "its rotation," and the earth not being supposed to rotate, he assumes that "earth" stands for "things on earth." The phrase חוג הארץ signifies therefore "the revolution of things on earth," referring to the species which through the constant change of individuals appear to be in a perpetual motion. The Hebrew חלילתה employed by Ibn Tibbon, and חלילה in the phrase which fol-

Again, למבול ישב ה׳, "The Lord sitteth upon the flood" (Psalm xxix. 10), *i.e.*, despite the change and variation of earthly objects, no change takes place with respect to God's relation (to the earth): His relation to each of the things which come into existence and perish again is stable and constant, for it concerns only the existing species and not the individuals. It should therefore be borne in mind, that whenever the term ישב is applied to God, it is used in this sense.

CHAPTER XII.

קום 1, *To stand.* 2, *To be confirmed.* 3, *To stir.*

THE term קימה is a homonym. In one of its significations[1] קום is the opposite of ישב, "to sit," as ולא קם ולא זע ממנו, "He did not rise nor move for him"

---

lows (ההוים בה חלילה) have the same meaning as the term has in the common phrase חוזר חלילה, "recurring by moving in a circle." The forms חללתה and בחללה in the printed editions of Tibbon's translation are misprints for חלילה and בה חלילה. See Moreh ha-moreh, page 161. Munk translates the passage thus: "Celui qui est perpétuel et stable au dessus du circuit de la terre ou de son *tour*, en faisant allusion aux choses qui y naissent *tour à tour*." Charizi translates דורא by בהקפת הגלגל, "by the revolution of the celestial sphere." Ibn Caspi and others explain the phrase likewise in that sense. This is incorrect; for things dependent on the revolutions of the sphere are transient, while Maimonides finds in the phrase חוג הארץ something permanent. Comp. ch. lxxii.

[1] Maimonides begins the explication of the homonyms with the "primary signification" (הנחתו הראשונה or עיקר הנחתו, and the like), when the second meaning has been derived from the first (הושאל, הרחיב בו הלשון etc.); when the first two or more significations of the term are, according to Maimonides, independent of each other, the first is not represented as the primary signification. In this chapter, therefore, he simply says, " and one of its meanings." (Comp. ch. xiii., xiv., xv., etc.) Comp. Munk, " Le Guide," p. 61, Note 1, who, like Shemtob and others, appears to have overlooked this distinction.

PART I.—CHAPTER XII.

(Esth. v. 9).[1] It further denotes the confirmation and verification of a thing, e.g.: יקם ח׳ את דברו, "The Lord will verify His promise" (1 Sam. i. 23); ויקם שדה עפרון, "The field of Ephron was made sure (as the property of Abraham)" (Gen. xxiii. 17). וקם הבית אשר בעיר, "The house that is in the walled city shall be established" (Lev. xxv. 30); וקמה בידך ממלכת ישראל, "And the kingdom of Israel shall be firmly established in thy hand" (1 Sam. xxiv. 20). It is in this sense that the term קום is always[2] employed with reference to the Almighty; as עתה אקום יאמר ח׳, "Now shall I rise, saith the Lord" (Ps. xii. 7), which is the same as saying, "Now shall I verify my word and my dispensation for good or evil." אתה תקום תרחם ציון, "Thou shalt arise and have mercy upon Zion" (Ps. cii. 13), which means: Thou wilt establish what thou hast promised, viz., that thou wouldst pity Zion.

Generally a person who resolves to set about a matter, accompanies his resolve by rising, hence the verb קום is employed to denote "to resolve" to do a certain thing; as, כי הקים בני את עבדי עלי, "That my son hath stirred up my servants against me" (1 Sam. xxii. 8). The word is figuratively used to signify the execution of a divine decree against a people sentenced to extermination, as וקמתי על בית ירבעם, "And I will rise against the

---

[1] This instance has been preferred to many others occurring in the Pentateuch and other books, because here the meaning of קום ("to rise") as the opposite of ישיבה "sitting," is best seen from the fact that ולא קם is opposed to ומרדכי ישב בשער המלך (v. 13). In verse 9, ישב must be supplied, and several MSS. read ישב בשער המלך.

[2] Here Maimonides states that קום, when applied to God, has *always* the meaning " to establish," and below two verses are quoted, in which he assigns another signification to the verb קום used in reference to God, viz., "to be determined to do" (התעורר). The difference may perhaps be that in the instances given for the second signification, the subject is "God," while in the two passages quoted subsequently the subject is "the decree" (גזרה, which in the interpretation of the passage is to be substituted for the personal pronoun).—Comp. ch. viii., p. 52, note 1, and beginning of ch. x. The Moreh ha-moreh (p. 162), in the resumé of this chapter, only speaks of two significations of the word.

house of Jeroboam" (Amos vii. 9); וקם על בית מרעים,
"but he will arise against the house of the evildoers"
(Isaiah xxxi. 2). Possibly, the phrase ערות אדם (Ps. xii. 7)
should be taken in this latter sense, as also הקום תרדם ציון
(ib. cii. 13), namely: Thou wilt rise up against her enemies.

There are many passages to be interpreted in this
manner, but in no way should it be understood that He
rises or sits—far be such a notion! Our Sages expressed this
idea in the formula, אין למעלה לא ישיבה ולא עמידה,[1] "In
the world above there is neither sitting nor standing;" for
עמד and קום are synonyms [and what is said about עמידה
also applicable to קימה].

CHAPTER XIII.

עמד 1, *To stand.* 2, *To cease.* 3, *To last.*

The term עמד is a homonym signifying "to stand upright," as בעמדו לפני פרעה, "When he stood before
Pharaoh" (Gen. xli. 46); אם יעמד משה ושמואל, "Though
Moses and Samuel stood" (Jer. xv. 1);[2] והוא עמד עליהם,
"He stood by them" (Gen. xviii. 8). It further denotes
"cessation and interruption," as כי עמדו לא ענו עוד, "but
they stood still and answered no more" (Job xxxii. 16);
ותעמד מלדת, "and she ceased to bear" (Gen. xxix. 35).
Next, עמד signifies "to be enduring and lasting,"
as, למען יעמדו ימים רבים, "that they may continue
many days" (Jer. xxxii. 14); ויכלת עמד; "Then shalt

[1] Talm. Babli. Chagigah 15a. The editions have לא ישיבה לא עורף ולא
עימוי (in accordance with Rashi). Maimonides appears to have read לא עמידה
ולא ישיבה. Comp. Maim. Comm. on Mishnah Sanhedrin X., I., third principle (יסוד).

[2] The phrase יעמד לפני, "stood before me," (i.e., before God), must
certainly be taken figuratively; it is here quoted as an instance for the primary
meaning of עמד, "to stand upright," in so far as it implies either
"standing" as distinguished from lying in the grave, or "standing" at
prayers.

thou be able to endure" (Exod. xviii. 23); עמד מעמד בו, "His taste remained in him" (Jer. xlviii. 11), *i.e.*, it has continued and remained in existence without any change; וצדקתו עמדת לעד, "His righteousness remaineth for ever" (Ps. cxi. 3), *i.e.*, it is permanent and everlasting. עמד applied to God must be understood in this latter sense, as ועמדו רגליו ביום ההוא על הר הזתים (lit. "And his feet shall stand in that day upon the Mount of Olives," Zech. xiv. 4), "His causes, *i.e.*, the events of which He is the cause,[1] will remain efficient," etc. This will be further elucidated when we speak of the meaning of רגל. (Vide *infra*, chap. xxviii.) In the same sense are used the phrases ואתה פה עמד עמדי, "But as for thee, stand thou here by me" (Deut. v. 28), and אנכי עמד בין ה' וביניכם, "I stood between the Lord and you"[2] (Deut. v. 5).

CHAPTER XIV.

אדם 1, *Adam.* 2, *Man.* 3, *Common people.*[3]

THE homonymous term אדם is the name of the first man, being, as Scripture indicates, derived from אדמה the "earth."[4] Next, it means "mankind," as לא ידון רוחי באדם

---

[1] אסבאבהו (Heb. סבותיו) lit. "his causes," signifies here "the things of which He is the cause." סבה appears to be used by homonymy in a double sense: *a*, cause; *b*, effect. In chapter xxviii., the term סבותיו is explained by הנפלאות אשר הוא ית' סבתם, "the wonders of which God is the cause" (page 97).

[2] The sense of the two passages accordingly is: "And thou remain firm in thy knowledge of Me," or "in the fulfilment of the command received of Me;" and "I remained firm in my mission between the Lord and you."

[3] According to the several commentators this chapter is a supplement to that on איש (ch. vi.), and is intended to throw light on some passages of the Maaseh Mercabhah (Ezek. i. 5, 8, 10, etc.) not mentioned here. They do not explain thereby the strange position of the chapter, which is "not the suggestion of the moment" (*supra*, page 20). As in mankind, so in each individual, a lower element (אדם), and a nobler one (איש) are contained. According to Maimonides the pronouns ואתה and אנכי in the last-mentioned passages (ch. xiii.) refer to the nobler element (the pure intellect) in Moses.

[4] It is not distinctly stated in the Bible that the name "Adam" is derived

"My spirit shall not strive with man" (Gen. vi. 3). Again, ומי יודע רוח בני האדם, "Who knoweth the spirit of the children of man" (Eccl. iii. 21); ומותר האדם מן הבהמה אין, "so that a man has no pre-eminence above a beast" (Eccl. iii. 19). אדם signifies also "the multitude," "the lower classes" as opposed to those distinguished from the rest, as גם בני אדם גם בני איש "Both low and high" (Psalm xlix. 3).

It is in this third signification that it occurs in the verses, ויראו בני האלהים את בנות האדם, "The sons of the higher order (Elohim) saw the daughters of the lower order (Adam)" (Gen. vi. 2); and אכן כאדם תמותון "Forsooth! as the humble man you shall die"[1] (Psalm lxxxii. 7).

CHAPTER XV.

נצב *and* יצב 1, *To stand.* 2, *To last.*[2]

ALTHOUGH the two radicals נצב and יצב are distinct, yet their meaning is identical, as you know from their various forms.

---

from אדמה, "earth," but Maimonides perhaps inferred it from Gen. ii. 7, "And God formed man, (האדם) out of the dust from the earth," (מן האדמה).

[1] This verse is quoted like the preceding, not only to explain the term "Adam," but also the expressions "elohim" and "b'ne elyon" which precede, and to show that the latter signify "the upper class of men," "the princes," etc., in contra-distinction to "adam," "the common people." According to Ibn Caspi, Narboni, etc., Maimonides here suggests that the biblical account of Adam is to be taken in a figurative sense, that it does not contain the history of the first man, but the development of man's moral and intellectual faculties. Abarbanel *ad locum* justly characterises this as הבל מעשה תעתועים.

[2] Proceeding with the interpretation of those anthropomorphic passages in the Pentateuch, which refer to space and motion, the author now directs our attention to the dream of Jacob, to the ladder by which the angels of the Lord go up and down, and on the top of which the Lord stood. Commentators and philosophers have long dwelt upon the explanation of this passage (Comp. Ibn Ezra, Nachmanides, Akedath Yitschak, etc., *ad locum*). Maimonides himself gives a different interpretation of the passage in Part II. x. Ibn Caspi says, that that passage deserves the name Maaseh Mercabhah, as much as the first chapter of Ezekiel. The interpretation of the words, "and behold the Lord stood upon it," led to the explanation of the phrase, ונצבת על הצור; and

PART I.—CHAPTER XV. 65

This homonym has several meanings: in some instances it signifies "to stand" or "to place oneself," as ותתצב אחתו מרחק, "And his sister stood afar off" (Exod. ii. 4); יתיצבו מלכי ארץ, "The kings of the earth set themselves" (Psalm ii. 2); יצאו נצבים, "They came out and stood" (Numb. xvi. 27). In other instances it denotes continuance and permanence, as דברך נצב בשמים, "Thy word is established in Heaven" (Ps. cxix. 89), *i.e.*, it remains for ever.

Whenever this term is applied to God it must be understood in the latter sense, as והנה ה' נצב עליו, "And, behold, the Lord stood upon it" (Gen. xxviii. 13), "stood," *i.e.*, appeared as eternal and everlasting "upon it," namely, upon the ladder, the upper end of which reached to heaven, while the lower end touched the earth. By means of this ladder all may climb up who wish to do so, and they must ultimately[1] attain to a knowledge of Him who is above the summit of the ladder, because He remains upon it permanently. It must be well understood that the term " upon it "[2] is employed by me in harmony with this metaphor. "Angels of God" who were going up represent the prophets. That

---

taking it figuratively, our author was obliged to find for צור an adequate signification. The next chapter, therefore, treats of the homonymity of the term "*tsur*."

[1] The expression צְרוּרָה (בחברה Tibbon, omitted by Charizi), "by necessity," is here ambiguous. Grammatically it can be connected with עליה (עליון Hebr.); so Munk: "celui qui est dessus nécessairement," explaining it in a note "l'être absolu et nécessaire," or with the verb ידרך (שישיג), in which case the sense of the passage would be, "till he who ascends step by step reaches the top and there necessarily attains a perception of the Supreme Being, as the latter remains permanently and eternally above the ladder." Those who join "necessarily" with "is upon it" (Munk, Moreh ha-moreh, etc.), make Maimonides use tautological language: God is upon the ladder necessarily, for He is upon it permanently. The reverse order would then certainly be more correct: God is upon it permanently, for He is there necessarily.

[2] In the translation of Tibbon, the words הנה עליו (=שמאמרי) שמאמ׳ have been misunderstood and have been transformed, in the printed editions, into שמאמר הנה ה' נצב עליו. In the Comm. of Ibn Caspi (cf. also other commentators), though he quotes הנה יי נצב עליו, the remark of Maimonides is referred to his own use of עליו, not to עליו occurring in the Biblical phrase. It is possible that here also the words יי נצב have erroneously been added by the copyist.

F

the name מלאך " angel," was applied to prophets may clearly be seen in the following passages: וישלח מלאך, "He sent an angel" (Numb. xx. 16); ויעל מלאך ח' מן הגלגל אל הבכים, "And an angel of the Lord came up from Gilgal to Bochim (Judges ii. 1).[1] How suggestive, too, is the expression עלים וירדים בו, "ascending and descending on it!" The ascent is mentioned before the descent, inasmuch as the "ascending" (עליה) and attaining a certain height of the ladder precedes the "descending," (ירידה), i.e., the application of the knowledge acquired in the ascent for the training and the instruction of mankind. This application is termed ירידה, "descent," in accordance with our explanation of the term (chapter x.).

To return to our subject. The phrase נצב עליו has reference to the permanence and constancy of God, not to the idea of physical position. This is also the sense of the phrase ונצבת על הצור, "Thou shalt stand upon the rock" (Ex xxxiii. 21). It is therefore clear that נצב and עמד are identical in their signification. Comp. הנני עומד לפניך שם על הצור בחורב, "Behold, I will stand before thee there upon the rock in Horeb" (Ex. xvii. 6).[2]

CHAPTER XVI.

צור 1, *Rock.* 2, *Flint.* 3, *Quarry.* 4, *Origin.*

THE word צור is a homonym. First, it denotes "a rock," as והכית בצור, "And thou shalt smite the rock" (Ex. xvii. 6).

---

[1] According to Maimonides, מלאך, in the first quotation, is Moses; in the second, some other prophet, not named. He does not, however, prove that "angel," in the two passages quoted, could not be taken in the ordinary sense of the word.

[2] Having stated that עמד and נצב, in their figurative application, denote the same thing, the author supports his interpretation of נצב in the phrase ונצבת על הצור, by extending the identity of the two terms to that of the phrases in which they are followed by על הצור. It is clear, that עמד על הצור, used in reference to God, has to be taken in a figurative sense; Maimonides concludes that ונצבת על הצור has the same meaning, although the subject in this phrase is Moses.

PART I.—CHAPTER XVI.

Then, "a hard stone," like the flint,[1] *e.g.*, חרבות צורים, "Knives of stone" (Josh. v. 2). It is next employed to signify the quarry from which the stones are hewn; comp. הביטו אל צור חצבתם, "Look unto the rock whence ye are hewn" (Isaiah li. 1).[2] From this latter meaning the term was afterwards employed to express "the root and origin" of all things. It is on this account that in the foregoing verse, after the words הביטו אל צור חצבתם, it is stated הביטו אל אברהם וגו', "Look unto Abraham your father," from which we evidently may infer that the words "Abraham your father" serve to explain "the rock whence ye are hewn;" and that the Prophet meant to say "Walk in his ways, put faith in his instruction, and conduct yourselves according to the rule of his life! for properties contained in the quarry should be found again in those things which are formed and hewn out of it."

It is in the latter sense that the Almighty is called "rock" (צור), He being the origin and the *causa efficiens* of all things besides Himself. Thus we read הצור תמים פעלו, "He is the Rock, His work is perfect" (Deut. xxxii. 4); צור ילדך תשי, "Of the Rock that begat thee thou art unmindful" (Deut. xxxii. 18); צורם מכרם, "Their Rock had sold them" (xxxii. 30); אין צור כאלהינו, "There is no rock like our God" (1 Sam. ii. 2): צור העולמים, "The Rock of Eternity" (Isaiah xxvi. 4). Again, ונצבת על הצור, "And thou shalt stand upon the rock" (Exod. xxxiii. 21), *i.e.*, Be firm and steadfast in the conviction that God is the source of all things (the "Primal Cause"), for this will lead you towards the knowledge of the Divine Being. We have shown that the words הנח מקום אתי contain the same idea.[3]

---

[1] כצור החלמיש (כאלצואן, Charizi), has no equivalent in the translation of Ibn Tibbon.

[2] This verse serves to prove the use of *tsur* in the sense of "quarry," and also its use in the figurative meaning, "origin." Having no other support for *tsur* denoting "quarry," Maimonides derives it, probably, from the verb חצבתם, which is used in reference to quarries (comp. אבני מחצב "minerals").

[3] Chapter viii. (p. 52), where *makom* is explained as denoting a certain degree in the development of the intellectual faculties of man (מדרגת עיון).

CHAPTER XVII.

ולא במעשה בראשית בשנים "*Do not expound Physics in the presence of two.*" (Talm. Bab. Chagigah 11 b.)

Do not imagine that only Metaphysics should be taught with reserve to the common people and to the uninitiated; for the same is also the case with most of the natural sciences.[1] In this sense we have repeatedly made use of the expression of the Sages, ולא במעשה בראשית בשנים, "Do not expound the chapter on the Creation in the presence of two," [*vide* Introd. page 7 and note 3]. This principle was not peculiar to our Sages; ancient philosophers and scholars of other nations were likewise wont to treat of the *principia rerum* obscurely, and to use figurative language in discussing such subjects. Thus Plato and his predecessors called Substance the female, and Form the male.[2]—(You are aware[3] that the elements of all existing transient things are three, *viz.*, Substance, Form, and Privation [of form]; the last-named element is always inherent in the substance, for otherwise the substance would be incapable of receiving a new form; and it is from this point of view that privation [of form] is included among the elements. As soon, then,

---

[1] This chapter appears to aim at justifying the use of figurative, and therefore less intelligible, expressions, such as "*Tsur*," instead of the more common appellations of the Supreme Being. It was here the proper place for Maimonides to make such a remark, because, according to his interpretation, the words ונצבת על הצור contain a figure which the reader, if left to himself, would not easily find in them. In addition to this, his interpretation of צור as "the source of all things," brings the Biblical passage into closer relation to physical science. (See Munk, note *ad locum*.)

[2] Comp. ἂν τὸ μὲν εἶδος λόγον ἔχει ἄρρενός τε καὶ πατρὸς ἃ δ' ὕλα, θηλεός τε καὶ ματέρος, "Of which the form has the relation of the male and the father, the substance that of the female and the mother." (Plat. Timaei Locri, 94, *b.*)

[3] The words "You are aware," etc., to "Treatises on Natural Science," are used parenthetically, containing, in opposition to the opinion of Plato —that the principles of all things were two, matter and form—the author's own opinion that three principles must be assumed, *viz.*, matter, form, and privation of form (*i.e.*, form *in potentia*, or the capacity of matter to receive a certain form).

as a substance has received a certain form, the privation of that form, namely, of that which has just been received, has ceased, and is replaced by the privation of another form, and so on with all possible forms, as is explained in treatises on natural philosophy.[1])—Now, if those philosophers who have nothing to fear from a lucid explanation of these metaphysical subjects still were in the habit of discussing them in figures and metaphors, how much more should we, having the interest of religion at heart, refrain from elucidating to the mass any subject that is beyond their comprehension, or that might be taken in a sense directly opposite to the one intended. This also deserves attention.[2]

CHAPTER XVIII.

נגש, נגע, קרב, *To approach, to touch,* 1, *physically;* 2, *mentally.*[3]

THE three words נגש, נגע, קרב sometimes signify "contact" or "nearness in space," sometimes the approach of man's know-

[1] See Arist. Phys., i. 6 and 7.

[2] In this phrase Narboni and other commentators discover an allusion to significations of the word צור not mentioned by Maimonides in this chapter. The causes of all things being four, and only one being given here, the word צור, denoting origin or beginning (that is, cause), must also include the other three causes (צורה, חומר, תכלית, form, matter, and purpose). More probably, however, the author reminds the reader that the explanations generally given of the passage quoted at the end of chapter xvi. are only for the common people, who would not understand the philosophical interpretation.

[3] In the preceding chapters Maimonides spoke of that knowledge of the Primal Cause, which man can attain, by gradually ascending the ladder of intellectual comprehension; he explains now the term "approaching God" as a metaphor expressing the same idea, especially in reference to the verse, "And Moses alone shall draw near to God, and they shall not draw near." The chapters which follow next contain the interpretation of expressions referring to manifestations of God in certain places: as "The glory of the Lord *filled* the tabernacle" (ch. xix.); "The Lord sitting upon the throne *high* and *exalted*" (ch. xx.); "And the Lord *passed* before his face" (ch. xxi.); "Behold, I *come* unto thee" (ch. xxii.); "The Lord *cometh* out from His place" (ch. xxiii.); "I will *go*, and I will *return* to my place" (ch. xxiv.); and the pleasure of him *who dwelleth* in the bush" (ch. xxv.).

ledge to an object, as if it resembled the physical approach of one body to another. As to the use of קרב in the first meaning, *viz.*, to draw near a spot, comp. כאשר קרב אל המחנה " As he drew near the camp" (Ex. xxxii. 19); ופרעה הקריב, "And Pharaoh drew near (Ex. xiv. 10). נגע in the first sense, *viz.*, expressing the contact of two bodies, occurs in ורתגע לרגליו "And she cast it at his feet" (Ex. iv. 25); ויגע על פי, "He caused it to touch my mouth" (Is. vi. 7).[1] And נגש in the first sense, *viz.*, the approach or motion of a man towards another, is found, *e.g.*, in ויגש אליו יהודה, "And Judah drew near unto him" (Gen. xliv. 1).

The second meaning of these three words is " approach by means of knowledge," or "contact by comprehension," but not in reference to space. As to נגע in this second sense, comp. כי נגע אל השמים משפטו, "for her judgment reacheth unto heaven" (Jer. li. 9).[2] An instance of קרב being used in this meaning is contained in the following passage, והדבר אשר יקשה מכם תקריבון אלי " And the cause that is too hard for you, bring it unto me" (Deut. i. 17); this is equivalent to saying, "Ye shall make it known unto me." The verb קרב (in the Hiphil) is thus employed in the sense of giving information concerning a thing.[3] The verb נגש is used figuratively in the phrase ויגש אברהם ויאמר, "And Abraham drew near, and said" (Gen. xviii. 23); this took place in a prophetic vision and in a trance, as will be explained;[4]

---

[1] By adding this instance, Maimonides appears to indicate that, although part of a prophetical vision, the words ויגע על פי, "and he caused (the coal) to touch my mouth," may be taken literally, because the Prophet really perceived that process in the vision.

[2] This phrase is generally taken as a hyperbolic expression, meaning "very great." According to Maimonides, the terms שמים and שחקים are here used in the sense of "the Most High," and משפטה as denoting "her sins deserve punishment" ("her sins became known to the Most High").

[3] This remark seems to be quite superfluous; there is no reason why it should be added after תקריבון אלי more than after the instances for נגע and נגש. The special figurative meaning of קרב is, perhaps, in this instance more clearly shown by the verb ושמעתיו " and I will hear it," which follows immediately.

[4] Pt. I., cap. xxi., and Pt. II., cap. xli.—The figurative meaning of נגש is

also in יען כי נגש העם הזה בפיו ובשפתיו, "Forasmuch as this people draw near me with their mouths and with their lips" (Isaiah xxix. 13). Wherever a word denoting approach or contact is employed in the prophetic writings to describe a certain relation between the Almighty and any created being, it has to be understood in this latter sense [viz., to approach mentally]. For, as will be proved in this treatise,[1] the Supreme is incorporeal, and consequently He does not approach nor draw near a thing, nor can aught approach or touch Him; for when a being is without corporeality, it cannot occupy space, and all idea of approach, contact, distance, conjunction, separation, touch, or proximity is inapplicable to such a being.

There can be no doubt respecting the verses קרוב ח׳ לכל קוראיו, "The Lord is nigh unto all them that call upon Him" (Ps. cxlv. 18); קרבת אלהים יחפצון, "They take delight in approaching to God" (Is. lviii. 2); קרבת אלהים לי טוב, "The nearness of God is pleasant to me" (Ps. lxxiii. 28); all such phrases intimate a spiritual approach, i.e., the attainment of some knowledge, not, however, approach in space. Thus also קרובים אליו, "who hath God so nigh unto him" (Deut. iv. 7); קרב אתה ושמע, "Draw thou near and

---

clearer in the instance which follows, the verb being joined to בפיו, "with their mouths;" and it is probably quoted to support the explanation of the phrase ויגש אברהם, "And Abraham approached mentally." This is in accordance with the view of Maimonides, that the communication between God and Abraham as related in Gen. xviii. 23-33, took place in a prophetic vision, although this circumstance is not distinctly stated in the Bible. Maimonides adds that it took place in תרדמה נבואית, "a prophetic trance;" the reader is not informed on what biblical passage this statement is based. The author nowhere proves that all divine communications were made to Abraham in that condition. The state of prophetic trance is different from a mere "vision," as is distinctly stated by Maimonides in Part II., chapter xli.

The preposition מן, meaning "in the same sense as the expression has in the following passage," or "of the same kind as," in Ibn Tibbon's version has no equivalent in the original. It is possible that it is a corruption of וכן. Some commentators join it with the preceding כמו שיתבאר, "as may be explained by referring to." Charizi has ואמר instead of מן.

[1] Pt. II., cap. iv.

hear" (Deut. v. 27); ובגש משה לבדו וגו׳, "And Moses alone shall draw near the Lord; but they shall not come nigh" (Ex. xxiv. 2).

If, however, you wish to take this expression ובגש משה "And Moses shall draw near" to mean that he approached a certain place in the mountain, whereon the Divine Light shone, or, in the words of the Bible, "where the glory of the Lord abode," you may do so, provided you do not lose sight of the truth that there is no difference whether a person stand at the centre of the earth or at the highest point of the ninth sphere, if this were possible; he is no further away from God in the one case, or nearer to Him in the other; those only approach Him who obtain a knowledge of Him; while those who remain ignorant of Him recede from Him. In this approach towards, or recession from God there are numerous grades one above the other, and I shall further elucidate, in one of the subsequent chapters of the Treatise,[1] what constitutes the difference in our perception of God.

In the passage גע בהרים ויעשנו, "Touch the mountains, and they shall smoke" (Ps. cxliv. 5), the verb גע is used in a figurative sense. "Let thy word touch them," as in the phrase וגע על עצמו, "Touch thou him himself" (Job ii. 5), the meaning of which is "Bring thy infliction upon him." In a similar manner נגע, in whatever form it may be employed, must in each place be interpreted according to the context; for in some cases it denotes contact of two material objects, in others knowledge and comprehension of a thing, as if he who now comprehends anything which he had not comprehended previously had thereby approached a subject which had been distant from him. This point is of considerable importance.[2]

[1] Part II., cap. xxxvi., and Part I., cap. lx.
[2] This remark is added, according to Efodi and others, to indicate that the two passages, "You shall not touch it" (Gen. iii.) and "No hand shall touch it" (Exod. xix.), are to be explained according to the same principle.

CHAPTER XIX.

מלא 1, *To fill.* 2, *To complete.* 3, *To reach the highest degree.*

THE term מלא is a homonym which denotes that one substance enters another, and fills it, as ותמלא כדה, "And she filled her pitcher" (Gen. xxiv. 16); מלא העמר לאחד, "An omer-full for each" (Ex. xvi. 32,),[1] and many other instances. Next, it signifies the expiration or completion of a fixed period of time, as וימלאו ימיה ללדת, "And when her days to be delivered were fulfilled" (Gen. xxv. 24); וימלאו לו ארבעים יום, "And forty days were completed for him" (Gen. l. 3). It further denotes attainment of the highest degree of excellency, as ומלא ברכת ח', "Full with the blessing of the Lord" (Deut. xxxiii. 23); מלא אותם חכמת לב, "Them hath he filled with wisdom of heart" (Ex. xxxv. 35); וימלא את החכמה ואת התבונה ואת הדעת. "He was filled with wisdom, and understanding, and cunning" (1 Kings vii. 14).[2] In this sense it is said מלא כל הארץ כבודו (lit. "The whole earth is full of his glory," Is. vi. 4), "All the earth gives evidence of His perfection," that is to say, leads to a knowledge of it.[3] Thus also וכבוד ח' מלא

---

[1] The editions of the Bible have מלא העמר ממנו. Either Maimonides himself or the copyists confounded the two passages שני העמר לאחד and מלא העמר ממנו (Ex. xvi. 21 and 32).

[2] According to Maimonides the meaning of these three passages is: "The greatest blessing of the Lord," "He gave them the highest degree of the wisdom of the heart," "He acquired the highest degree of wisdom," etc.

[3] It is difficult to see how Maimonides reconciles the grammatical construction of the sentence with his interpretation. Some authors (as Efodi and others) supply "the perfection" as the explanation of מלא, and give the meaning of the phrase as follows: "The perfection of the whole earth proves His perfection," so that in the words of Maimonides the principal part, the substitute for מלא, the theme of this chapter, is absent. It is possible that Maimonides in his interpretation of the passage paraphrases only the first three words מלא כל הארץ, excluding כבודו. According to this view the phrase is to be rendered, "The perfection of the whole earth is His glory," that is, "the perfection which the whole earth declares is His glory." The

את המשכן, "The glory of the Lord filled the tabernacle" (Ex. xl. 34);[1] and, in fact, every application of מלא to God must be interpreted in this manner; and not that He has a body occupying space. If, on the other hand, you prefer to think that (in this passage) by כבוד ח׳, "the glory of the Lord," a certain light created for the purpose is to be understood, that that light is always termed כבוד, and that the same "filled the tabernacle," we have no objection.[2]

CHAPTER XX.

רם and נשא, *High*, 1, *in space*; 2, *in estimation*.

THE word רם is a homonym, denoting elevation in space, and elevation in dignity, *i.e.*, greatness, honour, and power. It has the first meaning in ותרם התבה מעל הארץ, "And the ark was lifted up above the earth" (Gen. vii. 17); and the latter meaning in הרימותי בחור מעם, "I have exalted one chosen out of the people" (Ps. lxxxix. 20); יען אשר הרימתיך מתוך העפר,[3] "Forasmuch as I have exalted thee from amongst the dust" (1 Kings xvi. 2): יען הרימתיך מתוך העם, "Forasmuch as I exalted thee from among the people" (1 Kings xiv. 7).

Whenever the term רם is employed in reference to God, it must be taken in the second sense: רומה על שמים אלהים, "Be thou exalted, O God, above the heavens" (Ps. lvii. 12).

---

words אי תדל עליה have been added in order to substitute for תשחד ("is evidence," lit. "testifies,") another verb that implied the notion of "speaking" in a less degree. The suffix in עליה agrees with כמאל. Maimonides appears to have abandoned this somewhat forced interpretation of the passage in favour of the more simple one, "the whole earth is full of His praise." Comp. ch. lxiv. on the different meanings of כבוד.

[1] That is, according to the author, the perfection of the Lord appeared in the Tabernacle.

[2] Comp. chapter v., page 47, note 1.

[3] Our editions of the Bible have העפר כן.

PART I.—CHAPTER XX.

In the same manner נשא denotes both elevation in space and elevation in rank and dignity.[1] In the former sense it occurs in וישאו את שברם על חמריהם, "And they lifted up their corn upon their asses" (Gen. xlii. 26); and there are many instances like this in which the verb נשא has the meaning "to carry," "to move" from place to place; for this implies elevation in space. In the latter sense we have ותנשא מלכותו, "And his kingdom shall be exalted" (Num. xxiv. 7); וינטלם וינשאם, "And he bare them, and carried them" (Isaiah lxiii. 9); ומדוע תתנשאו, "Wherefore do ye exalt yourselves" (Num. xvi. 3).

Every expression including נשא when applied to God has this latter sense—e.g., הנשא שופט הארץ, "Lift up thyself, thou judge of the earth" (Ps. xciv. 2); כה אמר רם ונשא, "Thus saith the High and Exalted One" (Is. lvii. 15)— denoting elevation in rank, quality, and power;[2] not, however, in space.

You may be surprised that I employ the expression, "elevation in rank, quality, and power," and you may say, "How can you assert that several distinct expressions denote the same thing?"[3] It will be explained later on (ch. l. seqq.) that those

---

[1] The original אלחם is rendered החלק by Ibn Tibbon; it is the portion allotted to something; it is a synonym of מעלה and מדרגה; and יתרון החלק means "distinction of the portion" (scil. of honour, dignity, etc.) i.e., "distinction." Comp. ch. viii. page 51, note 2. Shemtob and others are of opinion that by יתרון החלק Maimonides meant to say that נשא implied a higher degree of elevation than רום.

[2] Ibn Tibbon appears to have read in the original ורפעה מנזלה ונלאלה תעזה in the edition of Munk מנזלה is omitted. The reading of Ibn Tibbon deserves the preference, for in the first place it harmonises better with the words which follow: ואל יקשה בעיניך אמרי גדולת מדרגה ומעלה ורוממות, and secondly the word רפעה, "elevation," is used by Maimonides in this chapter in its general meaning, referring both to space and to dignity, and was therefore most probably connected in this place with a qualifying genitive.

[3] The question here anticipated by Maimonides is not why the author employed the three synonyms מעלה, מדרגה, רוממות; first, because there were in the preceding chapters, even in the first part of this same chapter, opportunities for such a remark, and there is no reason why Maimonides should have reserved it for this place (see Shemtob ad locum); secondly, the answer that in

who possess a true knowledge of God do not consider that He possesses many attributes, but believe that these various attributes which describe His Might, Greatness, Power, Perfection, Goodness, etc., have one and the same sense, namely, that of His Essence, and not anything extraneous to His Essence. I shall devote special chapters to the Names and Attributes of God; our intention here is solely to shew that רם ונשׂא in the passage quoted denote elevation in rank, not in space.

CHAPTER XXI.

עבר, 1, *To pass.* 2, *To sound.* 3, *To appear.* 4, *To transgress.* 5, *To miss.*

In its primary signification[1] the word עבר refers to the motion of a body in space, and is chiefly applied[2] to living creatures moving at some distance in a straight line,[3] *e. g.,* וחוא עבר לפניהם, "And He passed over before

---

God all attributes are one and the same thing, is no reply to this question. The author has explained the expression נשׂא in nearly the same terms as רם; both occur together in the last mentioned instance; he therefore adds, Be not surprised that I explain two distinct attributes (ענינים רבים) to be identical (ענין אחד) for the Divine attributes, etc.; otherwise Maimonides would have said איך תשׂים ענין א' עינינים רבים. In addition to this reasoning we may add that Charizi omits those synonyms in his translation altogether. He has: כה אמר רם ונשׂא הכל לענין נדלה ועז ואם תאמר איך תשׂים עינים רבים מענין אחד.

[1] The Hebrew versions omit the words במעני אלעבור פי אל ערבי "in the signification of עבר in Arabic," as superfluous in a translation from Arabic into Hebrew.

[2] The Arabic is ומתאלה אלאול, lit., "and the first instance of it." Ibn Tibbon, ועקר הנחתו הראשונה, in some MSS. ודמיונו הראשׁון; Munk, Il désigne d'abord. מענאה אלאול is the first of the principal significations of the term; each of these may contain several different meanings, which are introduced by מתאלה אלאול, "the first instance of this primary meaning is." The first three significations given by Maimonides may be considered as variations of the primary meaning.

[3] Arabic: עלי בעד מא מסתקים; Ibn Tibbon, על רוחק אחד ישר. The word אחד, corresponding to the Arabic מא, does not here denote the numeral

them" (Gen. xxxiii. 3) ; עבר לפני העם, " Pass before the people" (Ex. xvii. 5). Instances of this kind are numerous. The term עבר was next applied to the passage of sound through air, as ויעבירו קול במחנה, " And they caused a sound to pass throughout the camp" (Ex. xxxvi. 6) ; אשר אנכי שמע מעברים עם ה׳, " That I hear the Lord's people spreading the report" (1 Sam. ii. 24).[1]

Figuratively it denoted the appearance of the Light and the Divine Presence (Shechinah) which the prophets perceived in their prophetic visions, as it is said והנה תנור עשן ולפיד אש אשר עבר בין הגזרים האלה, " And behold a smoking furnace, and a burning lamp that passed between those pieces " (Gen. xv. 17).[2] This took place in a prophetic vision, for the narrative commences ותרדמה נפלה על אברם, "And a deep sleep fell upon Abram." The verb has this latter meaning in ועברתי בארץ מצרים, " And I shall pass through the land of Egypt " (Ex. xii. 12),[3] and in all similar phrases.

The verb עבר is next employed to express that a person has gone too far, and transgressed the usual limit, in the performance of some act, as וכגבר עברו יין, " And as a man who in drinking wine has passed the proper limit "[4] (Jer. xxiii. 9).

"one," but rather the indefinite "a" or "some." The addition of מסתקים (ישר) " straight," implies that, strictly speaking, the verb עבר signifies " to go before another (at some distance) in a straight line."

[1] So Rashi also ; Targum: דרען עמא דיי (according to the reading quoted by Kimchi, דרגנין), "which the people of the Lord spread about." A. V., " Ye make the Lord's people to transgress."

[2] Maimonides does not appear to be consistent in these interpretations; "The smoking furnace and a burning lamp" were really seen by Abraham though in a vision, *passing* "between those pieces." The verb עבר, nevertheless, is said, in this instance, to have a figurative meaning, and even appears to serve as a support to the inference that in other passages, *e.g.*, ועברתי בארץ מצרים, the term עבר is likewise to be taken in this figurative sense. In speaking of the verb נגע (ch. xviii.), the passage וינע על פי (Isaiah vi. 7) was quoted as an instance of the primary meaning of the word, although the act was perceived by Isaiah in a vision. The author does not seem to use the expression " it was figuratively applied" in the same sense; and this signification of עבר is, in fact, the primary meaning of the word. (*See* p. 76, Note 2.)

[3] *i.e.*, My glory will reveal itself in the land of Egypt.

[4] Lit., " And like a man in whom the wine has passed the limit proper for

It is also used figuratively to denote: to abandon one aim,[1] and turn to a different aim and object, e.g., וחוא ירח חרצי לחעביר, "He shot an arrow, causing it to miss the aim"[2] (1 Sam. xx. 36). This is the sense, it appears to me, of עבר in the passage ויעבר ח' על פניו, (lit. "And the Lord passed by before him," Ex. xxxiv. 6,) the pronoun in the word פניו referring to God—also according to the opinion of our teachers פניו in this passage means "the face of God,," and, although this is found in the midst of Agadic interpretations[3] which would be out of place in this our work, yet it is some support of our view, that the suffix in פניו is employed as a substitute for the name of God—and the whole passage could in my opinion be explained as follows: Moses sought to attain to a certain perception which is called ראיית פנים "the perception of the Divine countenance," a term occurring in the phrase ופני לא יראו, "My face

him." The grammatical construction of the phrase has by no means been ignored by Maimonides, as Munk thinks ("L'auteur, en choisissent cet exemple, a négligé le sens grammatical du passage"). The question whether, according to Maimonides, נבר or ין is the subject of the sentence, was fully discussed by Ibn Caspi, Crescas, Abrabanel, and others.

[1] The original תכמי is treated by Munk as the fifth form of כמו, denoting "to advance," "to go before." This explanation is not in harmony with the instance which follows; for ויעבור ה' על פניו, according to Maimonides, means "God refused to grant the direct revelation called פנים;" and not "God passed before (or beyond) that revelation." ויחמיא, the rendering of Ibn Tibbon, (תכמ being derived from כמא), appears to be more correct; the Hiphil החמיא signifies "to cause to miss," "to turn away from a certain aim;" thus God 'turned away' from granting to Moses one gift and granted another.

[2] That is, he shot the arrow in such a manner that it should not come down where the lad stood. Some believe that according to Maimonides, the passage is to be explained as follows:—He shot the arrow, in order to divert the attention of the lad from the spot where David and Jonathan intended to have a farewell conversation. (See Ibn Caspi, Crescas and Abrabanel.)

[3] It is not clear to which passage in the Talmud, or in the Midrashim Maimonides refers. Munk thinks that Rosh ha-shanah 17b, is meant, where it is said ויעבור ה' על פניו מלמד שנתעטף הקב"ה כש"צ וכו'; and where נתעטף is a paraphrase of ויעבר (טליתו) על פניו. Maimonides appears to understand this metaphor in the sense, that God withheld the direct knowledge of Himself (פנים) from Moses.

cannot be seen;" but God vouchsafed to him a perception of a lower degree, *viz.*, that called ראיית אחור, "the seeing of the back," in the words וראית את אחורי, "And thou shalt see me from the back" (Ex. xxxiii. 23). We have mentioned this subject in our work Mischneh Torah.[1] Accordingly, it is stated in the above-mentioned passage that the Lord withheld from Moses that perception which is termed "the sight of the Divine face," and substituted for it another gift, *vis.*, the knowledge of the acts attributed to God, which, as I shall explain (ch. liv.), are considered to be different and separate attributes of the Supreme. In asserting that God withheld from Moses (the higher knowledge) I mean to say that this knowledge was unattainable, that by its nature it was inaccessible to Moses; for man, whilst able to gain perfection by applying his reasoning faculties to the attainment of what is within the reach of his intellect, either weakens his reason or loses it altogether[2] as soon as he ventures to seek a higher degree of knowledge—as I shall elucidate in one of the chapters[3] of this work—unless he be granted a special aid from heaven, as is described in the words, ושכתי כפי עליך עד עברי, "And I will cover thee with my hand until I pass by" (Ex. xxxiii. 23).

Onkelos, in translating this verse, adopts the same method which he applies to the explanation of similar subjects, *viz.*, every expression implying corporeality or corporal properties, when referring to God, is explained by assuming an ellipsis of a *nomen regens* before "God," thus connecting the expression (of corporeality) with another word which is supplied, governing the genitive "God;" *e.g.*, ותבח ח'

[1] See Maimonides, Mishneh Thorah, i.; Yesode hattorah, i. 8, 10. Comp. i. 38.

[2] The Arabic יהלך can, in the original, be referred both to אנסאן, and to אדראך, *i.e.*, either "the man dies," or "the perceptive power of the man dies;" the latter is more probable, as Munk rightly argues, because the author only treats here of intellectual failure and success. In Hebrew the two words, אדם, השגה having different genders, ימות must be joined with אדם.

[3] Chap. xxxii.

נצב עליו, "And behold the Lord stood upon it" (Gen. xxviii. 13), he renders יקרא דח' מעתד עלוהי, "The glory of the Lord stood arrayed above it." Again, יצף ח' ביני וביניך, "The Lord watch between me and thee" (Gen. xxxi. 49), he renders, יסך מימרא דח', "The word of the Lord shall watch." This is his ordinary method in explaining Scripture. He applies it also to the phrase ויעבר ח' על פניו ויקרא (Ex. xxxiv. 6), which he renders ואעבר ח' שכינתיה על אפוהי וקרא, "The Lord caused His Presence to pass before his face and called."[1] According to this rendering the thing which passed was unquestionably some physical object, the suffix in the word פניו referring to Moses, and the expression על פניו, being equivalent to לפניו, "before him." Comp. ותעבור המנחה על פניו, "So went the present over before him" (Gen. xxxii. 22). This is likewise an appropriate and satisfactory explanation; and I can adduce still further support for the opinion of Onkelos from the words בעבור כבודי, "while my glory passeth by" (Ex. xxxiii. 22), which expressly state that the passing object was something ascribed to God, not God Himself; and of this Divine glory it is also said עד עברי, "until I pass by," and ויעבור ח' על פניו, "And the Lord passed by before him."

Should it, however, be considered necessary to assume here an ellipsis, according to the method of Onkelos who supplies in some instances the term יקרא (glory), in others מימרא (word), and in others שכינה (Divine Radiance), as the context may require in each particular case, we can also supply here the word קול (voice), and explain ויעבור קול ח' על פניו ויקרא, "And a voice from the Lord passed before him and called." We have already shown that the verb עבר can be applied to the voice, as in ויעבירו קול במחנה, "And they caused a voice to pass through the camp" (Ex. xxxvi. 6). According to this explanation, it was the voice

---

[1] These three terms יקרא, מימרא, שכינתא express according to Efodi, three degrees of prophetic perception: the purely intellectual, the intellectual combined with physical hearing, and intellectual combined with physical sight.

which called. No objection can be raised to applying the expression קרא to קול (voice), for a similar phrase occurs in the Bible in reference to God's commands to Moses, וישמע את הקול מדבר אליו, "He heard the voice speaking unto him"; and, in the same manner as it can be said "the voice spoke," we may also say "the voice called" (קרא); indeed, we can even support this application of the verbs אמר and קרא to קול, by parallel passages,[1] as קול אמר קרא ואמר מה אקרא, "A voice saith 'Cry,' and it says 'What shall I cry'"[2] (Isaiah xl. 6). According to this view, the meaning of the passage under discussion would be: "A voice of God passed before him and called, 'Eternal, Eternal, All-powerful, All-merciful, and All-gracious!'" (The word Eternal is repeated; it is in the vocative,[3] for the Eternal is the one who is called. Comp. Moses, Moses! Abraham, Abraham!) This, again, is a very appropriate explanation of the text.

You will surely not find it strange that this subject, so profound and difficult, should bear various interpretations; for it will not impair the force of the argument with which we are here concerned. Either explanation may be adopted; you may take that grand scene altogether as a prophetic vision, and the whole occurrence[4] as a mental

---

[1] It is strange that Maimonides, in proving that קרא may be applied to קול draws an inference from the application of דבר to קול, while he at once could have adduced the parallel passage, קול קורא (Isa. xl. 3). Perhaps he prefers a proof from the Pentateuch to quotations from other Biblical books.

[2] A. V., "And he said, What shall I cry?" According to Maimonides, the words ואמר מה אקרא are not, as is generally believed, the answer of the prophet, but the continuation of what the voice says; and the first person of אקרא likewise refers to קול. It is not clear why the author chose this forced interpretation instead of quoting קול קורא (ib. ver. 3).

[3] It appears that, according to the first explanation ("God refused the direct comprehension"), Maimonides joined the two words, ויקרא ה׳, into one sentence, "and the Lord called." (So also Saadia; see Ibn Ezra, ad locum.) We are not told why, according to the second interpretation, ויקרא ה׳ could not be explained to be identical with ויקרא קול ה׳, "and the voice of the Lord called;" or why, according to the first, ה׳ ה׳, could not be in the vocative case.

[4] Charizi has והתרגש כלו; חרגש is here, probably, a synonym of

operation, and you may consider that what he required, what was withheld from him, and what he attained, were perceived by the intellect without the use of the senses (as we have explained above): or you may assume that in addition there was a certain ocular perception of a material object, the sight of which would assist intellectual perception. The latter is the view of Onkelos, unless he assumes that in this instance the ocular perception was likewise a prophetic vision, as was the case with "a smoking furnace and a burning lamp that passed between those pieces" (Gen. xv. 17), mentioned in the history of Abraham. You may also assume that in addition there was a perception of sound, and that there was a voice which passed before him, and was undoubtedly something material. You may choose either of these opinions, for our sole intention and purpose is to guard you against the belief that the phrase 'ויעבור ח "and the Lord passed," is analogous to עבור לפני העם, "pass before the people" (Ex. xvii. 5), for God, being incorporeal, cannot be said to move, and consequently the verb עבר, "to pass," cannot with propriety be applied to Him in its primary signification.

CHAPTER XXII.

בא 1, *To come.* 2, *To enter. Applied (a) to living creatures; (b) to incorporeal things.*[1]

In Hebrew, the verb בא signifies "to come" as applied to a living being, *i.e.* its arrival at a certain place, or approach

---

השתדלות, endeavour, exertion (comp. ברנש, Ps. lv. 16; רנשו, *ib.* ii. 1), corresponding to the Arabic אלרום. Munk believed that Charizi had, in the original, the reading אלחם instead of אלרום; he found the same reading in a Leyden MS.

[1] It is remarkable that the intermediate step, namely, "to come" used of life-

to a certain person, as בא אחיך במרמה, "Thy brother came with subtilty" (Gen. xxvii. 35). It next denotes (with regard to a living being) "to enter" a certain place,[1] e.g. ויבא יוסף הביתה, "And when Joseph came into the house" (Gen. xliii. 26); כי תבואו אל הארץ, "When ye come into the land" (Ex. xii. 25). The term was also employed metaphorically in the sense of "to come" applied to a certain event, that is, to something incorporeal, as כי יבא דבריך, "When thy sayings come to pass" (Judg. xiii. 17); מאשר יבאו עליך, "Of that which will come over thee" (Is. xlvii. 13). Nay, it is even applied to privatives,[2] e.g. ויבא רע, "Yet trouble came" (Job iii. 26); ויבא אופל, "And darkness came." Now, since the word has been applied to incorporeal things,[3] it has also been used in reference to God—to the fulfilment of His word, or to the manifestation of His Presence (the Shechinah). In this figurative sense it is said הנה אנכי בא אליך בעב הענן, "Lo, I come unto thee in a thick cloud" (Ex. xix. 9); כי ח' אלהי ישראל בא בו, "For the Lord the God of Israel enters through it" (Ex. xliv. 2). In these and all similar passages, the coming of the Shechinah is meant, while the explanation of ובא ח' אלהי, "And the Lord my God shall come" (Zech. xiv. 5) is יבא דברו, "His word will come," that is to say, the promises which He made

---

less corporeal beings, is omitted, although the author could have quoted several instances from the Bible; e.g., כספכם בא (Gen. xliii. 23); ובאו בה המים (Numb. v. 24).

[1] The object of the author in making this division in the significations of בא is not apparent, especially after having already mentioned "arrival at a certain place." The fact that no instance is quoted for "arrival at a certain place," suggests the idea that "arrival at a place," and "it signifies also to enter a place (used of living beings)" are only two variations of the same thing, and the one phrase was intended as a substitute for the other.

[2] (הערך) ערם) is the name applied to that class of terms which do not denote a thing really existing, but merely the absence of their opposite, e.g., darkness, as the absence of light; evil, as the absence of good.

[3] Lit. "To things which are not at all corporeal." This phrase has been added, because the usual formula ולפי זאת ההשאלה, "and in accordance with this use of the word," would refer to its being applied to things which have no real existence (הערדים), while it is his object to show the application of the word בא to God, to His word, or to His Shechinah, which have a real existence.

through the Prophets, will be fulfilled; therefore Scripture adds כל קדושים עמך, that is to say, "The word of the Lord my God will be performed, which has been spoken by all the holy ones who are with thee, *i.e.*, who address the Israelites." [1]

CHAPTER XXIII.

יצא 1, *To go out.*   2, *To manifest itself (of incorporeal beings).*
שוב 1, *To return.*   2, *To discontinue.*

יצא is the opposite of בא. The term יצא is applied to the motion of a body from a place in which it had previously rested, to another place (whether the body be a living being or not), *e.g.*, חם יצאו את העיר, "And when they were gone out of the city" (Gen. xliv. 4); כי תצא אש, "If fire break out" (Exod. xxii. 5). It was then figuratively employed to denote the appearance of something incorporeal, as הדבר יצא מפי המלך, "The word went out of the king's mouth" (Esth. vii. 8); כי יצא דבר המלכה על כל הנשים, "When this deed of the queen shall come abroad unto all women" (Esth. i. 17), that is to say, "the report will spread."[2] Again, כי מציון תצא תורה, "For out of Zion shall go forth the Law" (Is. ii. 3); further, השמש יצא על הארץ, "The sun had risen upon the earth" (Gen. xix. 23), *i.e.*, its light became visible.[3]

---

[1] מדברים in the version of Ibn Tibbon agrees with קדושים; in the original, the singular אלמאב is used. The author explains the suffix in עמך as referring to Israel, whom the prophets address.

[2] נפוד אלאמר, "The spreading of the word," or "of the command" has been rendered by Ibn Tibbon, עבור הטצוה, "the transgression of the king's order;" by Charizi, קיום מצות המלך, "The fulfilment of the king's order." Both assume that נפוד אלאמר explains the words דבר המלכה; but this is not necessary, since the principal thing to be mentioned here is the figurative application of the root יצא. The remark appears simply to imply that יצא is used of an incorporeal object—a word—and its proper place would have been after the instance which follows; after which the second figurative use, that of the light, is introduced by וכדלך (וכן) "and similarly."

[3] "The sun" is here taken in the sense of "light;" if taken literally "the

In this figurative sense we must take every expression of יצא relating to the Almighty, *e.g.*, הנה ה' יוצא ממקומו, (lit. "For, behold, the Lord cometh out of His place," Is. xxvi. 21) "The word of God, which until now has been in secret, cometh out, and will become manifest,"[1] *i.e.*, something will come into being which had not existed before; for everything new emanating from God is referred to His word. Comp. בדבר ה' שמים נעשו וברוח פיו כל צבאם, "By the word of the Lord were the heavens made, and all the host of them by the breath of His mouth" (Ps. xxxiii. 6). This is a simile taken from the conduct of kings, who employ the word as the means of carrying their will into effect. God, however, requires no instrument wherewith to operate in order to perform anything; the effect is produced solely by His will alone. He does not employ any kind of speech, as will be explained further on (ch. lv.).

The word יצא is thus employed to designate the manifestation of a certain work of God, as we noticed in our interpretation of the phrase הנה ה' יוצא ממקומו; in a similar manner the term שוב, "return," has been figuratively employed to denote the discontinuance of a certain act according to the will of God, as in אלך אשובה אל מקומי, "I will go and return to my place" (Hosea v. 15); that is to say, the Divine presence (Shechinah) which had been in our midst departed from us, the consequence of which has been the absence of Divine protection from amongst us. Thus the Prophet foretelling misfortune says והסתרתי פני מהם והיה לאכל, "And I will hide my face

---

sun came forth," it would be an instance of the first signification, and it is difficult to understand why Maimonides does not classify it so; perhaps because the sun is exactly over the earth at noon, while in the phrase of the passage quoted the morning is referred to; it may be on that account that he explains "The light became visible over the earth." The difficulty has been noticed by the several commentators, but the solution given by them is not satisfactory.

[1] That is, His word, which is able to perform certain acts visible to our eyes, whilst it does not act at present may be said to be hidden and invisible; when those acts are performed it becomes visible; this is therefore expressed by the phrase "The Lord will come forth from His place," that is, His word, which is now in its place, invisible to us, will appear.

from them, and they shall be devoured" (Deut. xxxi. 17); for, when man is deprived of Divine protection he is exposed (to all dangers), and becomes the butt of all fortuitous circumstances;[1] his fortune and misfortune then depend on chance. Alas! how terrible a threat!—This is the idea contained in the phrase אלך אשובה אל מקומי, "I will go and return to my place" (Hosea v. 15).

CHAPTER XXIV.

הלך, *To go, applied to,* 1, *living beings;* 2, *lifeless objects;* 3, *incorporeal beings.*

THE term הלך is likewise one of the words which denote movements performed by living beings, as in ויעקב הלך לדרכו, "And Jacob went on his way" (Gen. xxxii. 1), and in many other instances. This term was next employed in describing movements of objects less solid than the bodies of living beings, comp. והמים היו הלוך וחסור, "And the waters were gradually decreasing" (Gen. viii. 5); ותהלך אש ארצה, "And the fire ran along upon the ground" (Ex. ix. 23). Then it was employed to express the spreading and manifestation of something incorporeal, comp. קולה כנחש ילך, "The voice thereof shall go like a serpent" (Jer. xlvi. 22); again, קול ה' אלהים מתהלך בגן, "The voice of the Lord God walking in the garden" (Gen. iii. 8). It is "the voice" (קול) that is qualified by "walking" (מתהלך).

Whenever the word הלך, "to go," is used in reference to God, it must be taken in this figurative sense, *viz.*, applying to incorporeal things, and signifying either the manifestation of

---

[1] A similar view was held by Ibn Ezra, and he frequently refers to it in his writings; what Maimonides calls (מקרה) "chance," is to Ibn Ezra "fate," the necessary consequence of the natural influence of the heavenly bodies on things on earth." Comp. Ibn Ezra Literature, by Dr. M. Friedländer, iv. page 30.

PART I.—CHAPTER XXIV.

something ideal,[1] or the withdrawal of the Divine protection, an act corresponding to the departure of a living being, and effected by means of (הליכה) "walking." The withdrawal of God's protection is called in the Bible "the hiding of God's countenance," as in ואנכי הסתר אסתיר פני, "As for me, I will hide my countenance." On the same ground it has been designated הליכה, "going away," signifying "to move away from a thing," comp. אלך ואשובה אל מקומי, "I will depart and return to my place" (Hos. v. 15). But in the passage ויחר אף ח' וילך, "And the anger of the Lord was kindled against them, and he departed" (Num. xii. 9), the two meanings of הלך are combined, viz., the withdrawal of Divine protection,[2] expressed by אלך, and the revelation and manifestation of something, namely, of the anger which went forth and reached them, in consequence of which Miriam became "leprous, white as snow." The expression הלך, was further applied to conduct, which concerns only the inner life,[3] and which requires no bodily motion, as in the phrases והלכת בדרכיו, "And thou shalt walk in his ways" (Deut. xxviii. 9); אחרי ח' אלהיכם תלכו, "Ye shall walk after the Lord your God" (Deut. xiii. 5); לכו ונלכה באור ח', "Come ye, and let us walk in the light of the Lord" (Is. ii. 5).

[1] Both Hebrew translators understand אלאמר in this place in the sense of "thing" (ענין Tibbon, דבר Ch.); Munk wrongly translates "la divine parole"; for the only instance for this signification is ויחר אף יי בם וילך, where אלאמר is explained by יי אף, "The anger of the Lord;" if Maimonides had meant the Divine command he would have said (דברו אמרה).

[2] It is impossible to imagine how the verb וילך could be used here as implying two opposite motions at the same time (to come and to go away), each of which is related to a different subject: "The Lord (i.e., His protection) went away, and His anger came," unless we assume that Maimonides understood by וילך "He went," and said that the act manifested itself in two ways: in the withdrawal of the Divine protection and the manifestation of the Divine anger.

[3] אלסירה אלמצלה, "the higher walking," i.e., "the act as distinguished from the common walking with our feet," walking in a figurative, moral sense. Charizi does not translate אלמצלה at all; Tibbon by החשובים. It could not have escaped Maimonides that הלך בדרך is also used in a bad sense: "to walk in the ways of the wicked." Comp. Deut. viii. 19, etc.

CHAPTER XXV.

שכן To dwell, 1, literally ; 2, figuratively.

THE word שכן, as is well known, signifies "to dwell,"[1] as וחוא שכן באלני ממרא, " And he was dwelling in the plains of Mamre" (Gen. xiv. 13); ויחי בשכן ישראל, "And it came to pass, when Israel dwelt" (Gen. xxxv. 22). This is the most common meaning of the word. But "dwelling in a place" consists in the continued stay in a place, general or special; when a living being stays long in a place, we say that it rests in that place, although it unquestionably moves about in it, comp. וחוא שכן באלוני ממרא, "And he was dwelling in the plains of Mamre" (Gen. xiv. 13), and ויחי בשכן ישראל, "And it came to pass, when Israel dwelt" (Gen. xxxv. 22).

The term שכן was next applied metaphorically to inanimate objects, *i.e.*, to all things which have settled and remain fixed on an object, although the object on which the thing remains is not a place, and the thing itself is not a living being; for instance, תשכן עליו עננה, "Let a cloud dwell upon it" (Job iii. 5); there is no doubt that the cloud is not a living being, and that the day is not a corporeal thing, but a division of time.

In this sense the term is employed in reference to God, that is to say, to denote the continuance of His Divine Presence (Shechinah) or of His Providence in some place where the Divine Presence[2] manifested itself constantly, or in some object which was constantly protected

---

[1] The Arabic has here the simple translation of שכן, *viz.*, סכן; instead of which the Hebrew translations give the definition of שכן; hence Tibbon, חנות החונה במקום; Charizi, הוא התמדת העומד במקום אחר.

[2] The word שכינה appears to have been added by Ibn Tibbon (*see* Munk); but if it is not distinctly expressed in the original, it is certainly implied. The author mentions two things: שכינה (סכינה) and השגחה (ענאיה); these are further explained by the two sentences which follow in such a manner that the first sentence is related to שכינה, the second to השגחה; the ל in לכל דבר is connected with השגחתו, while the preposition ב is more applicable to שכינה. According to Munk, three kinds of manifestations are mentioned here: the

by Providence. Comp. 'וישכן כבוד ח, "And the glory of the Lord abode" (Ex. xxiv. 16); ושכנתי בתוך בני ישראל, "And I will dwell among the children of Israel" (Ex. xxix. 45); ורצון שכני סנה, "And for the goodwill of him that dwelt in the bush" (Deut. xxxiii. 16). Whenever the term שכן is applied to the Almighty, it must be taken consistently with the context in the sense either of the presence of His Shechinah (*i.e.*, of His light that was created for the purpose) in a certain place, or of the continuance of His Providence protecting a certain object.

CHAPTER XXVI.

דברה תורה כלשון בני אדם "*The Torah speaketh according to the language of man.*" (Talm. Babli., Baba Metsia, 31b.)[1]

You, no doubt, know the Talmudical saying, which includes in itself all the various kinds of interpretation connected with our subject. It runs thus: "The Torah speaketh

---

manifestation of the Shechinah, of Providence in a particular place, and of Providence in a certain object; but the difference between the last two is not discernible, and still less clear is the distribution of the three instances quoted by our author, between the three kinds of manifestation. In truth, Maimonides does not even seek to decide which of the various explanations is applicable to each instance, but rests satisfied with having shown that a figurative interpretation can be given, by which anthropomorphism may be avoided.

[1] The remarks on those anthropomorphic expressions which signify motion, or any other relation to space, are in this chapter brought to a conclusion with a discussion on the principle followed in the Bible, by which some terms including corporeality appear to have been applied to God figuratively, while others of an equally material character were excluded. According to Maimonides, all expressions which were believed by the common people to imply some kind of perfection were admitted; such are the terms explained in the preceding chapters. The expressions, on the other hand, which appeared to imply a notion of imperfection, are never used in the Bible with reference to God. Onkelos, in his version, observed a far stricter rule, and thought it necessary to paraphrase all the anthropomorphisms employed in Scripture. As, however, his principal object in paraphrasing such passages was to prevent misinterpretation and inferences leading to the belief that God possesses material properties, he retained the literal rendering where no such fears could be entertained. In chapter xxvii. this method of Onkelos is fully discussed.

according to the language of man,"[1] that is to say, expressions, which can easily be comprehended and understood by all, are applied to the Creator. Hence the description of God by attributes implying corporeality, in order to express His existence; because the multitude of people do not easily conceive existence unless in connection with a body, and that which is not a body nor connected with a body has for them no existence. Whatever we regard as a state of perfection, is likewise attributed to God, as expressing that He is perfect in every respect, and that no imperfection or deficiency whatever is found in Him. But there is not attributed to God anything which the multitude consider a defect or want;[2] thus He is never represented as eating, drinking, sleeping,[3] being ill, using violence,[4] and the like. Whatever, on the other hand, is commonly regarded as a state of

---

[1] The rabbinical principle דברה תורה כלשון בני אדם includes the following two rules:—(1.) The Bible must be interpreted by the same rules of grammar and logic as are generally applied to human language. In this sense the principle is frequently referred to in the Talmud (Talm. Babli. Berachoth, 31 b *et passim*). (2.) The language of the Bible is simple, and adapted to the average intelligence of man; anthropomorphic expressions are employed where purely metaphysical terms would not be intelligible to the majority of men. In this sense the words are employed by Maimonides. Ibn Caspi understands the rule in a wider sense, *viz*.,—"Things are frequently described in the Bible, not as they were in reality, but as they were believed to be by the common people." Comp. "And the men pursued *after them*" (Jos. ii. 7). The spies had, in fact, not yet left Jericho. "And the prophet Jeremiah said unto the *prophet* Hananiah" (Jer. xxviii. 5). Hananiah was not a prophet. Applying this rule to the anthropomorphisms of the Bible, Ibn Caspi says—"The prophetic authors had to choose of two evils the lesser one. The common people, not able to understand abstract ideas, had either to remain in entire ignorance of God or to receive imperfect notions of the Creator. The latter course was preferred, as admitting of gradual improvement."

[2] The words או העדר are not found in the version of Charizi, nor is the corresponding phrase found in the original. העדר is not used here in its strictly philosophical sense, but as a mere synonym to חסרון.

[3] "This assertion is not contradicted by the phrase עורה למה תישן, 'Awake, why sleepest Thou, O Lord?' (Ps. xliv. 24), because these words are equivalent to 'Awake, why dost Thou appear to us as if Thou wert asleep.'" (Shemtob and Caspi.) See Babyl. Talm. Sotah 48a, and Maimonides, Comm. on Mishnah Sotah ix. 6, and on Maaser Sheni v. 15.

[4] In Charizi's version these words (ולא בחולי ולא בחמס) are absent.

perfection is attributed to Him, although it is only a state of perfection in relation to ourselves; for in relation to God, what we consider to be a state of perfection, is in truth the highest degree of imperfection. If, however, men were to think that those human perfections were absent in God, they would consider Him as imperfect.

You are aware that locomotion is one of the distinguishing characteristics of living beings, and is indispensable for them in their progress towards perfection. As they require food and drink to supply animal waste, so they require locomotion, in order to approach that which is good for them and in harmony with their nature, and to escape from what is injurious and contrary to their nature.[1] It makes, in fact, no difference whether we ascribe to God eating and drinking or locomotion; but according to human modes of expression, that is to say, according to common notions, eating and drinking would be an imperfection in God, while motion would not, in spite of the fact that the necessity of locomotion is the result of some want.[2] Furthermore, it has been clearly proved,[3] that everything which moves is corporeal and divisible; it will be shown below that God is incorporeal and that He can have no locomotion;[4] nor can rest be ascribed to Him; for rest can only be applied to that which also moves. All expressions, however, which imply the

[1] The words הטוב לו ו and הרע לו ו מן in Ibn Tibbon's version are not found in Charizi's version, and have no corresponding words in the Arabic text. מורגל in Tibbon's version corresponds to the Arabic מואלף, "that which is familiar," or "which is joined," "friend." Charizi translates this word ממינו. In the second part (Introd.) both translators use instead of it הנאות. אלמבאלף is rendered by Tibbon כנגדו, "contrary to him," "against him;" by Charizi, הפכו, "the opposite of it."

[2] The words הצריך אליה החסרון, the correct rendering of the corresponding Arabic text, appear to have been misunderstood by Palquera in his Moreh ha-moreh, for, in criticising Ibn Tibbon's version, he understood חסרון in this phrase to signify "imperfection," while Ibn Tibbon used it here in its literal meaning, "want" (comp. בחסר כל, "in want of everything," Deut. xxviii. 48), corresponding to אפתקאר in the Arabic text.

[3] See Part II., Introduction, Proposition 7.

[4] Ibid, ch. 1 and 2.

various modes of movement in living beings, are employed with regard to God in the manner we have described and in the same way as life is ascribed to Him; although motion is an accident pertaining to living beings, and there is no doubt that, without corporeality, expressions like the following could not be imagined: "to descend, to ascend, to walk, to place, to stand, to surround, to sit, to dwell, to depart, to enter, to pass, etc."[1]

It would have been superfluous thus to dilate on this subject, were it not for the mass of the people, who are accustomed to such ideas. It has been necessary to expatiate on the subject, as we have attempted, for the benefit of those who are anxious to acquire perfection, to remove from them such notions as have grown up with them[2] from the days of youth.

CHAPTER XXVII.[3]

אסא אחות עמך למצרים "*I shall go down with thee into Egypt*" (Targum of Onkelos, Gen. xlvi. 4).

ONKELOS[4] the Proselyte, who was thoroughly acquainted with the Hebrew and Chaldaic languages, made it his task

---

[1] All the verbs of motion here alluded to, with the exception of סבב, have been mentioned and explained in the preceding chapters, though not in the same order. The verbs קום, קרב, נגש, and רום, explained above, are here omitted.

[2] המתחילות in Ibn Tibbon's version is here used in the sense of " which come in the beginning;" it implies the verb לבא or להגיע, and therefore the preposition אליהם is joined to it. Palquera suggests המחשבות הקודמות, in the sense of "ideas received indiscriminately." The term פשט in Charizi must be understood in its literal sense of "explicit."

[3] In the translation of Charizi this chapter is connected with the preceding one, and the chapters which follow are numbered accordingly. Ibn Caspi says in his notes הערבי בספר פרק הבדל בזה אין, " In the Arabic text the new chapter does not commence here." Palquera makes a similar remark.

[4] The theory of Maimonides as to the principle by which Onkelos was guided in paraphrasing some passages and rendering others literally, has been severely

to oppose the belief in God's corporeality. Accordingly, any expression employed in the Pentateuch in reference to God, and in any way implying corporeality, he paraphrases in consonance with the context. All expressions denoting any mode of motion, are explained by him to mean the appearance [1] or manifestation of a certain light that had been created [for the occasion], *i.e.*, the Shechinah (Divine Presence), or Providence. Thus he renders ירד יי (the Lord will come down), יתגלי יי, "The Lord will manifest Himself" (Exod. xix. 11); וירד יי (And God came down), ואתגלי יי, "And God manifested Himself" (*ib.* 20), and does not say ונחת יי (And God came down); ארדה נא ואראה, "I will go down now and see" (Gen. xviii. 21), he translates אתגלי כען ואחזה " I will manifest myself now and see." This is his rendering [of the verb ירד in reference to God] throughout his version, with the exception of the following passage אנכי ארד עמך מצרים, "I will go down with thee into Egypt" (Gen. xlvi. 4), which he

---

criticised by Nachmanides in his Commentary on the Pentateuch (Gen. xlvi. 4), and defended by Abrabanel in his Commentary on the Moreh Nebhuchim. About twenty objections are raised by Nachmanides, the strongest of which appears to be that which is founded on Gen. xxviii. 16. The circumstances accompanying the Divine promise to Jacob, mentioned in Gen. xxviii. 15 and in xlvi. 4, are the same; both were made in a dream (ויחלם), in a vision by night (במראת הלילה). Maimonides distinctly states in Part II. ch. xlv. that both visions were of one and the same category. He could certainly not have ignored Gen. xxviii. 15 while founding such an important principle on Gen. xlvi. 4. It appears that his commentators and objectors ignored the fact that Maimonides treats here only of expressions of motion (השמות הסורים על מין ממיני התנועה) which occur in a Divine communication received in a dream or nocturnal vision, and that the question whether apparent inconsistencies in the Targum in reference to other expressions were explained by Maimonides by the same rule or by another, or were not explained at all, is in no connection with the present chapter. It is noteworthy that the Targum Jonathan (on Gen. xlvi. 4) has the addition במימרי, "by my word."

[1] Charizi וגלוי שכינה, "the revelation of the Divine presence." Although the verb ואתגלי in the Targum is directly connected with the name of God (ואתגלי יי), it seems to imply the term יקרא or שכינה ("The Lord was revealed," *i.e.*, through יקרא or שכינה). Comp. Nachmanides, l.c.

translates (literally) אנא אחות עמך למצרים. A remarkable proof of this great man's talents, the excellence of his version, and the correctness of his interpretation! By this version he discloses to us an important principle as regards prophecy.

This narrative begins: "And God spake unto Israel in the visions of the night, and said, Jacob, Jacob, etc. And He said, I am God, etc , I will go down with thee into Egypt" (Gen. xlvi. 2, 3). Seeing that the whole narrative is introduced as a vision of the night, Onkelos did not hesitate to translate literally the words addressed (to Jacob) in the nocturnal vision, and thus gave a faithful account of the occurrence.[1] For the passage in question contains a statement of what Jacob was told, not what actually took place, as is the case in the words, "And the Lord came down upon Mount Sinai" (Exod. xix. 20). Here we have an account of what actually occurred in the physical world; the verb ירד is therefore paraphrased "to appear," and entirely detached from the idea of motion. Accounts of what happened in the imagination of man,[2] I mean of what he was told,[3] are not altered. A most remarkable distinction!

Hence[4] you may infer that there is a great difference

---

[1] Arabic והו אלצחיח; Charisi והאמת הנכון והוא; Ibn Tibbon והוא ספור האמת. Maimonides means to say that while in other instances the anthropomorphism diverges from positive truth, it is the actual truth in this instance, because Jacob really seemed to hear the Almighty speaking those words. Charisi, who took אלצחיח in the sense of "the right view," added the word הנכון. Munk likewise renders the phrase—*Et cela avec raison*.

[2] According to Maimonides, the most imperfect class of prophecies consists of those communicated to a prophet in a dream or nocturnal vision, when his *imagination* receives the Divine message. This form of prophecy is adapted to the nature of man's imagination, and therefore includes anthropomorphism. The highest degree of prophecy is a communion of man's *intellect* with the Supreme Being; in that case anthropomorphism is rigorously excluded.

[3] This phrase is to qualify the preceding sentence; not everything that passed in a dream, but only what the prophet was *told*, was rendered literally by Onkelos. Comp. page 92, note 4.

[4] That is, from the fact that Onkelos retains anthropomorphic expressions,

between a communication, designated as having been made in a dream, or a vision of the night, and a vision or a manifestation simply introduced [1] with phrases like "And the word of the Lord came unto me, saying;" "And the Lord spake unto me, saying."

According to my opinion, it is also possible that Onkelos understood אלהים in the above passage to signify "angel," and that for this reason he did not hesitate to translate literally אנא אחות עמך למצרים, "I will go down with thee to Egypt." Do not think it strange that Onkelos should have believed the אלהים, who says to Jacob, "I am God, the God of thy father" (ib. 3), to be an angel, for these words in the same form can also be spoken by an angel, as you can clearly see in the words (of Jacob), "And the angel of God spake unto me in a dream, saying, Jacob. And I said, "Here am I" etc. (Gen. xxxi. 11); the report of the angel's words to Jacob concludes, "I am the God of Bethel, where thou anointedst the pillar, and where thou vowedst a vow *unto me*" (ib. 13), although there is no doubt that Jacob vowed to God, not to the angel. It is the usual practice of prophets to relate words addressed to them by an angel in the name of God, as though God himself had spoken to them. Such passages are all to be explained by supplying the *nomen regens*,[2] and by considering them as identical with "I am the messenger of the God of thy father," "I am the messenger of God who appeared to thee in Bethel," and the like. Prophecy with its various de-

---

when the words heard by a prophet in a dream are related, but he paraphrases them when they occur in accounts of other visions and prophecies. This distinction shows that Onkelos believed in the existence of several degrees of prophecy. The least perfect form of prophecy was a vision in a dream, unfolded to the prophet's imagination; the most perfect form was that revealed to the intellect of the prophet. Comp. Part II. ch. xlv.

[1] Ibn Tibbon, סתם, without specifying that the words were perceived in a vision; Charizi, בדבר מוחלט, "by a decided word," *i.e.*, clearly, not in a dream. The Hebrew סתם corresponds better to the Arabic מטלקא.

[2] Ibn Tibbon, בחסרון הסמוך; Charizi, מכח השם הסמוך. Both phrases denote the same thing, *viz.*, the *nomen regens* which is to be supplied.

grees, and the nature of angels, will be fully discussed in the sequel, in accordance with the object of this treatise.[1]

CHAPTER XXVIII.

רגל,[2] 1, *Foot.* 2, *Suite.* 3, *Cause.* 4, *Effect.*[3]

THE term רגל is homonymous, signifying, in the first place, the foot of a living being; comp. רגל תחת רגל, "Foot for foot" (Exod. xxi. 24). Next it denotes an object which follows another; comp. וכל העם אשר ברגלך

---

[1] See Part II. ch. xlv.

[2] The next group of homonyms (ch. xxviii. to ch. xliv.) explained by Maimonides, consists of those which signify part of the body of man or of an animal. He begins with רגל, "foot," because it is related to expressions of motion, and after having made some remarks on the necessity of employing figurative language in speaking of God, and also on the importance of obtaining a correct notion of the incorporeality of God, he continues with פנים, "face," and אחור, "back," לב, נפש, רוח, חיים, "heart," "spirit," "soul," and "life," כנף, "wing," and concludes with עין, "eye." It is rather difficult to define what place ch. xxix. and ch. xxx. occupy in this group, and equally difficult to see the reason why the author introduced them here. The reader is probably to be prepared for the theory that any belief involving corporeality of God is equal to idolatry. For this purpose he begins with the explanation of רגל, and shows the consequence of the insufficient preparation and imperfect conception of the idea of God, in the instance of the nobles of Israel. According to tradition, as accepted by Maimonides (ch. v.), they were punished without having received any warning. By introducing next the phrase ויתעצב אל לבו, "And God was angry" (because of the wickedness of the generation of the flood, דור המבול) "without telling the people," he tacitly invites the reader to compare the causes of God's anger in both instances, and to conclude that a misconception of the nature of the Supreme Being is actually a sin. It can be avoided by suitable studies, which are as necessary for the mind as food is for the body (ch. xxx.). According to Abrabanel and others, Maimonides explains in ch. xxx. the word אכל occurring in the commandment given to Adam, "Of every tree of the garden thou mayest freely *eat*. But of the tree of the knowledge of good and evil, thou shalt not *eat* of it." That the reader is in fact expected to read between the lines, has expressly been stated by Maimonides in the Introduction. See page 8.

[3] Although Maimonides appears to give only three significations of the word, he evidently uses the word employed to express the third signification, סבה, in a double sense, cause and effect; לרגלי "because of me," and רגליו, "that caused by him."

"And all the people that follow thee " (*ib.* xi. 8). Another signification of רגל is "cause"; comp. ויברך יי אותך לרגלי, "And the Lord hath blessed thee, I being the cause" (Gen. xxx. 30), *i.e.*, for my sake; for that which exists for the sake of another thing has the latter for its final cause. Examples of רגל used in this sense are numerous. It has that meaning in לרגל המלאכה אשר לפני ולרגל הילדים, "because of the cattle that goeth before me, and because of the children" (Gen. xxxiii. 14).

Consequently, the words ועמדו רגליו ביום ההוא על הר הזתים (Zech. xiv. 4) can be explained to mean the following: "And the things caused by him on that day upon the Mount of Olives, that is to say, the wonders which will then be seen, and of which God will be the Cause or the Maker, will remain permanently." To this explanation does Jonathan ben Uziel[1] incline in translating the passage ואתגלי בגבורתיה ביומא ההוא על טורא דזיתיא, "And He will appear in His might on that day upon the Mount of Olives;" for expressions denoting those parts of the body by which contact and motion are effected,[2] he generally translates by בגבורתיה "His might," [when referring to God] because all such expressions denote acts done by Him.

As to the words ותחת רגליו כמעשה לבנת הספיר (Ex. xxiv. 10, lit., "And there was under his feet, as it were, a paved work of a sapphire stone"), Onkelos, as you know, in his version, considers רגליו, "his feet," as a figurative expression[3] for כסא, "throne," and the phrase ותחת רגליו he translates

---

[1] Jonathan ben Uziel is named in tradition as the author of the Chaldaic version of the books of the Prophets (Talm. Babli., Megillah, fol. 3.) The version known by this name is supposed to be a Babylonian Targum, and not the work of Jonathan. Comp. Zunz, "Gottesdienstliche Vorträge," 77 *sqq.*

[2] The Arabic נָארחה במש ותנקל, translated by Munk "Les mots désignant les membres dont on se sert pour saisir ou pour se transporter," is rendered by Ibn Tibbon מעשה מגע והעתק; by Charizi עסק ותנועה.

[3] The term כנוי in the Hebrew translations (צמיר in Arabic) generally means "a substitute for a proper name," and denotes therefore, 1, a pronoun; 2, a paraphrase. Here it is used in the second signification, referring to the substitution of כורסא, "throne," for רגל, "foot." The

וּתְחוֹת יְקָרֵיהּ ¹כֻּרְסֵא, "And under the throne of His glory." Consider this well and you will observe with wonder how Onkelos keeps free from the idea of the corporeality of God, and from everything that leads thereto, even in the remotest degree. For he does not say וּתְחוֹת כֻּרְסֵיהּ "and under His throne;" the direct relation of the throne to God, implied in the literal sense of the phrase "His throne" would necessarily suggest the idea that God is supported by a material object, and thus lead directly to the corporeality of God; he therefore refers the throne to His glory, i.e., to the Shechinah, which is a light created [for the purpose].²

Similarly, he renders כִּי יָד עַל כֵּס יָהּ (Exod. xvii. 16, "For my hand I lift up to the throne of God") מִן קֳדָם אֱלָהָא דִּשְׁכִינְתֵּיהּ עַל כֻּרְסֵא יְקָרֵיהּ, "by God whose Shechinah is upon the throne of His glory." This principle found also expression in the popular phrase³ כִּסֵּא הַכָּבוֹד, "the throne of the glory."

We have already gone too far away from the subject of

---

pronominal suffix הּ‎ֵ "his," is, as usual when it refers to God, rendered יְקָרֵיהּ, "of His glory." According to Munk, who takes (כנוי) צָמִיר to denote "suffix," Maimonides intended to say that וּתְחוֹת כֻּרְסֵי יְקָרֵיהּ, in the Targum, was the same as וּתְחוֹת רַגְלֵי כֻּרְסֵי יְקָרֵיהּ. But it is improbable that Onkelos should have omitted רַגְלֵי in that case, nor is it more probable that Maimonides should have omitted to call the reader's attention to this extraordinary anxiety of Onkelos to avoid anthropomorphism. It is remarkable that this passage has been considered by the Commentators as extremely difficult. Narboni says: "Not one of the learned men who discussed this passage understood it, as far as I know. When I was in Toledo, I had a conversation on it with Don Joseph Abubecr, and I found that he was at a loss to find a solution of the difficulty."

¹ כֻּרְסֵיהּ in the editions of Ibn Tibbon's version is a mistake for כֻּרְסֵא (as in the Arabic text) or for כֻּרְסֵי. See Luzzatto, Oheb Ger. (ad locum).

² Comp. ch. x. p. 57, note 4. According to Abarbanel, Maimonides distinguished by this phrase (אֲשֶׁר הוּא אוֹר נִבְרָא) the Shechinah revealed in this instance from other kinds. He says: "The term שְׁכִינָה in the Targum of Onkelos is a homonym; it is applied to three different things, to the intelligences, to physical light, and to Providence, according as the term is followed by 'heaven' or 'throne,' by the name of some place on earth, or by 'Israel.' Maimonides understood this correctly."

³ Charizi: עַל לְשׁוֹן כָּל עֲדָתֵנוּ; Ibn Tibbon עַל לְשׁוֹן כָּל הָעָם.

PART I.—CHAPTER XXVIII. 99

this chapter, and touched upon things which will be discussed in other chapters; we will now return to our present theme. You are acquainted with the version of Onkelos [of the passage quoted]. He contents himself with excluding from his version all expressions of corporeality in reference to God, and does not show us what they (the אֲצִילֵי בְּנֵי יִשְׂרָאֵל) perceived, or what is meant by that figure. In all similar instances Onkelos also abstains from entering into such questions, and only endeavours to exclude every expression implying corporeality, for the incorporeality of God is a demonstrative truth and an indispensable element in our faith; he could decidedly[1] state all that was necessary in that respect. The interpretation of a simile is a doubtful thing; it may possibly have that meaning, but it may also refer to something else. It contains besides very profound matter, the understanding of which is not a fundamental element in our faith, and the comprehension of which is not easy for the common people. Onkelos, therefore, did not enter at all into this subject.[2]

We, however, remaining faithful to our task in this treatise, find ourselves compelled to give our explanation. According to our opinion the expression וְתַחַת רַגְלָיו denotes "and under that of which He is the cause," "that which exists through Him," as we have already stated. They (the אֲצִילֵי בְּנֵי יִשְׂרָאֵל) therefore comprehended the real nature of the *materia prima*,[3] which emanated from Him, and of whose existence He is the only cause. Consider

---

[1] The verb גזר (in Ibn Tibbon's version) denotes here " to be decided," to speak in such a manner as to leave no doubt. Charizi: כדי לנגזור בו ולהבין על ענינו.

[2] Instead of לא חכנים עצמו בזה העניין, the reading of the editions of Ibn Tibbon's version, Palquera had in his text of the translation of Ibn Tibbon לא יטפל בזה העניין. The sense is the same in both phrases.

[3] Maimonides calls that substance which is the source of all things in the sublunary world, the first substance, (also the lowest התחתון, comp. Part II. ch. xxvi.) as being the nearest to the earth, and first perceived by man, in contradistinction to the substance of the heavenly spheres, which is more distant. It appears that the blame attached to the action of the nobles of Israel was, that they held the Creator to be in direct connection with the sublunary material

well the phrase כמעשה לבנת הספיר, "like the action of the whiteness of the sapphire stone." If the colour were the point of comparison, the words כלבנת הספיר "as the whiteness of the sapphire stone" would have sufficed; but the phrase כמעשה, "like the action," has been added, because matter, as such,[1] is, as you are well aware, always receptive[2] and passive, active only by some accident.[3] On the other hand, Form as such[1] is always active, and only passive by some accident,[3] as is explained in works on Physics.[4] This explains the addition of כמעשה "like the action"[5] in reference to the *materia prima*. As to the expression לבנת הספיר it refers to the transparency[6] not to the white *colour*; for "the whiteness" of the sapphire[7] is

---

world, without the intermediate beings, the intelligences, and the influence of the spheres. According to the author, their notion of the Supreme Being was impure; it included corporeality to some extent.

[1] Lit., "according to the consideration of its nature," or "according to its natural properties;" in Hebrew לפי בחינת טבעו, or בבחינת טבעו, and also בעצמו.

[2] Instead of מתפעל (Ibn Tibbon), we read in Charizi, מזולתו, "from without." On the passivity of matter and its capacity of receiving impressions from without, see *infra*, ch. xlvii. and Part III. viii.

[3] *I.e.*, the combination of matter and form; so long as they are not combined and continue in a free state, the one is active, the other passive; when combined, they are considered to participate in both qualities. The combination is an accident to the matter as well as to the form; it endows each with properties which are not essential to it.

[4] Charizi: בספרי הטבע. See Arist. *De Anima*, ii. 7. Maimonides explains it fully, Part III. ch. viii.

[5] This sentence is rather obscure. The connection of the word כמעשה with the difference between matter and form is not clear. The author intended, perhaps, to say that the כ of comparison ("like") qualifies the notion expressed by מעשה. "It resembled an action, but was not a real action," because the *materia prima* has no action of its own. Shemtob paraphrases the sentence as follows: ולכן יצדק שיש לו כמעשה ואיננו עושה, "Therefore it is correct to say that it has something similar to an action, but is not really acting."

[6] Ibn Tibbon: הזהר; Charizi more clearly: עבור העין בו; "the passing of the eye through it," "transparency."

[7] That is, the term "white," commonly applied to the sapphire (לובן, ביאץ), does not imply that the sapphire is of a white colour; it is described as "white" on account of its transparency, through the absence of all colour.

is not a white *colour* but the property of being transparent. Things, however, which are transparent, have no colour of their own, as is proved in works on Physics; for if they had a colour they would not permit all the colours[1] to pass through them nor would they receive colours; it is only when the transparent object is totally colourless, that it is able to receive successively all the colours. In this respect it (the whiteness of the sapphire) is like the *materia prima*, which as such[2] is entirely formless, and thus receives all the forms one after the other. What they (the אצילי בני ישראל) perceived was therefore the *materia prima*, whose relation[3] to God is distinctly mentioned, because it is the origin of those of His creatures which are subject to origination and destruction, and He created it. This subject also will be treated later on more fully.

Observe that you must have recourse to an explanation of this kind, even according to the rendering of Onkelos ותחות כורסא יקריה, "And under the throne of His glory;" for in fact the *materia prima* is also under the heavens, which are called "throne" (כסא) as we have remarked above. I should not have thought of this unusual interpretation, or hit on this argument were it not for an utterance of R. Eliezer ben Hyrcanus, which will be discussed in one of the parts of this treatise.[4] The primary object of every intelligent person must be to deny the corporeality of God, and to believe that all those perceptions (described in the above passage) were of a spiritual not of a material character. Note this and consider it well.

According to modern science, white is the combination of all different colours. Instead of ספיר, Charizi has הבדלח, corresponding to בלור of the Arabic text (bdellium).

[1] Charizi: אבל חיה מקבל אותם ומחזיקם, "But it would absorb them and keep them." The sense is the same.

[2] See note 1, on previous page.

[3] The word ויחסו in Ibn Tibbon's version is a noun, and is to be read וְיַחְסוֹ, "and its relation." Some read וְיִחֲסוּ "and they ascribed it to God;" this is not in accordance with the Arabic נסבתהא.

[4] Part II. ch. xxvi.

CHAPTER XXIX.

עצב, 1, Pain. 2, Grief. 3, Provocation.

THE term עצב is homonymous, denoting, in the first place, pain and trembling, as in בעצב תלדי בנים, "In sorrow thou shalt bring forth children" (Gen. iii. 16). Next it denotes anger; comp. ולא עצבו אביו מימיו, "And his father had not made him angry at any time" (1 Kings i. 6); כי נעצב אל דוד, "for he was angry for the sake of David" (1 Sam. xx. 34). The root עצב signifies also provocation;[1] comp. מרו ועצבו את רוח קדשו, "They rebelled, and vexed his holy spirit" (Is. lxiii. 10); יעציבוהו בישימון, "and provoke him in the desert" (Ps. lxxviii. 40); אם דרך עצב בי, "If there be any way of provocation in me" (*ib.* cxxxix. 24); כל היום דברי יעצבו, "Every day they rebel against my words" (*ib.* lvi. 6).

The words ויתעצב אל לבו (Gen. vi. 6) are to be explained either according to the second or according to the third signification of the word עצב. In the first case, the sense of the phrase is "God was angry with them on account of the wickedness of their deeds"; as to the words אל לבו used here, and also in the history of Noah ויאמר יי אל לבו, "And God said in his heart" (*ib.* viii. 21), I will here explain what they mean. With regard to man, we use the expression אמר אל לבו or אמר בלבו, "he said to himself" or "he said in his heart" in reference to a subject which he did not utter or communicate to any other person. Similarly the phrase ויאמר יי אל לבו, "And God said in His heart," is used in reference to an act which God decreed without mentioning it to any prophet at the time the event took place according to the will of God.[2] And a com-

---

[1] Charizi has here, as in many other instances, two words instead of one מרד ופשע.

[2] Tibbon כפי הרצון, "in accordance with the will of God;" Charizi בלא דבור, "without speaking."

parison in that respect is admissible, in accordance with the rule "the Torah speaketh in accordance with the language of man." This is plain and clear. In the Pentateuch no distinct mention is made of a message sent[1] to the wicked generation of the flood, cautioning or threatening them with death; therefore, it is said concerning them, that God was angry with them in His heart; likewise when He decreed that no flood should happen again, He did not tell a prophet to communicate it to others, and for that reason the words אל לבו " in His heart " are added.

Taking עצב in the third signification, we explain ויתעצב אל לבו, "And man rebelled[2] against God's will concerning him";[3] for לב also signifies "will," as we shall explain when treating of the homonymity of לב.

CHAPTER XXX.

אכל, 1, *To eat.* 2, *To destroy.* 3, *To learn.*

IN its primary meaning אכל is used in the sense of taking food by animals; this needs no illustration. It was afterwards observed that eating includes two processes—(1) the loss of the food,[4] *i.e.*, the destruction of its form, which first takes place; (2) the growth of animals, the preservation of their

---

[1] Instead of saying "no warning was given," Maimonides says "in the Pentateuch no *distinct* mention (התבאר) is made of a message," probably in opposition to the traditional explanation of the words והיו ימיו מאה ועשרים שנה, "yet his days shall be a hundred and twenty years" (Gen. vi. 3), *viz.*, that respite was given to the people that they might have a chance for repentance; and that they were also warned by Noah, who, during the long period when the ark was being constructed, told them for what purpose it was designed.

[2] Ibn Tibbon ומרות, in some editions המרות; the correct rendering, and perhaps also the correct reading, is ומרה, as in Charizi's version.

[3] The translation of the Arabic פה, "concerning him," *i.e.*, concerning Adam, has been omitted both by Ibn Tibbon and by Charizi. Munk is mistaken in referring the pronoun in פה to God.

[4] Ibn Tibbon הנאכל, Charizi אפס, והיותו.

strength and their existence, and the support of all their bodily forces, caused by the food they take.

The consideration of the first process led to the figurative use of אכל, in the sense of "losing," "destroying;" hence it includes all modes of depriving a thing of its form; comp. ואכלה אתכם ארץ איביכם, "And the land of your enemies shall destroy you" (Lev. xxvi. 38); ארץ אכלת יושביה, "A land that destroyeth the inhabitants thereof" (Num. xiii. 32); חרב תאכלו, "Ye shall be destroyed with the sword" (Is. i. 6); תאכל חרב, "Shall the sword destroy" (2 Sam. ii. 26); ותבער בם אש יי ותאכל בקצה המחנה, "And the fire of the Lord burnt among them, and destroyed them that were in the uttermost parts of the camp" (Num. xi. 1); אש אוכלה הוא, "(God) is a destroying fire" (Deut. iv. 24), that is, He destroys those who rebel against Him, as the fire destroys everything that comes within its reach. Instances of this kind are very frequent.

With reference to the second process connected with the act of eating, the word אכל is figuratively used for "acquiring wisdom," "learning;" in short, for all intellectual perceptions, by which the human form (reason) is constantly preserved in the most perfect manner, in the same way as by food the body is preserved in its best condition. Comp. לכו שברו ואכלו, "Come ye, buy and eat" (Is. lv. 1); שמעו שמע אלי ואכל טוב, "Hearken diligently unto me, and eat ye that which is good" (*ib.* 2); אכול דבש הרבה לא טוב, "It is not good to eat much honey" (Prov. xxv. 27); אכל בני דבש כי טוב ונופת מתוק לחכך כן דעה חכמה לנפשך "My son, eat thou honey, because it is good, and the honeycomb, which is sweet to thy taste; so shall the knowledge of wisdom be unto thy soul" (*ib.* xxiv. 13, 14).

This figure of using אכל in the sense of "acquiring wisdom" is frequently met with in the Talmud, *e g.*, "Come, eat fat meat at Raba's;"[1] also, "all expressions of 'eating' and 'drinking' found in this book (of Proverbs) refer to

---

[1] That is, Come, let us hear interesting discourses in the house of Raba, Babyl. Talm., Baba Bathra, fol. 22a.

wisdom," or, according to another reading, "to the Law."[1] Wisdom has also been frequently called "water," *e.g.*, חוי כל צמא לכו למים, "Ho, every one that thirsteth, come ye to the waters" (Is. lv. 1).

The figurative meaning of these expressions has been so general and common, that it was almost considered as its primitive signification, and led to the employment "of hunger" (רעב) and "thirst" (צמא), in the sense of "absence of wisdom and intelligence;" comp. "I will send a famine in the land, not a famine of bread, nor a thirst for water, but of hearing the words of the Lord;" "My soul thirsteth for God, for the living God" (Ps. xlii. 3). Instances of this kind occur frequently. The words ושאבתם מים בששון ממעיני הישועה, "With joy shall ye draw water out of the wells of salvation" (Is. xii. 3), are paraphrased by Jonathan ben Uziel thus: ותקבלון אולפן חדת בחדוא מבחירי צדיקיא, "You will joyfully receive new instruction from the chosen of the righteous." Consider how he explains מים "water" to indicate "the wisdom which will then spread," and מעיני as being identical with מֵעֵינֵי העדה "in the eyes of the congregation" (Num. xv. 24), in the sense of "the chiefs," *i.e.*, "the wise."[2] By the phrase מבחירי צדיקיא, "from the chosen of the righteous," he expresses his belief that righteousness is true salvation

---

[1] Comp. Midrash Rabba, Koheleth, iii. 13.

[2] According to Maimonides the Targum, in paraphrasing the word מעיני (lit. "sources of") by בחירי, "the best of," is supported by the similar figurative use of עין in the phrase מעיני העדה. Maimonides by no means overlooks the fact that מ in מַעֲיָנֵי is preformative, while in מֵעֵינֵי it is a preposition; the figurative use of the root עין in the two instances is the principal aim of Maimonides in this argument. Ibn Tibbon, misunderstanding this passage, remarks: נאים ושכיב רבינו וז״ל אמר זה הדבר, "while slumbering and lying down our teacher said this." Ibn Tibbon was justly rebuked in Moreh ha-moreh (p. 167) in the following words: ור׳ שמואל שתפשו לחנם תפשו שכתב כי נאים ושכיב מר אמר זה וחשדו בתנומה תפול עליו תרדמה. "R. Samuel censured him without reason when saying that he said this while slumbering and lying down; he suspected that Maimonides was slumbering, while he himself was in deep sleep." Comp. רבני סנהדרין the Targ. of עיני (Eccl. ii. 10).

(חישועה). You now see how he gives to every word in this verse some signification referring to wisdom and study. This should be well considered.

CHAPTER XXXI.

Man's intellect is limited.

KNOW[1] that the human mind has certain objects of perception which are within the scope of its nature and capacity; on the other hand, there are, amongst things which actually exist, certain objects which the mind can in no way and by no means[2] grasp: the gates of perception are closed against it. Further, there are things of which the mind understands one part, but remains ignorant of the other,[3] and when man is able to comprehend some things, it does not follow that he must be able to comprehend every-

---

[1] The arrangement in ch. xxxi. to ch. xxxvi. is as follows: Man's intellect is limited (xxxi.); a transgression of the limit is not only useless, but even dangerous (xxxii.). The limit is not the same for all. The study of Metaphysics, accessible to some, is too difficult for the ordinary capacity of man, and for novices in the study of philosophy (xxxiii.). Metaphysics is not a suitable subject for general instruction (xxxiv.). The doctrine of the incorporeality of God, though part of Metaphysics, must not be treated as an esoteric doctrine (xxxv.). Belief in the Corporeality of the Divine Being is equal to idolatry (xxxvi.).

[2] בונה of the original has been rendered בשום פנים by both Ibn Tibbon and Charisi; while בסבב is translated בסבה in the version of the former, and בשום סבה in that of Charisi. Munk, "D'une manière quelconque ni par une cause quelconque." Although בונה and בסבב are frequently used in the sense indicated by these translators "in some way," and "by some cause," the author would have added מא if he wished to say "in any way," or "by any cause" (בסבב מא and בונה מא). Besides, the antithesis, בונה and בסבב, leads to the suggestion that בונה is to be taken in its primary signification, "in face," i.e., "straight on," "directly," as opposed to בסבב, "indirectly." In the English translation the usual rendering has been retained, the sense being the same, "neither by any method," scil., of his own, "nor by any cause from without." Shemtob explains ולא בסבה אפילו בשמע אלהי, "not by any cause, even by Divine inspiration."

[3] The words וינהל חאלאת, "and he is ignorant of certain properties," have no corresponding rendering in Charisi's version.

thing. This also applies to the senses: they are able to perceive things, but not at every distance; and all other powers of the body are limited in a similar way. A man can, *e.g.*, carry two kikkar,[1] but he cannot carry ten kikkar. How individuals of the same species surpass each other in these sensations and in other bodily faculties is universally known, but there is a limit to them, and they cannot extend to every distance or to every degree.

All this is applicable to the intellectual faculties of man. There is a considerable difference between one person and another as regards these faculties, as is well-known to philosophers. While one man can discover a certain thing by himself, another is never able to understand it, even if taught by means of all possible expressions and metaphors, and during a long period; his mind can in no way grasp it, his capacity is insufficient for it. This distinction is not unlimited. A boundary is undoubtedly set to the human mind which it cannot pass. There are things (beyond that boundary) which are acknowledged to be inaccessible to human understanding, and man does not show any desire to comprehend them, being aware that such knowledge is impossible, and that there are no means of overcoming the difficulty; *e.g.*, we do not know the number of stars in heaven, whether the number is even or odd,[2] the number of animals, minerals, or plants, and the like. There are other things, however, which man very much desires to know, and strenuous efforts to examine and to investigate them[3] have been made by thinkers of all classes,[4] and at all times. They differ and disagree, and constantly raise new doubts with regard to

---

[1] A weight equal to 3,000 shekels.

[2] Comp. Gen. xv. 5, "And tell the stars, if thou be able to number them."

[3] Munk, "Et les scruter," referring the suffix in ענהא to אשיא, "les choses;" Ibn Tibbon, ולחפשה, the suffix agreeing with אמתת. Charizi, treating the Arabic ותסלט (Ibn Tibbon והתגברות) as a finite verb, begins with ואלבחת ענהא (Ibn Tibbon והחקירה עליהם) a new sentence. וירדוף השכל אחרי ידיעת אמתתם, והחקירה עליהם היא מצואה.

[4] Ibn Tibbon adds here the word אומה, "nation;" the words כת מעינת must then be considered to be in apposition to אומה and to qualify it.

them, because their minds are bent on comprehending such things, that is to say, they are moved by desire; and every one of them believes that he has discovered the way leading to a true knowledge of the thing, although human reason is entirely unable to demonstrate the fact by convincing evidence.—For a proposition which can be proved by evidence is not subject to dispute, denial, or rejection; none but the ignorant would contradict it, and such contradiction is called "denial of a demonstrated proof."[1] Thus you find men who deny the spherical form of the earth, or the circular form of the line in which the stars move,[2] and the like; such men[3] are not considered in this treatise. This confusion prevails mostly in metaphysical subjects, less in problems relating to physics, and is entirely absent from the exact sciences. Alexander Aphrodisius[4] said that there are three causes which prevent men from discovering the exact truth: first, arrogance and vainglory; secondly, the subtlety, depth, and difficulty of any subject which is being examined; thirdly, ignorance and want of capacity to comprehend what might be comprehended. These causes are enumerated by Alexander. At the present time there is a fourth cause not mentioned by him, because it did not then prevail,[5]

---

[1] According to the definition of Ibn Tibbon in his Glossary, "a contradiction against a proposition established by proof."

[2] The spherical form of the earth and the circular motions of the stars were asserted and generally accepted by the ancients. The past tense עאנדרוא implies, perhaps, that Maimonides referred rather to former generations than to his own age.

[3] The pronoun והאולא, Hebrew אלה, refers to the persons who denied established truths. In Charizi's translation ואלה הדברים is undoubtedly a mistake.

[4] Alexander Aphrodisius, a commentator of the works of Aristotle, flourished at the end of the second and the beginning of the third century. His writings were eagerly studied by the philosophers of the Arabic schools. Comp. Maimonides' letter to R. Samuel Ibn Tibbon, Epistle of Maimonides, Miscellany of Hebrew Literature, First Series, page 225.

[5] Our training, education, and surroundings undoubtedly produce in our minds certain prepossessions, which make our researches less absolute or independent; and Alexander perhaps included shortcomings from this source in the first class of obstacles. Maimonides was anxious to expose the folly of his opponents, and, as though the three causes of opposition could not sufficiently

PART I.—CHAPTER XXXI. 109

namely, habit and training.¹ We naturally like what we have been accustomed to, and are attracted towards it. This may be observed amongst villagers; though they rarely enjoy the benefit of a douche or a bath, and have few enjoyments, and pass a life of privation,² they dislike town life and do not desire³ its pleasures, preferring the bad to which they are accustomed, to the good to which they are strangers; it would give them no satisfaction to live in palaces, to be clothed in silk, and to indulge in baths, ointments, and perfumes.

The same is the case with those opinions of man to which he has been accustomed from his youth; he likes them, defends them, and shuns the opposite views. This is likewise one of the causes which prevent men³ from finding truth, and which make them cling to their habitual opinions. Such is, *e.g.*, the case with the vulgar notions with respect to the corporeality of God, and many other metaphysical questions, as we shall explain. It is the result of long familiarity⁴ with passages of the Bible,⁵ which they are

account for their obstinacy, he finds for them a special fourth cause in the ideas and words with which their minds were imbued by the authority of the Bible taken in its literal sense. This point is repeatedly urged by Maimonides. Comp. ch. xxxv. If, however, for Bible we substitute the sacred books and traditions of each nation, every one will be found to be subject to similar errors and contradictions. According to Narboni, the four divisions correspond to the "four who entered into the garden" (see next chapter).

¹ אלאלף is translated by Ibn Tibbon ההרגל, "the training;" by Charizi, החברה, "the society." The root אלף denotes both " to be joined" and "to be accustomed."

² Ibn Tibbon ממיעוט רחיצת ראשם ונופם והעדר ההנאות וצוק הפרנסה; Charizi הטירוף appears מן המירוף והניוול וחסרון התענוגים ורע המאכלים. to be a mistake of the copyist for הטינוף.

³ Palquera uses a stronger expression, ויתעוור, "he makes himself blind as regards."

⁴ Palquera כל זה מפני ההרגל וסתרנות (?) על פסוקים התישבה הנדלחם בהם וההצדקה. In a note he adds: " In the same way as man's progress in his search for truth is impeded by false ideas imbibed in his youth, so the apprehension of religious truths is difficult for those who have exclusively devoted themselves to science and have ignored the teaching of religion."

⁵ Ibn Tibbon כתובים, " Biblical texts;" Charizi ענינים, " subjects;" Original נצוץ, " Scriptures."

accustomed to respect and to receive as true, and the literal sense of which implies the corporeality of God and other false notions; in truth, however, these words were employed as figures and metaphors for reasons to be mentioned below. Do not imagine that what we have said of the insufficiency of our understanding and of its limited extent is an assertion founded only on the Bible; for philosophers likewise assert the same, and perfectly understand it, without having regard to any religion[1] or opinion. It is a fact which is only doubted by those who ignore things fully proved. This chapter is intended as an introduction to the next.

CHAPTER XXXII.

Man's intellect is injured when forced beyond its natural limits.

You must consider, when reading this treatise, that mental perception, because connected with matter,[2] is subject to conditions similar to those to which physical perception is subject. That is to say, if your eye looks around, you can perceive all that is within the range of your vision; if, however, you overstrain your eye, exerting it too much by attempting to see an object which is too distant for your eye, or to examine writings or engravings too small for your sight, and forcing it to obtain a correct perception of them, you will not only weaken your sight with regard to that special object, but also for those things which you otherwise are able to perceive: your eye will have become too weak

---

[1] Ibn Tibbon, דעת, "knowledge," "opinion," "character;" Charizi דת, "religion." Arabic, מדהב, "doctrine."

[2] The intellectual perceptions are here called נתלות בחומר, "attached to, or connected with matter," in so far as the mind is connected with the human body, and is, as it were, residing in it. The "ideas," of the intellect are generally considered by Maimonides as independent of the body, but he does not speak here of the intellect in the strictly philosophical sense of the word, as he distinctly states at the end of this chapter. נתלות בחומר is according to the Moreh ha-moreh opposed to טבועות בחומר, "intimately connected with matter"; the latter is applied to the five senses.

PART I.—CHAPTER XXXII. 111

to perceive what you were able to see before you exerted yourself and exceeded the limits of your vision.

The same is the case with the speculative faculties of one who devotes himself to the study of any science.[1] If a person studies too much and exhausts his reflective powers, he will be confused, and will not be able to apprehend even that which had been within the power of his apprehension. For the powers of the body[2] are all alike in this respect.

The mental perceptions are not exempt from a similar condition. If you admit the doubt, and do not persuade[3] yourself to believe that there is a proof for things which cannot be demonstrated, or to try at once[4] to reject and positively to refute an assertion the opposite of which has never been

---

[1] The words (Hebr. חאלה פי חאל אלתפכר (ענינו בענין מחשבה) are generally understood to be a qualification of (Heb. אלנאצר (כל מעיין); Munk translates the phrase "lorsqu'il se livre à la meditation." The purpose, however, of this qualification would not be obvious; those who study any science must necessarily think or meditate. The principal object of the author in the present chapter is to show that the solution of metaphysical problems is possible only within certain limits; he supports this assertion by examples taken from the action of man's senses, and the study of the speculative sciences. The words חאלה פי חאל אלתפכר are in the objective case, governed by the verb ינד (יטצא).

According to Maimonides (the Eight Chapters), the rational faculties of man are divided into מעשיי, "practical," and עיוני, "speculative." The former class includes two kinds, מלאכת מחשבת, "artisanship," and מחשבי, (Arab. סכרי) "theoretical faculty." The מלאכת מחשבת is defined as follows: היא הכח אשר בו ילמד המלאכות כננרות ועבודת האדמה והרפואות והמלחות, "it is man's capacity of learning a trade, as, e.g., carpentry, husbandry, medicine, and navigation." Respecting מחשבי, he says: הוא הכח אשר בו יסתכל בדבר אשר ירצה לעשות אם אפשר לעשות או לא ואם אפשר לעשותו היאך צריך לעשותו, "The capacity for theoretical science is that faculty by which man reflects on a thing he desires to do, whether it is possible or not, and if possible, how it is to be done."

[2] The capacity for the study of theoretical science is called by Maimonides a faculty of the body (כח גופני), because it concerns physical objects, and is more a matter for the imagination (also a כח גופני, comp. Part II. chap. xxxvi.) than for the pure intellect.

[3] Ibn Tibbon ולא תונה, "and you will not deceive." Charizi ואל תשיא, "and do not mislead."

[4] The phrase ולא תתחיל לדחות, lit. "do not begin to reject," in the trans-

proved, or attempt to perceive things which are beyond your perception, then you have attained the highest degree of human perfection, then you are like R. Akibha,[1] who "in peace entered [the study of these theological problems], and came out in peace." If, on the other hand, you attempt to exceed the limit of your perceptive power, or at once to reject things as impossible which have never been proved to be impossible, or which are in fact possible, though their possibility be very remote, then you will be like Elisha Acher;[2] you will not only fail to become perfect, but you will become exceedingly imperfect. Ideas founded on mere imagination will prevail over you, you will incline toward defects, and towards base and degraded habits, on account of the confusion which troubles the mind, and of the dimness of its light, just as weakness of sight [3] causes invalids to see many kinds of unreal images, especially when they have looked for a long time at dazzling or at very minute objects.

Respecting this it has been said, "Hast thou found honey? eat so much as is sufficient for thee, lest thou be filled therewith, and vomit it" (Prov. xxv. 16). Our Sages also applied this verse to Elisha Acher.[4]

---

lation of Ibn Tibbon has the meaning "Do not reject at once, in the beginning of thy research."

[1] R. Akibha was one of the four scholars, of whom it is related in the Babyl. Talmud (Chagigah 14b), also in Jerus. Talmud (*ibid.*, ch. ii.), that they ventured into the garden of speculative philosophy, and met with different fates, viz., "Ben Azai gazed and was killed; Ben Zoma gazed and was hurt; Acher cut down the young plants; R. Akibhah went in and came out unhurt." See Grätz, Gnosticismus, 56 and 95.

[2] Elisha was probably called אחר from the fact that he was no longer the same Elisha as before (Comp. 1 Sam. x. 6, "and shall be turned into another man," איש אחר); his opinions were quoted as authoritative; but this was probably only the case with such decisions as were expressed by him before he seceded from his former colleagues.

[3] Both Hebrew versions render אלרוח אלבאצר "the spirit of sight" ("l'esprit visuel," M.), according to the sense, by כח הראות, but some MSS., and the editio princeps of Ibn Tibbon's version, have הרוח הראות (Munk). *Spiritus visionis* is the term used by Scholastics for "sight."

[4] This verse is applied in the Babylonian Talmud to Ben Zoma, in the Jerusalem Talmud to Ben Azai, in Midrash Yalkut (*at locum*, Prov. xxv.)

PART I.—CHAPTER XXXII.   113

How excellent is this simile! In comparing knowledge to food (as we observed in chapter xxx.), the author of Proverbs mentions the sweetest food, namely, honey, which has the further property of irritating the stomach, and of causing sickness. He thus fully describes the nature of knowledge. Though great, excellent, noble and perfect, it is injurious if not kept within bounds or not guarded properly; it is like honey which gives nourishment and is pleasant, when eaten in moderation, but is totally thrown away when eaten immoderately. Therefore, it is not said "lest thou be filled and loathe it," but "lest thou vomit it." The same idea is expressed in the words, "It is not good to eat much honey" (Prov. xxv. 27); and in the words, "Neither make thyself over-wise; why shouldst thou destroy thyself?" (Eccl. vii. 16); Comp. "Keep thy foot when thou goest to the house of God" (*ibid.* v. 1). The same subject is alluded to in the words of David, "Neither do I exercise myself in great matters, or in things too high for me" (Ps. cxxxi. 2), and in the saying of our Sages: "Do not inquire into things which are too difficult for thee, do not search what is hidden from thee; study what you are allowed to study, and do not occupy thyself with mysteries."[1] They meant to say, Let thy mind only attempt things which are within human perception; for the study of things which lie beyond man's comprehension [2] is extremely injurious, as has been already stated. This lesson is also contained in the Talmudical passage, which begins, "He who considers four things," etc., and concludes, "He who does not regard the honour of his Creator;"[3] here also is given the advice which

---

to both of them; to Acher the following verse is applied: "Suffer not thy mouth to cause thy flesh to sin" (Eccl. v. 6).

[1] The Arabic MSS. have התבונן and בנפלאות instead of דרוש and בנסתרות, as in the editions of the Babyl. Talmud (Chagigah 13a, cited from the book of Ben Sira, iii. 18).

[2] Charizi adds מפני חולשת השכל, "because of the weakness of the intellect."

[3] The whole passage referred to runs as follows: כל המסתכל בד׳ דברים ראוי לו כאלו לא בא לעולם מה למעלה מה למטה מה לפנים מה לאחור

I

we have already mentioned, viz., that man should not rashly engage in speculation with false conceptions, and when he is in doubt about any thing, or unable to find a proof for the object of his enquiry, he must not at once abandon, reject and deny it; he must modestly keep back, and from regard to the honour of his Creator, hesitate [from uttering an opinion] and pause. This has already been explained.

It was not the object of the Prophets and our Sages in these utterances[1] to close the gate of investigation entirely, and to prevent the mind from comprehending what is within its reach, as is imagined by simple and idle people, whom it suits better to put forth their ignorance and incapacity as wisdom and perfection, and to regard the distinction and wisdom of others as irreligion and imperfection, thus taking darkness for light and light for darkness. The whole object of the Prophets and the Sages was to declare that a limit is set for human reason where it must halt. Do not criticise the words used in this chapter and in others in reference to the mind, for we only intended to give some idea of the subject in view, not to describe the essence of the intellect;[2] for other chapters have been dedicated to this subject.

CHAPTER XXXIII.

The study of Metaphysics is injurious to beginners.

You must know that it is very injurious to begin with this branch of philosophy, viz., Metaphysics; or to explain [at first] the sense of the similes occurring in prophecies, and interpret the metaphors which are generally employed in orations

---

"He who reflects on four things, viz., what is above, what is below, what is in front, what is behind, should better not have seen the light of the world" (Mishnah, Chagigah ii. 1).

[1] Arab. אלנצוץ, "sentences;" Ibn Tibbon, הכתובים; Charizi, הכתובים והדברים, referring the one term to "Prophets," the other to "Sages," mentioned before. Comp. ch. xxxi., p. 109, note 5.   [2] See p. 110, note 2.

and which abound in the writings of the Prophets. On the contrary, it is necessary to initiate the young and to instruct the less intelligent according to their comprehension; those who appear to be talented and to have capacity for the higher method of study, *i.e.*, that based on proof and on true logical argument, should be gradually advanced towards perfection, either by tuition or by self-instruction. He, however, who begins with Metaphysics, will not only become confused in matters of religion, but will fall into infidelity.[1] I compare such a person to an infant fed with wheaten bread, meat and wine; it will undoubtedly die, not because such food is naturally unfit for the human body, but because of the weakness of the child, who is unable to digest the food,[2] and cannot derive benefit from it. The same is the case with the true principles of science. They were presented in enigmas, clad in riddles, and taught by all wise men in the most mysterious way that could be devised, not because they contain some secret evil, or are contrary to the fundamental principles of the Law (as fools think who are only philosophers in their own eyes), but because of the incapacity of man to comprehend them at the beginning of his studies: only slight allusions have been made to them to serve for the guidance of those who are capable of understanding them. These sciences were, therefore, called Sodoth (mysteries), and Sithre Thorah (Secrets of the Law),[3] as we shall explain.

This also is the reason why "the Torah speaks the language of man," as we have explained,[4] for it is the object of the Torah to serve for the instruction of the young, of

---

[1] The original תעטיל מחץ Ibn Tibbon renders במול לנמרי, Charizi מינות אמיתית; both mean the same thing—the entire rejection of the authority of the Bible. Munk translates תעטיל "irreligion."

[2] Charizi has here the additional explanatory phrase, כי לא יוכל הגוף למחון אותם, "The body is not able to grind them."

[3] סודות וסתרי תורה (comp. Ps. xxv. 14, סוד יי ליראיו), "secrets and hidden portions of the Law," that is, instruction contained in Scripture, but not for him who only reads it superficially.

[4] See p. 90, note 1.

women, and of the common people; and as all of them are incapable to comprehend the true sense of the words, tradition was considered sufficient to convey all truths which were to be established; and as regards ideals, only such remarks were made as would lead towards[1] a knowledge of their existence, though not to[1] a comprehension of their true essence.[2] When a man attains to perfection, and arrives at a knowledge of the "Secrets of the Law," either through the assistance of a teacher or by self-instruction, being led by the understanding of one part to the study of the other, he will belong to those who faithfully believe in the true principles, either because of conclusive proof, where proof is possible,[3] or by forcible arguments, where argument is admissible; he will have a true notion of those things which he previously received in similes and metaphors, and he will fully understand their sense. We have frequently mentioned in this treatise the principle of our Sages "not to discuss the Maaseh Mercabhah even in the presence of one pupil, except he be wise and intelligent; and then only the headings of the chapters are to be given to him." We must, therefore, begin with teaching these subjects according to the capacity

---

[1] In the Arabic text two different prepositions are used to express the direction, נחו and עלי, "towards," "to." In the Hebrew this variation has been imitated by Ibn Tibbon who renders the two prepositions by אל and על. Some MSS., however, have in both places אל (Comp. Munk, page 416, note 4).

[2] The suffix in ונורה (Hebr. מציאותו) and מאהיתה (Hebr. מהותו) does not refer to "God," as has been assumed by most Commentators, but to תצור (Hebr. ציור), "ideal." The preposition עלי in the Arabic text before מה יסדר (Hebr. מה שיישיר) is co-ordinate with the same preposition before אלתקליד (Hebr. הקבלה), both the prepositions being governed by the verb אקתצר, the Hebrew equivalent for which, הספיקה, being a personal verb, does not require any preposition. Charizi appears to have misunderstood the passage, and translates it inaccurately as follows:— היה לו די מהם הקבלה בכל סברא אמיתית אשר יבקשו להצדיקה ובכל מחשבה וציור השכל כמו שיורה הרעיון על מציאות הבורא לא להשיג אמתת מהותו.

[3] Charizi omits the words במה שאפשר בו מופת, "where proof is possible."

of the pupil, and on two conditions, first, that he be wise, *i.e.*, that he should have successfully gone through the preliminary studies, and secondly that he be intelligent, talented, clear-headed, and of quick perception, that is, "have a mind of his own" מבין מדעתו, as our Sages termed it.

I will now proceed to explain the reasons why we should not instruct the multitude in pure metaphysics, or begin with describing to them the true[1] essence of things, or with showing them that a thing must be as it is, and cannot be otherwise.[2] This will form the subject of the next chapter; and I proceed to say:

CHAPTER XXXIV.

Metaphysics cannot be made popular.

THERE are five reasons why instruction should not begin with metaphysics, but should at first be restricted to pointing out what is fitted for notice and what may be made manifest to the multitude.

First Reason.—The subject itself is difficult, subtle and profound, "Far off and exceeding deep, who can find it out" (Eccl. vii. 24). The following words of Job may be applied to it: "Whence then cometh wisdom? and where is the place of understanding?" (Job xxviii. 20). Instruction should not begin with abstruse and difficult subjects.

---

[1] The pronoun in עליה—the Hebrew equivalent of which, עליו, is frequently omitted in the Hebrew versions—agrees with the relative מא (Hebr. מה), lit., "in that (manner) in which it is," *i.e.*, "truly" or "fully." כפי זה אשר עליו הוא (Char. על פי) is equal to כפי מה שהוא עליו.

[2] The words אלא אם כן אביאהו in the version of Tibbon are not to be joined together; כן is the end of a sentence, and אביאהו begins a new one. אלא אם has perhaps the same meaning as the Biblical כי אם.—Charizi translates thus ומוכרח להיות כן כמו שיתבאר בפרק הבא אחר כן.

In one of the similes contained in the Bible,[1] wisdom is compared to water, and amongst other interpretations given by our Sages of this simile,[2] occurs the following: He who can swim may bring up pearls from the depth of the sea, he who is unable to swim will be drowned, therefore only such persons as have had proper instruction should expose themselves to the risk.

Second Reason.—The intelligence of man is at first limited; for he is not endowed with perfection at the beginning, but at first possesses perfection only *in potentiâ*, not in fact. Thus it is said, "And man is born a wild ass" (Job xi. 12). If a man possesses a certain faculty *in potentiâ*, it does not follow that it must become in him a reality. He may possibly remain deficient either on account of some obstacle, or from want of training in practices which would turn the possibility into a reality. Thus it is distinctly stated in the Bible, "Not many are wise" (*ib.* xxxii. 9); also our Sages say, "I noticed how few were those who attained to a higher degree of perfection."[3] There are many things which obstruct the path to perfection, and which keep man away from it. Where can he find sufficient preparation and leisure to learn all that is necessary in order to develope that perfection which he has *in potentiâ*?

Third Reason.—The preparatory studies are of long duration, and man in his natural desire to reach the goal, finds them frequently too wearisome, and does not wish to be

[1] Arab. פי מלתנא; Ibn Tibbon, באמתנו; Charizi, בתורתנו; Munk, "dans (les traditions de) notre nation."

[2] See end of ch. xxx.; Babyl. Talm. Baba Kama 62a; Midrash Yalkut on Is. lv. 1, *et passim*. The following are a few examples: "The Law has been compared to water; as water leaves the high places and seeks the lower ones, so the knowledge of the Law leaves the proud and is only found with the meek." "Water comes down by drops, and is collected into rivers and streams; in like manner the knowledge of the Law is acquired step by step." "Nobody is too proud to ask for a drop of water; so nobody need be ashamed in asking another person for instruction;" etc. The application made by Maimonides of this simile does not appear to have been taken from Talmud or Midrash.

[3] ראיתי בני עליה והנם מועטים Babyl. Talm. Succah 45 b.

troubled by them. Be convinced that, if man were able to reach the end without preparatory studies, such studies would not be preparatory but tiresome and utterly superfluous. Suppose you awaken any person, even the most simple, as if from sleep, and you say to him, Do you not desire to know what the heavens are, what is their number and their form; what beings are contained in them; what the angels are; how the creation of the whole world took place; what is its purpose, and what is the relation of its various parts to each other; what is the nature of the soul; how it enters the body; whether it has an independent existence, and if so, how it can exist independently of the body; by what means[1] and to what purpose, and similar problems. He would undoubtedly say "Yes," and show a natural desire for the true knowledge of these things; but he will wish to satisfy that desire and to attain to that knowledge by listening to a few words from you. Ask him to interrupt his usual pursuits for a week, till he learn all this, he would not do it, and would be satisfied[2] and contented with imaginary and misleading notions; he would refuse to believe that there is anything which previously requires great research and persevering study.

You, however, know how all these subjects are connected together; for there is nothing else in existence but God and His works, the latter including all existing things besides Him; we can only obtain a knowledge of Him through His works; His works are an evidence of His existence, and of what must be assumed concerning Him, that is to say, of what must be attributed to Him either affirmatively or negatively. It is thus necessary to examine all things according to their essence,[3] to infer from

[1] "By what means," *i.e.*, how man can ensure the eternal separate existence of the soul after death.—Munk (p. 120, note 1) explains these questions as follows: (1) Has each soul an individual existence, or do all form one substance? (2) How is the immortality of the soul obtained—by speculation or by religious practice? (3) Is it the end of the soul to unite with the active intellect or with God?

[2] Charizi adds בעצלתו, "in his laziness."

[3] See ch. xxxiii., page 117, note 1.

every species such true and well-established propositions as may assist us in the solution of metaphysical problems. Again, many propositions based on the nature of numbers and the properties of geometrical figures,[1] are useful in examining things which must be negatived in reference to God, and these negations will lead us to further inferences. You will certainly not doubt the necessity of studying astronomy and physics, if you are desirous of comprehending the relation between the world and Providence as it is in reality, and not according to imagination. There are also many subjects of speculation, which, though not preparing the way for metaphysics, help to train the reasoning power, enabling it to understand the nature of a proof, and to test truth by characteristics essential to it.[2] They remove the confusion arising in the minds of most thinkers, who confound[3] accidental with essential properties, and likewise the wrong opinions resulting therefrom. We may add, that although they do not form the basis for metaphysical research, they assist in forming a correct notion of these things, and are certainly useful in many other things connected with that discipline. Consequently he who wishes to attain to human perfection, must therefore first study Logic,[4] next the

---

[1] Instances of inferences drawn from mathematical truths for theological propositions are given by the author of Moreh ha-moreh (p. 18); the properties of the unity which admits of no division, multiplication, etc., is the basis of all numbers, etc.; similarly he refers to the nature of the circle, which is one continuous line without beginning and without end. Comp. Ibn Ezra Literature, IV., page 21, note 1.

[2] The pronoun לה (Hebrew לו) refers to אלחק (אמת), "truth," according to others to מופת, "proof." In the translation of Charizi it is paraphrased by המורים על עצם הבורא, "things which refer to the Essence of the Creator."

[3] הסתפק "to become doubtful" in Ibn Tibbon's Version, corresponding to the Arabic אלתבאס, has here the same meaning as התערב "to be confounded" in Charizi's Version, and in Palquera's Moreh ha-moreh (page 150).

[4] Logic, e.g., assists man in finding the truth in various branches of science connected though indirectly with Metaphysics. See Introduction, page 3, note 3.

PART I.—CHAPTER XXXIV. 121

various branches of Mathematics[1] in their proper order, then Physics, and lastly Metaphysics. We find that many who have advanced to a certain point in the study of these disciplines become weary, and stop; that others, who are endowed with sufficient capacity, are interrupted in their studies by death, which surprises them while still engaged with the preliminary course. Now, if no knowledge whatever had been given to us by means of tradition, and if we had not been brought to the belief in a thing through the medium of similes, we would have been bound to form a perfect notion of things with their essential characteristics, and to believe only what we could prove: a goal which could only be attained by long preparation. In such a case most[2] people would die, without having known whether there was a God or not, much less that certain things[3] must be asserted about Him, and other things denied as defects. From such a fate not even "one of a city or two of a family" (Jer. iii. 14) would have escaped.

As regards the privileged few, "the remnant whom the Lord calls" (Joel iii. 5), they only attain the perfection at which they aim after due preparatory labour. The necessity of such a preparation and the need of such a training for the acquisition of real knowledge, has been plainly stated by King Solomon in the following words: "If the iron be blunt, and he do not whet the edge, then must he put to more strength; and it is profitable to prepare for wisdom" (Eccl. x. 10); "Hear counsel, and receive instruction, that thou mayest be wise in thy latter end" (Prov. xix. 20).

There is still another urgent reason why the preliminary disciplines should be studied and understood. During the study many doubts present themselves, and the difficulties,

[1] Lit., "Elementary Disciplines," which must be learnt and which admit of no speculation, especially mathematics and astronomy. Comp. Introd., page 3, note 1.

[2] Charizi: כל בני אדם, "all people."

[3] Arabic חכם, "judgment," "wisdom," or "relation."—The Hebrew versions דבר, "something" (perhaps in the sense of λόγος).

that is, the objections to certain assertions, are soon understood, for this may be compared to the demolition of a building;[1] while, on the other hand, it is impossible to prove an assertion, or to remove any doubts, without having recourse to several propositions taken from these preliminary studies. He who approaches metaphysical problems without proper preparation is like a person who journeys towards a certain place, and on the road falls into a deep pit, out of which he cannot rise, and he must perish there; if he had not gone forth, but had remained at home, it would have been better for him.

Solomon has expatiated in the book of Proverbs on sluggards and their indolence, by which he figuratively refers to indolence in the search after wisdom. He thus speaks of a man who desires to know the final results, but does not exert himself to understand the preliminary disciplines which lead to them, doing nothing else but desire. "The desire of the slothful killeth him; for his hands refuse to labour. He coveteth greedily all the day long; but the righteous giveth, and spareth not" (Prov. xxi. 25, 26); that is to say, if the desire killeth the slothful, it is because he neglects to seek the thing which might satisfy his desire, he does nothing but desire, and hopes to obtain a thing without using the means to reach it. It would be better for him were he without that desire. Observe how the end of the simile throws light on its beginning. It concludes with the words "but the righteous giveth, and spareth not;" the antithesis of "righteous" and "slothful" can only be justified on the basis of our interpretation. Solomon thus indicates that only such a man is righteous who gives to everything its due portion; that is to say, who gives to the study of a thing the whole time required for it, and does not devote any part of that time to another purpose. The passage may therefore be paraphrased thus: "And the righteous man devotes his days to wisdom, and does not withhold any of

[1] That is, it is easier to raise objections to an assertion, than to prove it, as it is easier to demolish a house, than to build it.

them." Comp. "Give not thy strength unto women" (Prov. xxxi. 3).

The majority of scholars, that is to say, the most famous in science, are afflicted with this failing, viz., that of hurrying at once to the final results, and of speaking about them, without treating of the preliminary disciplines. Led by folly or ambition to disregard those preparatory studies, for the attainment of which they are either incapable or too idle, some scholars endeavour to prove that these are injurious or superfluous. On reflection the truth will become obvious.

The Fourth Reason is taken from the physical constitution of man. It has been proved that moral conduct[1] is a preparation for intellectual progress; and that only a man whose character is pure, calm and steadfast, can attain to intellectual perfection; that is, acquire correct conceptions. Many men are naturally so constituted as to make all perfection impossible; e.g., he whose heart is very warm and is himself very powerful, is sure to be passionate, though he tries to counteract that disposition by training; he whose ὀρχίπεδα are warm, humid, and vigorous, and the organs connected therewith are surcharged, will not easily refrain from sin, even if he makes great efforts to restrain himself. You also find persons of great levity and rashness, whose excited manners and wild gestures prove that their constitution is in disorder, and their temperament so bad that it cannot be cured.[2] Such persons can never attain to perfection; it is utterly useless to occupy oneself

---

[1] What Maimonides here calls מעלות המדות is called in Yad hachazakah דעות, and a whole section הלכות דעות is devoted to this subject. In the second, of the "Eight Chapters" the excellencies of man are divided into מעלות המדות "morals," and מעלות השכליות, "intellectual faculties." In both works M. points out that the highest development of the intellectual faculties (viz., השגת הבורא) is impossible, if the moral dispositions of man have not been regulated by good training and exercise. The two classes of virtues correspond to the Greek ἀρηταί ἠθικαί and ἀρηταί διανοητικαί.

[2] Arabic, אן יעבר ענהו, "that it should pass away from him;" Ibn Tibbon: שיפורש, "that it should be separated;" Charizi: להפריש אותו, Munk: "Dont on ne peut rendre compte," "qui échappe à l'analyse."

with them on such a subject [Metaphysics]. For this science is, as you know, different from the science of Medicine and of Geometry, and, from the reason already mentioned, it is not every person who is capable of approaching it. It is impossible for a man to study it successfully without moral preparation; he must acquire the highest degree of uprightness and integrity, "for the froward is an abomination to the Lord, but His secret is with the righteous" (Prov. iii. 32). Therefore it was considered inadvisable to teach it to young men; nay, it is impossible for them to comprehend it, on account of the heat of their blood and the flame of youth, which confuses their minds; that heat, which causes all the disorder, must first disappear; they must have become moderate and settled, humble in their hearts, and subdued in their temperament; only then will they be able to arrive at the highest degree of the perception of God, i.e., the study of Metaphysics, which is called Maaseh Mercabhah. Comp. "The Lord is nigh unto them that are of a broken heart" (Ps. xxxiv. 18); "I dwell in the high and lofty place, with him also that is of a contrite and humble spirit; to revive the spirit of the humble, and to revive the heart of the contrite ones" (Is. lvii. 15).

Therefore the rule מוסרין לו ראשי פרקים, "the headings of the sections may be confided to him," is further restricted in the Talmud, in the following way: The headings of the sections must only be handed down to an Abh-beth-din (President of the Court), whose heart[1] is full of care, i.e., in whom wisdom is united with humility, meekness, and a great dread of sin. It is further stated there: "The secrets of the Law can only be communicated to a יועץ חכם חרשים ונבון לחש, counsellor, scholar, and good orator."[2] These qualities can only be acquired if the physical constitution of the student favour their development. You certainly know that some persons, though exceedingly able,

---

[1] Our editions of the Babyl. Talmud (Chagigah, 13a) have the reading וכל מי, "and to every one, who."

[2] Lit., a person that is skilled in whispering (or speaking on secret things).

are very weak in giving counsel, while others are ready with proper counsel and good advice in social and political matters. A person so endowed is called "counsellor" (יוֹעֵץ), and may be unable to comprehend purely abstract notions, even such as are similar to innate ideas.[1] He is unacquainted with them, and has no talent whatever for them; we apply to him the words: "Wherefore is there a price in the hand of a fool to get wisdom, seeing he hath no heart to it?" (Prov. xvii. 16.) Others are intelligent and naturally clear-sighted, able to convey complicated ideas in concise and well-chosen language,[2]— they are called "good orators" (נבון לחש)—but they have not been engaged in the pursuit of science, or acquired any knowledge of it. Those who have actually acquired a knowledge of the sciences, are called "wise in arts" (or "scholars"); the Hebrew term חכם חרשים has been explained in the Talmud as implying, that when such a man speaks, all become, as it were, speechless.[3]

Now, consider how, in the writings of the Rabbis,[4] the admission of a person to discourses on metaphysics is made dependent on distinction in social qualities, and study of philosophy, as well as on the possession of clear-sightedness, intelligence, eloquence, and ability to communicate things by slight allusions. If a person satisfies these requirements, the secrets of the Law are confided to him. In the

[1] המושכלות הראשונות, "The first ideas," the *intelligibilia prima*, those ideas which man possesses even before he is able to reason logically; "the innate notions."—מושכלות (Arab. מעקולות) are matters which are grasped only by the intellect (שכל, עקל), not by the senses.

[2] Munk: Qui maitrisse les sujets les plus obscurs en l'exprimant, etc. He explains אכם׳ in the Arabic text to be an adjective, signifying "the most hidden." Ibn Tibbon and Charizi explain it as being an infinitive, signifying "to hide," and in accordance with this interpretation the literal translation of נבון לחש would be "secretary."

[3] חֲרָשִׁים is explained by them as identical with חֵרְשִׁים "deaf" (Babyl. Talm. Chagigah 14a).

[4] בנץ כתאב, "with the text of the Bible," or "in the traditional explanations of the Bible." Charizi: הביאו מדברי הכתוב; Ibn Tibbon: התנו בספריהם; Munk: "En se servant d'un texte sacré."

same place we also read the following passage:—R. Jochanan said to R. Elasar, "Come, I will teach you Maaseh Mercabhah." The reply was, "I am not yet old," or in other words, I have not yet become old, I still perceive in myself the hot blood and the rashness of youth. You learn from this that, in addition to the above-named good qualities, a certain age is also required. How, then, could any person speak on those metaphysical themes in the presence of ordinary people, of children, and of women?

Fifth Reason.—Man is disturbed in his intellectual occupation by the necessity of looking after the material wants of the body, especially if the necessity of providing for wife and children be superadded; much more so if he seeks superfluities in addition to his ordinary wants, for by custom and bad habits these become a powerful motive. Even the perfect man to whom we have referred, if too busy with these necessary things—much more so if busy with unnecessary things, and filled with a great desire for them—must weaken or altogether lose his desire for study, to which he will apply himself with interruption, lassitude, and want of attention. He will not attain to that for which he is fitted by his abilities, or he will acquire imperfect knowledge, a confused mass of true and false ideas. For these reasons it was proper that the study of Metaphysics should have been exclusively cultivated by privileged persons, and not entrusted to the common people. They are not for the beginner, and he[1] should abstain from them, as the little child has to abstain from taking solid food and from carrying heavy weights.

[1] In the translation of Ibn Tibbon the following phrase is added here: מי שאינו ראוי להם, "He who has not the capacity for those studies."

CHAPTER XXXV.

The Incorporeality of God should be made known to all.

Do not think that what we have laid down in the preceding chapters on the importance, obscurity, and difficulty of the subject, and its unsuitableness for communication to ordinary persons, includes the doctrine of God's incorporeality and His exemption from all affections ($\pi\acute{a}\theta\eta$).[1] This is not the case. For in the same way as all people must be informed, and even children must be trained in the belief that God is One, and that none besides Him is to be worshipped, so must all be taught by simple authority that God is incorporeal; that there is no similarity in any way whatsoever between Him and His creatures; that His existence is not like the existence of His creatures, His life not like that of any living being, His wisdom not like the wisdom of the wisest of men; and that the difference between Him and His creatures is not merely quantitative, but absolute[2] [as between two individuals of two different classes]; I mean to say that all must understand that our wisdom and His, or our power and His, do not differ quantitatively or qualitatively, or in a similar manner; for two things, of which the one is strong and the other weak, are necessarily similar, belong to the same class, and can be included in one definition. The same is the case with all other comparisons; they can only be made between two things belonging to the same class, as has been shown in works on natural science.[3] Anything predicated of God is totally different from our attributes; no definition can comprehend

---

[1] See below, ch. lv.

[2] Lit., "In the class of existence."—The word פקט (Hebr. בלבד), "merely," is superfluous, because according to Maimonides there is no quantitative difference whatever between God and His creatures.

[3] Comp. Arist. Phys., vii. 4, and below, chap. lii. and lvi.

both; therefore His existence and that of any other being totally differ from each other, and the term existence (מציאות) applied to both is homonymous, as I shall explain.

This suffices for the guidance of children and of ordinary persons who must believe that there is a Being existing, perfect, incorporeal, not inherent in a body as a force of it—God, who is above all kinds of deficiency, above all affections. But the question concerning the attributes of God, their inadmissibility, and the meaning of those attributes which are ascribed to Him; concerning the Creation, His Providence, in which He provides for everything; concerning His will, His perception, His knowledge of everything; concerning prophecy and its various degrees; concerning the meaning of His names which imply the idea of unity, though they are more than one; all these things are very difficult problems, the true "Secrets of the Law," the secrets (סודות) mentioned so frequently in the Books of the Prophets and in the words of our Teachers, the subjects of which we should only mention the headings of the chapters, as we have already stated, and only in the presence of a person satisfying the above-named conditions.[1]

That God is incorporeal, that He cannot be compared with His creatures, that He is not subject to external influence; these are things which must be explained to everyone according to his capacity, and they must be taught by way of tradition to children and women, to the stupid and ignorant, as they are taught that God is One, that He is eternal, and that none but He is to be worshipped. Without incorporeality there is no unity, for a corporeal thing is in the first case not simple, but composed of matter and form which are two separate things by definition,[2] and secondly, as it has

---

[1] See preceding chapter.—Instead of המתואר in the translation of Ibn Tibbon, Charizi employed the phrase ולמי שהוא ראוי לזה.

[2] Arab. באלחד; Ibn Tibbon: בגדר; Charizi: בגבול המנין, "by the definition of the number." Maimonides adds this qualifying phrase, because substance and form are in reality not found as two separate things. It is only in the definition of a thing that they appear to be separable.

extension it is also divisible.¹ When persons have received this doctrine, and have been trained in this belief, and are in consequence at a loss to reconcile it with the writings of the Prophets, the meaning of the latter must be made clear and explained to them by pointing out the homonymity and the figurative application of certain terms discussed in this part of the work. Their belief in the unity of God and in the words of the Prophets will then be a true and perfect belief.

Those who are not sufficiently intelligent to comprehend the true interpretation of these passages in the Bible, or to understand that the same term admits of two different interpretations, may simply be told that the scriptural passage is clearly understood by the wise, but that they should content themselves with knowing that God is incorporeal, that He is never subject to external influence, as passivity implies a change, while God is entirely free from all change, that He cannot be compared to anything besides Himself, that no definition includes Him together with any other being, that the words of the Prophets are true, and that difficulties met with in them can be explained on this principle. This will suffice for that class of persons, and it is not proper[2] to leave them in the belief that God is corporeal, or that He has any of the properties of material objects, just as there is no need to leave them in the belief that God does not exist, that there are more Gods than one, or that any other being may be worshipped.

CHAPTER XXXVI.

Belief in the Corporeality of God is equal to the sin of Idolatry.

I SHALL explain to you, when speaking on the attributes of

[1] Arabic: מנקסם קאבל אלתגזיה; Hebr.: מתחלק מקבל החלוקה; Munk: "divisible et susceptible d'être partagé."

[2] The expression אין צריך here and in several other passages in the translation of Ibn Tibbon does not signify "it is not necessary," but "it is necessary that . . . . not," *i.e.*, it is not proper, equal in sense to the phrase אין ראוי

K

God,[1] in what sense we can say that a particular thing pleases Him, or excites His anger and His wrath, and in reference to certain persons that God was pleased with them, was angry with them, or was in wrath against them. This is not the subject of the present chapter; I intend to explain in it what I am now going to say. You must know, that in examining the Law and the books of the Prophets, you will not find the term חרון אף "burning anger," כעס "provocation," or קנאה "jealousy" applied to God except in reference to idolatry;[2] and that none but the idolater is called "enemy," "adversary," or "hater of the Lord." Comp. "And ye serve other gods, ... and then the Lord's wrath will be kindled against you" (Deut. xi. 16, 17); "Lest the anger of the Lord thy God be kindled against thee," etc. (ib. vi. 15); "To provoke Him to anger

---

employed in these passages by Charizi.—The Arabic ינבגי has both meanings: "it is necessary" and "it is proper."

[1] See below, chap. liv. sqq.

[2] It has not escaped the critical eyes of the Commentators that the phrase חרה אף also occurs in the Bible when the anger of God does not appear to have been directed against idolatry. Comp. Exod. iv. 14; xxii. 24; Num. xii. 9. Either we must assume there is no rule without exception (אין למדין מן הכללות), or that Maimonides found in these examples a deviation from the true belief in God, which would, in his view, be equal to idolatry. Thus, Moses thought that God could not accomplish the deliverance of the Israelites from Egypt through him, on account of the impediment in his speech; Miriam and Aaron believed their conception of God equal to the most perfect notions held by Moses; the Israelites, in oppressing the stranger, would not believe that God is the father and protector of the poor and the helpless. Ibn Caspi, though he believes that Maimonides did not ignore those passages, and himself fully explained them in Maskiyoth Kesef, admits the possibility that men like Maimonides could forget parts of the Bible. He says: ואם חם ושלום שכח המורה, כי לא לאלהים הוא כמו שכתבתי פרק י״ט והיה גם האם אין שכחה, or as quoted in Mekor Chayim on Numbers xii., זה עמהם: לפני כסא כבודו ז״ל והנה משה רבינו ע״ה שכח עצמו במי מריבה אבל האמת אין איש אשר לא יחמא וכל יתרון החכמים הוא במיעוט תעיותיו "Why should we assume that Maimonides was free from errors, seeing that even Moses our Teacher made a mistake at the waters of Meribhah. The truth is, that no man is free from error, and the distinction of wise men consists in the smaller number of their mistakes."

through the work of your hands" (*ib.* xxxi. 29); "They have moved me to jealousy with that which is not God; they have provoked me to anger with their vanities" (*ib.* xxxii. 21); "For the Lord thy God is a jealous God" (*ib.* vi. 15); "Why have they provoked me to anger with their graven images, and with strange vanities?" (Jer. viii. 19); "Because of the provoking of his sons and of his daughters" (Deut. xxxii. 19); "For a fire is kindled in mine anger" (*ib.* 22); "The Lord will take vengeance on His adversaries, and He reserveth wrath for His enemies" (Nah. i. 2);[1] "And repayeth them that hate Him" (Deut. vii. 10); "Until He hath driven out His enemies from before Him" (Num. xxxii. 21); "Which the Lord thy God hateth" (Deut. xvi. 22); "For every abomination to the Lord, which He hateth, have they done unto their gods" (*ib.* xii. 31). Instances like these are innumerable; and if you examine all the examples met with in the holy writings, you will find that they confirm our view.

The Prophets in their writings laid special stress on this, because it concerns errors in reference to God, *i.e.*, it concerns idolatry. For if any one believes[2] that, *e.g.*, Zaid is standing, while in fact he is sitting, he does not deviate from truth so much as one who believes that fire is under the air, or that water is under the earth[3] or that the earth is a plane[4] or things similar to these. The latter does not deviate so much from truth as one who believes that the sun consists of fire, or that the heavens form a hemisphere, and similar things; in the third instance the deviation from truth is less than the deviation of a man who believes that angels

---

[1] In our editions of the Bible we read נקם ה' לצריו ונוטר הוא לאויביו, while the Arabic MSS. as well as the Hebrew translations have הוא instead of ה', and ומשלם instead of ונוטר.

[2] It appears that Maimonides in the selection of these instances, took two examples with reference to the earth, two with reference to the spheres above, and two with reference to immaterial beings. (Efodi.)

[3] On the belief in this arrangement of the four elements, comp. Arist., Phys. iv. 5, and De Cœlo, iv. 5. Comp. chap. lxxii.

[4] This instance is not mentioned by Charizi.

eat and drink, and the like. The latter again deviates less from truth than one who believes that something besides God is to be worshipped; for ignorance and error concerning a great thing, *i.e.*, a thing which has a high position in the universe,[1] are of greater importance than those which refer to a thing which occupies a lower place;[1]—by "error" I mean the belief that a thing is different from what it really is; by "ignorance," the want of knowledge respecting things the knowledge of which can be obtained.

If a person does not know the measure of the cone,[2] or the sphericity of the sun,[3] it is not so important as not to know

---

[1] Ibn Tibbon מן לה מרתבה דון דלך and מן לה מרתבה מתמכנה Arabic מי שיש לו מדרגה למטה ממנו, and מי שיש לו מדרגה חזקה במציאה.

[2] The cubic contents of the cone, the sphere and the cylinder of the same base and height are in the proportion of 1 : 2 : 3, ($\tfrac{1}{3}r^2\pi$, $\tfrac{4}{3}r^3\pi$, $2r^3\pi$). מכרום אלאסטואנה is explained to be the cone of the cylinder (Ibn Tibbon, מחודד האיצטוונה, lit. "the pointed portion of the column or 'cylinder'"), *i.e.*, the cone standing with the cylinder on the same base, and having the same height. He therefore, who thinks that such a cone is half of that cylinder is mistaken, the proportion being 1 : 3. Charizi, however, translates למוד מוצק העמור בחציו. According to the Glossary prefixed to the translation of Charizi, מוצק is the base (יסוד); in this sense מוצק would give no sense, nor would it correspond to the Arabic מכרום; מוצק is here used in the meaning of "narrow," "pointed," (מחודד), and מוצק העמוד is likewise the cone included in a cylinder. As it is not likely that Charizi was ignorant of the above proportions, he either meant that the contents of the cone are half of the sphere included in the cylinder, or that the area of the surface of the cone, forming a triangle, is half of the base of the triangle multiplied by the height.

In More ha-moreh, p. 171, the following explanation is given, ואמר מחודד האיצטוונה חציה, קרא האיצטוונה עמוד (הוא) האמת כי (שני חלקים) האיצטוונה בכל עצם פרדי הם שני חלקים עד שישוב לנקודה:

"He says "the pointed portion of the cylinder (*i.e.*, the cone) is half of it." (he calls the pillar איצטוונה). The right proportion, however, is, that the portion taken away from the cylinder in order to leave a cone [of the same base and the same height] is equal to two-thirds of the cylinder." The same author gives a clearer explanation (*ibid.*) in the following words:—אצטוונה הוא עמוד והוא עשוי כעגול כעין פירון בלעז ואם תרצה להשיבה בנקודה ילכו ב' חלקים וישאר השליש האי מהעמוד, ואם יחשוב אדם שישאר חצי האצטוונה הוא טועה.

[3] Charizi: עגולה, כי אין השמש עגולה, "that the sun is not spherical." עגולה in Ibn Tibbon's version means a circle; Charizi uses it in the sense of "sphere." Moreh ha-moreh: או שהשמש איננה מסיבה, "or that the sun does not go round." According to Munk איננה has been added, as it is not found in the

whether God exists, or whether the world exists without a God; and if a man assumes that the cone is half (of the cylinder), or that the sun is a circle, it is not so injurious as to believe that God is more than One. You must know that idolaters when worshipping idols do not believe that there is no God besides them; and no idolater ever did assume or ever will assume that any image made of metal, stone, or wood has created the heavens and the earth, and still governs them. Idolatry is founded on the idea that a particular form represents the agent between God and His creatures. This is plainly said in passages like the following: "Who would not fear thee, O king of nations?" (Jer. x. 7); "And in every place incense is offered unto my name" (Mal. i. 11); by "my name" allusion is made to the Being which is called by them [*i.e.*, the idolaters] "the First Cause." We have already explained this in our larger work,[1] and none of our fellow believers can doubt it.

The infidels, however, though believing in the existence of the Creator, attack the exclusive prerogative of God, namely, the service and worship which was commanded, in order that the belief of the people in His existence should be firmly established, in the words, "And you shall serve the Lord," etc. (Exod. xxiii. 25). By transferring that prerogative to other beings, they cause the people, who only notice the rites, without comprehending their meaning or the true character of the being which is worshipped, to renounce their belief in the existence of God. They were therefore punished with death; Comp. "Thou shalt save alive nothing that breatheth" (Deut. xx. 16). The object of this commandment, as is distinctly stated, is to extirpate that false opinion, in order that other men should not be corrupted by it any more; in the words of the Bible "that they teach you not," etc. (*ib.* 18). They are called "enemies,"

MSS. As, however, the sun was believed to move round the earth, the negation איננה, may perhaps not be without foundation.

[1] See Mishneh Torah, Book I., Hilchoth Akum (on Idolatry), ch. i.

"foes," "adversaries;" by worshipping idols they are said to provoke God to jealousy, anger, and wrath. How great, then, must be the offence of him who has a wrong opinion of God himself, and believes Him to be different from what He truly is, i.e., assumes that He does not exist, that He consists of two elements, that He is corporeal, that He is subject to external influence, or ascribes to Him any defect whatever! Such a person is undoubtedly worse than he who worships idols in the belief that they, as agents,[1] can do good or evil.

Therefore bear in mind that by the belief in the corporeality or in anything connected with corporeality, you would provoke God to jealousy and wrath, kindle His fire and anger, become His foe, His enemy, and His adversary in a higher degree than by the worship of idols. If you think that there is an excuse for those who believe in the corporeality of God on the ground of their training, their ignorance or their defective comprehension, you must make the same concession to the worshippers of idols; their worship is due to ignorance, or to early training, "they continue in the custom of their fathers."[2] You will perhaps say that the literal interpretation of the Bible causes men to fall into that doubt, but you must know that idolaters were likewise brought to their belief by false imaginations and ideas. There is no excuse whatever for those who, being unable to think for themselves, do not accept [the doctrine of the incorporeality of God] from the true philosophers. I do not consider those men as infidels who are unable to prove the incorporeality, but I hold those to be so who do not believe it, especially when they see that Onkelos and Jonathan avoid [in reference to God] expressions implying corporeality as much as possible. This is all I intended to say in this chapter.

---

[1] Ibn Tibbon, אמצעית; Charizi, קשר אמצעות, "link, intermediate."

[2] מנהג אבותיהם בידיהם is a Talmudical phrase employed in demonstrating that the idolatry practised by the heathens in the Talmudical age was no real idolatry; men only followed the practice of previous generations, without having any intention of worshipping idols (Talm. Babl., Chullin 13a).

CHAPTER XXXVII.

פנים, 1, *Face.* 2, *Anger.* 3, *Presence.* 4, *Before (place).* 5, *Before (time).* 6, *Attention.*

The term פנים is homonymous; most of its various meanings have a figurative character.[1] It denotes in the first place the face of a living being; comp. ונהפכו כל פנים לירקון, "And all *faces* are turned into paleness" (Jer. xxx. 6); מדוע פניכם רעים, "Wherefore are your *faces* so sad?" (Gen. xl. 7). In this sense the term occurs frequently.

The next meaning of the word is "anger;" comp. ופניה לא היו לה עוד, "And her *anger*[2] was gone" (1 Sam. i. 18). Accordingly, the term is frequently used in reference to God in the sense of anger and wrath; comp. פני יי חלקם, "The *anger* of the Lord hath divided them" (Lam. iv. 16); פני יי בעשי רע, "The *anger* of the Lord is against them that do evil" (Ps. xxxiv. 17); פני ילכו והניחתי לך, "Mine anger shall go[3] and I will give thee rest" (Ex. xxxiii. 14); ושמתי אני את פני, "Then I will set mine anger" (Lev. xx. 3), and many other instances.

Another meaning of the word פנים is "the presence and existence of a person;" comp. על פני כל אחיו נפל, "He died in the *presence* [*i. e.*, in the lifetime] of all his brethren"[4] (Gen. xxv. 18); ועל פני כל העם אכבד, "And in the *presence*

---

[1] Lit., "are borrowed," see Introduction, p. 5, note 2. Maimonides does not state here which of the six significations of פנים are metaphorical, and which are really homonymous. Even in the author's own interpretations the several meanings of the term are intimately connected with the original signification. The only case, perhaps, not included in the phrase, "most of its meanings," is its use in the sense of "attention," and its application to the Providence of God.

[2] Comp. Rashi *ad locum*, ופניה של זעם, and Targum, ואפין בישין.

[3] Comp. Targ. Pseudo-Jonathan, סבר אפין דרוגזא; Ibn Ezra cites the Gaon's explanation חמתי, "my anger." Comp. Babyl. Talm., Berachoth, fol. 7a.

[4] Comp. Ibn Ezra *ad locum*. Here, and in many other instances, Maimonides does not follow the authority of the Targum.

of all the people I will be glorified" (Lev. x. 3); אם לא על
פניך יברכך, "And he will curse Thee while Thou existest,"
i.e., in Thy presence (Job i. 11). In the same sense the word is
used in the following passage, וידבר יי אל משה פנים אל פנים,
"And the Lord spake unto Moses face to face," *i.e.*, both
being present, without any intervening medium[1] between
them. Comp. לכה נתראה פנים, "Come, let us look one
another in the face" (2 Kings xiv. 8); and also פנים בפנים
דבר יי עמכם, "The Lord talked with you face to face"
(Deut. v. 4); instead of which we read more plainly in
another place, "Ye heard the voice of the words, but saw
no similitude; only ye heard a voice" (*ib.* iv. 12). The
hearing of the voice without seeing any similitude is termed
פנים בפנים, "face to face." Similarly do the words "And
the Lord spake unto Moses face to face" correspond[2] to
"There he heard the voice of one speaking unto him"
(Num. vii. 89), in the description of God's speaking to
Moses. Thus it will be clear to you that the perception
of the Divine voice without the intervention of an angel is
called "face to face" (פנים בפנים). In the same sense the
word פנים must be understood in ופני לא יראו, "And my
face shall not be seen" (Ex. xxxiii. 23); *i.e.*, my true existence,[3] as it is, cannot be comprehended.

The word פנים is also used as an adverb of place, in the
sense of "before," or "between the hands of."[4] In this
sense it is frequently employed in reference to God; also in
the phrase ופני לא יראו, according to Onkelos, who renders it

[1] Ibn Caspi, מבלתי אמצעי כח המדמה, "without the agency of the representative faculty."

[2] See ch. xxviii. p. 97, note 3 on the meaning of the word כנוי, "paraphrase," "substitute."

[3] See ch. xxxiii. p. 117, note 1.

[4] Arabic טרף מכאן אלמקול ענה פי אלערביה אמאמך או בין ידיך, "an adverb of place expressed in Arabic by אמאמך or בין ידיך." This passage is certainly misunderstood by Charizi, when he translates it כנוי מקום ונקרא בל׳ ערב כלי מקום כנון לפניך אשר ירצה לומר בין ידיך. More correctly Ibn Tibbon, who omits the words "in Arabic," כלי מקום שענינו לפניך או בין ידיך.

PART I.—CHAPTER XXXVII.

ודקדמי לא יתחזון,[1] "And those before me shall not be seen." He finds here an allusion to the fact, that there are also higher created beings of such superiority that their true nature cannot be perceived by man; viz., the ideals, separate intellects,[2] which in their relation to God are described as being constantly before Him, or between His hands, i.e., as enjoying uninterruptedly the closest attention of Divine Providence. He, i.e. Onkelos, considers that the things which are described as completely perceptible are those beings which, as regards existence, are inferior to the ideals, viz., substance and form; in reference to which we are told, ותחזה ית דבתראי, "And thou shalt see that which is behind Me" (ibid.), i.e., beings, from which, as it were, I turn away, and which I leave behind Me. This figure is to represent the utter remoteness of such beings from the Deity. You shall afterwards (ch. liv.) hear my explanation of what Moses, our teacher, asked for.

פנים is also used as an adverb of time, meaning "before." Comp. לפנים בישראל, "In former time in Israel" (Ruth iv. 7); לפנים הארץ יסדת, "Of old hast thou laid the foundation of the earth" (Ps. cii. 25).[3]

Another signification of the word is "attention and regard."[4] Comp. לא תשא פני דל, "Thou shalt not have

[1] Abravanel classifies the six various renderings of פנים by Onkelos, viz., רוגזי, שכנתי, אפי שכנתי, דקדמי, ממלל, אפין, and assigns to each a special meaning. When Maimonides, e.g., says, that according to Onkelos, the knowledge of God and of the ideals was withheld from Moses, Abravanel finds this indicated in the circumstance that ומני is once rendered אפי שכנתי, and once דקדמי.

[2] Maimonides treats more explicitly of the ideals (דעות נפרדות or שכלים נפרדים) in Part II., ch. iv. It appears that according to Maimonides these are comprehensible to human understanding, while Onkelos is of opinion that man cannot directly understand them.

[3] Ibn Caspi thinks that this verse has the same meaning as Genesis i. 1; if, therefore, פנים is an adverb of time, בראשית must likewise be an adverb of time, and when Maimonides, in Part II., xiii. and xxx., gives a different interpretation of the term בראשית, this is an inconsistency which may be attributed to the seventh cause mentioned in the Introduction, p. 24 and p. 26.

[4] Arab. רעאיה ועואיה, Ibn Tibbon הזהרה והשגחה, "attention and Providence;" Charizi, הדור וכבוד, "honor and glory," and in a similar sense

regard to the poor" (Lev. xx. 15); ונשׂא פנים, "And a person receiving attention" (Isa. iii. 3); אשׁר לא ישׂא פנים וכו׳, "Who does not show regard," etc. (Deut. x. 17, etc.). The word פנים has a similar signification in the blessing, ישׂא יי פניו אליך וישׂם לך שׁלום, "The Lord turn His face to thee" (i.e., Let His providence accompany thee), "and give thee peace."

CHAPTER XXXVIII.

אחר, 1, *Back*. 2, *After (time)*. 3, *According to (the will)*.

אחר is a homonym. It is a noun, signifying "back." Comp. אחרי המשׁכן, "Behind the tabernacle" (Exod. xxvi. 12); ותצא החנית מאחריו, "The spear came out behind him" (2 Sam. ii. 23).

It is next used in reference to time, signifying "after;" ואחריו לא קם כמוהו, "neither after him arose there any like him" (2 Kings xxiii. 25); אחר הדברים האלה, "After these things" (Gen. xv. 1). In this sense the term occurs frequently.

The term אחר includes also the idea of assimilation and of conformity with the moral principles of some other being. Comp. אחרי יי אלהיכם תלכו, "Ye shall walk after the Lord, your God" (Deut. xiii. 5); אחרי יי ילכו, "They shall walk after the Lord" (Hos. xi. 10), i.e., follow His will, walk in the way of His actions, and imitate His virtues; הלך אחרי צו, "He walked after the commandment" (*Ib.* v. 11). In this sense the word occurs in וראית את אחרי, "And thou shalt' see My back" (Exod. xxxiii. 23); thou shalt perceive that which follows Me, is similar to Me, and is the result of My will, i.e., all things

---

Palquera, זוהר, "splendour." It is difficult to see how the Arabic רעאיה could be translated הדור or זוהר.

created by Me,[1] as will be explained in the course of this treatise.[2]

CHAPTER XXXIX.

לב, 1, *Heart.* 2, *Middle.* 3, *Thought.* 4, *Resolution.* 5, *Will.* 6, *Intellect.*

THE word לב is a homonymous noun, signifying that organ which is the source of life to all beings possessing it. Comp. ויתקעם בלב אבשלום, "And thrust them through the heart of Absalom" (1 Sam. xviii. 14).

This organ being in the middle of the body, the word has been figuratively applied to express "the middle part of a thing." Comp. עד לב השמים, "unto the midst of heaven" (Deut. iv. 11); לבת אש, "the midst of fire"[3] (Exod. iii. 2).

It further denotes "thought." Comp. לא לבי הלך, "Went not mine heart with thee?" (2 Kings v. 26), *i.e.*, I was with thee in my thought when a certain event happened. Similarly must be explained ולא תתורו אחרי לבבכם, "And that ye seek not after your own heart" (Numb. xv. 39), *i.e.*, after your own thoughts; אשר לבבו פונה היום, "Whose heart (*i.e.*, his thought), turneth away this day" (Deut. xxix. 18).

The word לב has also the signification "resolution." Comp. כל שארית ישראל לב אחד להמליך את דוד, "All the rest of Israel were of one heart (*i.e.*, had one determination) to make David king" (1 Chron. xii. 38); ואוילים בחסר לב

[1] Either two explanations of אחרי have been combined, *viz.*, 1, that which follows the ways of God and is similar to Him; 2, that which His will brought into existence, "all His creatures;" or the author alludes here to the ideals שכלים נפרדים which follow the ways of God, are similar to Him, have been created by Him, and are themselves the cause of the existence of the whole universe. Comp. *infra* ch. xlix., and Part II., ch. vi.

[2] See ch. liv., Part I.

[3] Generally לבת is considered to be a contracted form of להבת, "flame." According to Ibn Ezra, it is also a feminine form of לב; comp. Ez. xvi. 30.

ימותו, "but fools die for want of heart," *i.e.*, of counsel[1]; לא יחרף לבבי מימי, "My heart (*i.e.*, my counsel) shall not turn away from this so long as I live" (Job xxvii. 6); for this sentence is preceded by the words, "My righteousness I hold fast, and will not let it go;" and then follows, "my heart shall never turn away from this."—As regards the expression יחרף,[2] I think that it may be compared with the same verb in the phrase שפחה נחרפת לאיש, "a handmaid betrothed to a man" (Lev. xix. 20), where נחרפת is similar in meaning to the Arabic מנחרפה, "turning away," and signifies "turning from the state of slavery to that of marriage."

לב denotes also "will;" comp. ונתתי לכם רעים כלבי, "And I shall give you pastors according to My will,"[3] Jer. iii. 15) היש את לבבך ישר כאשר עם לבבי, "Is thine heart right as my heart is?" (2 Kings x. 15), *i.e.*, is thy will right as my will is? In this sense the word has been figuratively applied to God. Comp. כאשר בלבבי ובנפשי יעשה, "That shall do according to that which is in Mine heart and in My soul" (1 Sam. ii. 35), *i.e.*, according to My will; והיה עיני ולבי שם כל הימים, "And Mine eyes and Mine heart (*i.e.*, My providence and My will) shall be there perpetually" (1 Kings ix. 3).[4]

לב is also used in the sense of "understanding." Comp. ואיש נבוב ילבב, "For vain man will be endowed with a heart" (Job xi. 12), *i.e.*, will be wise; לב חכם לימינו, "A wise man's heart is at his right hand" (Eccles. x. 2), *i.e.*, his understanding is engaged in perfect thoughts, the highest problems. Instances of this kind are numerous. It is in this sense, namely, that of understanding, that the

---

[1] וכן אמרו ואוילים בחסר לב ימותו כלומר בחסרון עצה is omitted by Charizi.

[2] חרף, according to Maimonides, "to turn away," "to change." According to others "to abandon," "to give over," also "to blame."

[3] לב, in this instance, is applied to God. The passage is here out of place; it belongs to the next group introduced by the words, "In this sense the word has been figuratively applied to God."

[4] This instance has been omitted by Charizi.

word לב is used whenever figuratively applied to God; but exceptionally it is also used in the sense of "will." It must, in each passage, be explained in accordance with the context. Also, in the following and similar passages, לב signifies "understanding": וחשבת אל לבבך, "Consider it in thine heart" (Deut. iv. 39); ולא ישיב אל לבו, "And none considereth in his heart" (Is. xliv. 19). Thus, also ולא נתן יי לכם לב לדעת, "Yet the Lord hath not given you an heart to perceive," is analogous in its meaning to "Unto thee it was shown that thou mightest know"[1] (Deut. iv. 35).

As to the passage, ואהבת את יי אלהיך בכל לבבך, "And thou shalt love the Lord thy God with all thine heart" (Ib. vi. 5), I explain "with all thine heart" to mean "with all the powers of thy heart," that is, with all the powers of the body, for they all have their origin in the heart; and the sense of the entire passage is: make the perception of God the aim of all thy actions, as we have stated in our Commentary on the Mishnah, and in our Mishneh Torah.[2]

CHAPTER XL.

רוח, 1, *Air.* 2, *Wind.* 3, *Breath.* 4, *Soul.* 5, *Inspiration.* 6, *Will.*

רוח is a homonym, signifying, "air," that is, one of the four elements. Comp. ורוח אלהים מרחפת, "And the air[3] of God moved" (Gen. i. 2).

It denotes also, "wind." Comp. ורוח הקדים נשא את הארבה, "And the east wind brought the locusts" (Exod. x. 13); רוח ים, "west wind" (*ib.* 19). In this sense the word occurs frequently.

---

[1] This instance is added to throw light on the signification of לב in the preceding quotation, to show that it means "understanding," "comprehension."

[2] Book I. Yesode ha-torah, ii. 2. See also Shemonah Perakim, ch. v.

[3] Generally "the spirit." Comp. Part II., ch. xxx.

Next, it signifies "breath."[1] Comp. רוח הולך ולא ישוב, "A breath that passeth away, and does not come again" (Ps. lxxviii. 39); אשר בו רוח חיים, "wherein is the breath of life" (Gen. vii. 15).

רוח signifies also that which remains of man after his death, and is not subject to destruction. Comp. והרוח תשוב אל האלהים אשר נתנה, "And the spirit shall return unto God who gave it" (Eccl. xii. 7).

Another signification of רוח is "the divine inspiration of the prophets whereby they prophesy"—as we shall explain, when speaking on prophecy, as far as it is opportune to discuss this subject in a treatise like this.—Comp. ואצלתי מן הרוח אשר עליך ושמתי עליהם, "And I will take of the spirit which is upon thee, and will put it upon them" (Num. xi. 17); ויהי כנח עליהם הרוח, "And it came to pass, when the spirit rested upon them" (*ib.* 25); רוח יי דבר בי, "The spirit of the Lord spake by me" (2 Sam. xxiii. 2). רוח is frequently used in this sense.

The meaning of "intention," "will," is likewise contained in the word רוח. Comp. כל רוחו יוציא כסיל, "A fool uttereth all his spirit" (Prov. xxix. 11), *i.e.*, his intention and will; ונבקה רוח מצרים בקרבו ועצתו אבלע, "And the spirit of Egypt shall fail in the midst thereof, and I will destroy the counsel thereof" (Isa. xix. 3), *i.e.*, her intentions will be frustrated, and her plans will be obscured; מי תכן את רוח יי ואיש עצתו יודיענו, "Who has comprehended the spirit of the Lord, or who is familiar with His counsel that he may tell us"?[2] (Isa. xl. 13), *i.e.*, Who knows the order fixed by His will, or perceives the system of His Providence in the existing world, that he may tell us? as we shall explain in the chapters in which we shall speak on Providence.[3]

Thus רוח, when used in reference to God, has generally the fifth signification; sometimes, however, as explained

---

[1] Munk, "l'esprit vital."
[2] The pronominal suffix in יודיענו can be either 3rd sing. (יודיענהו=יודיענו) or 1st pl. (=יודענו). Maimonides takes it to be the latter.
[3] See Part III. ch. xviii.

above, the last signification, viz., "will." The meaning of the word is therefore to be gathered from the context.

CHAPTER XLI.

נפש, 1, *Vitality.* 2, *Blood.* 3, *Reason.* 4, *Soul.* 5, *Will.*

נפש[1] is a homonymous noun, signifying the vitality which is common to all living, sentient beings. Comp. אשר בו נפש חיה, "wherein there is a living soul" (Gen. i. 30). It denotes also "blood," as in לא תאכל הנפש עם הבשר, "Thou shalt not eat the blood with the meat" (Deut. xii. 23). Another signification of the term is "reason," that is, the distinguishing characteristic of man, as in חי יי אשר עשה לנו את הנפש הזאת, "As the Lord liveth that made us this soul" (Jer. xxxviii. 16). It has also the meaning of "soul," the part of man that remains after death; comp. והיתה נפש אדוני צרורה בצרור החיים, "But the soul of my lord shall be bound in the bundle of life" (1 Sam. xxv. 29). Lastly, it denotes "will;" comp. לאסור שריו בנפשו, "To bind his princes at his pleasure" (Ps. cv. 22); also אל תתנני בנפש צרי, "Thou wilt not deliver me unto the will of my enemies" (Ps. xli. 3);[2] and also, according to my opinion, in the passage אם יש את נפשכם לקבור את מתי, "If it be your will that I should bury my dead" (Gen. xxiii. 8); אם יעמד משה ושמואל

[1] Maimonides here distinguishes three kinds of נפש, "soul": 1, that which constitutes animal life in general: vitality, blood; 2, that which constitutes human life in particular, beginning with the birth and ending with the death of each individual: reason, will; 3, that part of man's individuality which exists independently of his body: soul. The first is common to all living creatures; the second is possessed by all human beings; it enables them to acquire the intellect which is the third kind of נפש, and is here stated by Maimonides to be immortal. These three kinds correspond to some extent to the Biblical expressions, 1, נפש; 2, רוח; 3, נשמה. See Ibn Ezra on Eccles. vii. 3.

[2] The original quotation appears to have been אל תתנהו בנפש אויביו (Ps. xli. 3), which the copyists gradually replaced by אל תתנני בנפש צרי (*Ib.* xxvii. 12). (Munk.)

לפני אין נפשי אל העם הזה, "Though Moses and Samuel stood before me, yet my will could not be toward this people" (Jer. xv. 1), that is, I had no pleasure in them, I did not wish to preserve them. When נפש is used in reference to God, it has the meaning "will," as we have already explained with reference to כאשר בלבבי ובנפשי יעשה, "That shall do according to that which is in my will and in mine intention" (1 Sam. ii. 35). Similarly we explain the phrase ותקצר נפשו בעמל ישראל, "And his will to trouble Israel ceased" (Jud. x. 16). Jonathan, the son of Uzziel [in the Targum of the Prophets], did not translate this passage,[1] because he understood נפשו to have the first signification, and finding, therefore, in these words sensation ascribed to God, he omitted them in the translation. If, however, נפש be here taken in the last signification, the sentence can well be explained. For in the passage which precedes, it is stated that Providence abandoned the Israelites, and left them on the brink of death; then they cried and prayed for help, but in vain. When, however, they had thoroughly repented, when their misery had increased, and their enemy had had power over them, He showed mercy to them, and His will to continue their trouble and misery ceased. Note it well, for it is remarkable. The preposition ב in בעמל ישראל has the force of מ; בעמל ישראל has here the same meaning as מעמל ישראל.[2] Grammarians give many instances of this use of the pre-

[1] Kimchi likewise says in his Commentary on Judges x. 16, that Jonathan did not translate this passage; but in our editions of the Targum the passage is translated as follows: ועקת לנפשיה בעמל ישראל. Perhaps the words are a later addition. Ibn Caspi, in his Commentary on the More, asserts that he found the translation in several MSS. In one MSS. of the Targum Jonathan (Arc. fonds. hébr. No. 57, fol. 118a), the Hebrew text is given instead of the translation (Munk).

[2] The instances quoted are not to be compared with this; for there the ב is used instead of מ to indicate the whole, of which a part is taken, while in the present instance the preposition מ is governed by the verb קצר; it means "from," and cannot be replaced by ב. The preposition should rather be translated "through," "because of," and would lead to the same interpretation of the passage.

position ב: וְהַנּוֹתָר בַּבָּשָׂר וּבַלֶּחֶם, "And that which remaineth of the flesh and of the bread" (Lev. viii. 32); אִם מְעַט נִשְׁאַר בַּשָּׁנִים, "If there remains but few of the years" (ib. xxv. 52); גֵּר וְאֶזְרַח הָאָרֶץ, "Of the strangers and of those born in the land"[1] (Exod. xii. 19).

CHAPTER XLII.

חַיִּים 1, *Life.* 2, *Recovery.* 3, *Virtue.*
מָוֶת 1, *Death.* 2, *Illness.* 3, *Vice.*

חַי ("living") signifies a sentient organism (lit. "growing," "having sensation,")[2] comp. כָּל רֶמֶשׂ אֲשֶׁר הוּא חַי, "Every moving thing that liveth" (Gen. ix. 3); it also denotes recovery from a severe illness: וַיְחִי מֵחָלְיוֹ, "And was recovered of his sickness" (Is. xxxviii. 9); בַּמַּחֲנֶה עַד חֲיוֹתָם, "In the camp till they recovered" (Jos. v. 8); בָּשָׂר חַי, "quick, raw flesh" (Lev. xiii. 10).

מָוֶת signifies "death" and "severe illness," as in וַיָּמָת לִבּוֹ בְּקִרְבּוֹ וְהוּא הָיָה לְאָבֶן, "That his heart died within him, and he became as a stone" (1 Sam. xxv. 37), that is, his illness was severe. For this reason it is stated concerning the son of the woman of Zarephath, וַיְחִי חָלְיוֹ חָזָק מְאֹד עַד אֲשֶׁר לֹא נוֹתְרָה בּוֹ נְשָׁמָה, "And his sickness was so sore, that there was no breath left in him" (1 Kings xvii. 17). The simple expression וַיָּמָת would have given the idea that he was very ill, near death, like Nabal when he heard what had taken place.

Some of the Andalusian authors[3] say that his breath was suspended, so that no breathing could be perceived at all, as

---

[1] This instance is omitted in our editions of Ibn Tibbon's translation.

[2] צוֹמֵחַ (organic growth) and מַרְגִּישׁ (sensation) are the two characteristics of the animal world; man is distinguished from the rest of the animal world by being מְדַבֵּר (a speaking or thinking being).

[3] אֶחָד מִן הַסְּפָרַדִים, "One of the Sephardim," Charizi.

sometimes an invalid[1] is seized with a fainting fit[2] or an attack of asphyxia, and it cannot be discovered whether he is alive or dead; in this condition the patient may remain one day or two.[3]

The term חי has also been employed in reference to the acquisition of wisdom. Comp. ויחיו חיים לנפשך, "So shall they be life unto thy soul" (Prov. iii. 22); כי מוצאי מצא חיים, "For whoso findeth me findeth life" (ib. viii. 35); חיים הם למוצאיהם, "For they are life to those that find them" (ib. iv. 22). Such instances are numerous. In accordance with this metaphor, true principles are called life, and corrupt principles, death. Thus the Almighty says, "See, I have set before thee this day life and good and death and evil" (Deut. xxx. 15), showing that "life" and "good," "death," and "evil," are identical, and then He explains these terms.[4] In the same way I understand

---

[1] Charizi, לרוב חולים, "to most invalids."

[2] Charizi, מפגע הרחם והוא חולי יארע לנשים.

[3] The remark of the Andalusian author is not cited in reference to the last-mentioned phrase לא נותרה בו נשמה, but in support of Maimonides' explanation of the verb מות in וימת לבו, i.e., the term which forms the subject of this chapter. It shows that וימת is appropriately said of Nabal when he was more like a dead man than like a living one. (Comp. Abravanel ad locum.) Some critics (Munk and others) believe that the remark refers to the passage עד אשר לא נותרה בו נשמה, misled probably by the use of נשימתו and נשימה in that explanation. If this were correct, Maimonides would by this quotation destroy his own argument that the two meanings of מות correspond to the two meanings of חי, and he would not have omitted to make some remarks in defence of his own view. Much less is it probable that Maimonides hid his own opinion under the cover of the Andalusian authority, from fear of being accused of heresy. (Comp. Narboni, Ibn Caspi, ad locum; also letter of R. Jehudah ibn Alfachar to R. David Kimchi, in קובץ תשובות הרמב״ם, ed. Lichtenberg, Leipzig, 1859, page 2a). In such case our author would have been silent on the point, as there was no necessity for introducing the explanation of מות with the remark of the Andalusian scholar.

[4] The subject to צרח (Hebrew באר) and ובינהמא (Hebrew ופרשם) is ית׳, "God." The term צרח refers to the juxtaposition of החיים והטוב, המות והרע; the expression ובינהמא refers to the further explanation of the terms given in the verses which follow. Munk renders the first by: "Où l'on explique clairement," and leaves the second without translation.

His words, למען תחיון, "That ye may live" (ib. v. 33), in accordance with the traditional interpretation of למען ייטב לך וכו', "That it may be well with thee"[1] (ib. xxii. 7). In consequence of the frequent use of this figure in our language our Sages said,[2] "The righteous even in death are called living, while the wicked even in life are called dead." Note this well.

CHAPTER XLIII.

כנף 1, *Wing.* 2, *Corner (of garment).* 3, *Distant countries.* 4, *Cover.*

כנף is a homonym; most of its meanings are metaphorical.[3] Its primary signification is "wing of a flying creature." Comp. כל צפור כנף אשר תעוף בשמים, "Any winged fowl that flieth in the air" (Deut. iv. 17).

The term was next applied figuratively to the wings or corners of garments; comp. על ארבע כנפות כסותך, "upon the four corners of thy vesture" (ib. xxii. 12).

It was also used to denote the ends of the inhabited part of the earth, and the corners that are most distant from our habitation. Comp. לאחז בכנפות הארץ, "That it might take hold of the ends of the earth" (Job xxxviii. 13); מכנף הארץ זמירות שמענו, "From the uttermost part of the earth have we heard songs" (Is. xxiv. 16).

Ibn Ganach[4] says that כנף is used in the sense of "concealing," in analogy with the Arabic כנפת אלשי, "I have

---

[1] "Life" being identical with "good" or "good actions," (and "death" with "evil" or "bad actions,") it may also denote "the immortal soul," the synthesis of the moral and intellectual perfections of man.—Comp. Pseudo-Jon., *ad locum* בדיל דיוטב לך בעלמא הדין ותוריך יומין בעלמא דאתי.

[2] See Babyl. Talm. Berachoth 18.

[3] Comp. p. 135, note 1.

[4] R. Jonah Ibn Ganach, the Grammarian and Lexicographer, lived in the beginning of the 11th century. See Munk, Notice sur Aboul-Walid, etc.

hidden something," and accordingly explains, ולא יכנף עוד מוריך, "And thy teacher will no longer be hidden or concealed "[1] (Is. xxx. 20). It is a good explanation, and I think, that כנף has the same meaning in ולא יגלה כנף אביו, "He shall not take away the cover of his father" (Deut. xxiii. 1); also in ופרשת כנפיך על אמתך, "Spread, therefore, thy cover over thine handmaid" (Ruth iii. 9). In this sense, I think, the word is figuratively applied to God and to angels (for angels are not corporeal, according to my opinion, as I shall explain).[2] The passage אשר באת לחסות תחת כנפיו, must therefore be translated "Under whose protection thou art come to trust" (Ruth ii. 12); and wherever כנף occurs in reference to angels, it means concealment. You have surely noticed the words of Isaiah, בשתים יכסה פניו ובשתים יכסה רגליו (Is. vi. 2), "With twain he covered his face, and with twain he covered his feet." Their meaning is this: The cause of his existence (that of the angel) is hidden and concealed; this is meant by the covering of the face. The things of which he (the angel) is the cause, and which are called his feet (as I stated in speaking of the homonym רגל), are likewise concealed;[3] for the actions of the intelligences[4] are not seen, and their ways[5] are, except after long study, not understood, on account of two reasons—the one of which is contained in their own properties, the other in ourselves; that is to say, because our perception is imperfect and the ideals are difficult to be fully comprehended. As regards the phrase ובשתים יעופף, I shall explain in a special chapter (xlix.) why flight has been attributed to angels.

His Grammar Sefer ha-rikmah was published by Kirchheim and Goldberg (Frankfort, 1856); his Lexicon by A. Neubauer (Oxford, 1875).

[1] See "The Book of Hebrew Roots by Abu'l-Walid Marwân ibn Janâh," ed. Ad. Neubauer (Oxford, 1875), page 325.

[2] See Part II., ch. vi.

[3] Charizi adds here מכחות השכל, "from the powers of the intellect."

[4] The terms שכלים and מלאכים are identical, according to Maimonides.

[5] אתרחא, lit., "forces" or "impressions"; Ibn Tibbon, ענינם.

CHAPTER XLIV.

עין 1, *Well.* 2, *Eye.* 3, *Attention.*

עין is a homonym, signifying "fountain;" comp. על עין חמים, "By a fountain of water" (Gen. xvi. 7). It next denotes "eye";[1] comp. עין תחת עין, "Eye for eye" (Ex. xxi. 24). Another meaning of עין is "providence," as it is said concerning Jeremiah, קחנו ועיניך שים עליו, "Take him and direct thine attention to him" (Jer. xxxix. 12). In this figurative sense it is to be understood when used in reference to God; comp. והיו עיני ולבי שם כל הימים, "And My providence and My pleasure shall be there perpetually" (1 Kings ix. 3), as we have already explained (page 140); תמיד עיני יי אלהיך בה, "The eyes, *i.e.*, the Providence of the Lord thy God, are always upon it (Deut. xi. 12); עיני יי המה משוטטים בכל הארץ[2] "They are the eyes of the Lord, which run to and fro through the whole earth" (Zech. iv. 10), *i.e.*, His providence is extended over everything that is on earth, as will be explained in the chapters,[3] in which we shall treat of Providence. When, however, the word "eye" (עין) is connected with the verb "to see" (ראה or חזה) as in פקח עיניך וראה, "Open thine eyes, and see" (1 Kings xix. 16); עיניו יחזו, "His eyes behold" (Ps. xi. 4), the phrase denotes perception of the mind, not that of the senses; for every sensation is a passive state, as is well known to you, and God is active, not passive, as will be pointed out.[4]

---

[1] It deserves notice that the signification "eye," which is generally believed to be the original meaning of עין, is placed by Maimonides after that of "fountain." According to Munk, this was done because "eye" is more similar to the metaphorical "providence," which follows next, than "fountain."

[2] In the Arabic text and in the translation of Ibn Tibbon the fem. form משוטטות is quoted instead of משוטטים as we have in the several editions of the Bible.   [3] See Part III. xvii.   [4] *Infra*, ch. lv.

CHAPTER XLV.

שמע 1, To hear. 2, To accept. 3, To understand.[1]

שמע is used homonymously with several meanings, signifying "to hear" and also "to obey." As regards the first signification, comp. לא ישמע על פיך "Neither let it be heard out of thy mouth" (Ex. xxiii. 13); וחקל נשמע בית פרעה, "And the fame thereof was heard in Pharaoh's house" (Gen. xlv. 16). Instances of this kind are numerous.

Equally frequent are the instances of שמע being used in the sense of "to obey:" ולא שמעו אל משה, "And they hearkened not unto Moses" (Ex. vi. 9). אם ישמעו ויעבדו, "If they obey and serve him" (Job xxxvi. 11); ולכם הנשמע "Shall we then hearken unto you" (Neh. xiii. 27); אשר לא ישמע את דבריך, "Whosoever will not hearken unto thy words" (Jos. i. 18).

The verb שמע also signifies "to know" ("to understand"), comp. גוי אשר לא תשמע לשונו, "A nation whose tongue, i.e., his language, thou shalt not understand" (Deut. xxviii. 49). The expression שמע, used in reference to God, must be taken in the sense of perceiving, which is part of the third signification, whenever, according to the literal interpretation of the passage, it appears to have the first meaning:

---

[1] The interpretation of homonymous terms signifying parts and organs of the body is properly followed by a discussion of the figurative use of verbs of sensation in reference to God. In accordance with the method adopted in the preceding chapter to select from the organs of sense, one (עין the eye) for special discussion, the author selected the verb שמע, "to hear," to serve as an example of verbs of sensation. He then explains that the use of such verbs in reference to God serves to convey to man the notion of God's existence (xlvi.); but some expressions though in reality exactly the same as all the rest, were never applied to God (xlvii.); Onkelos, in his Targum of the Law, makes a similar distinction, even as regards the verbs "to hear" and "to see," שמע and ראה (xlviii.). Ibn Caspi remarks בזה ממנו בבחירה השלים והמורה כאלו אמר שמע בני מה שאמרתי עד עתה מן השתומים. "The author selected שמע for the concluding chapter, as if to say, Listen, my son, to all that has been said so far on the use of homonymous expressions."

comp. וישמע יי, "And the Lord heard it" (Num. xi. 1); בשמעו את תלנתיכם, "For that He heareth your murmurings" (Ex. xvi. 7). In all such passages mental perception is meant. When, however, according to the literal interpretation the verb appears to have the second signification,[1] it implies, that God responded to the prayer of man and fulfilled his wish, or did not respond and did not fulfil his wish: שמע אשמע צעקתו, "I will surely hear his cry" (Ex. xxii. 23); ושמעתי כי חנון אני, "I will hear, for I am gracious" (ib. 27); הטה אזנך ושמע, "Bow down thine ear, and hear" (2 Kings xix. 16); ולא שמע יי בקלכם ולא האזין אליכם, "But the Lord would not hearken to your voice, nor give ear unto you" (Deut. i. 45); גם כי תרבו תפלה איננו שומע, "Yea, when ye make many prayers, I will not hear" (Is. i. 15); כי אינני שומע אותך, "For I will not hear thee" (Jer. vii. 16). There are many instances in which שמע has this sense.[2]

Remarks will now be presented to you on these metaphors and similes, which will quench your thirst, and explain to you all their meanings without leaving a doubt.

CHAPTER XLVI.

Senses are ascribed to God in order to express that He exists.

WE have already stated, in one of the chapters of this treatise,[3] that there is a great difference between bringing to view the existence of a thing and demonstrating its true essence. We can lead others to notice the existence of an

---

[1] It appears that Maimonides found an anthropomorphism in the application of the verbs "to accept," "to listen" to God, there being implied in those verbs a kind of influence exercised upon God (הפעלות), which is not implied in the phrase "to reply to the prayer of a man."

[2] Maimonides probably refers to what he is going to explain in ch. xlvi.—ch. xlviii., as to the use of similes and metaphors in reference to God.

[3] See ch. xxxiii., p. 116.

object by pointing to its accidents, actions, or even most remote relations to other objects,[1] *e.g.*, if you wish to describe the king of a country to one of his subjects who does not know him, you can give a description and an account of his existence in many ways. You will either say to him, the tall man with a fair complexion and grey hair is the king, thus describing him by his accidents; or you will say, the king is the person round whom are seen a great multitude of men on horse and on foot, and soldiers with drawn swords, over whose head banners are waving, and before whom trumpets are sounded; or it is the person living in the palace in a particular region of a certain country; or it is the person who ordered the building of that wall, or the construction of that bridge; or by some other similar acts and things relating to him. His existence can be demonstrated in a still more indirect way, *e.g.*, if you are asked whether this land has a king, you will undoubtedly answer in the affirmative. "What proof have you?" "The fact that this banker here, a weak and little person, stands before this large mass of gold pieces, and that poor man, tall and strong, who stands before him asking in vain for alms of the weight of a carob-grain,[2] is rebuked and is compelled to go away by the mere force of words; for had he not feared the king he would, without hesitation, have killed[3] the banker, or pushed him away and taken as much of the money as he held in his hand."[4] Consequently, this is a proof that this country has a ruler, and his existence is proved by the well-

---

[1] Maimonides mentions here first, "His actions," and then "His relations to others"; in the instance subsequently given for illustration the order is reversed.

[2] Arabic בְּרוּבָּה; Charizi פרוטה, "an obolus;" Ibn Tibbon משקל שעורה, "the weight of a barley corn." Munk, "un grain de caroube." According to Munk one בְּרוּבָּה is equal in weight to four grains of barley.

[3] Arabic לבאדר בקטלה, "he could have surprised and killed him;" Ibn Tibbon היה מתחיל בהריגתו, "he would have commenced to kill him (that is before being pushed away by the rich man);" Charizi היה יבול להרנו, "he could have killed him."

[4] Ibn Tibbon literally, מה שבידו; Charizi, מה שלפניו; Munk, "qu'il a

regulated affairs of the country, on account of which the king is respected and the punishments decreed by him are feared. In this whole example nothing is mentioned that indicated his characteristics, and his essential properties, by virtue of which he is king. The same is the case with the information concerning the Creator given to the ordinary classes of men in all prophetical books and in the Law.[1] For it was found necessary to teach all of them that God exists, and that He is in every respect the most perfect Being, that is to say, He exists not only in the sense in which the earth and the heavens exist, but He exists and possesses life, wisdom, power,[2] activity, and all other properties which our belief in His existence must include, as will be shown below. That God exists was then shown to ordinary men by means of similes taken from physical bodies;[3] that He is living by a simile taken from motion, because ordinary men consider only the body as fully, truly, and undoubtedly existing; that which is connected with a body but is itself not a body, although believed to exist, has a lower degree of existence on account of its dependence on the body for existence. That, however, which is neither itself a body, nor a force

---

entre les mains." The suffix in בידו either refers to the rich man or to the poor, in the latter case supply לקחת, " to take" (he would have taken as much as he could).

[1] It deserves notice that the books of the Prophets are mentioned before the Law. By תורה, the author perhaps means both the written law and the oral, or a climax was intended by the phrase ובתורה, "and even in the Law," the book which is to serve as a practical guide to all the educated as well as the uneducated, "figurative language was unavoidable."

[2] In the illustration which follows, this term יכול is passed over in silence. The figurative expressions for the existence and the life of God are discussed first; and then His wisdom or knowledge and His activity. These four attributes are fully treated in ch. lvii.

[3] The phrase מושג במחשבות גופיות of Charizi has the same meaning as דמיון הגשמות of Ibn Tibbon. מחשבה, and the verbs חשב are not used in the sense of "thought" or "thinking," but are employed in reference to man's imagination, a faculty considered to be intermediate between the purely physical action of the senses and the purely intellectual operations of the mind. מחשבה signifies "image," and מחשבות גופיות " images taken from physical bodies." Comp. chap. xxxii., page 111, note 1.

within a body, is non-existent according to man's original notions, and is above all excluded from the range of imagination. In the same manner motion is considered by the ordinary man as identical with life; what cannot move voluntarily from place to place has no life, although motion is not part of the definition of life, but an accident connected with it.[1] The perception by the senses, especially by hearing and seeing, is best known to us; we have no idea or notion of any other mode of communication between the soul of one man and that of another than by means of speaking, *i.e.*, by the sound produced by lips, tongue, and the other organs of speech. When, therefore, we are to be informed[2] that God has *a knowledge* of things, and that communication is made by Him to the Prophets who convey it to us, they represent Him to us as seeing and hearing, *i.e.*, as perceiving and knowing those things which can be seen and heard. They represent Him to us as speaking, *i.e.*, that communications from Him reach the Prophets; that is to be understood by the term "prophecy," as will be fully explained.[3] God is described as active, because we do not know any other mode of producing a thing except by direct action. He is said to have a soul in the sense that He is living, because all living beings are generally supposed to have a soul; although[4] the term soul (נפש) is, as has been shown,[5] a homonym.

[1] See ch. xlii., where חי "living" is defined as being צומח טרגיש, "growing and having sensation." Living beings, therefore, do not move because they have life, but their motion is owing to the circumstance (מקרה) that it serves living beings as the means of acquiring perfection (שלמות בעלי חיים). Comp. ch. xxvi., p. 91.

[2] Charizi, וכאשר הורו רבותינו, "And when our teachers taught."

[3] See Part II. ch. xxxii. *sqq.*

[4] That is to say, the Prophets were justified in applying this term to God, since it is homonymous, but its application to God had also the purpose mentioned here.—The explanation of נפש as being equal to חי is here out of place, and was probably added parenthetically, when the chapter was revised by the author; the sentence beginning "Again since we perform" appears to have originally followed the words "by direct action."

[5] *Supra*, ch. xli. The Arabic תבין has been rendered inaccurately by Ibn Tibbon as well as Charizi, יתבאר (fut.) instead of נתבאר (past).

Again, since we perform all these actions only by means of corporeal organs, we figuratively ascribe to God the organs of locomotion, as feet, and their soles;[1] organs of hearing, seeing, and smelling, as ear, eye, and nose; organs and substance[2] of speech, as mouth, tongue, and sound; organs for the performance of work, as hand, its fingers, its palm, and the arm. In short, these organs of the body are figuratively ascribed to God, who is above all imperfection, to express that He performs certain acts; and these acts are figuratively ascribed to Him to express that He possesses certain perfections different from those acts themselves. *E.g.*, we say that He has eyes, ears, hands, a mouth, a tongue, to express that He sees, hears, acts, and speaks; but seeing and hearing are attributed to Him to indicate simply that He perceives. You thus find in Hebrew instances in which the perception of the one sense is named instead of the other; thus, "See the word of the Lord" (Jer. ii. 31), in the same meaning as "Hear the word of the Lord," for the sense of the phrase is, "Perceive what He says;" similarly the phrase, "See the smell of my son" (Gen. xxvii. 27) has the same meaning as "Smell the smell of my son," for it relates to the perception of the smell. In the same way are used the words, "And all the people saw the thunders and the lightnings" (Exod. xx. 15), although the passage also contains the description of a prophetical vision, as is well known and understood by every one among the people.[3] Action and speech are like-

---

[1] כפותם is expressly added in reference to Ezek. xliii. 7.

[2] The "sound" or "voice" (קול) is, as it were, the substance of which the speech or the words are formed (חומר הדבור) through the organs of speech. Charizi כח החניון, "the faculty of utterance"; the root הגה being here used in its primary signification, "to utter." "Mouth" and "tongue" refer to "organs of speech."

[3] Two explanations are given by Maimonides for the use of the verb ראים, with the object את הקלות, viz.: (a) ראה, signifies "to perceive," and may be used in the sense of "to hear," "to see," "to smell," etc.; (b) a prophetical vision is described in this verse, not a real physical perception, and therefore the verb ראה can be applied to both thunder and lightning. For the Arabic

wise figuratively applied to God to express that a certain influence has emanated from Him, as will be explained (ch. lxv. and ch. lxvi.). The physical organs which are attributed to God in the writings of the Prophets are either organs of locomotion, indicating life; organs of sensation, indicating perception; organs of touch,[1] indicating action; or organs of speech, indicating the divine inspiration[2] of the Prophets, as will be explained.[3]

The object of all these indications[4] is to establish in our minds the notion of the existence of a living being, the Maker of everything,[5] who also possesses a knowledge of the things which He has made. We shall explain, when we come to speak of the inadmissibility of Divine attributes, that all these various attributes convey but one notion, viz., that of the essence of God. The sole object of this chapter is to explain in what sense physical organs are ascribed to the Most Perfect Being, namely, that they are mere indications of the actions generally performed by means of these organs, which actions, being perfections respecting ourselves, are predicated of Him, because we wish to express[6] that He is most perfect in every respect, as we remarked above[7] in explaining the Rabbinical phrase, "The language of the Torah is like the language of man." Instances of organs

---

in (המקום) אלמקאם, probably taking המאמר has Ibn Tibbon ,אלמקאם term the sense of "the passage" or "the verse." Munk conjectures that he read אלמקאל, but this is not at all necessary. Charizi translates המעמד, but certainly the whole phrase מעמד הר סיני, "the standing round the mount Sinai," though principally referring to the act of divine revelation, cannot be considered as indicating a mere "vision."

[1] Charizi, כלי הפעולה, "the organs of actions."
[2] Lit., "the transmission of ideas" (intelligence); Ibn Tibbon השכלים; Charizi, דעת נאצל, "abstract knowledge."
[3] Part II. ch. xii.
[4] Charizi, הסמיכות, "metaphors." Ibn Tibbon, ההערות, "indications."
[5] The attribute of being omnipotent יכול, mentioned above is omitted here.
[6] Ibn Tibbon, בעבור שנודה, "that we may confess." According to Munk we should read שֶׁנֻגָּרָה, "that we be guided," corresponding to the Arabic לנדל. Charizi, כדי להורות.   [7] See ch. xxvi.

of locomotion being applied to the Creator occur as follows:—
"My footstool" (Is. lxvi. 1); "the place of the soles of My feet"[1] (Ez. xliii. 7). For examples of organs of touch[2] applied to God, comp. "the hand of the Lord" (Ex. ix. 3); "with the finger of God" (*ib.* xxxi. 18); "the work of Thy fingers" (Ps. viii. 4); "And Thou hast laid Thine hand upon me" (*ib.* cxxxix. 5); "The arm of the Lord" (Is. liii. 1); "Thy right hand, O Lord" (Exod. xv. 6). In instances like the following, organs of speech are attributed to God: "The mouth of the Lord has spoken" (Is. i. 20); "And He would open His lips against thee" (Job xi. 5); "The voice of the Lord is powerful" (Ps. xxix. 4); "And His tongue as a devouring fire" (Is. xxx. 27). Organs of sensation are attributed to God in instances like the following: "His eyes behold, His eyelids try" (Ps. xi. 4); "The eyes of the Lord which run to and fro"[3] (Zech. iv. 10); "Bow down Thine ear unto me, and hear" (2 Kings xix. 16); "You have kindled a fire in My nostril" (Jer. xvii. 5). Of the inner parts of the human body only the heart is figuratively applied to God, because "heart" is a homonym, and denotes also "intellect";[4] it is besides the source of animal life. In phrases like המו מעי לו, "My bowels are troubled for him" (Jer. xxxi. 20); המון מעיך, "The sounding of Thy bowels" (Is. lxiii. 15), the term מעי, "bowels," is used in the sense of לב, "heart;" for מעי[5] is used both in a general and in a specific meaning; it denotes specifically "bowels," but more generally it can be used as the name of any inner organ, including "heart." The correctness of this argument can be proved by the phrase ותורתך בתוך מעי, lit., "And Thy law is within my bowels" (Ps. xl. 9),

---

[1] This instance is omitted in the translation of Ibn Tibbon.
[2] See p. 156, note 1.
[3] Comp. ch. xliv., p. 149, note 2.   [4] See ch. xxxix., p. 140.
[5] מעי is either the supposed singular form of the word, or the plural form contained in מֵעָי and מֵעֶיךָ. Munk believes that מעי is Arabic. This is not the case, as the meanings contained in a root in Arabic, are not necessarily implied in the same root in Hebrew. Maimonides would not have introduced an Arabic word without mentioning that it is Arabic.

which is identical with ותורתך בתוך לבי, "And Thy law is within my heart." For that reason the prophet employed in this verse the phrase המו מעי (and המון מעיך;[1]) the verb חמה is in fact used more frequently in connection with לב, "heart," than with any other organ; comp. חומה לי לבי, " My heart maketh a noise in me" (Jer. iv. 19). Similarly,[2] the shoulder is never used as a figure in reference to God, because it is known as a mere instrument of transport, and also comes into close contact with the thing which it carries. With far greater reason the organs of nutrition[3] are never attributed to God; they are at once recognised as signs of imperfection. In fact all organs, both the external and the internal, are employed in the various actions of the soul; some, as *e.g.*, all inner organs, are the means of preserving the individual for a certain time; others, as the organs of generation are the means of preserving the species; others are the means of improving the condition of man and bringing his actions to perfection, as the hands, the feet, and the eyes, all of which tend to render motion, action, and perception more perfect. Animate beings require motion in order to be able to approach that which is conducive to their welfare, and to move away from the opposite; they require the senses in order to be able to discern what is injurious to them and what is beneficial. In addition, man requires various kinds of handiwork, to prepare his food, clothing, and dwelling; and he is compelled by his physical constitution to perform such work, namely, to prepare what is good for him. Some kinds of work also occur among certain animals, as far as such work is required by those animals. I do not believe that any man can doubt the correctness of the assertion that the Creator is not in need of anything for the con-

[1] The second instance המון מעיך, appears to be a later addition on account of בזה הפסוק, " in this verse," which refers only to one instance.

[2] *I.e.*, Like the inner organs, with the exception of the heart, the shoulders are generally considered as too material to be employed in a figurative sense in reference to God.

[3] See ch. xxvi.

tinuance of His existence, or for the improvement of His condition. Therefore, God has no organs, or, what is the same, He is not a body; His actions are accomplished by His Essence, not by any organ, and as undoubtedly physical forces are connected with the organs, He does not possess any forces, that is to say, He has, besides His Essence, nothing[1] that could be the cause of His action, His knowledge, or His will; for attributes are nothing but forces under a different name.[2] It is not my intention to discuss the question in this chapter. Our Sages laid down a general[3] principle, by which the literal sense of the physical attributes of God mentioned by the prophets is rejected; a principle which evidently shows that our Sages were far from the belief in the corporeality of God, and that they did not think any person capable of misunderstanding it, or entertaining any doubt about it.[4] For that reason they employ in the Talmud and the Midrashim phrases similar to those contained in the prophecies,[5] without any circumlocution; they knew

[1] By this phrase the author means to say that God does not possess any qualities or attributes; and therefore the author continues, "for attributes are the same as forces."

[2] *I.e.*, In the same way as physical forces are denied to God, all attributes or qualities must be denied, for to assume that God is בעל תוארים, "possessing attributes," is the same as to say God is בעל כח, "possessing (physical) force." Both phrases imply a dualism—God, and forces or qualities. Those who apply to God תוארים, "attributes," while decrying כחות, "forces," are mistaken, because they only substitute one name for another, without weakening the original objection. Munk explains the sentence thus: The attributes of God—the term generally used—are nothing else but the sum total of forces which only differ in name, but in reality are the same thing—the essence of God. Maimonides could not have meant this; for instead of justifying the use of the term בעל כחות, or בעל תוארים, he constantly reproaches those who use it.

[3] Munk: "D'une grande portée."—Ibn Tibbon, כולל.

[4] Munk: "Et qu'il n'y a chez eux rien qui puisse faire naître l'erreur ou le doute." This is wrong. There are passages in the Talmud which may seem to imply a belief in the corporeality, and Maimonides does not deny this. (Comp. end of ch. xxxi.) Maimonides says that the belief in the corporeality (ענין ההגשמה) was too absurd for them to assume that the use of metaphors would lead a person to accept it.

[5] Charizi: המקרא והנבואה.

that there could not be any doubt about their metaphorical character, or any danger whatever of their being misunderstood; and that all such expressions would be understood as figurative [language], employed to communicate to the intellect the notion of His existence. Now, it was well known that in figurative language God is compared to a king who commands, cautions, punishes, and rewards, his subjects, and whose servants and attendants publish his orders, so that they might be acted upon, and they also execute whatever he wishes. Thus the Sages adopted that figure, used it frequently, and introduced such speech, consent, and refusal[1] of a king, and other usual acts of kings, as became necessary by that figure. In all these instances they were sure that no doubt or confusion would arise from it. The general[2] principle alluded to above is contained in the following saying of our Sages, mentioned in Bereshith Rabba (c. xxvii.), "Great was the power of the Prophets; they compared the creature to its Creator; comp. 'And over the resemblance of the throne was a resemblance like the appearance of man'" (Ezek. i. 26). They have thus plainly stated that all those images which the Prophets perceived, *i.e.*, in prophetic visions, are images created by God. This is perfectly correct; for every image in our imagination has been created.[3] How pregnant is the expression גדול כחן, "Great is their boldness!" They indicated by it, that they themselves found it very remarkable; for whenever they perceived a word or act difficult to explain, or apparently objectionable, they used that phrase; *e.g.*, a certain rabbi has performed the act (of

---

[1] פי אלאמר "respecting a thing" (omitted in the English translation as superfluous) refers alike to speech, consent, and refusal. Ibn Tibbon renders the Arabic אלתרדד by החזרה; the latter does not mean "repetition," but "refusal" (Munk: "inculquer des ordres"); but a separate term for giving orders is not required here, it is implied in "speech."—Charizi: לשוב, "to return."

[2] See p. 159, note 3.

[3] The images of our imagination, as distinguished from the ideals, are our creation; but the images in the imagination of the Prophets in a prophetic vision are created by God, and produced directly by His will in their minds.

"chalitsah") with a slipper, alone and by night. Another Rabbi, thereupon exclaimed כמה רב גובריה, "How great is his boldness to have followed the opinion of the minority."[1] The phrase רב גובריה in Chaldee has the same sense as גדול כחו in Hebrew. Hence, in the preceding quotation, the sense is, How remarkable is the language which the Prophets were obliged to use[2] when they speak of God the Creator in terms signifying properties of beings created by Him. This deserves attention. Our Sages have thus stated in distinct and plain terms that they are far from believing in the corporeality of God; and in the figures and forms seen in a prophetical vision, though belonging to created beings, the Prophets, to use the words of our Sages, "compared the creature to its Creator." If, however, after these explanations, any one wishes out of malice to cavil at them, and to find fault with them, though their method is neither comprehended nor understood by him, they will sustain no injury by it.

CHAPTER XLVII.

Only some sensations were metaphorically attributed to God.

WE have already stated several times[3] that the prophetic books never attribute to God anything which ordinary men

[1] Babyl. Talm., Yebhamoth 104a.—Raba bar Chiya of Ktesiphon, broke three rules in allowing the act of chalitsah (Deut. xxv. 9) to be performed—*a*, with a slipper (of cloth) instead of sandal (of leather); *b*, when alone instead of in the presence of several Rabbis; *c*, by night instead of by day.—Instead of ביחידאה, "following the opinion of the minority," the reading of Charizi and of our editions of the Talmud, the Arabic text (according to the edition of Munk), and the translation of Ibn Tibbon have the reading ביחידאה, "by himself" ("en particulier," Munk). This is wrong. For it could only be in reference to the expression ביחידאה that the minority was described (*ibid.*) as having consisted of R. Shimeon and R. Jochanan, or, according to another interpretation, of R. Jishmael b. R. Jose.

[2] *I.e.*, the Prophets have done something which we do not know how to justify.

[3] פעמים, the literal rendering of מראת in Ibn Tibbon's Version, has here the same meaning as פעמים רבות, employed by Charizi. See ch. xxvi. and xlvi.

M

consider a defect, or which they cannot in their imagination combine with the idea of the Almighty,[1] although such terms may not otherwise be different from those which were employed as metaphors in relation to God. Indeed all things which are attributed to God are considered in some way to be perfection,[2] or can at least be imagined [1] [as appertaining to Him].

We must now show why, according to this principle,[3] the senses of hearing, sight and smell, are attributed to God, but not those of taste and touch. He is equally elevated above the use of all the five senses; they are all defective as regards perception,[4] even for those who have no other source of knowledge; because they are passive, receive impressions from without,[5] and are subject to interruptions and sufferings, as much as the other organs of the body. By saying that God sees, we mean to state that He perceives visible things; "He hears" is identical with saying "He perceives audible things"; in the same way we might say, "He tastes and He touches," in the sense of "He perceives objects which man perceives by means of taste and touch." For, as regards perception, the senses are identical; if we deny the existence of one sensation in God, we must deny that of all other sensations, *i.e.*, the perceptions of the five senses; and if we attribute the existence of one sensation to Him, *i.e.*, the perception appertaining to one of the senses, we must attribute all the five sensations. Nevertheless, we find in Holy Writ, "And

---

[1] This condition is neither mentioned in ch. xxvi., nor in ch. xlvi., nor is it illustrated by any instance in this chapter. It is perhaps a repetition of the first condition in different words.

[2] Charizi, כחות הגוף, "faculties of the body." The whole sentence must accordingly be translated as follows: "For all figures which are applied to God cause men to believe that God possesses physical properties."

[3] Ibn Tibbon, לפי ההנחה הזאת; Charizi, לפי השיעור הזה. Both phrases have the same meaning, "according to this assumption."—The two different readings found in MSS. of the Arabic text, אלתקריר and אלתקדיר, correspond to these two different translations in Hebrew. (Munk.)

[4] Charizi, בבחינת השכל, "if compared with reason."

[5] This seems to have been added as an explanation of "passive." It is omitted in the translation of Ibn Tibbon.

God saw" (Gen. vi. 5); "And God heard" (Num. xi. 1); "And God smelt" (Gen. viii. 21); but we do not meet with the expressions, "And God tasted," "And God touched." According to our opinion, the reason of this is to be found in the idea, which has a firm hold in the minds of all men, that God does not come into contact with a body in the same manner as one body comes into contact with another, since He is not even seen by the eye. While these two senses, namely, taste and touch, only act when in close contact with the object, by sight, hearing, and smell, even distant objects[1] are perceived. These, therefore, were considered by the multitude appropriate expressions [to be figuratively applied to God].[2] Besides, the object in figuratively applying the sensations to Him, could only have been to express that He perceives our actions; but hearing and sight are[3] sufficient for that, namely, for the perception of what a man does or says. Thus our Sages, among other admonitions, gave the following advice and warning: "Know what is above thee, a seeing eye, and a hearing ear." (Mishnah Abhoth, ii. 1.)

You, however, know that, strictly speaking, the condition of all the sensations is the same, that the same argument which is employed against the existence of touch and taste in God, may be used against sight, hearing, and smell; for they all are material perceptions and impressions which are subject to change. There is only this difference, that the former, touch and taste, are at once recognised as deficiencies, while the others are considered as perfections. In a similar manner the defect of the imagination is easily seen, less easily that of thinking and reasoning. Imagination (רעיון),

[1] Lit., "the substances having (or bearing) those qualities," i.e., those qualities which are the cause of the sensations of sight, hearing, and smell.

[2] The words, "to be figuratively applied to God," correspond to the Hebrew phrase ליחסם לשם in Ibn Tibbon's translation. The Arabic text and Charizi's translation do not contain the phrase.

[3] In the Arabic and the two Hebrew translations the two senses, hearing and seeing, are treated as one faculty; therefore we have מספיק, "sufficient," and בו, "by it," in the singular.

therefore, was never[1] employed as a figure in speaking of God, while thought and reason (מחשבה and תבונה) are figuratively ascribed to Him.[2] Comp. "The thoughts (מחשבותיו) which the Lord thought" (Jer. xlix. 20); "And with His understanding (ובתבונתו) He stretched out the heavens" (ib. x. 12). The inner senses were therefore treated in the same way as the external; some are figuratively applied to God, some not. All this is according to the language of man; he ascribes to God what he considers a perfection, and does not ascribe to Him what he considers a defect. In truth, however, no real attribute, implying an addition to His essence, can be applied to Him, as will be proved.[3]

CHAPTER XLVIII.

קבל, שמיע קדם = שמע
חזא, גלי קדם = ראה } in Targum.

WHENEVER in the Pentateuch the term שמע, "to hear," is applied to God, Onkelos, the Proselyte, does not translate it literally, but paraphrases it, merely expressing that a certain speech reached Him, i.e., He perceived it, or that He accepted or did not accept, when it refers to supplication and prayer as its object. The phrase שמע יי is therefore rendered by him regularly either שמיע קדם יי, "It was heard before the Lord," or [קבל, "He accepted"] when it is employed in relation to supplication and prayer; [e.g.] קבלא אקבל, "I will surely accept," corresponding to the original, שמוע אשמע צעקתו, "I will surely hear his crying" (Exod. xxii. 22).

[1] Ibn Caspi: ואם אמצא אם לא כאשר דמיתי אינו מענין כח המדמה רק כמו שחשבתי. "When we find in Isaiah (xiv. 24) דמיתי applied to God, it does not mean 'I imagined,' but 'I thought.'"—In the Moreh ha-moreh this is considered an oversight on the part of Maimonides: ולא נזכר למורנו ז״ל אם לא וגו׳, "And our Teacher did not think of the passage," etc.

[2] The whole of this sentence is omitted in Charizi's translation.
[3] See ch. li. sqq.

PART I.—CHAPTER XLVIII.   165

This principle is followed by Onkelos in his translation of the Pentateuch without any exception. But as regards the term ראה, "to see," his renderings vary in a remarkable manner,[1] and I was unable to discern his principle or method. In some instances he translates וירא יי by וחזא יי, "and God saw;" in others by וגלי קדם יי, "it was revealed before the Lord." The use of the phrase וחזא יי is sufficient evidence that the term חזא in Chaldee is homonymous, and that it denotes mental perception as well as the sensation of sight. This being the case, I am surprised that, in some instances avoiding the literal rendering, he substituted for it וגלי קדם יי, "And it was revealed before the Lord." When I, however, examined the various readings in the version of Onkelos, which I either saw myself or heard from others during the time of my studies, I found that the term "to see," ראה, when connected with wrong, injury, or violence, was paraphrased by וגלי קדם יי, "It was manifest before the Lord." There is no doubt that the term חזא in that language denotes complete apprehension and reception of the object in the state in which it has been perceived.[2] When Onkelos, therefore, found the verb "to see" connected with the object "wrong," he did not render it חזא, but וגלי קדם. Now, I noticed that in all instances of the Pentateuch where ראה is referred to God, he

[1] The Arabic תלון פי הלך תלונה עניבא "He had in this a great variety of colours." Ibn Tibbon, פירש בו פירושים מופלאים, "He explained it by explanations distinguished" (from each other), or "He explained it in an extraordinary way."—Charizi, נהפך בה מצד אל צד הפוך מופלא, "He turned respecting it from one side to the other in a wonderful manner."

[2] According to Maimonides, the term חזא in Chaldee implies a closer and longer contact between subject and object than the Hebrew ראה.—The literal translation of the Arabic is: The verb חזא in Chaldee denotes the perception and the fixing of the thing perceived in the manner in which it has been perceived, i.e., the verb, חזא, "to look on," implies, besides the mere act of perceiving, also the act of retaining impressions left after the object has been withdrawn.—Munk: חזא, implique indubitablement l'idée de percevoir et d'avouer (אקראר) la chose perçue telle qu'elle a été perçue.— Charizi renders the Arabic אקראר by להושיב, "to settle," or "to fix;" Ibn Tibbon by ידיעת, "knowledge of," i.e., the retaining of the image of the object perceived, and also by ישוב, see infra, which expresses this idea more clearly.

translated it by חזא, except those instances which I will mention to you: ארי גלי קדם (Gen. xxix. 32), כי ראה יי בעניי, יי עלבוני, "For my affliction was revealed before the Lord;" (ibid. xxxi. 12), כי ראיתי את כל אשר לבן עומה לך, ארי גלי קדמי ית כל די לבן עבד לך, "For all that Laban doeth unto thee is revealed before me;"—although the first person in the sentence refers to the angel [and not to God], Onkelos does not ascribe to him that perception which implies complete comprehension of the object, because the object is "iniquity"—וירא אלהים את בני ישראל (Exod. ii. 25), וגלי קדם יי שיעבודא דבני ישראל "The oppression of the children of Israel was known to the Lord;" ראה ראיתי את עני עמי אשר במצרים (Exod. iii. 7), מיגלא גלי קדמי ית שעבודא דעמי, "The oppression of My people was surely known to Me;" וגם ראיתי את הלחץ (ib. 9), גלי קדמי ית דוחקא, "The affliction is known to Me;" (ibid. iv. 31), וכי ראה את ענים, ארי גלי קדמי שעבודהון, "Their oppression is known to Me;" ראיתי את העם הזה (ib. xxxii. 9), גלי קדמי עמא חדין, "This people is known to Me," i.e., their rebellion is known to Me—comp. the Targum of the phrase וירא אלהים את בני ישראל which is equal to וירא את ענים ואת עמלם, "He saw their affliction and their trouble"—וירא יי וינאץ (Deut. xxxii. 19), וגלי קדם יי, "And it was known to the Lord, and He abhorred them;" כי יראה כי אזלת יד (Deut. xxxii. 36), ארי גלי קדמוהי, "It was known to Him that their power was gone;" in this instance the object of the perception is likewise the wrong done to the Israelites, and the increasing power of the enemy. In all these examples Onkelos is consistent,[1] following the maxim expressed in the words "Thou canst not look on iniquity" (Hab. i. 13); wherefore he renders the verb "to see" when connected with oppression or rebellion, גלי קדמוהי, גלי קדמי, etc. This appropriate and satisfactory explanation, the correctness of which I do not doubt, is weakened by three passages, in which, according to this view, I expected to find the verb "to see" rendered by גלי קדם יי, but found instead וחזא יי in the various copies of the

[1] Charizi, נמשך ונראה בו, Ibn Tibbon, נוהג מנהג נכון כפי מה שאמרנו.

Targum. The following are the three passages: "And God saw that the wickedness of man was great upon the earth" (Gen. vi. 6); "And the Lord saw the earth, and behold it was corrupt" (ibid. vi. 12); "and God saw that Leah was hated"[1] (ibid. xxx. 31). It appears to me that in these passages there is a mistake, which has crept into the copies of the Targum, since we do not possess the Targum in the original manuscript of Onkelos, for[2] in that case we should have assumed that he could have given a proper explanation of it.

In rendering אלהים יראה לו חשה by קדם יי גלי אמרא, "the lamb is known to the Lord" (Gen. xxii. 8), he either wished to indicate that the Lord was not expected to seek and to bring it, or he considered it inappropriate[3] in Chaldee to connect the divine perception with one of the lower animals.

However, the various copies of the Targum must be carefully examined with regard to this point, and if you still find those passages the same as I quoted them, I cannot explain what he meant.[4]

CHAPTER XLIX.

On figurative expressions applied to angels.

THE angels are likewise incorporeal; they are intelligences without matter,[5] but they are nevertheless created beings,

[1] Pseudo-Jonathan translates וגלי קדם יי.—Some editions of Onkelos have in the first-mentioned passage וגלי קדם יי.

[2] *I.e.*, if we were sure that Onkelos deviated from this rule in these three passages, we might have tried to find some particular reason; but as we are not sure, this is not necessary.

[3] Charizi, נמנע, "inadmissible," "impossible."

[4] The reason might perhaps be that in these passages the verb ראה is not so closely connected with the word "evil." In the first instance the object perceived by God is the circumstance that the evil was great, not the evil itself; in the second the notion of corruption is expressed in another sentence; in the third instance the circumstance that Leah was hated, is said to have been perceived, not the hatred itself, nor Leah the hated one.

[5] Lit., "separated from matter." Charizi, מכח הגוף, "distinguished from physical force."

and God created them, as will be explained below.[1] In Bereshith Rabbah (on Gen. iii. 24) we read the following remark of our Sages; "The angel is called 'the flame of the sword which turned every way' (להט החרב, Gen. iii. 24), in accordance with the words, 'His ministers a flaming fire' (Ps. civ. 4); the attribute המתהפכת, 'which turned every way' is added, because angels are changeable in form;[2] they appear at one time as males,[3] at another as females;[4] now as spirits;[5] now as angels."[6] By this remark they clearly showed that angels are incorporeal, and have no permanent bodily form independent of the mind [of him who perceives them], they exist entirely in prophetic vision, and depend on the action of the imaginative power, as will be explained when speaking on the true meaning of prophecy.[7] As to the words "at another time as females," which imply that the Prophets in prophetical vision perceived angels also in the form of women, they refer to the vision of Zechariah (v. 9), "And, behold, there came out two women, and the wind was in their wings." You know very well, how difficult it is for men to form a notion of anything immaterial, and entirely devoid of corporeality, except after considerable training: it is especially difficult for those who do not distinguish between objects of the intellect and objects of the imagination, and depend mostly on the mere apprehensive power. They believe that all imagined things exist or at least have the possibility of existing; but that which cannot be imagined does not exist, and cannot exist.[8] For persons of this class — and the majority of thinkers belong to it — cannot arrive at the true solution of any question, or at the explanation of anything doubtful. On account of this difficulty the prophetic

[1] See Part II. vi.
[2] The author speaks of the form which the angels of the Bible assume, and which exists only in the mind of him who perceives them, and not of their real form.
[3] Gen. xviii. 2.   [4] Zech. v. 9.   [5] 1 Kings xxii. 21.
[6] I.e., as divine messengers or as supernatural beings.
[7] Part II. xvi. sqq.   [8] See Ch. lxxiii., Propos. 10.

books contain expressions which, taken literally, imply that angels are corporeal, moving about, endowed with human form, receiving commands of God, obeying His word and performing whatever He wishes, according to His command. All this only serves to lead to the belief that angels exist, and are alive and perfect in the same way as we have explained in reference to God.[1] If the figurative representation of angels were limited to this, their true essence would be believed to be the same as the essence of God, since, in reference to the Creator expressions are likewise employed, which literally imply that He is corporeal, living, moving and endowed with human form. In order, therefore, to give to the mind of men the idea that the existence of angels is lower than the divine existence, certain forms of lower animals were introduced in the description of angels. It was thereby shown, that the existence of God is more perfect than that of angels, as much as man is more perfect than the lower animals. Nevertheless no organ of the brute creation was attributed to the angels, except wings. Without wings the act of flying appears as impossible as that of walking without legs; for these two modes of motion can only be imagined in connection with these organs. The motion of flying has been chosen as a symbol to represent that angels possess life, because it is the most perfect and most sublime movement of the brute creation. Men consider this motion a perfection to such an extent that they themselves wish to be able to fly, in order to escape easily what is injurious, and to obtain quickly what is useful, though it be at a distance. For this reason this motion has been attributed to the angels.

There is besides another reason. The bird in its flight is sometimes visible, sometimes withdrawn from our sight; one moment near to us, and in the next far off; and these are exactly the circumstances which we must associate with the idea of angels, as will be explained below. This imaginary perfection, the motion of flight, being the exclusive

[1] See ch. xlvi.

property of the brute creation, has never been attributed to God. You must not be misled by the passage, "And he rode upon a cherub, and did fly" (Ps. xviii. 10), for it is the cherub that did fly, and the simile only serves to denote the rapid arrival of that which is referred to in that passage.[1] Comp.: "Behold, the Lord sitteth upon a swift cloud, and shall come into Egypt" (Is. xix. 1); that is, the punishment[2] alluded to will come down quickly upon Egypt. Nor should expressions like "the face of an ox," "the face of a lion," "the face of an eagle," "the sole of the foot of a calf," found in the prophecies of Ezekiel (i. 10, 7) mislead you; for all these are explained in a different manner, as you will learn later,[3] and besides, the prophet only describes the animals (Chajoth).[4] The subject will be explained, though by mere hints, as far as necessary for directing your attention to the true interpretation.[5]

The motion of flying, frequently mentioned in the Bible, necessitates, according to our imagination, the existence of wings; wings are therefore given to the angels as symbols expressive of their existence, not of their true essence. You must also bear in mind that whenever a thing moves very quickly, it is said to fly, as that term implies great velocity of motion. Comp. "As the eagle flieth" (Deut. xxviii. 49). The eagle flies and moves with greater velocity than any other bird, and therefore it is introduced in this simile. Furthermore, the wings are the organs [lit. causes] of flight; hence the number of the wings of angels in the prophetic vision corresponds to the number of the causes which set a thing in motion,[5] but this does not belong to the theme of this chapter.

[1] Charizi, רדת שבינתו. [2] Charizi, "His anger," קצפו.
[3] Part III. ch. i.
[4] The Chayoth do not represent angels but the spheres.
[5] The four causes of the motion of the spheres are the form of sphere, the soul, the intellect, and the longing for the highest intellect (God) כדוריתו ונפשו ושכלו ותשוקת שכלו (Efodi). Comp. Part II. ch. iv. and x.

CHAPTER L.

Faith consists in inmost conviction, not in mere utterances.[1]

When reading my present treatise, bear in mind that by "faith" we do not understand merely that which is uttered with the lips, but also that which is apprehended by the soul, the conviction that the object [of belief] is exactly as it is apprehended. If, as regards real or supposed truths, you content yourself with giving utterance to them in words, without apprehending them or believing in them, especially if you do not seek real truth, you have a very easy task as, in fact, you will find many ignorant people professing articles of faith without connecting any idea with them.

If, however, you have a desire to rise to a higher state, *viz.*, that of reflection, and truly to hold the conviction that God is One and possesses true unity, without admitting plurality or divisibility in any sense whatever, you must understand that God has no essential[2] attribute in any form or in any sense whatever, and that the rejection of corporeality implies the rejection of essential attributes. Those who believe that God is One, and that He has many attributes, declare the unity with their lips, and assume

---

[1] Before commencing his interpretation of the attributes of God (ch. li. to lx.), he discusses what faith is, and states that he who declares God to be one, and at the same time believes Him to be בעל תארים, to possess attributes, believes in the unity of God only in words, but not in reality. In ch. li. the reason is given why the rejection of the attributes of God is proved here. The author then proceeds to show the nature of attributes (lii.); and that the so-called attributes of God are qualifications of the actions of God (liii., liv.); comparison between God and His creatures is impossible (lv.); attributes imply a comparison between all individual beings possessing the same attribute (lvi.); even such attributes as חי "living," יכול "mighty," רוצה "willing," חכם "wise," אחד "one," are as attributes inadmissible (lvii.); only negative attributes are admissible (lviii.); and the more negative attributes man applies correctly to God, the nearer he comes to truth (lix. and lx.).

[2] By "essential attributes," we must understand attributes which are not mere metaphors, but really exist in connection with the essence of God.

plurality in their thoughts. This is like the doctrine of the Christians, who say that He is one and He is three, and that the three are one. Of the same character is the doctrine of those who say that God is One, but that He has many attributes, and that He with His attributes are One, although they deny corporeality and affirm His most absolute freedom from matter; as if our object were to seek forms of expression, not subjects of belief. For belief is only possible after the apprehension of a thing; it consists in the conviction that the thing apprehended has its existence beyond the mind [in reality] exactly as it is conceived in the mind.[1] If in addition to this we are convinced that the thing cannot be different in any way from what we believe it to be, and that no reasonable argument can be found for the rejection of the belief or for the admission of any deviation from it, then the belief is true. Renounce desires and habits, follow your reason, and study what I am going to say in the chapters which follow on the rejection of the attributes; you will then be fully convinced of what we have said; you will be of those who truly conceive the Unity of God, not of those who utter it with their lips without thought, like men of whom it has been said, " Thou art near in their mouth, and far from their reins " (Jer. xii. 2). It is right that a man should belong to that class of men who have a conception of truth and understand it, though they do not speak of it. Thus the pious are advised and addressed, " Commune with your own heart upon your bed and be still. Selah." (Ps. iv. 5.)

CHAPTER LI.

On the necessity of proving the inadmissibility of attributes in reference to God.

THERE are many things whose existence is manifest and obvious; some of these are innate notions or objects of

[1] This sentence is omitted in the translation of Charizi.

PART I.—CHAPTER LI.   173

sensation, others are nearly so;[1] and in fact they would require no proof if[2] man had been left in his primitive state. Such are the existence of motion,[3] of man's free will,[4] of phases of production and destruction, and of the natural properties of things perceived by the senses, e.g., the heat of fire, the coldness of water, and many other similar things. False notions, however, may be spread either by a person labouring under error,[5] or by one who has some particular end[6] in view, and who establishes theories contrary to the real nature of things, by denying the existence of things perceived by the senses, or by affirming the existence of what does not exist. Philosophers are thus required to establish by proof things which are self-evident, and to disprove the existence of things which only exist in man's

---

[1] In Milloth higgayon, viii., four kinds of assertions are enumerated that require no proof: *a*, המוחשים, those which are perceived by the senses; *b*, המושכלות הראשונות, innate notions; *c*, המפורסמות, general opinions; *d*, המקובלות, traditions.

[2] עד שאפילו הונח האדם כמו שהוא, Ibn Tibbon; quand-même on le laisserait tel qu'il est, Munk. More correct is the rendering of Charizi, ואילו יניחו אדם עטם: if man had been left to follow exclusively his innate notions, and the perception of his senses, he would have believed in the existence of motion, etc., without demanding any proof. Man, however, has been misled by false theories and perverse methods to believe in things contrary to the experience of his senses and to common sense. Therefore it became necessary to prove the most obvious truths. The renderings of Munk and Ibn Tibbon imply that at the present time the proof is less necessary, as man has not been left in his primitive state. The contrary is the case. The Arabic פלו admits both renderings, "and if," "and although."

[3] Motion has been denied by Zeno (Arist. Phys., vi. 2); the power of man to act according to his free will was denied by the fatalists (Ashariyah). See Part III. xvii. 3. Production and destruction (γένεσις καὶ φθορά) of the forms of things was mere appearance according to the Eleatic school (Parmenides). The same school denied the truth and reality of all variety and plurality of existing things.   [4] Comp. lxxiii., Propos. 6.

[5] מפני מטעה in the translation of Charizi is certainly a mistake.

[6] According to Shemtob, the support of some religious dogma which is contrary to what is perceived by the senses, or understood by common sense; or, the obtaining of superiority by overthrowing well-founded theories. Comp. Crescas (*ad locum*): "as, *e.g.*, the Mutakallemim, who employ it to support their doctrine of the *creatio ex nihilo*."

imagination.[1] Thus Aristotle gives a proof for the existence of motion, because it had been denied; he disproves the reality of atoms, because it had been asserted.[2]

To the same class belongs the rejection of essential attributes[3] in reference to God. For it is a self-evident truth that the attribute is not inherent in the object to which it is ascribed, but it is superadded to its essence, and is consequently an *accident*; if the attribute denoted the essence [τὸ τί ἦν εἶναι] of the object, it would be either mere tautology, as if, *e.g.*, one would say "man is man," or the explanation of a name, as, *e.g.*, "man is a speaking animal"; for the words "speaking animal" include the true essence of man, and there is no third element besides life and speech that constitutes man; when he, therefore, is described by the attributes of life and speech, these are nothing but an explanation of the name "man," that is to say, that the thing which is called man, consists of life and speech.[4] It will now be clear that the attribute

---

[1] אשיא אלמצ׳נונאת, in Hebrew דברים הנחשבים (Ibn Tibbon), are things which are only imagined, opposed to things which exist in reality. Charizi translates rather freely המחשבות הרקים ההם, "these empty thoughts."

[2] It is remarkable that Maimonides, after having mentioned motion, man's will, production and destruction, and physical properties of things, almost ignores this classification, and speaks only of motion and atoms. The above instances are, perhaps, a later addition. For proofs of the existence of motion, *see* Aristotle Phys., vi. 2, and viii. 8; his objections to the atomic theory are found, *ib.*, vi. 1. Instead of החלק שאינו מתחלק, "atom" (Arab. ג׳ז), Charizi has השדים, "genii" (he read, perhaps, נין). Comp. Narb., מי שכנהו על השר אחוהו שד, "he who refers it to genii is mad."

[3] That is to say, for those who believe in the Unity of God, and agree with Maimonides in respect to the definition of the term "Unity." In its general acceptation we also apply the term to beings which have many properties.

[4] The logical definition, consisting of the genus (סוג, *e.g.*, החי, "the living") and the differentia (הבדלו, *e.g.*, מדבר, "speaking"), is called "the explanation of the name," it contains all the constituent elements of the thing (עצם הדבר). Thus דבור, "the peculiar faculty of man," is explained in Milloth higgayon x. הכח אשר בו תצירנה המשכלות, "the power by which ideas are conceived," *i.e.*, mind or reason. *Ibid.* x., the דבור, "speech," is divided into three kinds: 1, intellect (הנפש המדברת); 2, the conceived notions (הדבור הפנימי); 3, speech in its literal sense (דבור חיצוני).

must be one of two things, either the essence of the object described—in that case it is a mere explanation of a name, and on that account we might admit the attribute in reference to God, but we reject it from another cause as will be shown[1]— or the attribute is something different from the object described, some extraneous superadded[2] element; in that case the attribute would be an accident, and he who merely rejects the appellation "accidents" in reference to the attributes of God, does not thereby alter their character;[3] for everything superadded to the essence of an object joins it without forming part of its essential properties, and that constitutes an accident.[4] Add to this the logical consequence of admitting many attributes, viz., the existence of many eternal beings.[5] There cannot be any belief in the unity of God except by admitting that He is one simple substance, without any composition or plurality of elements; one from whatever side you view it, and by whatever test you examine it; not divisible into two parts in any way and by any cause, nor capable of any form of plurality either objectively or subjectively, as will be proved in this treatise.[6]

Some thinkers[7] have gone so far as to say that the attributes of God are neither His essence nor anything extraneous

---

[1] See chapter lii. An explanation—without being a strict logical definition—is admissible in reference to the name of God; a strict definition is shown in the next chapter to be impossible.

[2] The Arabic זאיד (part. act.) is rendered מוסיף by Ibn Tibbon, נוסף by Charizi.

[3] That is to say, although they do not expressly call it "accident" (מקרה), it is the same thing, and remains inadmissible.

[4] That is, everything not included in the definition. The Hebrew name מקרה, here corresponds to "accident" in its original meaning, "befalling," "coming to," although in the Bible it is used in the sense of "chance."

[5] That is, the attributes are inadmissible, because they are "accidents;" and even if they were not "accidents" they could not be admitted; because in that case they would eternally coexist with the essence, and this is contrary to the belief in the perfect unity of God.

[6] See II. xxii.

[7] "Thinkers" is to be understood in an ironical sense. The Mutakallemim are meant.

to His essence. This is like the assertion of some theorists, that the ideals, *i.e.*, the *universalia*, are neither existing nor non-existent,[1] and like the views of others, that the atom does not fill a definite place, but keeps an atom of space occupied;[2] that man has no freedom at all, but has acquirement.[3] Such things are only said; they exist only in words, not in thought, much less in reality. But as you know, and as all know who do not delude themselves, these theories are preserved by a multitude of words,[4] by misleading similes sustained by declamation and invective, and by numerous methods borrowed both from dialectics and

---

[1] This is a kind of compromise (like the conceptualists) between the nominalists and realists; the universalia are neither rejected nor entirely admitted; they assumed *universalia in re* (Abaelardus). Comp. Part III., ch. xviii.

[2] The atom cannot occupy any definite space; it is infinitely small, otherwise it would be divisible, and cease to be an atom; but each atom added to a body changes the limits of that body. The different positions of a point constitute successively a line, a surface, and a body; in a similar way the different positions of atoms constitute the body, and have dimensions. The Arabic ישגל אלחיז (Heb. ימריד הנבול, Tibbon), means literally "it keeps the atom of space occupied," so that a second atom must occupy a neighbouring unit of space, and so on; thus implying the idea of extension, which is excluded by the first part of the proposition, "the atom is not in a place." As to the difference between מכאן and חיז see Munk *ad locum*; Charizi, כולל המקום, "it includes some idea of space." The contradiction implied here is, that on the one side no measurable dimension is given to the atom, and on the other side, each additional atom increases the magnitude of the body. Comp. lxxii., Propos. 5. The proposition cited here as contradictory in itself occurs in some different form in the monadic theory of Leibnitz. Comp. also Aaron b. Eliya, Ets-Chayim, ch. iv.

[3] Some of the Fatalists (the sect of the Ashariyah) modified their creed and admitted man's will as granted specially for each action; these successive productions of the will of man are called הקניה, "acquirement," or ריוח, "space" to move about, according to Aaron b. Eliyah, in Ets-Chayim (ch. iv. and lxxxvi.). The rendering of Charizi, יחס וערך, is by no means literal; it expresses vaguely the sense of the original, that there is some relation between man and his actions.

[4] The words במאמרים שמשתדל אומרם לשטרם ברוב דברים, in the translation of Tibbon, are superfluous, as pointed out by Munk (p. 187, note 2); בהוצאת דפות (not רבות as in some editions) והרחקת is a combination of two different renderings of the original אלתשניעת.

sophistry.[1] If after uttering them and supporting them by such words a man were to examine for himself his own belief on this subject, he would see nothing but confusion and stupidity in an endeavour to prove the existence of things which do not exist, or to find a mean between two opposites that have no mean. Or is there a mean between existence and non-existence, or between the identity and non-identity of two things? But, as we said,[2] to such absurdities men were forced by the great licence given to the imagination, and by the fact that every existing material thing is necessarily imagined as a certain substance possessing several attributes; for nothing has ever been found that consists of one simple substance without any attribute. Guided by such imaginations, men thought that God was also composed of many different elements, *viz.*, of His essence[3] and of the attributes superadded to His essence. Following up this comparison,[4] some believed that God was corporeal, and that He possessed attributes; others abandoning this theory, denied the corporeality, but retained the attributes. The adherence to the literal sense of the text of Holy Writ is the source of all this error, as I shall show in some chapters devoted to this theme.[5]

[1] Ibn Tibbon, מחלוקת נצוח והטעאה : Char., והכחשת האמת הנ׳ סופסטא "and the refutation of truth, which is called sophistry."

[2] See ch. xlix. page 168. Comp. page 94, note 2; page 111, note 1.

[3] Instead of עצמיים in the ordinary editions of Ibn Tibbon's version, the editio princeps and the MSS. have עצמו (Munk).

[4] Charizi: רחקו סמנו הדמות, "did not admit similarity," the Arabic, מרדוא אלתשביה, admits of both interpretations: "they pushed forward" (*poussant plus loin*, M.), and "they pushed away."

[5] See ch. liii. The licence given to the imagination has been represented above as the source of the corporification of God; here the anthropomorphisms employed in the Bible are said to lead to these errors. Maimonides distinctly states, in ch. liii., that not reasoning, but the Biblical anthropomorphism created the belief in the attributes of God. He probably meant to say, if people would follow reason more than imagination, they would easily find out the correct interpretation of the metaphors employed in reference to God.

CHAPTER LII.

Classification of Attributes.

EVERY description of an object by an affirmative attribute, which includes the assertion that an object is of a certain kind, must be made in one of the following five ways[1]:—

First. The object is described by its *definition*, as *e.g.*, man is described as a being that lives and has reason; such a description, containing the true essence of the object, is, as we have already shown, nothing else but the explanation of a name. All agree that this kind of description cannot be given of God; for there are no previous causes[2] to His existence, by which He could be defined: and on that account it is a well-known principle, received by all the philosophers who are precise in their statements,[3] that no definition can be given of God.

Secondly. An object is described by *part of its definition*, as when, *e.g.*, man is described as a living being or as a rational being. This kind of description includes the neces-

---

[1] The attributes are divided by Maimonides into five classes: 1, those which include all the essential properties of an object; 2, those which include only part of them; 3, those which denote non-essential properties [quality]; 4, those which express the relation of an object to something else [relation]; 5, those which refer to the action of the object [action]. The ten Aristotelian categories appear to be included in these five classes, the first two of which refer to the substance (עצם), while the remaining three include all the rest. Quantity, quality and passiveness are here included in "quality;" relation, place and time, and property are included in "relation;" position and action are united in "action."

[2] The definition, consisting of the *genus* and the *differentia*, is inapplicable to God; *genus* and *differentia* are at the same time represented as the causes (סבות) of the existence of the thing defined (Οὐ μόνον τὸ ὅτι δεῖ τὸν ὁριστικὸν λόγον δηλοῦν, ὥσπερ οἱ πλεῖστοι τῶν ὅρων λέγουσιν, ἀλλὰ καὶ τὴν αἰτίαν ἐνυπάρχειν καὶ ἐμφαίνεσθαι, Arist. De animâ, II. ii. § 1). For the apparent contradiction, see ch. li., page 175, note 1.

[3] אלנטאר אלמחצלין למא יקולונה is rendered by Ibn Tibbon, according to ed. pr. and MSS. by והמעיינים (Ch.) המשכילים) המברדים למה שיאמרוהו "the philosophers, who are particular in what they say." Munk. The several editions of Ibn Tibbon's Version erroneously read, המדברים instead of המברדים.

sary connection [of the two ideas];[1] for when we say that every man is rational, we mean by it that every being which has the characteristics of man must also have reason. All[2] agree that this kind of description is inappropriate in reference to God; for if we were to speak of a portion of His essence, we should consider His essence to be a compound. The inappropriateness of this kind of description in reference to God is the same as that of the preceding kind.

Thirdly. An object is described by something different from its true essence, by something that does not complement or establish the essence of the object. The description, therefore, relates to a *quality;* but quality, in its most general sense,[3] is an accident. If God could be described in this way, He would be the substratum of accidents: a sufficient reason for rejecting the idea that He possesses quality, since it diverges from the true conception of His essence. It is surprising how those who admit the application of attributes to God can reject, in reference to Him, comparison and qualification. For when they say "He cannot be qualified," they can only mean that He possesses no quality; and yet every positive essential attribute of an object either constitutes its essence,—and in that case it is identical with the essence,—or it contains a quality of the object.

There are, as you know, four kinds of quality;[4] I will

---

[1] אלתלאום in Arabic, and החיוב (Ibn Tibbon) or ההצמדה (Char.) in Hebrew, denote the closest and inseparable connection between two things, here between "man" and "reason," the latter forming part of the definition of the former.

[2] That is, even those who are not particular (אלמחצלין) in their speech.

[3] Quality is one of the categories of which nine are said to be accidents (מקרים), and quality (איכות), being one of these, is consequently an accident. The categories are called in Hebrew מאמרות, also סוג העליון or מין העליון.

[4] These four kinds of quality correspond to the Aristotelian subdivision of this category into: 1. ἕξις καὶ διάθεσις. 2. ὅσα κατὰ δύναμιν φυσικὴν ἢ ἀδυναμίαν λέγεται. 3. παθητικαὶ ποιότητες καὶ πάθη. 4. σχῆμά τε καὶ ἡ περὶ ἕκαστον ὑπάρχουσα μορφή (psychological, physical, emotional and mathematical properties). The first of these four kinds of properties, ἕξις and διάθεσις, includes those that concern the soul of man (נפש), and those that concern

give you instances of attributes of each kind, in order to show you that this class of attributes cannot possibly be applied to God. (*a.*) A man is described by any of his intellectual or moral qualities, or by any of the dispositions appertaining to him as an animate being, when, *e.g.*, we speak of a person who is a carpenter, or who shrinks from sin, or who is ill.[1] It makes no difference whether we say, a carpenter, or a sage, or a physician;[2] by all these we represent certain physical dispositions; nor does it make any difference whether we say "sin-fearing" or "merciful." Every trade, every profession, and every settled habit of man are certain physical dispositions. All this is clear to those who have occupied themselves with the study of Logic. (*b.*) A thing is described by some physical quality it possesses, or by the absence of the same,[3] *e.g.*, as being soft or hard. It makes no difference whether we say "soft or hard," or "strong or weak;" in both cases we speak of physical conditions. (*c.*) A man is described by his passive qualities, or by his emotions; we speak, *e.g.*, of a person who is passionate, irritable, timid, merciful, without implying that these conditions have become permanent. The description of a thing by its colour, taste, heat, cold, dryness, and moisture,[4] belongs also to this

---

the body as the seat of the soul (בעל נפש). Those which concern the soul are either intellectual or moral (מדות or עיונים). Charizi renders אלבלקיאה (מדות, "moral qualities," in the Hebrew Version of Ibn Tibbon) by היצוריות "the formative capacities." Although the Arabic, כלק, admits of both meanings, the instances which are given by the author to illustrate these terms apply only to "moral qualities."

[1] The three instances refer to the three kinds of qualities mentioned before in the same order. Carpentry means here the knowledge of carpentry, and as such is considered as an intellectual quality.

[2] Arabic אלחכים, Hebr. הרופא; according to Munk, "the wise" or "the learned;" this is the more improbable, as the word אלעאלים, "the sage," which precedes, has almost the same meaning.

[3] The Arabic קוה לא כח (לא Ibn Tibbon) appears to be the literal translation of the Greek ἀδυναμίαν.

[4] It is remarkable that colour, taste, etc., are classified together with the emotions; they were probably considered as momentary effects produced by some external force, as the rays of the sun, the wind, etc. It is true that colours in the face of man come from affections (see Munk *ad locum*), but that

class of attributes. (d.) A thing is described by any of its qualities resulting from quantity as such;[1] we speak, e.g., of a thing which is long, short, curved, straight, etc.

Consider all these and similar attributes, and you will find that they cannot be employed in reference to God. He is not a magnitude that any quality resulting from quantity as such could be possessed by Him; He is not affected by external influences, and therefore does not possess any quality resulting from emotion. He is not subject to physical conditions, and therefore does not possess strength or similar qualities; He is not an animate being, that He should have a certain disposition of the soul, or acquire certain properties, as meekness, modesty, etc., or be in a state to which animate beings as such are subject, as, e.g., in that of health or of illness. Hence it follows that no attribute coming under the head of quality in its widest sense, can be predicated of God. Consequently, these three classes of attributes, describing the essence of a thing, or part of the essence, or a quality of it, are clearly inadmissible in reference to God, for they imply composition, which, as we shall prove,[2] is out of question as regards the Creator. We say, with regard to this latter point, that He is absolutely One.[3]

Fourthly. A thing is described by its *relation* to another thing, e.g., to time, to space, or to a different individual; thus we say, Zaid, the father of A, or the partner of B, or who dwells at a certain place, or who lived at a stated time. This kind of attribute does not necessarily imply plurality or change in the essence of the object described; for the

---

is not the meaning here, because it is not "man" but "the thing" (אלשׁי, in Hebr. הדבר) that is described by these qualities.

[1] That is, the mathematical properties of the thing, the qualities resulting from its abstract form. It is uncertain whether כמות "quantity" is here to be understood as the category of quantity, or in the particular sense of geometrical magnitude. All the instances given refer to geometrical forms, and besides the Aristotelian name σχῆμα καὶ μόρφη apply only to these.

[2] See II. i.

[3] This sentence does not occur in some MSS., nor in the version of Charizi.

same Zaid, to whom reference is made, is the partner of Amru, the father of Becr, the master of Khalid, the friend of Zaid, dwells in a certain house, and was born in a certain year. Such relations are not the essence of a thing, nor are they so intimately connected with it as qualities. At first thought, it would seem that they may be employed in reference to God, but after careful and thorough consideration we are convinced of their inadmissibility. It is quite clear that there is no relation between God and time or space.[1] For time is an accident connected with motion, in so far as the latter includes the relation of anteriority and posteriority, and is expressed by number,[2] as is explained in books devoted to this subject; and since motion is one of the conditions to which only material bodies are subject, and God is immaterial, there can be no relation between Him and time. Similarly there is no relation between Him and space.[3] But what we have to investigate and to examine is this: whether some real relation exists between God and any of the substances created by Him, by which He could be described? That there is no correlation between Him and any of His creatures can easily be seen; for the characteristic of two objects correlative to each other is the equality of their reciprocal relation.[4] Now, as God

---

[1] See II. xiii.

[2] That is, motion can be considered as a series of successive positions of a moving body, and can thus be reduced to number or measure. The idea of succession, of before and after, or of earlier and later, necessarily includes the idea of time. Time is called an accident connected with motion; it does not form a constituent element, but it is inseparable from it. Comp. II. xiii.: "Time depends on motion" (והזמן נמשך אחר התנועה), and 'Ἀριθμὸς κινήσεως κατὰ τὸ πρότερον καὶ ὕστερον. (Arist. Phys., iv. 11.)

[3] That is, space is an accident connected with bodies; God is not material, the relations of space are therefore inapplicable to Him.

[4] The relation between two things is either perfect or imperfect. In the first case the two things being equal in other respects equally participate in it, and are equally essential in that relation; it is, therefore, out of question in reference to God, whose very existence is different from that of all other beings. When the relation is imperfect (קצת יחס אמתי), and does not require the fulfilment of that condition, its application to God may seem less objectionable, but it is in reality equally inadmissible. According to Munk, the condition of

has absolute existence, while all other beings have only possible existence, as we shall show,[1] there consequently cannot be any correlation [between God and His creatures]. That a certain kind of relation does exist between them is by some considered possible, but wrongly. It is impossible to imagine a relation between intellect and sight, although, as we believe, the same kind of existence is common to both; how, then, could a relation be imagined between any creature and God, who has nothing in common with any other being; for even the term existence is applied to Him and other things, according to our opinion,[2] only by way of pure homonymity. Consequently there is no relation whatever between Him and any other being. For[3] whenever we speak of a relation between two things,[4] these belong to the same species;[5] but when two things belong to different species though of the same class, there is no relation between them. We therefore do not say, this red compared with that green, is more, or less, or equally

---

התהפך בשווי, "la parfaite réciprocité," consists in inverting the relation "A is the master of B," into "B is the servant of A." If this were meant by Maimonides, he has not proved the inadmissibility of that relation in reference to God, by referring to the difference between the existence of God and that of of His creatures, as that difference is entirely unconnected with the reciprocity which he mentions. Besides, the relation "A is the master of B," *always* implies the inversion B is the servant of A; both sentences meaning one and the same thing. The verb אנעכאס (Hebrew התהפך) does not signify "to be inverted," but "to form the opposite," and the phrase אנעכאס באלתכאפו (Hebrew התהפך בשווי) means "to form equally the opposite to each other," *i.e.* to have the same relation though in opposite directions, to the mean between them.

[1] Comp. II., Introd. Propos. 19.

[2] According to the opinion of those who believe in the *creatio ex nihilo*. Those who believe in the eternity of the Universe, need not consider the term existence as homonymous when applied to God and to the Universe.

[3] This passage from "For whenever we speak" to "the greatest of all differences" contains a mere repetition of the argument just concluded with the words "Consequently there is no relation," etc. The conjunction "for" does not appear to refer to that which closely precedes, but to the phrase "but wrongly." The two forms of the arguments may be due to the corrections and alterations in the text made by the author.   [4] Comp. ch. xxxv.

[5] The species (מין קרוב) is that which is nearest to the individual beings of a class. It is called in Milloth higgayon, ch. x., "the last species" (המין האחרון).

intense, although both belong to the same class—colour; when they belong to two different classes,[1] there does not appear to exist any relation between them, not even to a man of ordinary intellect, although the two things belong to the same category; *e.g.*, between a hundred cubits and the heat of pepper there is no relation, the one being a quality, the other a quantity; or between wisdom and sweetness, between meekness and bitterness, although all these come under the head of quality in its more general signification. How, then, could there be any relation between God and His creatures, considering the important difference between them in respect to true existence, the greatest of all differences. Besides, if any relation existed between them, God would be subject to the accident of relation; and although that would not be an accident to the essence of God, it would still be, to some extent, a kind of accident. You would, therefore, be wrong if you applied affirmative attributes in their literal sense to God, though they contained only relations; these, however, are the most appropriate of all attributes, to be employed, in a less strict sense, in reference to God, because they do not imply that a plurality of eternal things exists,[2] or that any change takes place in the essence of God, when those things change to which God is in relation.

Fifthly. A thing is described by its *actions*; I do not mean

[1] The word עליונים in the version of Tibbon has no equivalent in the Arabic text, and yet it does not appear to have been put in by error. In the instance which follows, two סוגים עליונים (categories) are mentioned, *viz.*, quality and quantity. Besides, there is some confusion in the order of the instances. We should expect, for the sake of the climax, which the author undoubtedly intended, the following order: Two things of two divisions of the same species, of two species of the same class, of two classes of the same category, and then of two categories. The whole passage seems to have undergone frequent corrections and alterations.—The words אין ספק ש and שאין ספק לשום אדם are not found in the MSS., nor their equivalents in the original (Munk).

[2] Ibn Tibbon renders the Arabic תכתיר אלקדים by רבוי הקדמות "a multitude of eternal things," Charizi רבוי הקדמון, "the plurality of the eternal." The latter takes אלקדים as referring to God, Ibn Tibbon in the general sense of "eternal thing."

by "its actions" the inherent capacity for a certain work, as is expressed in "carpenter," "painter,"[1] or "smith"—for these belong to the class of qualities which have been mentioned above[2]—but I mean the action the latter has performed; we speak, *e.g.*, of Zaid, who made this door, built that wall, wove that garment. This kind of attributes is separate from the essence of the thing described, and, therefore, the most appropriate to be employed in describing the Creator, especially since we know that these different actions do not imply that different elements must be contained in the substance of the agent, by which the different actions are produced, as will be explained.[3] On the contrary, all the actions of God emanate from His essence, not from any extraneous thing superadded to His essence, as we have shown.[4]

What we have explained in the present chapter is this: that God is one in every respect, containing no plurality or any element superadded to His essence: and that the many attributes of different significations applied in Scripture to God, originate in the multitude of His actions, not in a plurality existing in His essence, and are partly employed with the object of conveying to us some notion of His perfection, in accordance with what we consider perfection, as has been explained by us.[5] The possibility of one simple substance excluding plurality, though accomplishing different actions, will be illustrated by examples in the next chapter.

CHAPTER LIII.

The arguments on which the Attributists found their theory.

THE circumstance which caused men to believe in the existence of divine attributes is similar to that which caused others to believe in the corporeality of God. The latter have not arrived at that belief by speculation, but

---

[1] The painter is not mentioned in the Arabic text.
[2] In the elucidation of the first class of qualities by examples.
[3] Ch. liii.   [4] Ch. xlvi., page 159.   [5] Ch. xxvi., xlvi., xlvii.

by following the literal sense of certain passages in the Bible. The same is the case with the attributes; when in the books of the Prophets and of the Law,[1] God is described by attributes, such passages are taken in their literal sense, and it is then believed that God possesses attributes; as if He were to be exalted above corporeality, and not above things connected with corporeality, *i.e.*, the accidents, I mean psychical dispositions,[2] all of which are qualities [and connected with corporeality]. Every attribute[3] which the followers of this doctrine assume to be essential to the Creator, you will find to express, although they[4] do not distinctly say it, a quality similar to[5] those which they are accustomed to notice in the bodies of all living beings. We apply to all[6] such passages the principle, "The Torah speaketh

[1] Here, as in several other passages, the books of the Prophets are mentioned before the books of the Pentateuch. See ch. xlvi. page 153, note 1.

[2] Of the several classes of attributes described in the preceding chapter, only the psychical properties (תכונות בנפש) are named here, because the essential attributes—the admissibility of which is denied by Maimonides, but asserted by his opponents—are those of life, power, wisdom, and will, all of which are (תכונות הנפש) psychical dispositions. All other attributes are either not essential, or, if essential, too evidently material to be applied to God by any class of thinkers. The words, I mean "psychical dispositions," seem to be out of place; for it is entirely unnecessary to explain these by the additional phrase "all of which are qualities." From the sentence which follows it is evident that Maimonides describes "the things connected with corporeality" or "accidents" as "qualities," and further limits this term by "psychical dispositions." The words אעני אלהיאת אלנפסאניה "I mean psychical dispositions," appear therefore to include the qualification of אלתי הי כלהא כיפיאת, "all of which are qualities," and not *vice versa*.

[3] That is, occurring in the books of the Bible.

[4] *I.e.*, the followers of this doctrine. According to Munk, "the Prophets," because in the original text the plural יצרחוא "they say distinctly" does not agree with the singular מעתקד, "the follower." But in reference to the Prophets this remark of Maimonides would be superfluous; they had no occasion to declare what the attributes which occurred in their writings were, while those philosophers who believed in the existence of essential attributes, might in discussing them, have stated whether these attributes were qualities or not.

[5] Ibn Tibbon renders תשביהא by the adjective דומה, "similar;" Charizi by כדי להדמות, "in order to make a comparison." The sense is the same in both.

[6] That is, of whatever kind the attributes occurring in those passages are, whether they seem to be essential or not.

in the language of man," and say that the object of all these terms is to describe God as the most perfect being, not as possessing those qualities which are only perfections in relation to created living beings. Many of the attributes express different acts of God, but that difference does not necessitate any difference as regards Him from whom the acts proceed. This fact, viz., that from one agency different effects may result, although that agency has not free will, and much more so if it has free will, I will illustrate by an instance taken from our own sphere. Fire melts certain things and makes others hard, it boils and consumes,[1] it bleaches and blackens. If we described the fire as bleaching, blackening, consuming, boiling, hardening and melting, we should be correct, and yet he who does not know the nature of fire, would think that it included six different elements, one by which it blackens, another by which it bleaches, a third by which it boils, a fourth by which it consumes, a fifth by which it melts, a sixth by which it hardens things—actions which are opposed to one another, and of which each has its peculiar property. He, however, who knows the nature of fire, will know that by virtue of one quality in action, namely, by heat, it produces all these effects. If this is the case with that which is done by nature,[2] how much more is it the case with regard to those who act by free will, and still more with regard to God, who is above all description. If we, therefore, perceive in God certain relations of various characters—for wisdom in us is different from power, and power from will—it does by no means follow that different elements are really contained in Him, that He contains one element by which He knows, another by which He wills, and another by which He exercises power, as is, in fact, the signification of the attributes [of God] according to the Mutakallemim. Some of them express it plainly, and enumerate the attributes as elements added to the essence. Others, however, are more reserved with regard

---

[1] That is, it prepares one thing for our use, and nature destroys another.
[2] Charizi has here the addition ואין לו חפץ, "and nature has no will."

to this matter, but indicate their opinion, though they do not express it in distinct and intelligible words. Thus, *e.g.*, some of them say: "God is omnipotent by His essence, wise by His essence, living by His essence, and endowed with a will by His essence."[1] (I will mention to you, as an instance, man's reason, which being one faculty and implying no plurality, enables him to know many arts and sciences; by the same faculty man is able to sow, to do carpenter's work, to weave, to build, to study, to acquire a knowledge of geometry, and to govern a state. These various acts resulting from one simple faculty, which involves no plurality, are very numerous; their number, that is, the number of the actions originating in man's reason,[2] is almost infinite. It is therefore intelligible how in reference to God, those different actions can be caused by one simple substance, that does not include any plurality or any additional element. The attributes found in Holy Scripture are either qualifications of His actions, without any reference to His essence, or indicate absolute perfection, but do not imply that the essence of God is a compound of various elements.)[3] For in not admitting the *term* "compound," they do not reject the *idea* of a compound[4] when they admit a substance with attributes.

There still remains one difficulty which led them to that error, and which I am now going to mention. Those who

[1] This is not clear, as it is not distinctly stated whether the repetition of בעצמו " by His essence " four times, refers to four different kinds of essence, or to one and the same essence ; Maimonides appears to understand it in the first sense. According to Shemtob Palquera בעצמו means " exclusively," no other power being possessed of life, wisdom, power, will. (Moreh ha-moreh, p. 151.)

[2] That all these actions originate in man's reason (כח המדבר) is distinctly stated by Maimonides in his Shemonah Perakim, ch. i.

[3] The passage beginning "I will mention to you as an instance," etc., to "of various elements" is here out of place, and the words "for in not admitting" etc., are to be joined with the sentence, "Others, however, are more reserved with regard to this matter, but indicate their opinion," etc. The sentence in parenthesis contains an elucidation of the words " how much more is that the case as regards those who act with free will."

[4] ענינים or ענינם in the editions of the version of Tibbon is a misprint for ענינה (Munk).

PART I.—CHAPTER LIII. 189

assert the existence of the attributes do not found[1] their opinion on the variety of God's actions; they say it is true that one substance can be the source of various effects, but His essential attributes[2] cannot be qualifications of His actions, because it is impossible to imagine that the Creator created Himself. They vary with regard to the so-called essential attributes—I mean as regards their number—according to the text of the Scripture[3] which each of them follows. I will enumerate those on which all agree, and the knowledge of which they believe that they have derived from reasoning, not from some words of the Prophets, namely, the following four:—life, power, wisdom, and will. They believe that these are four different things, and such perfections as cannot possibly be absent in the Creator, and that these cannot be qualifications of His actions.[4] This is their opinion. But

---

[1] Munk: Ne les admittent pas (seulement) à cause de la multiplicité. The word "seulement" is decidedly wrong. The plurality of actions was no reason whatever for believing in the existence of attributes, as is distinctly stated in the text.

[2] The essential attributes (התארים העצמיים, Ibn Tibbon; המדות הדבקות ב, Char.) are closely connected with the essence, and are opposed to attributes which are qualifications of actions; the arguments in favour of their existence appear to be as follows: these four attributes (life, power, wisdom, will) are inseparable from the idea of God; to think of God without them, would be the same as to think of Him without existence. Hence, if these attributes were mere qualifications of actions, they could not have existed before the respective actions, and the Creator would by His actions produce them, which amounts, in the opinion of those philosophers, to saying that God created Himself or His own essence. The commentators have introduced much abstruse discussion, in connection with these simple words of the text. Munk says of this passage, " L'auteur s'est exprimé ici d'une manière tronquée et obscure."

[3] This refers to the Koran, as Maimonides here chiefly thinks of the Mahomedan philosophers who believed in the attributes. The numerous attributes were reduced by some of them to seven:—life, knowledge, will, might, word, hearing, sight. (Munk.)

[4] These words are undoubtedly a mere repetition of what was already shown above, namely, why the Mutakallemim believe that the essential attributes are not qualifications of God's actions. Munk is less accurate in rendering the first מא הי מן אפעאלה, " ne sont pas de (ceux qui viennent de) ses actions," and here נמלה מן הדה תכון אן יסוג ולא אפעאלה, " et qui ne sauraient être comptées au nombre de ses actions." The question of neuter and transitive attributes is not touched upon in this passage.

you must know[1] that wisdom and life in reference to God are not different from each other; for in every being that is conscious of itself, life and wisdom are the same thing,[2] that is to say, if by wisdom we understand the consciousness of self. Besides, the subject and the object of that consciousness are undoubtedly identical [as regards God]; for according to our opinion, He is not composed of an element that apprehends, and another that does not apprehend; He is not like man, who is a combination of a conscious soul and an unconscious body. If, therefore, by " wisdom " we mean the faculty of self-consciousness, wisdom and life are one and the same thing. They, however, do not speak of wisdom in this sense, but of His power to apprehend His creatures. There is also no doubt that power and will do not exist in God in reference to Himself; for He cannot have power or will as regards Himself; we cannot imagine such a thing. They take these attributes as different relations between God and His creatures, signifying that He has power in creating things, will in giving to things existence as He desires, and wisdom in knowing what He created. Consequently, these attributes do not refer to the essence of God, but express relations between Him and His creatures.

Therefore we, who truly believe in the Unity of God, declare, that as we do not believe that some element is included in His essence by which He created the heavens, another by which He created the [four] elements, a third by which He created the ideals, in the same way we reject the idea that His essence contains an element by which He has power, another element by which He has will, and a third by which He has a knowledge of His creatures. On the contrary, He is a simple essence, without any additional element whatever; He created the universe, and knows it, but not by any

[1] Maimonides wishes to show the error of these philosophers, by demonstrating, that wisdom, power, and will, if their object is God Himself, must be one and the same thing; but if, as those philosophers assume, they have reference to other objects, they are qualifications of actions, as all other attributes.

[2] Apprehension ($αἰσθάνεσθαι$, $νοεῖν$) is the characteristic of both life and wisdom. Comp. ch. xlii., and Arist. Metaph., xii. 7.

extraneous force. There is no difference whether these various attributes refer to His actions or to relations between Him and His works; in fact, these relations, as we have also shown, exist only in the thoughts of men.[1] This is what we must believe concerning the attributes occurring in the books of the Prophets; some may also be taken as expressive of the perfection of God by way of comparison with what we consider as perfections in us, as we shall explain.

CHAPTER LIV.[2]

On Exodus xxxiii. 13, to xxxiv. 7.

THE wisest man,[3] our Teacher Moses, asked two things of God, and received a reply respecting both. The one thing he asked was, that God should let him know His true essence; the other, which in fact he asked first,[4] that God should let him know His attributes. In answer to both these petitions God promised that He would let him know all His attributes, and that these were nothing but His actions. He also told him that His true essence could not be perceived, and pointed out a method by which he could obtain the utmost knowledge of God possible for man to acquire. The knowledge obtained by Moses has not been

---

[1] *I.e.*, they are employed as figurative expressions, and are not meant to be taken literally as real relations between God and His creatures.

[2] In this chapter Maimonides shows that all the attributes communicated to Moses by God Himself were qualifications of actions.

[3] Moses is here called "the wisest man," (lit. the prince of the wise men), and not as usually "the greatest prophet," because, according to Maimonides, in the vision referred to in this chapter, Moses was shown the method (מקום עיון) of solving the most difficult metaphysical problems, and the limits of human reason.

[4] The logical order in describing an object is to speak first of the essence of the object, and then of its properties; in practice we frequently arrive at the knowledge of things in the reverse order, by perceiving first the properties and then the object itself. Maimonides, therefore, in mentioning the two petitions of Moses, followed the logical order, while Moses is said to have asked first for that which he considered easier to obtain.

possessed by any human being before him or after him. His petition to know the attributes of God is contained in the following words: "Show me now Thy way, that I may know Thee, that I may find grace in Thy sight" (Exod. xxxiii. 13). Consider how many excellent ideas found expression in the words, "Show me Thy way, that I may know Thee." We learn from them that God is known by His attributes, for Moses believed that he knew Him, when he was shown the way[1] of God. The words "That I may know Thee," imply that He who knows God will find grace in His eyes. Not only[2] is he acceptable and welcome to God, who fasts and prays, but everyone who acquires a knowledge of Him. He who has no knowledge of God is the object of His wrath and displeasure. The pleasure and the displeasure of God, the approach to Him and the withdrawal from Him are proportional to the amount of man's knowledge or ignorance concerning the Creator. We have already gone too far away from our subject, let us now return to it.

Moses prayed to God to grant him knowledge of His attributes, and also pardon for His people; when the latter had been granted, he continued to pray for the knowledge of God's essence in the words, "Show me Thy glory" (*ib.* 18), and then received, respecting his first request "Show me Thy way," the following favourable reply, "I will make all My goodness to pass before thee" (*ib.* 19); as regards the second request, however, he was told, "Thou canst not see My

---

[1] דְּרָכֶךָ is generally taken to be the singular, but Maimonides seems to have understood it as being identical with the plural דְּרָכָיךָ,

[2] According to Abravanel, Maimonides does not describe those who fast and say prayers as unacceptable to God, but declares that, besides them, all those who have obtained a true knowledge of God are acceptable to Him. Narboni says that the common people approach God by fasting and saying prayers, ומי יתן ויתעסקו בהם ברורנו זה, and would that this were done at present! The philosopher, however, must aim at the knowledge of God as his highest blessing. Munk refers the limiting פקט "only" to the phrase "who fast and pray," but the words כל מן, "all those who," which follow, show that פקט is to be joined with לא מן; "not only those who . . . , but all those who . . ."

PART I.—CHAPTER LIV. 193

face" (*ib.* 20). The words "all my goodness" (כל טובי) imply that God promised to show him the whole creation, concerning which it has been stated, "And God saw everything that He had made, and, behold, it was very good" (Gen. i. 31); when I say "to show him the whole creation," I mean to imply that God promised to make him comprehend the nature of all things, their relation to each other, and the way they are governed by God both in reference to the universe as a whole and to each creature in particular.[1] This knowledge is referred to when we are told of Moses, "he is firmly established[2] in all Mine house" (Num. xii. 7); that is, "his knowledge of all the creatures in My universe is true and firmly established"; for false opinions are not firmly established. Consequently the knowledge of the works of God is the knowledge of His attributes,[3] by which He can be known.[4] The fact that God promised Moses to give him a knowledge of His works, may be inferred from the circumstance that God taught him such attributes as refer exclusively to His works, *viz.*, "merciful and gracious, longsuffering and abundant in goodness," etc. (Exod. xxxiv. 6). It is therefore clear that the ways which Moses wished to know, and which God taught him, are the actions emanating from God. Our Sages call them *middoth* (qualities), and speak of the thirteen *middoth*[5] of God; they

---

[1] Charizi והחבור בהם והפרוד, "and their combination and separation."

[2] The word נאמן appears to be understood in the sense of "firm," "sure," "possessed with a true knowledge."

[3] Lit., "are His attributes." This is inaccurate; after "consequently," we must either repeat "the knowledge of" (אדראך Hebrew השגת) before "His attributes," and substitute "is" for "are," or omit the phrase altogether. That the text is corrupt is proved by the various readings found in the MSS., which, however, do not give a better sense than the one adopted by Munk. In Charizi's version the difficulty has been removed: כי הרעות שאינם אמתיות לא תתקים השנתם והפעלים ההם הם מדותיו. (In the printed edition אם כן has wrongly been added. Munk.)

[4] That is to say, the knowledge referred to in the prayer of Moses in the words "Show me Thy ways that I may know Thee" (Ex. xxxiii. 13).

[5] *I.e.*, the thirteen attributes mentioned in Exod. xxxiv. 6-7. Contrary to the traditional interpretation, Maimonides does not count the repetition of the

o

used the term also in reference to man;[1] comp. ארבע מדות בחולכי בית המדרש, "there are four different *middoth* (characters) among those who go to the house of learning;" ארבע מדות בנותני צדקה, "There are four different *middoth* (characters) among those who give charity."[2] They do not mean to say that God really possesses *middoth*[3] (qualities), but that He performs actions similar to such of our actions as originate in certain qualities, *i.e.*, in certain psychical dispositions; not that God has really such dispositions. Although Moses was shown "all His goodness," *i.e.*, all His works, only the thirteen *middoth* are mentioned, because they include those acts of God which refer to the creation[4] and the government of mankind, and to know these acts was the principal object of the prayer of Moses. This is shown by the conclusion of his prayer, "that I may know Thee, that I may find grace in Thy sight, and consider that this nation is Thy people" (Exod. xxxiii. 16), that is to say, the people whom I have to rule by certain acts in the performance of which I must be guided by Thy own acts in governing them. We have thus shown that "the ways" [דרכים in the Bible], and "*middoth*" [used by our Sages], are identical, denoting the acts emanating from God in reference to the universe.

Whenever any one of His actions is perceived by us, we ascribe to God that emotion which is the source of the act when performed by ourselves, and call Him by an epithet which is formed from the verb expressing that action. We see, *e.g.*, how well[5] He provides for the life of the embryo of living beings; how He endows with certain faculties both the embryo itself and those who have to rear it after its birth,

---

name of God as a separate attribute, and includes in the number "visiting the iniquity," etc. Comp. Babyl. Talm. Rosh ha-shanah, 17b, and Tosafoth beg. שלש עשרה.

[1] Char., הכחות והטבעים.
[2] Mishnah Abhoth v. 13 and 14.
[3] Char., בעל טבעים ומנהגים ומדות.
[4] Charizi's version contains two different renderings of this sentence.
[5] According to Charizi טוב, "good," "well;" Ibn Tibbon דקות, "minutely," "carefully."

in order that it may be protected from death and destruction, guarded against all harm, and assisted in the performance of all that is required [for its development]. Similar acts, when performed by us, are due to a certain emotion and tenderness called mercy (רחמנות and חמלה). God is, therefore, said to be merciful (רחום); *e.g.*, "Like as a father is merciful (כרחם) to his children, so the Lord is merciful (רחם) to them that fear Him" (Ps. ciii. 13); "And I will spare (וחמלתי) them, as a man spareth (יחמל) his own son that serveth him" (Mal. iii. 17). Such instances do not imply that God is influenced by a feeling of mercy, but that acts similar to those which a father performs for his son, out of pity, mercy and real affection, emanate from God solely for the benefit of His pious men, and are by no means the result of any impression or change [produced in God].—When we give something to a person who has no claim upon us, we perform an act of grace (חנינה); *e.g.*, חנונו אותם, "Grant them graciously unto us" (Judges xxi. 22).[1] [The same term is used in reference to God, *e.g.*] אשר חנן אלהים, "which God hath graciously given" (Gen. xxxiii. 5); כי חנני אלהים, "Because God hath dealt graciously with me" (*ib.* 11). Instances of this kind are numerous. God creates and guides beings who have no claim upon Him to be created and guided by Him; He is therefore called gracious (חנון).—His actions towards mankind also include great calamities, which overtake individuals and bring death to them, or affect whole families and even entire regions, spread death, destroy generation after generation, and spare nothing whatsoever.[2] Hence there occur inundations, earthquakes, destructive storms, expeditions of one nation against the other for the sake of destroying it with the sword and blotting out its memory, and many other evils of the same kind. Whenever such evils are caused by us to any person, they originate

[1] Instead of חנונו אותם, as in the original, Ibn Tibbon quotes חנני אתם רעי from Job xix. 21.

[2] Lit., "Neither field nor offspring." Charizi, ולא תשאיר זרע ולא חריש. In Arabic חרת ונסל is a phrase which means "every thing."

in great anger, violent jealousy, or a desire for revenge. God is therefore called, because of these acts, "jealous" (קנוא), "revengeful" (נוקם), "wrathful" (בעל חמה), and "keeping anger" (נוטר, Nah. i. 2); that is to say, He performs acts similar to those which, when performed by us, originate in certain psychical dispositions, in jealousy, desire for retaliation, revenge, or anger; they are in accordance with the guilt of those who are to be punished, and not the result of any emotion; for He is above all defect! The same is the case with all divine acts; though resembling those acts which emanate from our passions and psychical dispositions, they are not due to anything superadded to His essence.—The governor of a country, if he is a prophet,[1] should conform to these attributes. Acts [of punishment] must be performed by him moderately and in accordance with justice, not merely as an outlet of his passion. He must not let loose his anger, nor allow his passion to overcome him; for all passions are bad,[2] and they must be guarded against as far as it lies in man's power. At times and towards some persons he must be merciful and gracious, not only from motives of mercy and compassion, but according to their merits; at other times and towards other persons he must evince anger, revenge, and wrath in proportion to their guilt, but not from motives of passion. He must be able to condemn a person to death by fire without anger, passion, or loathing against him, and must exclusively be guided by what he perceives of the guilt of the person, and by a sense of the great benefit which a large number will derive from such a sentence. You have, no doubt, noticed in the Torah how the commandment to annihilate the seven nations, and "to save alive nothing that breatheth" (Deut. xx. 16) is followed im-

---

[1] The words "if he is a prophet" seem to be superfluous; there is no reason why only prophets should conform to these conditions. נביא of the Arabic text is perhaps a mistake, the correct reading being נביהא, "noble," and the sense of the phrase is: "if he is (or desires to be) noble."

[2] That is, in so far as they prevent man from following the dictates of reason, and prompt him to act in accordance with momentary impulses.

mediately by the words "That they teach you not to do after all their abominations, which they have done unto their gods; so should you sin against the Lord your God" (*ib.* 18); that is to say, you shall not think that this commandment implies an act of cruelty or of retaliation; it is an act demanded by the tendency of man to remove everything that might turn him away from the right path, and to clear away all obstacles in the road to perfection, that is, to the knowledge of God. Nevertheless, acts of mercy, pardon, pity, and grace should more frequently be performed by the governor of a country than acts of punishment; seeing that all the thirteen *middoth* of God are attributes of mercy with only one exception, namely, פקד עון אבות על בנים, "visiting the iniquity of the fathers upon the children" (Exod. xxxiv. 7); for the meaning of ונקה לא ינקה is "and He will not utterly destroy;"[1] comp. ונקתה לארץ תשב, "And she will be utterly destroyed, she shall sit upon the ground" (Is. iii. 26). When it is said that God is visiting the iniquity of the fathers upon the children, this refers exclusively to the sin of idolatry, and to no other sin. That this is the case may be inferred from what is said in the ten commandments, "upon the third and fourth generation of My enemies"[2] (לשנאי, Exod. xx. 5), none except idolaters being called "enemy" (שנא); comp. also כל תועבת יי אשר שנא, "every abomination to the Lord, which He hateth" (Deut. xii. 31). It was, however, considered sufficient to extend the punishment to the fourth generation, because

---

[1] Generally, "He will not hold guiltless." It appears that Maimonides wished especially to point out, that among the principal attributes of God, there is one of punishment and severity. Otherwise he would no doubt have explained the phrase פקד עון אבות על בנים as being an attribute of mercy, and implying that God delays the punishment and gives the sinner an opportunity to improve.

[2] Maimonides appears to have understood the word לשנאי "to my enemies," in the sense of "to those whom I hate," contrary to the traditional interpretation, *viz.*, "to those who hate me." Therefore he quotes another passage, in which God is said to hate idolatry. Comp. ch. xxxvi., page 131, where the same verse is quoted in support of the view that the idolater is an enemy (שונא) of God.

the fourth generation is the utmost a man can see of his posterity; and when, therefore, the idolaters of a place are destroyed, the old man worshipping idols is killed, his son, his grandson, and his great-grandson, that is, the fourth generation. By the mention of this attribute[1] we are, as it were, told that His commandments, undoubtedly in harmony with His acts, include the death even of the little children of idolaters because of the sin[2] of their fathers and grandfathers. This principle we find frequently applied in the Law, as, *e. g.*, we read concerning the city that has been led astray to idolatry, "destroy it utterly, and all that is therein" (Deut. xiii. 15). All this has been ordained in order that every vestige of that which would lead to great injury should be blotted out, as we have explained.

We have gone too far away from the subject of this chapter, but we have shown why it has been considered sufficient to mention only these (thirteen) out of all His acts; namely, because they are required for the good government of a country; for the chief aim of man should be to make himself, as far as possible, similar to God: that is to say, to make his acts similar to the acts of God, or as our Sages expressed it in explaining the verse, "Ye shall be holy"[3] (Lev. xxi. 2): "He is gracious, so be you also gracious; He is merciful, so be you also merciful."

The principal object of this chapter was to show that all attributes ascribed to God are attributes of His acts, and do not imply that God has any qualities.

[1] That is, by mentioning to Moses the attribute פקד עון אבות על בנים.

[2] In Arabic פי נמאר, or פי נמר ; most of the editions of the Hebrew Versions have בחמא, "by the sin." According to Munk, "Pêle-mêle avec leur pères," etc. The MSS. of Tibbon's version and the ed. princeps have the reading בתוך ; the version of Charizi has בחיי (in MS., the printed ed. has בחמא).

[3] Although the words (Lev. xix. 2), "Ye shall be holy, for I am holy," admit of reflections similar to those quoted here, these remarks are made in the Talmud in reference to the words "Ye shall walk after the Lord" (Deut. xiii. 5. Comp. Babyl. Talm., Sota, 14a). Maimonides (Yad ha-chazakah, Hilchoth Deoth, i. 6), quotes והלכת בדרכיו, "And thou shalt walk in His ways" (Deut. xxviii. 9).

CHAPTER LV.[1]

On Attributes implying Corporeality, Emotion, Non-existence, and Comparison.

WE have already, on several occasions, shown in this treatise that everything that implies corporeality or passiveness, is to be negatived in reference to God, for all passiveness implies change; and the agent producing that state is undoubtedly different from the object affected by it; and if God could be affected in any way whatever, another being beside Him would act on Him and cause change in Him. All kinds of non-existence must likewise be negatived in reference to Him; no perfection whatever can therefore be imagined to be at one time absent from Him, and at another present in Him : for if this were the case, He would [at a certain time] only be potentially perfect. Potentiality always implies non-existence,[2] and when anything has to pass from potentiality into reality, another thing that exists in reality is required to effect that transition. Hence it follows that all perfections must really exist in God, and none of them must in any way be a mere potentiality. Another thing likewise to be denied in reference to God, is similarity to any existing being. This has been generally accepted, and is also mentioned in the books of the Prophets; *e.g.,* "To whom, then, will you liken me?" (Is. xl. 25); "To whom, then, will you liken God?" (*ib.* 18); "There is none like unto Thee" (Jer. x. 6). Instances of this

---

[1] Having shown in the preceding chapter that the thirteen *middoth* are qualifications of those acts which are the consequence of certain emotions when performed by man, the author points out in the present chapter that it is not sufficient to exclude from the idea of God everything leading to corporeality, all emotions and changes, transitions from δύναμις to ἐνέργεια, and comparison with material objects, but the necessity of their exclusion must be established by scientific proof.

[2] This sentence is here out of place; its object is not clear. The author intended, perhaps, to justify the substitution of potentiality for non-existence in this argument.

kind are frequent. In short, it is necessary to demonstrate by proof that nothing can be predicated of God that implies any of the following four things: corporeality, emotion or change, non-existence,—*e.g.*,[1] that something would be potential[2] at one time and real at another—and similarity with any of His creatures. In this respect our knowledge of God is aided by the study of Natural Science. For he who is ignorant of the latter cannot understand the defect implied in emotions, the difference between potentiality and reality, the non-existence implied in all potentiality,[3] the inferiority of a thing that exists *in potentia* to that which moves in order to cause its transition from potentiality into reality, and the inferiority of that which moves to that for the sake of whose realisation it moves.[4] He who knows these things, but without their proofs, does not know the details which logically result from these general propositions; he will not be able to prove that God exists, or that the [four] things mentioned above are inadmissible in reference to God.

Having premised these remarks, I shall explain in the next chapter the error of those who believe that God has essential attributes; those who have some knowledge of Logic and Natural Science will understand it.

[1] Charizi, כדי שלא, "that not." The negation is a repetition of the negation contained in "nothing can be predicated."

[2] Lit. "not real," according to the Arabic and Ibn Tibbon's versions. Charizi has בכח. A Leyden MS. of the Arabic has likewise באלקוה.

[3] An object does not possess a property which it is *capable* of acquiring, the property is therefore absent; the possibility and the absence of a property are thus always associated with each other. It has already been mentioned that absence is required as a link between matter and form, without which the combination of matter and form could not take place. (Comp. ch. xvii. pag. 68, note 3.)

[4] Three stages are here assumed, before any special form is combined with a substance; first, the στέρησις, or the absence of the form from the respective substance, and the capacity of the latter to receive the form; secondly, the κίνησις, the motion of the form toward the matter; and thirdly, the real combination of both.

CHAPTER LVI.

Existence, Life, Power, Wisdom, and Will are homonymously ascribed to God and His Creatures.

SIMILARITY[1] is based on a certain relation between two things; if between two things no relation can be found, there can be no similarity between them, and there is no relation between two things that have no similarity to each other; *e.g.*, we do not say this heat is similar to that colour, or this voice is similar to that sweetness. This is self-evident. Since the existence of a relation between God and man, or between Him and other beings has been denied, similarity must likewise be denied. You must know that two things of the same kind—*i.e.*, whose essential properties are the same, distinguished from each other by greatness and smallness, strength and weakness, etc.—are necessarily similar, though different in a certain particular point; *e.g.*, a grain of mustard and the sphere of the fixed stars are similar as regards the three dimensions, although the one is exceedingly great, the other exceedingly small, the property of having [three] dimensions is the same in both; or wax melted by the heat of the sun and wax melted by the heat of fire,[2] are similar as regards heat; although the heat is exceedingly great in the one case, and exceedingly small in the other, the existence of that quality is the same in both. Thus those who believe in the existence of essential attributes in reference to God, *viz.*, Existence, Life, Power,[3] Wisdom, and Will, should know that these attributes, when applied to God, have not the same meaning

---

[1] A comparison between God and His creatures is rejected by all thinkers; the Mutakallemim are therefore wrong in ascribing to God essential attributes in the same sense as applied to man; for this necessarily leads to a comparison between God and man as regards the degree, quantity, intensity, etc., of those qualities. (Comp. ch. xxxv.)

[2] Lit., "the heat of the element fire."

[3] Ibn Tibbon adds here ידוע, which is identical with חכם.

as when applied to us, and that the difference does not only consist in magnitude, or in the degree of perfection, stability, and durability. It cannot be said, as they practically believe, that His existence is only more stable, His life more permanent, His power greater, His wisdom more perfect, and His will more general than ours, and that the same definition applies to both. This is in no way admissible, for the expression "more than" is used in comparing two things as regards a certain attribute predicated of both of them in exactly the same sense,[1] and consequently implies similarity [between God and His creatures]. When they ascribe to God essential attributes, these so-called essential attributes should not have any similarity to the attributes of other things, and should according to their own opinion, not be included in one and the same definition, in the same manner as there is no similarity between the essence of God and that of other beings. They do not follow this principle, for they hold that one definition may include them, and that, nevertheless, there is no similarity between them.[2] Those who are familiar with the meaning of similarity will certainly understand that the term existence, when applied to God and to other beings, is perfectly homonymous. In like manner, the terms Wisdom, Power, Will, and Life are applied to God and to other beings by way of perfect homonymity, admitting of no comparison whatever. Nor must you think that the homonymity of these terms is doubtful.[3] For an expression, the

[1] An adjective applied in the same sense to two things admits of comparison, but if it is applied to two things in different significations, the two cannot be compared with each other; תואטו (Hebr. הסכמה) means complete agreement between the significations of a word in the several instances in which it is employed, and is opposed to שתוף or ספוק, complete or partial homonymity of expressions. Comp. Introd., p. 5, note 2.

[2] The contradiction which Maimonides desires here to point out in the theory of his opponents is this: on the one hand they declare that God cannot be compared, and on the other hand by applying attributes to Him in the same sense as they are applied to man, they admit comparison.

[3] Comp. Introd., page 5, note 2, on hybrid terms (מסופקים). A term is sometimes applied to different objects, which have a certain non-essential

homonymity of which is uncertain, is applied to two things which have a similarity to each other in respect to a certain relation which is in both of them an accident, not an essential, constituent element. The attributes of God, however, are not considered as accidental by any intelligent person, while all attributes applied to man are accidents, according to the Mutakallemim.[1] I am therefore at a loss to see how they can find any similarity [between the attributes of God and those of man]; how their definitions can be identical, and their significations the same! This is a decisive proof that there is, in no way or sense, anything common to the attributes predicated of God, and those used in reference to ourselves; they have only the same names, and nothing else is common to them. Such being the case, it is not proper to believe, on account of the identity in those names, that there is in God something additional to His essence, similar to the properties which are joined to our essence. This is most important for those who understand it. Keep it in memory, and study it thoroughly, in order to be well prepared for that which I am going to explain to you

CHAPTER LVII.

The Essence of God and His Attributes are identical.

ON attributes; remarks more recondite than the preceding.[2]

---

property in common; it may therefore be a question regarding that term, whether it is in all its significations of the same origin. As the property expressed by that term is an accident (מקרה), and not part of the constituent elements of the object, it can in no way be ascribed to God. Comp. ch. lii., pag. 179.

[1] See ch. lxxiii., Propos. 4.

[2] The first words "on attributes; remarks more recondite than the preceding," seem to be connected with the conclusion of the preceding chapter, "which I am going to explain to you." The subject of this chapter is said to be more subtle than that of the preceding. In the present chapter he proves the necessity of even excluding the attributes of existence, unity, and eternity

It is known that existence is an accident[1] appertaining to all things, and therefore an element superadded to their essence. This must evidently be the case as regards everything the existence of which is due to some cause; its existence is an element superadded to its essence. But as regards a being whose existence is not due to any cause—God alone is that being, for His existence, as we have said, is absolute—existence and essence are perfectly identical; He is not a substance to which existence is joined as an accident, as an additional element. His existence is always absolute, and has never been a new element or an accident in Him. Consequently God exists without possessing the attribute of existence.[2] Similarly He lives, without possessing the attribute of life; knows, with-

---

from God as attributes, although they are generally considered as inseparable from the idea of God.—Comp. "The investigation of this subject, which is almost too subtle for our understanding, must not be based on current expressions employed in describing it, for these are the great source of error" (*infra* pp. 205-6).

[1] Of all the things we notice in the universe, we predicate that they exist; we also speak of the things before they come into existence, or after they have ceased to exist, and say that they did not or that they do not exist. We have, therefore, in our mind two separate ideas: the idea of the thing itself and the idea of existence, which we can imagine as being combined, or separate. The idea of God, however, is inseparable from the idea of existence. How far this separation of the things from their existence is in reality possible, their relation to each other and similar problems, were the subject of much discussion among the philosophers of the Middle Ages. Ibn Sina assumed that existence was an accident of the thing itself, so that the thing must for some time have been without existence. If there is to be any sense in this theory, we must combine it with the Platonic theory of ideals (αὐτὸ καθ' αὑτό.) Ibn Roshd, on the other hand, contended that the thing itself, its essence, was inseparable from existence, without which the thing is nothing. He therefore declares the existence to be a part of the essence of the thing. Maimonides follows Ibn Sina in this point. He accordingly holds that existence is an element that is superadded to the thing, and distinguishes between the thing *in potentiâ* and the thing in reality; in the first case the thing is said to be without existence, and to pass over into the state of reality, when existence is combined with it as an accident. (Comp. ch. xvii. and lv.)

[2] That is, we say of God that He exists; but we deny that existence is in Him an attribute or an accident, as it is in the things created by God; the term "existence" is applied to God in the sense of denying His non-existence.

out possessing the attribute of knowledge; is omnipotent without possessing the attribute of omnipotence; is wise, without possessing the attribute of wisdom; all this reduces itself to one and the same entity; there is no plurality in Him, as will be shown. It is further necessary to consider that unity and plurality are accidents supervening to an object according as it consists of many elements or of one. This is fully explained in the book called Metaphysics.[1] In the same way as number is not the substance of the things numbered, so is unity not the substance of the thing which has the attribute of unity, for unity and plurality are accidents belonging to the category of discrete quantity,[2] and supervening to such objects as are capable of receiving them.

To that being, however, which has truly simple, absolute existence, and in which composition is inconceivable, the accident of unity is as inadmissible as the accident of plurality; that is to say, God's unity is not an element superadded, but He is One without possessing the attribute of unity. The investigation of this subject, which is almost too subtle for our

[1] According to Aristotle (Metaphys. v. 6), there are two kinds of unity, τὰ κατὰ συμβεβηκὸς ἓν λεγόμενα, καὶ τὰ καθ' αὑτὰ ἓν λεγόμενα, accidental unity, or the combination of different things into one body without forming an organic whole, and the absolute unity, or the combination of the constituent elements into one organic whole. In both cases the property of forming one whole may properly be described an accident superadded (מקרה קרה) to the single constituent elements. Unity in this sense is not different from plurality, in its relation to the essence of the thing. Ideal unity, which is inseparable from the idea of the thing itself, or rather identical with it, is not here referred to, but unity as the correlative of plurality, expressive, like plurality, of a certain property of the things as regards their relation to the ideal unity. (Comp. Narboni *ad locum*). The two principal philosophers of the Mahomedan schools, Ibn Sina and Ibn Roshd, differed from each other in that respect. While Ibn Sina considers the ideal unity as an accident, Ibn Roshd treated it as the essence of the thing. Comp. p. 204, note 1.

[2] במות המתפרק, Ibn Tibbon; כמות הנבדל, Char.; both terms have the same meaning. Here we see clearly that Maimonides had in view numerical unity as correlative of plurality; and that he does not, as some believe (see Munk *ad locum*), confound the two kinds of unity; the term "number," used here as distinguished from "unity," is to be understood as equal to "the rest of the numbers," which are generally admitted to be "accidents;" and since unity as such is part of the series of numbers, it is likewise an "accident."

understanding,[1] must not be based on current expressions employed in describing it, for these are the great source of error. It would be extremely difficult for us to find, in any language whatsoever, words adequate to this subject, and we can only employ inadequate language. In our endeavour to show that God does not include a plurality, we can only say "He is one," although "one" and "many" are both terms which serve to distinguish quantity. We therefore make the subject clearer, and show to the understanding the way of truth by saying He is one but does not possess the attribute of unity.

The same is the case when we say God is the First (קדמון), to express that He has not been created; the term קדמון, "First," is decidedly inaccurate, for it can in its true sense only be applied to a being that is subject to the relation of time; the latter, however, is an accident to motion which again is connected with a body. Besides the attribute קדמון ("first" or "eternal") is a relative term,[2] being in regard to time the same as the terms "long" and "short" are in regard to a line.[3] Both expressions, "created" and "eternal" (or "first"), are equally inadmissible in reference to any being to which the attribute of time is not applicable, just as we do not say "crooked" or "straight" in reference to taste, "salted" or "insipid" in reference to the voice. These subjects are not unknown to those who have accustomed themselves to seek a true understanding of the things, and to establish their properties in accordance with the abstract notions which the mind has formed of them, and who are not misled by the

---

[1] Comp. beginning of this chapter.

[2] The two relative terms are מחודש, "beginning at a certain time," and קדמון, "preceding," "anterior," viz., to every מחודש. According to Maimonides, such a comparison or relation, as regards time, is inadmissible between God and His creatures.

[3] The Arabic عرض admits of two renderings, "accident," and "extension" or "measure." Ibn Tibbon translates it by מקרה, "accident."—Ibn Palquera, in "Moreh ha-moreh," considers that it should be rendered by מדה or רוחב: Munk, adopting the latter intepretation, distinguishes between עֲרָץ, "extension," and עֲרָץ, "accident."

inaccuracy[1] of the words employed. All attributes, such as "the First," "the Last," occurring in the Scriptures in reference to God, are as metaphorical as the expressions "ear" and "eye." They simply signify that God is not subject to any change or innovation whatever; they do not imply that God can be described by time, or that there is any comparison between Him and any other being as regards time, and that He is called on that account "the first" and "the last." In short, all similar expressions are borrowed from the language commonly used among the people. In the same way we use "One" (אחד), in reference to God, to express that there is nothing similar to Him, but we do not mean to say that an attribute of unity is added to His essence.

CHAPTER LVIII.

The true attributes of God have a negative sense.

THIS chapter is even more recondite than the preceding.[2] Know that the negative attributes of God are the true attributes: they do not include any incorrect notions[3] or any

---

[1] Some MSS. have, instead of באלתנמל, lit. "in the general sense," or "in the comprehensive meaning," באלתנסים, "in a material sense."—Ibn Tibbon renders it בכללות; Char. בחבור; both expressions have the same signification. The sense of the sentence is this: The words admit of many interpretations. In order to understand the nature of any particular thing, inquiry must be directed to the nature of the object, and not solely to the signification of the word by which it is described.

[2] In this chapter Maimonides shows the propriety of applying negative attributes to God, and of rejecting all positive attributes without any exception. He says that this chapter is more subtle than the preceding, probably on account of the difficulty of understanding how a Being with the most absolute and the most positive existence could be described by mere negations, which cannot give a positive idea of the object which is to be described.

[3] The negative attributes fully express what we have to say; we need not content ourselves with inadequate terms as is the case when we attempt to describe God by positive attributes. Charizi renders אלתסאמח (Ibn Tibbon דבר ההקל, "inaccuracy,") by ספק, "doubt."

deficiency whatever in reference to God, while positive attributes imply polytheism,[1] and are inadequate, as we have already shown. It is now necessary to explain how negative expressions can in a certain sense be employed as attributes, and how they are distinguished from positive attributes. Then I shall show that we cannot describe the Creator by any means except by negative attributes. An attribute does not exclusively belong to the one object to which it is related; while qualifying one thing, it can also be employed to qualify other things, and is in that case not peculiar to that one thing. *E.g.*, if you see an object from a distance, and on enquiring what it is, are told that it is a living being, you have certainly learnt an attribute of the object seen, and although that attribute does not exclusively belong to the object perceived, it expresses that the object is not a plant or a mineral. Again, if a man is in a certain house, and you know that something is in the house, but not exactly what, you ask what is in that house, and you are told, not a plant nor a mineral. You have thereby obtained some special knowledge of the thing; you have learnt that it is a living being, although you do not yet know what kind of living being it is. The negative attributes have this in common with the positive, that they necessarily circumscribe the object to some extent, although such circumscription consists only in the exclusion of what otherwise would not be excluded. In the following point, however, the negative attributes are distinguished from the positive. The positive attributes, although not peculiar to one thing, describe a portion of what we desire to know, either some part of its essence or some of its accidents; the negative attributes, on the other hand, do not, as regards the essence of the thing which we desire to know, in any way tell us what it is, except it be indirectly, as has been shown in the instance given by us.

After this introduction, I would observe that—as has already

[1] By admitting positive essential attributes, we assume that, besides the essence of God, other things co-existed with Him from eternity. (Compare ch. xxxvi. pag. 134.)

been shown—God's existence is absolute, that it includes no composition, as will be proved,[1] and that we comprehend only the fact that He exists, not His essence.[2] Consequently it is a false assumption to hold that He has any positive attribute; for He does not possess existence[3] in addition to His essence; it therefore cannot be said that the one[4] may be described as an attribute [of the other]; much less has He [in addition to His existence] a compound essence,[5] consisting of two constituent elements to which the attribute could refer; still less has He accidents, which could be described by an attribute. Hence it is clear that He has no positive attribute whatever. The negative attributes, however, are those which are necessary to direct the mind to the truths which we must believe concerning God; for, on the one hand, they do not imply any plurality, and, on the other, they convey to man the highest possible knowledge of God; e.g., it has been established by proof that some being must exist besides those things which can be perceived by the senses, or apprehended by the mind;[6] when we say of this being, that it exists, we mean that its non-existence is impossible. We thus perceive that such a being is not, for instance, like the four elements, which are inanimate, and we therefore

[1] See Part II., ch. i.

[2] That is, we only comprehend that He exists (ὅτι or *quod*), but not what he is (τί or *quid*); we cannot give a logical definition of God, which consists of the *genus* and specific difference (comp. ch. lii., pag. 178, note 2).

[3] This is according to the Arabic text, and the reading of Ibn Tibbon's version in some MSS.; the printed editions of the latter have the reverse, אין לו מהות חוץ לישותו, "He has besides His existence, no essence." This reading appears to be preferable; it conforms more to the phrase which follows: "Much less has He a compound *essence*"; and also to the preceding sentence: "We comprehend only the fact that He exists, not His essence." Charizi in accordance with the Arabic renders the passage thus: אין לו הויה יוצאת חוץ מנבול מהותו.

[4] "One of them" (Tibbon and Charizi: אחת מהם), that is, either the ישות, "existence" (ὅτι), or the מהות, "essence" (τί), the one being considered as the substance, the other as its accident.

[5] That is, besides His existence, e. g., *genus* and specific difference.

[6] *I.e.*, corporeal objects, or their forms, relations, and properties.

P

say it is living, expressing thereby that it is not dead. We call such a being incorporeal, because we notice that it is unlike the heavens, which are living, but material.[1] Seeing that it is also different from the intellect, which, though incorporeal and living, owes its existence to some cause,[2] we say it is the first (קדמון), expressing thereby that its existence is not due to any cause. We further notice, that the existence, that is, the essence, of this being is not limited to its own existence;[3] many existences emanate from it, and its influence is not like that of the fire in producing heat, or that of the sun in sending forth light, but consists in constantly giving them stability and order by well-established rule, as we shall show:[4] we say, on that account, it has power, wisdom, and will, *i.e.*, it is not feeble or ignorant, or hasty, and does not abandon its creatures; when we say that it is not feeble, we mean that its existence is capable of producing the existence of many other things; by saying it is not ignorant, we mean "it perceives" or "it lives,"—for everything that perceives is

[1] The heavens, though different from the sublunary elements, and consisting of the fifth element which is a kind of ether, are nevertheless material. Comp. Arist. De Cœlo, i. 2.

[2] The intellect owes its existence to some cause; both the acquired intellect (שכל הנקנה), which comes into existence by certain intellectual actions of man, and the active intellect, שכל הפועל, which is the source of the intellectual faculty existing in man, and which emanates from immaterial beings of a higher order created by God (see Part II. ch. iv.) have a beginning, while God is without a beginning.

[3] Lit., "As regards this existing Being, it does not content itself with its existence, which is the same as its essence, that it should exist alone." The word מציאות, generally a feminine noun, is here used by Tibbon as a masculine noun (מספקת in the editions of Ibn Tibbon's version is a mistake; the correct reading is מספיק), with the express purpose of leaving it undefined whether the original requires that מאתו is to agree with נמצא or with מציאות (as stated by him in a note on this passage; Munk *ad locum*). It does not make any difference as regards the sense of the passage. The words עצמו and מציאותו have the same meaning as מחותו and ישותו used before.

[4] The difference here pointed out is as follows: heat comes from fire, light from the sun, as a natural consequence of the properties of fire and of the sun. There is no intention or will in either of them; but that which comes from God emanates from His will (בהנהגה מתוקנת). See Part II., ch. xvii. *sqq*.

alive[1]—by saying "it is not hasty, and does not abandon its creatures," we mean that all these creatures preserve a certain order and arrangement; they are not left to themselves, or produced aimlessly, but whatever condition they receive from that being is given them with design and intention. We thus learn that there is no other being like unto God, and we say that He is One, *i.e.*, there are not more Gods than one.

It has thus been shown that every attribute predicated of God either denotes the quality of an action, or—when the attribute is intended to convey some idea of the Divine Being itself, and not of His actions—the negation of the opposite.[2] Even these negative attributes must not be formed and applied to God, except in the way in which, as you know, sometimes an attribute is negatived in reference to a thing, although that attribute can naturally never be applied to it[3] in the same sense, as, *e.g.*, we say, "This wall does not see." Those who read the present work, are aware that, notwithstanding all the efforts of the mind, we can obtain no knowledge of the essence of the heavens,—a revolving substance which has been measured by us in spans and cubits, and examined even as regards the proportions of the several spheres to each other and respecting most of their motions—although we know that they must consist of matter and form; but the matter not being the same as sublunary matter, we can only describe the heavens in terms expressing negative properties, but not in terms denoting positive qualities.[4] Thus we say that the heavens are not light, not

[1] Comp., ch. lii., pag. 178.

[2] Lit., "The negative of the absence of that attribute," that is, the negation of the opposite, *e.g.*, "wise" means "not ignorant;" "strong" means "not weak," etc.

[3] That is, absolute negation. We can never affirm of God that which we have denied of Him, in the same way as in reference to the wall, of which we say "This wall does not see," it is impossible ever to assert, "This wall does see."

[4] The Arabic ניר מחצלה and אלמחצל, signify respectively, "without clearness," or "not distinct," and "with clearness," or "decided." Ibn Tibbon renders the two phrases, בלתי מקיימים and מקיימים; Palquera,

heavy, not passive and therefore not subject to impressions, and that they do not possess the sensations of taste or smell; or we use similar negative attributes. All this we do, because we do not know their substance. What, then, can be the result of our efforts, when we try to obtain a knowledge of a Being that is free from substance, that is most simple, whose existence is absolute, and not due to any cause, to whose perfect essence nothing can be superadded, and whose perfection consists, as we have shown, in the absence of all defects. All we understand, is the fact that He exists, that He is a Being to whom none of all His creatures is similar, who has nothing in common with them, who does not include plurality, who is never too feeble to produce other beings, and whose relation to the universe is that of a steersman to a boat; and even this is not a real relation, a real simile, but serves only to convey to us the idea that God rules the universe; that is, that He gives it duration, and preserves its necessary arrangement. This subject will be treated more fully.[1] Praised be He! In the contemplation of His essence, our comprehension and knowledge prove insufficient; in the examination of His works, how they necessarily result from His will, our knowledge proves to be ignorance, and in the endeavour to extol Him in words, all our efforts in speech are mere weakness and failure!

שאינם מיושבים, and המיושב; both reproduce fairly the sense of the original; Char., שאינם כוללים, "That are not general," and כולל, "That is general," a term that is a common noun, and includes many things in its signification; he understands the passage to imply that we can employ only a proper noun for that unique substance of the heaven, not a common noun.

[1] Comp. *infra* ch. lxx., and Part II., ch. xvii.

CHAPTER LIX.

On Differences in the Knowledge of God which consists of Negations.

THE following question might perhaps be asked: Since there is no possibility of obtaining a knowledge of the true essence of God, and since it has also been proved that the only thing that man can apprehend of Him is the fact that He exists, and that all positive attributes are inadmissible, as has been shown; what is the difference among those who have obtained a knowledge of God? Must not the knowledge obtained by our teacher Moses, and by Solomon,[1] be the same as that obtained by any one of the lowest class of philosophers, since there can be no addition to this knowledge? But, on the other hand, it is generally accepted among theologians and also among philosophers, that there can be a great difference[2] between the knowledge of God obtained by two different men. Know that this is really the case, that those who have obtained a knowledge of God differ greatly from each other; for in the same way as by each additional attribute an object is more specified, and is brought nearer to the true apprehension of the observer, so by each additional negative attribute you advance toward the knowledge of God, and you are nearer to it than he who does not negative, in reference to God, those qualities which you are convinced by proof must be negatived. There

---

[1] It has been stated above (ch. liv.), that Moses surpassed all men in his knowledge of God. For the ability which Solomon possessed to comprehend and to unfold the secrets of the Law, see Introduction, pag. 14. According to Shemtob, Moses and Solomon are mentioned here as representing the two methods by which men can obtain knowledge of God—revelation and study; by both alike, only negative knowledge is obtained. This explanation is not correct; Maimonides does not consider revelation and study as two different methods of obtaining true knowledge. According to his opinion revelation or prophecy cannot be obtained without preparation and study.

[2] Comp. Part II., ch. xxxii., xxxvii., *seqq.*

may be a man who after having earnestly devoted many years to the pursuit of one science, and to the true understanding of its principles, till he is fully convinced of its truths, has obtained as the sole result of that science the conviction that a certain quality must be negatived in reference to God, and the means of demonstrating that there is no reason for applying that quality to Him. Superficial thinkers will have no proof for this, will doubt it and ask, Is that quality existing in the Creator, or not? And those who are deprived of sight will positively ascribe it to God, although it has been clearly shown that He does not possess it. *E.g.*, while I show[1] that God is incorporeal, other persons doubt and are not certain whether He is corporeal or incorporeal; others even positively declare that He is corporeal, and appear before the Lord (פני יי) with that belief.[2] Now see how great the difference is between those three men; the first is undoubtedly nearest to the Almighty; the second is remote, and the third still more distant from Him. If there be a fourth person who holds himself convinced by proof that emotions are impossible in God, while the first, who rejects the corporeality, is not convinced of that impossibility, that fourth person is undoubtedly nearer the knowledge of God than the first, and so on, so that a person who, convinced by proof, negatives a number of things in reference to God, which according to our belief may possibly be in Him or emanate from Him, is undoubtedly a more perfect man than we are, and would surpass us still more if we positively believed these things to be properties of God. It will now be clear to you, that every time you establish by proof the negation of a thing in reference to God, you become more perfect, while with every additional positive assertion you follow your imagination and recede from the true knowledge of

---

[1] Part II., ch. i.
[2] Ibn Tibbon, ויקדים פני הבורא בזאת הכוונה. Char. ויראה פני אלהיו. Palq., וישליך האלה בזו האמונה.—בזאת האמונה. "And he loses thereby his belief in God."

God. Only by such ways must we approach the knowledge of God, and by such researches and studies[1] as would show us the inapplicability of what is inadmissible as regards the Creator, not by such methods as would prove the necessity of ascribing to Him anything extraneous to His essence, or asserting that He has a certain perfection, when we find it to be a perfection in relation to us. The perfections are all to some extent acquired properties, and a property which must be acquired does not exist in every thing capable of making such acquisition.[2]

You must bear in mind, that by affirming anything of God, you are removed from Him in two respects; first, whatever you affirm, is only a perfection in relation to us; secondly, He does not possess any thing superadded to the essence; His essence includes all His perfections, as we have shown.[3] Since it is a well-known fact that even that knowledge of God which is accessible to man cannot be attained except by negations, and that negations do not convey a true idea of the being to which they refer, all men, both of past and present generations,[4] declared that God cannot be the object of human comprehension, that none but Himself comprehends what He is, and that our knowledge consists in knowing that we are unable truly to comprehend Him. All philosophers say, "He has overpowered us by His grace, and is invisible to us through the intensity of His light," like

---

[1] This word is omitted in Ibn Tibbon's version. Char. בחקירה ובבקשה.

[2] There can be no doubt that the sense of this passage is as follows:—We predicate of God certain positive attributes, as an expression of our conviction that God is the most perfect being; these positive attributes, whatever perfection they describe as regards ourselves, must not be understood in the same sense as regards God. For the term "perfection" itself implies, in reference to ourselves, the *acquisition* of some quality which we did not possess before; and what is to be *acquired* is not yet possessed in reality, and by some it is not acquired at all, though they have the capacity of acquiring it. Perfection, in this sense, namely, as an acquisition, cannot be ascribed to God. It is remarkable how the Commentators could find any difficulty in the understanding of these words; Munk says of this passage, "un peu obscur."

[3] Comp. ch. lii.

[4] The expression (והבאים ואלאתון) is not quite exact; he means the present age; but literally אלאתון signifies "future generations."

the sun which cannot be perceived by eyes which are too weak to bear his rays.[1] Much more has been said on this topic, but it is useless to repeat it here. The idea is best expressed in the book of Psalms: לך דמיה תהלה, "Silence is praise to Thee" (lxv. 2). It is a very expressive remark on this subject; for whatever we utter with the intention of extolling and of praising Him, contains something that cannot be applied[2] to God, and includes derogatory expressions; it is therefore more becoming to be silent, and to be content with intellectual reflection,[3] as has been recommended by men of the highest culture,[4] in the words "Commune with your own heart upon your bed, and be still" (Ps. iv. 4). You must surely know the following celebrated passage in the Talmud[5]—would that all passages in the Talmud were like that!—although it is known to you, I quote it literally, as I wish to point out to you the ideas contained in it: "A certain person, reading prayers in the presence of Rabbi Chaninah, said, האל הגדול הגבור והנורא האדיר החזק והאמיץ, 'God, the great, the valiant and the tremendous, the powerful, the strong, and the mighty.'[6] — The rabbi said to him, Have you finished all the praises of your Master? The three epithets, האל הגדול הגבור והנורא, 'God, the great, the valiant and the tremendous,' we should not have applied to God, had Moses not mentioned them in the Law, and had not the men of the Great Synagogue[7] come forward subse-

[1] Comp. Chobhoth ha-lebhabhoth, i. 10.

[2] Arabic חמל, "burden;" Ibn Tibbon, מעמס; Charizi, נגרע, "diminished." Comp. Speyer, Notes on Charizi's version of Moreh Nebhuchim *ad locum*.

[3] Some editions of Ibn Tibbon have ההשתקפות, "reflection," instead of ההסתפקות. Char. ולהסתפק.

[4] This term does not refer to David, the author of Psalm iv., but to those wise men who recommended silent praise of God in the words of David: ודמו and אמרו בלבבכם. Char. has כאשר נצטוו השלמים, "as the wise men have been recommended." [5] Babyl. Talm. Berachoth 33 b.

[6] In our editions of the Talmud we read האל הגדול הגבור והנורא והאדיר והאמיץ והעזוז האמתי והיראוי החזק והנכבד, המתין לו עד דסיים. Charizi quotes it in a varied form, and Ba'bya, in Chobhoth ha-lebhabhoth (I. ch. x.), again in another form.

[7] The principal prayer (the eighteen blessings) is generally believed to have

quently and established their use in the prayer; and you say all this! Let this be illustrated by a parable. There was once an earthly king, possessing millions of gold coin; he was praised for owning millions of silver coin; was this not really dispraise to him?" Thus far the opinion of the pious rabbi. Consider, first, how repulsive[1] and annoying the accumulation of all these positive attributes was to him; next, how he has shown that, if we had only to adapt our speech to our reason,[2] we should never have composed them,[3] and we should not have uttered any of them. It has, however, become necessary to address men in words that should leave some idea in their minds, and, in accordance with the saying of our Sages, "The Torah speaks in the language of men," the Creator has been described to us in terms of our own perfections; but we should not on that account have uttered any other than the three abovementioned attributes, and we should not have used them as names of God except when meeting with them in reading the Law. Subsequently, the men of the Great Synagogue, who were prophets, introduced these expressions also into the prayer, but we should not on that account use [in our prayers] any other attributes of God. The principal lesson to be derived from this passage is that there are two reasons for our employing those phrases in our prayers: first, they occur in the Pentateuch; secondly, the Prophets introduced them into the prayer. Were it not for the first reason, we should never have uttered them; and were it not for the second reason, we should not have copied them from the

---

been introduced by the men of the Great Synagogue, the origin of which is not certain; it was probably instituted in the days of Ezra. Comp. Babyl. Talm. Berachoth 33a; Megillah 17b.

[1] Ibn Tibbon, שִׁתְּקוּ וּמֵאֲסוּ, "his silencing and rejecting:" Charizi, רוב דאגתו וכעסו, "his great uneasiness and anger."

[2] Some editions of Ibn Tibbon's version have אלו הונחו לשכלנו, "if they (i.e., the attributes) had been left to depend on our own reason," to decide whether we should employ them or not. Char. אלו הונחו לפשט שכלנו.

[3] Char. לא השכלנו (according to the reading עקלנאה in some of the MSS. of the original text), "we should not have thought of them."

Pentateuch to recite them in our prayers; how then could we approve of the use of those numerous attributes! You also learn from this that we ought not to mention and employ in our prayers all the attributes we find applied to God in the books of the Prophets; for he does not say, "Were it not that Moses, our Teacher, said them, we should not have been able to use them;" but he adds another condition—"and had not the men of the Great Synagogue come forward and established their use in the prayer," because only for that reason are we allowed to use them in prayer. We cannot approve of what those foolish persons do who are extravagant in praise, fluent and prolix in the prayers they compose, and in the hymns they make in the desire to approach the Creator. They describe God in attributes which would be an offence if applied to a human being; for those persons have no knowledge of these great and important principles, which are not accessible to the ordinary intelligence of man. Treating the Creator as a familiar object, they describe Him and speak of Him in any expressions they think proper; they eloquently continue to praise Him in that manner, and believe that they can thereby influence Him and produce an effect on Him. If they find some phrase suited to their object in the words of the Prophets they are still more inclined to consider that they are free to make use of such texts—which should at least be explained—to employ them in their literal sense, to derive new expressions from them, to form from them numerous variations, and to found whole compositions on them. This license is frequently met with in the compositions of the singers, preachers, and others who imagine themselves to be able to compose a poem. Such authors write things which partly are real heresy, partly contain such folly and absurdity that they naturally cause those who hear them to laugh, but also to feel grieved at the thought that such things can be uttered in reference to God. Were it not that I pitied the authors[1] for their

[1] According to Sachs, Ha-techiyah I. 58, II. 19, Ibn Gabirol is meant.

defects, and did not wish to injure them, I should have cited some passages to show you their mistakes; besides, the fault of their compositions is obvious to all intelligent persons. You must consider it, and think thus: If slander and libel is a great sin, how much greater is the sin of those who speak with looseness of tongue in reference to God, and describe Him by attributes which are far below Him; and I declare that they not only commit an ordinary sin, but unconsciously at least incur the guilt of profanity and blasphemy. This applies both to the multitude that listens to such prayers, and to the foolish man that recites them. Men, however, who understand the fault of such compositions, and, nevertheless, recite them, may be classed, according to my opinion, among those to whom the following words are applied: "And the children of Israel used words that were not right against the Lord their God" (2 Kings xvii. 9); and "utter error against the Lord" (Is. xxxii. 6). If you are of those who regard the honour of their Creator,[1] do not listen in any way to them, much less utter what they say, and still less compose such prayers, knowing how great is the offence of one who hurls aspersions against the Supreme Being.[2] There is no necessity at all for you to use positive attributes of God with the view of magnifying Him in your thoughts, or to go beyond the limits which the men of the Great Synagogue have introduced in the prayers and in the blessings, for this is sufficient for all purposes, and even more than sufficient,[3] as Rabbi Chaninah said. Other attributes, such as occur in the books of the Prophets, may be uttered when we meet with them in reading those books; but we must bear in mind what has already been explained, that they are either attributes of God's actions, or expressions implying the negation

---

[1] A phrase taken from Mishnah Chag. ii. 1, שלא חס על כבוד קונו.

[2] A phrase taken from Babyl. Talm., Succah, 53a, הטיח דברים כלפי מעלה.

[3] Char. עליו אין להוסיף וממנו אין לגרוע, "nothing can be added, nothing taken away." (Eccl. iii. 14.)

of the opposite. This[1] likewise should not be divulged to the multitude; but a reflection of this kind is fitted for the few only who do not consider that the glorification of God does not consist in *uttering* what is *not* proper, but in *reflecting* what *is* proper.

We will now conclude our exposition of the wise words of R. Chaninah. He does not employ any such simile as: "A king who possesses millions of gold denarii, and is praised as having hundreds;" for this would imply that God's perfections, although more perfect than those ascribed to Him, are still of the same kind; but this is not the case, as has been proved. The excellence of the simile consists in the words: "who possesses golden denarii, and is praised as having silver denarii;" this implies that these attributes, though perfections as regards ourselves, are not such as regards God; in reference to Him they all include defects, as is distinctly suggested in the remark, " Is this not an offence to Him?"

I have already told you that all these attributes, whatever perfection they may denote according to your idea, imply defects in reference to God, if applied to Him in the same sense as they are used in reference to ourselves. Solomon has already given us sufficient instruction on this subject by saying, "For God is in heaven, and thou upon earth; therefore let thy words be few" (Eccl. v. 2).

CHAPTER LX.

On the Difference between Positive and Negative Attributes.

I WILL give you in this chapter some illustrations, in order that you may better understand the propriety of forming as many negative attributes as possible, and the impropriety

[1] That is, the theory that the attributes are mere qualifications of God's actions, or negations of the opposite, must not be made familiar to the multitude because they would not understand it.

of ascribing to God any positive attributes. A person may know for certain that a "ship" is in existence, but he may not know to what object that name is applied, whether to a substance or to an accident; a second person then learns that the ship is not an accident; a third, that it is not a mineral; a fourth, that it is not a plant growing in the earth; a fifth, that it is not a body whose parts are joined together by nature; a sixth, that it is not a flat object like boards or doors; a seventh, that it is not a sphere; an eighth, that it is not pointed;[1] a ninth, that it is not round-shaped,[2] nor equilateral; a tenth, that it is not solid. It is clear that this tenth person has almost arrived at the correct notion of a "ship" by the foregoing negative attributes, as if he had exactly the same notion as those have who imagine it to be a wooden substance which is hollow, long, and composed of many pieces of wood, that is to say, who know it by positive attributes. Of the other persons in our illustration, each one is more remote from the correct notion of the ship than the next mentioned, so that the first knows nothing about it but the name. In the same manner you will come nearer to the knowledge and comprehension of God by the negative attributes. But you must be careful, in what you negative, to negative by proof, not by mere words, for each time you ascertain by proof that a certain thing, believed to exist in the Creator, must be negatived, you have undoubtedly come one step nearer to the knowledge of God.

It is in this sense that some men come very near to God, and others remain exceedingly remote from Him, not in the sense of those who are deprived of vision, and believe that God occupies a place,[3] which man can physically approach or from which he can recede. Examine this well, know it, and be content with it. The way which will bring you

---

[1] *I.e.*, a cone.   [2] *I.e.*, a cylinder.

[3] Lit., "that there is a place." Ibn Tibbon, לא שיש לשם מקום, "not that God is occupying a place," or "not that there (לשָׁם, Arabic חֹם) is a place." Char. לא שיש למעלה קרבת מקום. Palq. לא ששם מקום.

nearer to God has been clearly shown to you; walk in it, if you have the desire. On the other hand, there is a great danger in applying positive attributes to God. For it has been shown that every perfection we could imagine, even if existing in God in accordance with the opinion of those who assert the existence of attributes, would in reality not be of the same kind as that imagined by us, but would only be called by the same name, according to our explanation;[1] it would in fact amount to a negation. Suppose, e.g., you say He has knowledge, and this knowledge, which admits of no change and of no plurality, embraces many changeable things; His knowledge remains unaltered, while new things are constantly formed, and His knowledge of a thing before it exists, while it exists, and when it has ceased to exist, is the same without the least change: you would thereby declare that His knowledge is not like ours; and similarly that His existence is not like ours. You thus necessarily arrive at some negation, without obtaining a true conception of an essential attribute; on the contrary, you are led to assume that there is a plurality in God, and to believe that He, though one essence, has several unknown attributes. For if you intend to affirm them, you cannot compare them with those attributes known by us, and they are consequently not of the same kind. You are, as it were, brought by the belief in the reality of the attributes,[2] to say that God is one subject of which several things are predicated; though the subject is not like ordinary subjects, and the predicates are not like ordinary predicates.[3] This

---

[1] Chap. lvi. pag. 201.

[2] The editions of Ibn Tibbon's version have העיון בהיות התוארים, "the reflection on the existence of the attributes," which appears to be a corruption of הענין בחיוב התוארים, as rendered by Charizi.

[3] Charizi: ואין המוסד ההוא כאלו הנשואים, "and that subject is not like those predicates." The Arabic original (ed. Munk) has likewise לא דלך אלמוצוע מתל הדה אלמחמולאת. Munk prefers this reading to that of other MSS.: לא דלך אלמוצוע מתל הדה אלמוצועאת ולא תלך אלמחמולאת מתל הדה אלמחמולאת. The version of Ibn Tibbon agrees with the latter reading, which appears to be the correct one. The object of the author is to show

PART I.—CHAPTER LX.

belief would ultimately lead us to associate other things with God,[1] and not to believe that He is One. For of every subject certain things can undoubtedly be predicated, and although in reality subject and predicate are combined in one thing, by the actual definition they consist of two elements, the notion contained in the subject not being the same as that contained in the predicate. In the course of this treatise[2] it will be proved to you that God cannot be a compound, and that He is simple in the strictest sense of the word.

I do not merely declare[3] that he who affirms attributes of God has not sufficient knowledge concerning the Creator, admits some association with God, or conceives Him to be different from what He is; but I say that he unconsciously loses his belief in God. For he whose knowledge concerning a thing is insufficient, understands one part of it while he is ignorant of the other, as, *e. g.*, a person who knows that man possesses life, but does not know that

---

that the whole theory of the attributes consists in the fact that something is predicated of God; and although they confess that subject and predicate are above comparison with anything known to us, the fact remains that they assume a duality, or even a plurality: a subject and one or several predicates. If the author had wished to express the idea that subject and predicate are two distinct things, he would probably not have used the phrase "that subject is not *like* those predicates," but "subject and predicate are not identical" (עצם אחד). For the assertion that two things are not alike does not include that they are not two distinct objects.

[1] According to Shemtob and Efodi, "homonymity;" this cannot be the meaning of the word here; because from the reason which follows it is clear that Maimonides meant here an association or a combination of several elements (the subject and the predicate) into one whole. Subject and predicate may form one whole in reality, but they are defined each by its own separate definition. The Arabic שרך and the Hebrew שתוף admit of several significations: 1, association or participation of two subjects in a certain thing; 2, homonymity (the participation of two different things in the same name); 3, combination of various elements to form one whole.

[2] Comp. Part II., i. 4.

[3] Maimonides does not say here, that the Attributists could refute the three charges mentioned here, as Munk believes, but merely that he does not bring these three charges against them, as they would imply that the Attributists have some knowledge of God; but Maimonides is of opinion that they do not possess any such knowledge.

man possesses understanding; but in reference to God, in whose real existence there is no plurality, it is impossible that one thing should be known, and another unknown. Similarly he who associates an object with [the properties of] another object, conceives a true and correct notion of the one object, and applies that notion also to the other; while those who admit the attributes of God, do not consider them as identical with His essence, but as extraneous elements.[1] Again, he who conceives an incorrect notion of an object, must necessarily have a correct idea of the object to some extent; he, however, who says that taste belongs to the category of quantity has not, according to my opinion, an incorrect notion of taste, but is entirely ignorant of its nature, for he does not know to what object the term "taste" is to be applied.—This is a very difficult subject; consider it well.

According to this explanation you will understand, that those who do not recognise, in reference to God, the negation of things, which others negative by clear proof, are deficient in the knowledge of God, and are remote from comprehending Him. Consequently, the smaller the number of things is which a person can negative in relation to God, the less he knows of Him, as has been explained in the beginning of this chapter; but the man who affirms an attribute of God, knows nothing but the name; for the object to which, in his imagination, he applies that name, does not exist; it is a mere fiction and invention, as if he applied that name to a non-existing being, for there is, in reality, no such object. *E.g.*, some one has heard of the elephant, and knows that it is an animal, and wishes to know its form and nature. A person, who is either misled

[1] The association of some other being with God would mean that some being is endowed with properties or qualities like those possessed by God. Those who believe in such an association seem to have some knowledge of God, but wrongly transfer what they know of God to other beings. The Attributists, when they speak of one divine Being endowed with attributes, have no knowledge whatever of God, and the divine being, consisting of substance and attributes, exists only in their imagination.

or misleading, tells him it is an animal with one leg, three wings, lives in the depth of the sea, has a transparent body; its face is wide like that of a man, has the same form and shape, speaks like a man, flies sometimes in the air, and sometimes swims like a fish. I should not say, that he described the elephant incorrectly, or that he has an insufficient knowledge of the elephant, but I would say that the thing thus described is an invention and fiction, and that in reality there exists nothing like it; it is a non-existing being, called by the name of a really existing being, and like the griffin, the centaur, and similar imaginary combinations for which simple and compound names have been borrowed from real things. The present case is analogous; namely, God, praised be His name, exists, and His existence has been proved to be absolute and perfectly simple, as I shall explain. If such a simple, absolutely existing essence were said to have attributes, as has been contended, and were combined with extraneous elements, it would in no way be an existing thing, as has been proved by us; and when we say that that essence, which is called "God," is a substance with many properties by which it can be described, we apply that name to an object which does not at all exist. Consider, therefore, what are the consequences of affirming attributes of God! As to those attributes of God which occur in the Pentateuch, or in the books of the Prophets, we must assume that they are exclusively employed, as has been stated by us, to convey to us some notion of the perfections of the Creator, or to express qualities of actions emanating from Him.

CHAPTER LXI.[1]

On the Names of God.

It is well known that all the names of God occurring in Scripture, are derived from His actions,[2] except one, namely the Tetragrammaton, which consists of the letters *yod, hé, vau* and *hé*. This name is applied exclusively to God, and is on that account called *Shem ha-meforash*,[3] "The proper name." It is the distinct and exclusive designation of the Divine Being; whilst His other names are common nouns, and are derived from actions, to which some of our own are similar, as we have already explained. Even the name

---

[1] In this chapter and those which follow (lxi.—lxx.), the author explains the names of God: *viz.*, (1) those which refer to His essence and existence (lxi.—lxiv.); and (2) those which express His relation to the universe (lxv.—lxx.). Ch. lxiv. is a sequel to the explanation of the phrase "What is His name?" (ch. lxiii.); ch. lxv.—lxvii. a preparation for ch. lxviii.—lxx.

[2] Maimonides does not mean to say that all the names of God are derived from verbs, since אדני is derived by him from ארנות, but that they refer to certain actions, and therefore include a whole class rather than one individual being.

[3] שם המפורש, lit., "the name which is made clear," or "the name which is separated," *i. e.*, is exclusively applied to one Being, and therefore distinctly indicates which being the speaker means; while other nouns, as appellatives, apply to a whole class, and in using them we do not distinctly indicate the special object of our thought. The usual term for a proper name is שם המיוחד (or שם עצם פרטי), the name exclusively applied to one thing; but as in reference to God's name the term שם המפורש is used in the Mishnah (Yoma, 6, 2), and in the Gemara (*ib.*, 39, 2; Sota, 38 *a*), the author gives it the preference. Munk is mistaken in saying, "Les mots שם המפורש (Mishnah, Yoma 6, 2), signifient sans doute le nom de Dieu distinctement prononcé." There is no doubt that פרש also denotes "to pronounce distinctly;" but if the word had this signification in the passage quoted, the author of the Mishnah, instead of saying שם המפורש שהוא יוצא מפי כהן גדול would have said שם שהוא יוצא מפורש מפי וגו׳. In the Boraitha, quoted in the Gemara, the term שם המפורש is explained by שם המיוחד לי, "the name especially applied to Me," and is contradistinguished from כנוי, "substitute."

PART I.—CHAPTER LXI.

אדני (*Adonaï*, "Lord,"), which has been substituted for the Tetragrammaton,[1] is derived from the appellative "lord;" comp. דבר האיש אדני הארץ אתנו קשות : " The man who is the lord of the land spake roughly to us " (Gen. xliii. 30). The difference between *Adoni* (אֲדֹנִי, "my lord"), with *chirek* under the *nun*, or *Adonaï* (אֲדֹנָי) with *kamets*, is similar to the difference between *Sari* (שָׂרִי), "my prince," and *Saraï*, Abraham's wife (*ib.* xvi. 1), the latter form denoting majesty and acknowledged distinction.[2] An angel is also addressed as "*Adonaï;*" *e.g.*, אדני אל נא תעבור, "*Adonaï* (My lord), pass not away, I pray thee"[3] (*ib.* xviii. 3). I have restricted my explanation to the term *Adonaï*, the substitute for the Tetragrammaton, because it is more commonly applied to God than any of the other names which are in frequent use, like *dayyan* (דַּיָּן, "judge"), *shaddai*

---

[1] It appears that Maimonides refrains as much as possible from writing, not only the Tetragrammaton, but also the name (*Adonaï*) substituted for it, and therefore he paraphrases it as above.—This mode of expression continues to be used by many Jews.

[2] עמום, Heb. כללות, is synonymous with תפכים, Heb. הדור; Maimonides says that the syllable *ai* (ִי or ָ), in words like Saraï, is not a pronominal suffix but a noun-termination. By the omission of the limiting pronoun "my," and saying "Lord," "Prince," instead of "my Lord," and "my Prince," the speaker expresses his conviction that the title is recognised generally, and not by himself alone. The commentators (see Munk) think that, according to the opinion of Maimonides, the ending *ai* (ִי) indicates two things—1, Pluralis majestatis; 2, the character of the noun itself (אדון, שרה) as an appellative, including a whole class of individuals. The introduction of the second signification is entirely out of place here, where the difference between the suffixes ִ and ַ is to be defined. Besides, it has already been stated that *Adonai* is an appellative; and lastly, the instance quoted, *viz.*, שָׂרִי, would not illustrate the explanation. The names given to persons generally include some element of honour and distinction; in the present case this is shown by the example of שָׂרִי. An objection has been raised by some commentators that *Sarah* is described as more honourable than *Saraï;* but this does not exclude the fact that "*Saraï*" likewise served as an expression of distinction.

[3] In the Massorah this is marked as קדש, "holy," that is, referring to God, and not to an angel; the same is stated by Maimonides himself in Yad hachazakah (Yesode ha-torah, vi. 9). In the latter work, where he describes the laws, he adheres strictly to the traditional explanation; in this philosophical work he sometimes deviates from it.

228   GUIDE OF THE PERPLEXED.

(שדי, "almighty"),[1] *tsaddik* (צדיק, "righteous"), *channun* (חנון, "gracious"), *rachum* (רחום, "merciful"), and *elohim* (אלהים, "chief"); all these terms are unquestionably appellatives and derivatives. The derivation of the name, consisting of *yod, hé, vau,* and *hé,*[2] is not positively known,[3] the word having no additional signification. This sacred name, which, as you know, was not pronounced except in the sanctuary by the appointed priests, when they gave the sacerdotal blessing,[4] and by the high priest on the Day of Atonement,[5] undoubtedly denotes something which is peculiar to God, and is not found in any other being. It is possible that in the Hebrew language, of which we have now but a slight knowledge, the Tetragrammaton, in the way it was pronounced, conveyed the meaning of "absolute existence." In short, the majesty of the name and the great dread of uttering it, are connected with the fact that it denotes God Himself, without including in its meaning any names of the things created by Him. Thus our Sages say : " ' My name ' (שמי, Numb. vi. 27) means the name which is peculiar to Me." All other names of God have reference to qualities, and do not signify a simple substance, but a substance with attributes, they being derivatives. On that account it is believed that they imply the presence of a plurality in God, I mean to say, the presence of attributes, that is, of some extraneous element superadded to His essence. Such is the meaning of all derivative names ; they imply the presence of some attribute and its substratum, though this be not distinctly named.[6] As, how-

[1] This instance is absent in the Arabic and in the version of Charizi.

[2] Char. ה״א אשר יהגו בו יו״ד ה״א וא״ו ה״א, which they pronounce "*yod hé vau hé.*" Comp. Yad ha-chazakah II., xiv. 10, השם הנהגה מיו״ד ה״א וא״י ה״א.

[3] The verb היה is generally assumed to be the root of the Tetragrammaton, although the exact meaning of the word is not known. Maimonides admits that it may signify "absolute existence" or "essence," but does not venture to say that it is connected with the verb היה.

[4] Mishnah Sotah, vii. 6, and Yoma vi. 2.

[5] Babyl. Talmud Sotah, 38a.

[6] That is, the adjective used as a noun, *e.g.*, "the great," includes two

PART I.—CHAPTER LXI.   229

ever, it has been proved,[1] that God is not a substratum capable of attributes, we are convinced that those appellatives when employed as names of God, only indicate the relation of certain actions to Him, or they convey to us some notion of His perfection.[2]

Hence R. Chaninah would have objected to the expression הגדול הגבור והנורא "the great, the mighty, and the tremendous," had it not been for the two reasons mentioned by him; because such expressions lead men to think that the attributes are essential, *i.e.*, they are perfections actually present in God. The frequent use of names of God derived from actions, led to the belief that He had as many [essential] attributes as there were actions from which the names were derived. The following promise was therefore made, implying that mankind will at a certain future time understand this subject, and be free from the error it involves: "In that day will the Lord be One, and His name One" (Zech. xiv. 9). The meaning of this prophecy is this: He being One, will then be called by one name, which will indicate the essence of God; but it does not mean that His sole name will be a derivative [*viz.*, "One"].[3] In the Pirke Rabbi Eliezer (ch. iii.), occurs the following passage: "Before the universe was created, there was only the Almighty and His name." Observe, how clearly the author states that all these appellatives employed as names of God came into existence after the Creation. This is true; for they all refer to actions connected with the Universe. If, however, you consider His essence as separate and as abstracted from all actions, you will not describe it by an appellative, but

---

elements: the quality, and the substratum to which the quality is attached, although that substratum is not mentioned and must be supplied.

[1] See II. ch. i., *sqq.*   [2] See ch. lix.

[3] Arabic לא אנה משתקא; אנה is governed by יעני. The translation of Munk: "et ce ne sera point un nom dérivé," is inaccurate. Comp. Targum ארי שמיה יציב בעלמא ולית בר מניה, "for His name will be firmly established in the world, and there will be none besides Him." Ibn Ezra holds that the tetragrammaton is meant.

by a proper noun, which exclusively indicates that essence. Every other name of God is a derivative, except this Tetragrammaton, which is a real *nomen proprium*,[1] and must not be considered from any other point of view. You must beware of sharing the error of those who write amulets (*kameoth*). Whatever you hear of them, or read in their works, especially in reference to the names which they form by combination, is utterly senseless; they call these combinations *shemoth* (names), and believe that their pronunciation demands sanctification and purification, and that by using them they are enabled to work miracles. Rational persons ought not to listen to such men, nor in any way believe their assertions. No other name is called *shem ha-meforash* except this Tetragrammaton, which is written, but is not pronounced according to its letters. The words כה תברכו את בני ישראל, "Thus shall ye bless the children of Israel" (Numb. vi. 23) are interpreted in Siphri[2] as follows: "'*Thus*,' in the holy language; again '*thus*,' with the *shem ha-meforash*." The following remark is also found there: "In the sanctuary [the name of God is pronounced] as it is spelt, but elsewhere by its substitutes." In the Talmud,[3] the following passage occurs: "'*Thus*' (כה), *i.e.*, with the *shem ha-meforash*.—You say [that the priests, when blessing the people, had to pronounce] the *shem ha-meforash*; this was perhaps not the case, as they may have used other names instead.—We infer it from the words ושמו את שמי: 'And they shall put My name' (Numb. vi. 27), *i.e.*, My name, which is peculiar to Me." It has thus been shown that the *shem ha-meforash* (the proper name of God) is the Tetragrammaton, and that this is the only name which includes nothing but His essence, and therefore our Sages in referring to this sacred term said "'*My name*' means the one which is peculiar to Me alone."

[1] The other names, *Yah* and *Ehyeh*, apparently derived from the same root (היה), are regarded by Maimonides as appellatives. See chapter lxiii.
[2] *Ad locum* (Numb. vi. 22).
[3] Talm. Babyl. Sotah 38a.

In the next chapter I will explain the circumstances which brought men to a belief in the power of *Shemoth* (names of God); I will point out the main subject of discussion, and lay open to you its mystery, and not any doubt will be left in your mind, unless you prefer to be misguided.

CHAPTER LXII.

On the divine Names of God composed of four, twelve, and forty-two letters.

WE were commanded that,[1] in the sacerdotal blessing, the name of the Lord should be pronounced as it is written[2] in the form of the Tetragrammaton, *i.e.*, the *Shem ha-meforash*. It was not known to every one how the name was to be pronounced, what vowels were to be given to each consonant, and whether some of the letters capable of reduplication[3] should receive a dagesh. Wise men successively transmitted the pronunciation of the name[4]; it was only communicated to a distinguished disciple once in seven years. I must, however, add that the statement, "The wise men communicated the Tetragrammaton to their children and their disciples once in seven years,"[5] does not only refer to the pronunciation but also to its meaning, which makes the name a *nomen proprium* of God, and includes metaphysical knowledge.

[1] Numb. vi. 22, *sqq*. As to the detailed rules, see Yad ha-chazakah Book II. (Sepher ahabha) Hilchoth Tefillah, xiv. The act of pronouncing the blessing is generally called נשיאות כפים "lifting up the hands," or דוכן, lit. "dais," from the circumstance that the priests ascend some elevated place and lift up their hands when pronouncing the blessing.

[2] See Babyl. Talm., Sotah 37b and 38a; Comp. also preceding chapter.

[3] That is, *vau* and the second *hé*; for *yod* can have no *dagesh* being the first letter of the word, and the first *hé* does not take *dagesh*, as *hé* can only take a *dagesh* at the end of a word. Charizi או רפות, "or without a *dagesh*."

[4] Char., ענין למודו, "how it is to be learnt."

[5] Babyl. Talm. Kiddushin, 71a. The portion from "I must, however," to "once in seven years" is omitted in Charizi's version.

232   GUIDE OF THE PERPLEXED.

Our Sages knew in addition a name of God which consisted of twelve letters,[1] inferior in sanctity to the Tetragrammaton. I believe that this was not a single noun, but consisted of two or three words, the sum of their letters being twelve, and that these words were used by our Sages as a substitute for the Tetragrammaton, whenever they met with it in the course of their reading the Scriptures, in the same manner as we at present substitute for it *aleph, daleth*, etc. [*i.e., Adonaï*]. There is no doubt that this name also, consisting of twelve letters, was in this sense more distinctive than the name *Adonaï*: it was never withheld from any of the students; whoever wished to learn it, had the opportunity given to him without any reserve:[2] not so the Tetragrammaton; those who knew it did not communicate it except to a son or a disciple, once in seven years. When, however, unprincipled men[3] had become acquainted with that name which consists of twelve letters, and in consequence had become corrupt in faith—as is sometimes the case when persons with imperfect knowledge become aware that a thing is not such as they had imagined—the Sages concealed also that name, and only communicated it to the worthiest among the priests, that they should pro-

---

[1] Babyl. Talm., Kiddushin 71a. The name consisting of twelve letters is not given in the Talmud. Maimonides, therefore, conjectures that it did not consist of a single word but of an entire phrase. Narboni, in his Commentary, is surprised that Maimonides ignored the form of that name which is mentioned in the Sefer ha-bahir, in the name of R. Nechunyah ben Hakanah, and which consisted of the tetragrammaton pronounced in three different ways, according to יִפְעַל, יְפַעֵל, יֻפְעַל.—The suffix in עֲנְדְהָם, "with them," refers to the חֲכָמִים, "wise men," mentioned before.

[2] ולא מצנונא בה, lit., "and there was no stint in it." The phrase is not translated in the version of Ibn Tibbon. It is said in contradistinction to the rule laid down concerning the tetragrammaton (Kiddushin 71a) viz., "that it should be kept a secret."

[3] Arab. מסיבון, "free," "following their own course"; Ibn Tibbon, פרוצים; Charizi adds, ומשולחים, "unrestricted" or "easy," not feeling any regret at the renunciation of the principles in which they have been brought up, the opposite of the שלם, the well-trained, who would be perplexed (נבון), and seek relief in a proper solution of the difficulty. See Introduction, page 6.

nounce it when they blessed the people in the Temple; for the Tetragrammaton was no longer uttered in the sanctuary on account of the corruption of the people. There is a tradition, that with the death of Simeon the Just, his brother priests discontinued the pronunciation of the Tetragrammaton in the blessing;[1] they used, instead, this name of twelve letters. It is further stated,[2] that at first the name of twelve letters was communicated to every man; but when the number of impious men increased it was only entrusted to the worthiest among the priests, whose voice, in pronouncing it, was drowned amid the singing of their brother priests. Rabbi Tarphon said, "Once I followed my grandfather[3] to the daïs [where the blessing was pronounced]; I inclined my ear to listen to a priest [who pronounced the name], and noticed that his voice was drowned amid the singing of his brother priests."

There was also a name of forty-two letters[4] known among them. Every intelligent person knows that one word of forty-two letters is impossible. But it was a phrase of several words which had together forty-two letters. There is no doubt that the words had such a meaning as to convey a correct notion of the essence of God, in the way we have stated. This phrase of so many letters is called a name because, like other proper nouns, they represent one single object, and several words have been employed in order to explain more clearly the idea which the name represents; for an idea can more easily be comprehended if expressed in

---

[1] Babyl. Talm., Yoma, 39 b, and Menachoth, 109 b. In the Talmud the discontinuance of pronouncing the Holy Name in the Temple is represented as connected with the death of Simeon the Just, but it is not stated what this had to do with the degeneration of the people.

[2] Babyl. Talm. Kiddushin, 71a.

[3] In our editions of the Talmud, אחי אימה, "the brother of the mother."

[4] This name likewise appears to have been unknown in the time of Maimonides; it was described in cabbalistic books, which Maimonides ignored. See Comment. of Narboni, אב״ג יתש״ץ קרע״ שטמ״ן נג״ד יכש״ש פצ״ר צת״ג חק״ר בנ״ע יג״ל פז״ק שק״ו צי״ת. According to R. Hai Gaon, the letters were well known, but not the way in which they should be pronounced. See Taam Zekenim by Eliezer Ashkenazi, page 57.

many words. Mark this and observe now that the instruction in regard to the names of God extended to the signification of each of those names, and did not confine itself to the pronunciation according to letters which, in themselves, are destitute of an idea. *Shem ha-meforash* applied neither to the name of forty-two letters[1] nor to that of twelve, but only to the Tetragrammaton, the proper name of God, as we have explained. Those two names must have included some metaphysical ideas. It can be proved that one of them conveyed profound knowledge, from the following rule laid down by our Sages: "The name of forty-two letters is exceedingly holy; it can only be entrusted to him who is modest, in the midway of life, not easily provoked to anger, temperate, gentle, and who speaks kindly to his fellow men. He who understands it, is cautious with it, and keeps it in purity, is loved above and is liked here below; he is respected by his fellow men; his learning remaineth with him, and he enjoys both this world and the world to come."[2] So far in the Talmud. How grievously has this passage been misunderstood! Many believe that the forty-two letters are merely to be pronounced mechanically; that by the knowledge of these, without any further interpretation, they can attain to those exalted ends, although it is stated that he who desires to obtain a knowledge of that name must be trained in the virtues named before, and go through all the great preparations which are mentioned in that passage. On the contrary, it is evident that all this preparation aims at a knowledge of Metaphysics, and includes ideas which constitute the "secrets of the Law" (סתרי תורה), as we have explained.[3] In works on Metaphysics[4] it has

---

[1] Although in the MSS. the order is reversed, this seems to be the correct sequence, because הו״א (Hebr. זה) agrees better with the preceding name of forty-two letters, than with that of twelve letters. In the order adopted in the MSS. the demonstrative should either be omitted, or be in the plural.

[2] See Talmud Babli. Kiddushin, 71 a.

[3] See ch. xxxv., page 128.

[4] See Arist. de Anima, iii. 5; Shahrastani, Part II. on the philosophical system of Ibn Sina.

been shown that no knowledge gained in this science, *i.e.*, no knowledge of the active intellect[1] can ever be forgotten; and this is meant by the phrase "his learning remaineth with him."[2]

When bad and foolish men were reading such passages, they considered them to be a support of their false pretensions and of their assertion that they could, by means of an arbitrary combination of letters, form a *shem* (שם, "name") which would act and operate miraculously when written or spoken in a certain particular way. Such fictions, originally invented by foolish men, were in the course of time committed to writing, and came into the hands of good[3] but weak-minded and ignorant persons who were unable to discriminate between truth and falsehood, and who made a secret of those *shemoth*. When after the death of such persons those writings were discovered among their papers, it was believed that they contained truths; for, "The simple believeth every word" (Prov. xiv. 15).

We have already gone too far away from our interesting subject and recondite inquiry, endeavouring to refute a perverse notion, the absurdity of which everyone must perceive who gives a thought to the subject. We have, however, been compelled to mention it, in treating of the divine names, their meanings, and the opinions commonly held concerning them. We shall now return to our theme. Having shown that all names of God, with the exception of the Tetragrammaton (*Shem ha-meforash*), are appellatives, we must now, in a separate chapter, speak on the phrase *Ehyeh Asher Ehyeh* (אהיה אשר אהיה), because it is connected with the difficult subject under discussion, namely, the inadmissibility of divine attributes.

---

[1] Comp. "The intellect in action, which emanates from the active intellect, and through which we attain a knowledge of the active intellect." Part II., ch. iv.

[2] The acquired abstract knowledge or metaphysical truths form the substance of the immortal soul, or the intellect in action. Comp. ch. xli. and ch. lxviii. Also Ibn Ezra Literature, IV., page 44 *sqq.*, and page 22, note 2.

[3] This epithet is omitted in the version of Charizi.

CHAPTER LXIII.

On Ehyeh, Yah and Shaddai.

BEFORE approaching the subject of this chapter,[1] we will first consider the words of Moses, "And they shall say unto me, What is His name? what shall I say unto them?" (Exod. iii. 13). How far was this question, anticipated by Moses, appropriate, and how far was he justified in seeking to be prepared with an answer? Moses was correct in declaring, "But, behold, they will not believe me, for they will say, The Lord hath not appeared unto thee" (*ib.* iv. 1); for any man claiming the authority of a prophet must expect to meet with such an objection so long as he has not given a proof of his mission.[2] Again, if the question, as appears at first sight, referred only to the name, as a mere utterance of the lips, the following dilemma would present itself: either the Israelites knew the name, or they had never heard it; if the name was known to them, they would perceive in it no argument in favour of the mission of Moses, his knowledge and their knowledge of the divine name being the same. If, on the other hand, they had never heard it mentioned, and if the knowledge of it was to prove the

---

[1] That is, to explain the name *Ehyeh asher ehyeh*. The author has shown in the last chapter, that the importance and significance of God's names consist in the amount of metaphysical knowledge they convey concerning the First Cause. He now attempts to prove that the great anxiety of Moses when he anticipated the question of the Israelites, "What is His name?" was not to learn the word to be used as God's name, and its pronunciation, but to obtain such knowledge concerning God, and such proofs concerning His existence, as would enable him to convince his brethren of the truth of his belief. When the name was communicated to him, he further asked for the means of making the Israelites believe in his mission; and it was for that purpose that the miracles were shown to him.

[2] According to Maimonides, the question of the Israelites, "What is his name?" if referring only to the name, must have been addressed to Moses in order to test the truth of his words; while it has generally been considered as an expression of mere curiosity to know the name of Him by whose order Moses addressed the people.

mission of Moses, what evidence would they have that this was really the name of God? Moreover, after God had made known that name to Moses, and had told him, "Go and gather the elders of Israel,...and they shall hearken to thy voice," (*ib.* xvi. 18), he replied, "Behold, they will not believe me nor hearken unto my voice," although God had told him, "And they will hearken to thy voice"; whereupon God answered, "What is that in thine hand?" and he said, "A rod" (*ib.* iv. 2). In order to obviate this dilemma,[1] you must understand what I am about to tell you. You know how widespread were in those days the opinions of the Sabeans;[2] all men, except a few individuals, were idolaters, that is to say, they believed in spirits, in man's power to direct the influences of the heavenly bodies, and in the effect of talismans.[3] Anyone who in those days laid claim to authority, based it[4] either, like Abraham,[5] on the fact that, by reasoning and by proof he had been convinced of the existence of a Being who rules the whole Universe, or that some spiritual power was conferred upon him by a star, by an angel, or by a similar agency; but no one could establish his claim on prophecy,[6] that is to say, on the fact

[1] Char., כל סתום, "all mystery;" Tibbon, כל ספק, "every doubt."

[2] The Sabeans (probably from צבא, "host" of heaven, stars ; according to Shahrastani from the Arabic צבא, "to turn away," *scil.* from truth), though believing in the unity of the Supreme Being, worshipped the hosts of the heavens, and thought that by certain formulæ and images they could direct the influences of the stars upon mundane affairs in any way they desired. The Chaldeans are known to have held the same doctrine.

[3] Char. והיו המאמינים בכחות הכוכבים ועושים כוונים למלאכת השמים (אסתנזאל) (compare the Arab. להזיל כחם והיו עושים תמונות בשעוה. "They believed in the powers of the stars, and made images for the host of heaven, in order to direct their influences, and also made images in wax." Ibn Tibbon adds, as an explanation of טליסמאות, the words צורות מדברות, "figures that speak." Comp. Ibn Ezra Literature, IV., p. 36, note 1.

[4] רעוי in the Arabic original is rendered in the version of Ibn Tibbon by דבר (Char., טענת); most of the editions have כבר (Munk).

[5] Comp. Bereshith Rabba, ch. xxxviii.

[6] The definition here given of a prophet, as a person who had received a divine mission to communicate to his fellowmen, agrees with the fact that the book of Daniel, though containing predictions, was excluded from the number

that God had spoken to him, or had entrusted a mission to him; before the days of Moses no such assertion had ever been made.[1] You must not be misled by the statements that God spoke to the Patriarchs, or that He had appeared to them. For you do not find any mention of a prophecy [2] which appealed to others, or which directed them. Abraham, Isaac, or Jacob, or any other person before them did not tell the people, "God said unto me you shall do this thing, or you shall not do that thing," or "God has sent me to you." Far from it! for God spoke to them on nothing but of what especially concerned them, i.e., He communicated to them things relating to their perfection, directed them in what they should do, and foretold them what the condition of their descendants would be; nothing beyond this. They guided their fellow-men by means of argument and instruction, as is implied, according to the interpretation generally received amongst us, in the words ואת הנפש אשר עשו בחרן "and the souls that they had gotten in Haran" (Gen. xii. 5).[3] When God appeared to our Teacher Moses, and commanded him to address the people and to bring them the message, Moses replied that he might first be asked to prove the existence of God in the Universe, and that only after doing so he would be able to announce to them that God had sent him. For all men, with few

---

of prophetical books; because Daniel was not charged by God with any message to deliver to his fellowmen.

[1] Maimonides is in so far correct, as no direct mission is mentioned in the Biblical records prior to Moses; indirect commandments, however, to exercise his influence on fellowmen, by word and example, were, according to tradition, given to Noah when he was commanded to build the ark, in order that he might have an opportunity of exhorting the people, and of showing them the folly of their conduct. See Rashi on Gen. vi. 4. An opportunity appears to have been given to Abraham for exhorting his fellowmen; comp. Gen. xviii. 19, "that he will command his children, and his household after him, and they shall keep the way of the Lord," etc.

[2] Char. ענין נבואת מרע״ה ר״ל שיורה, "the purpose of the prophecy of Moses, namely, that he should instruct," etc.

[3] Comp. the version of Onkelos, וית נפשתא דשעבדו לאורייתא, "and those whom they had won for the true faith."

exceptions, were ignorant of the existence of God; their highest thoughts did not extend beyond the heavenly sphere, its forms or its influences. They could not yet emancipate themselves from sensation, and had not yet attained to any intellectual perfection. Then God taught Moses how to teach them, and how to establish amongst them the belief in the existence of Himself, namely, by saying אהיה אשר אהיה (*Ehyeh asher Ehyeh*), a name derived from the verb היה in the sense of "existing," for היה denotes "to be," and in Hebrew no difference is made between the verbs "to be" and "to exist." The principal point in this phrase is that the same word which denotes "existence," is repeated as an attribute. The word אשר, "that," corresponds to the Arabic אלדי and אלתי, and is an incomplete noun that must be completed by another noun;[1] it may be considered as the subject of the predicate which follows. The first noun which is to be described is אהיה; the second, by which the first is described, is likewise אהיה, the identical word, as if to show that the object which is to be described and the attribute by which it is described are in this case necessarily identical. This is, therefore, the expression of the idea that God exists, but not in the ordinary sense of the term; or, in other words, He is "the existing Being which is the existing Being," that is to say, whose existence is absolute. The proof which he was to give consisted in demonstrating that there is a Being of absolute existence, that has never been and never will be without existence. This I will clearly prove.[2]

God thus showed Moses the proofs by which His existence would be firmly established among the wise men of His people. Therefore the explanation of the name is followed by the words, "Go, gather the elders of Israel," and by the assurance that they (the elders) would understand what God had shown to him, and they would accept it, as is stated in the words, "And they will hearken to thy voice." Then

---

[1] That is, the relative is the substitute for a noun with which it agrees. אשר אהיה is the same as אהיה אהיה.

[2] See II. Introd., Propos. 20, and ch. i.

Moses replied as follows: They will accept the doctrine that God exists through these intelligible proofs, but by what means shall I be able to show that this existing God has sent me? Thereupon God gave him the sign.[1] We have thus shown that the question, "What is His name?" means "Who is that Being, which according to thy belief has sent thee?" The sentence "What is His name," (instead of, Who is He), has here been used as a tribute of praise and homage, as though it had been said, Nobody can be ignorant of Thy essence and of Thy real existence; if, nevertheless, I ask[2] what is Thy name, I mean, What idea is to be expressed by the name? (Moses considered it inappropriate to say to God that any person was ignorant of God's existence, and therefore described the Israelites as ignorant of God's name, not as ignorant of Him who was called by that name.[3])—The name *Jah* (יה), likewise implies eternal existence.[4] *Shaddai*, however, is derived from די, "enough;" comp. והמלאכה היתה דים, "for the stuff they had was sufficient" (Ex. xxxvi. 7); the *shin* (ש) is equal to אשר, "which," as in שכבר, "which already" (Eccl. ii. 16). The name *Shaddai*, therefore, signifies "he who is sufficient;" that is to say, He does not require the existence of what He created, or the conservation of any other being; His existence is self-sufficient. In a similar manner the name חסין implies "strength"; comp. חסון הוא כאלונים, "he was strong as the oaks" (Amos ii. 9); also צור, "rock," is a homonym, as we have explained.[5] It is, therefore, clear that all these names of God are appellatives, or applied by way of homonymy, like צור

---

[1] Exod. iv. 1, *et seq.*

[2] The original סאלת, active; Munk substitutes סילת, the passive; in the version of Tibbon וישאל can be Kal as well as Niphal. Char. ישאלוני, "they ask me."

[3] This appears to be a mere repetition of the preceding sentence in another form. One of the two was probably the original, and the other the corrected form which was intended to be substituted for it.

[4] That is, like *ehyeh*, the following names of God are also common nouns. The derivation of יה is not indicated here by Maimonides; but probably derived from היה. Comp. Yad ha-chazakah, Yesode ha-torah, vi. 4.

[5] See ch. xvi.

and others,[1] the only exception being the tetragrammaton, the *Shem ha-meforash* (the *nomen proprium* of God), which is not an appellative; it does not denote any attribute of God, nor does it imply anything except His existence. Absolute existence includes the idea of eternity, *i.e.* the necessity of existence. Note well the results at which we have arrived in this chapter.

CHAPTER LXIV.

(יי) שם 1, *The name of God.* 2, *God.* 3, *The Word of God.*
(יי) כבוד 1, *The Glory of God.* 2, *God.* 3, *The praise of God.*

KNOW that in some instances by the phrase "the name of the Lord," nothing but the name alone is to be understood; comp. "Thou shalt not take the name of the Lord thy God in vain" (Ex. xx. 7); "And he that blasphemeth the name of the Lord" (Lev. xxiv. 16). This occurs in numerous other passages. In other instances it means the essence and reality of God himself,[2] as in the phrase "They shall say to me, What is His name"? Sometimes it stands for "the word of God," so that "the name of God," "the word of God," and "the command of God," are identical phrases; comp. כי שמי בקרבו, "for My name is in him" (Ex. xxiii. 21), that is, My word or My command is in him, *i.e.* he is the instrument of My desire and will. I shall explain this fully in treating of the homonymity of the term מלאך "angel."[3]—The same is the case with כבוד יי, "The glory of the Lord." The phrase sometimes signifies "the material light,"[4] which God caused to rest on a certain place in order to show the

---

[1] In the version of Ibn Tibbon, and in some MSS. of the Arabic text צור ואמת. Munk conjectures that ואמת is a corruption of ואמתאלה, because אמת is not employed in the Bible as a name of God.

[2] שם with a suffix (in the same manner as נפש with a suffix), has frequently the meaning of a personal pronoun. Comp. מי שמך, "Who art thou?" Judges xiii. 17.

[3] See II., vi. and xxxiv.   [4] See ch. x., pag. 57, note 4.

R

distinction of that place, *e.g.*, "And the glory of the Lord (כבוד יי) abode upon Mount Sinai and the cloud covered it" (Ex. xxiv. 16): "And the glory of the Lord filled the tabernacle" (*ib.* xl. 35). Sometimes the essence, the reality of God is meant by that expression, as in the words of Moses, "Show me *Thy glory*" (*ib.* xxxiii. 18), to which the reply was given, "For no man shall see *Me* and live" (*ib.* xx.). This shows that the glory of the Lord in this instance is the same as He Himself, and that "Thy glory" has been substituted for "Thyself," as a tribute of homage;[1] an explanation which we also gave of the words, "And they shall say unto me, What is His name?" Sometimes the term כבוד "glory," denotes the glorification of the Lord by man or by any other being.[2] For the true glorification of the Lord consists in the comprehension of His greatness, and all who comprehend His greatness and perfection, glorify Him according to their capacity, with this difference, that man alone magnifies God in words, expressive of what he has received in his mind, and what he desires to communicate to others. Things not endowed with comprehension, as *e.g.*, minerals,[3] may also be considered as glorifying the Lord, for by their natural properties they

[1] That is, instead of saying "Show me Thyself," Moses says "Show me Thy glory," as if to express thereby his conviction that "God Himself cannot be shown," only "His glory can be shown." See preceding chapter.

[2] Lit. "By any other being besides the Almighty." Char. וכל מה שהוא זולתו להדרו ולרוממו. Munk: "Ou plutôt de la part de tout ce qui est en dehors de lui, car tout sert à le glorifier." In a note he gives the following literal rendering: "ou plutôt, tout ce qui est en dehors de lui le glorifie."— The sense of the passage is as follows: Not only man's praises but also those of all who glorify Him, are called כבוד; *e.g.*, the praises of the pure intelligences (שכלים הנפרדים) and the angels. They do not speak, but this is not essential in praising God. For in the perception of God's greatness consists His praise; men require speech to communicate with each other. This is not the case with immaterial, purely spiritual beings. After having mentioned man and spiritual beings, both of which are capable of perceiving God's greatness, the author treats of inanimate beings, of which likewise it is said figuratively that they praise God.

[3] Char., כאבנים ומה שאין בו רוח חיים, "as, *e. g.*, stones and inanimate beings."

testify to the omnipotence and wisdom of their Creator,[1] and cause him who examines them to praise God, by means of speech or without the use of words, if the power of speech be wanting.[2] In Hebrew this license has been extended still further, and the use of the verb "to speak" (אמר) has been admitted as applicable in such a case; things which have no comprehension are therefore said to give utterance to praise, *e.g.*, "All my bones shall say, Lord, who is like unto Thee?" (Ps. xxxv. 10). Because a consideration of the properties of the bones leads to the discovery of that truth, and it is through them that it became known, they are represented as having uttered the divine praise; and since[3] this [cause of God's praise] is itself called כבוד "praise," it has been said מלא כל הארץ כבודו, "the fulness of the whole earth is His praise[4]" (Is. vi. 3), in the same sense as ותהלתו מלאה הארץ, "the earth is full of His praise" (Hab. iii. 3). As to כבוד being employed in the sense of praise, comp. תנו ליי אלהיכם כבוד, "Give praise to the Lord your God" (Jer. xiii. 16); also ובחיכלו כלו אומר כבוד, "and in His temple does everyone speak of His praise" (Ps. xxix. 9), etc. Consider well this homonymity of the term כבוד, and explain it in each instance in accordance with the context; you will thus escape great embarrassment.

CHAPTER LXV.

On the phrases "God spake," "God said."

AFTER you have advanced thus far,[5] and truly comprehended that God exists without having the attribute of

---

[1] Char., מציאותו, "of His existence."

[2] See page 242, note 2.

[3] לפיכך, in Ibn Tibbon's version, is probably a mistake; the correct reading is ולפי קרוא; Char., וכפי קריאת.

[4] See chapter xix., page 73, note 3.

[5] That is, if a person is convinced that even the attributes of existence and unity are not predicated of God, in the ordinary sense of these terms, because

existence, and that He is One, without having the attribute of unity, I do not think that I need explain to you the inadmissibility of the attribute of speech in reference to God, especially since our people generally believe that the Law, *i.e.*, the word ascribed to Him, was created.[1] Speech is attributed to Him, in so far as the word which Moses heard, was produced and brought to existence by God in the same manner as He produced all His other works and creations. As we shall have to speak more fully on prophecy,[2] we shall here merely show that speech is attributed to God in the same way as all other actions, which are similar to our own. When we are told that God addressed the Prophets and spoke to them, our minds are merely to receive a notion that there is a Divine knowledge to which the Prophets attain; we are to be impressed with the idea that the things which the Prophets communicate to us come from the Lord, and are not altogether the products of their own conceptions and ideas. This subject, which we have already mentioned above,[3] will receive further explanation. It is the object of this chapter to show that the verbs דבר, "to speak," and אמר, "to say," are synonyms denoting (*a*) "Speech;" as, *e.g.*, משה ידבר, "Moses shall speak" (Exod. xix. 19); ויאמר פרעה, "And Pharaoh said" (*ib.* v. 5);

---

every notion of a real attribute is inadmissible in reference to Him, he need not be told that speech, as an attribute, is inadmissible; for many would admit the attribute of existence and unity, and would still reject that of speech. Some of the Mahomedan Theologians considered the Word of God as an attribute co-existing with Him from eternity to eternity. According to the theory of some Jewish philosophers, the Word of God emanated from Him, as all His other acts, and on that account it cannot be considered as an attribute of God. Although the Divine Word, or the Torah, is said in the Talmud and the Midrash to have existed two thousand years (not as Munk, p. 290, note 1, paraphrases, "de toute éternité") anterior to the creation of the universe, it was believed to be a thing created and limited in time. As to the meaning of "two thousand years," see Motot and Ohel Joseph on Ibn Ezra's Comm. on the Pentat., Introd. Fourth Method.

[1] That is to say, it did not exist from eternity.
[2] See II., xxxv. and xxxvi.
[3] See I., ch. xlvi., page 154.

(b) "Thought" as formed in the mind without being expressed in words; *e.g.*, ואמרתי אני בלבי, "And I thought in my heart" (Eccles. ii. 15); ודברתי בלבי, "And I thought in my heart" (*ib.*); ולבך ידבר, "And thy heart will contrive" (Prov. xxiii. 33); אמר לבי, "Concerning Thee my heart thought" (Ps. xxvii. 8); ויאמר עשו בלבו, "And Esau thought in his heart" (Gen. xxvii. 41); examples of this kind are numerous; (c) Will; *e.g.*, ויאמר להכות את דוד, "And he said to slay David" (2 Sam. xxi. 16), that is to say, he wished or he intended to slay him;[1] הלהרגני אתה אומר, "Dost thou desire to slay me" (Ex. ii. 14); ויאמרו כל העדה לרגום אותם, "And the whole congregation intended to stone them" (Numb. xiv. 10). Instances of this kind are likewise numerous.

The terms אמר and דבר applied to God, can only have one of the two significations mentioned last, *viz.*, the will and desire, or the thought, and there is no difference whether the divine thought became known to man by means of an actual voice,[2] or by one of those kinds of inspiration which I shall explain. We must not suppose that in speaking God employed voice or sound, or that He has a soul in which the thoughts reside,[3] and that these thoughts are things superadded to His essence; but we ascribe and attribute to Him thoughts in the same manner as we ascribe to Him any other attributes. The use of אמר and דבר in the sense of will and desire, is based, as I have explained, on the homonymity of these terms. In addition they are figures

[1] Lit., "As if he said, And he wished to kill him, that is to say, he intended to kill him." This additional explanation appears to be superfluous; it is a mere variation of the preceding words; it is improbable that both have originally formed part of the same text.

[2] Lit., "created," that is, created for the purpose; a sound was produced in a supernatural manner, that reached the ears of the Prophet or of the Israelites when they received the Decalogue. Comp. Jehudah Hallevi in Kusri, I., 89. Saadia in Emunoth we-deoth, II., 8. Abravanel, Comm. on Exod. xx. 18.

[3] That is, we must neither imagine, that God speaks, and that a sound is produced by some organs of speech, nor that He conceives ideas or thoughts, which form the substance of speech; for the first would lead directly to corporeality, the latter would be contrary to the idea of absolute unity.

borrowed from our common practices, as has been already pointed out.[1] For we cannot, at a first glance, see how anything can be produced by a mere desire; we think that he who wishes to produce a thing, must perform a certain act,[2] or command some one else to perform it. Therefore the command is figuratively ascribed to God when that takes place which He wishes, and we then say that He commanded that a certain thing should be accomplished. All this has its origin in our comparing the acts of God to our own acts, and also in the use of the term אמר in the sense of רצה, "He desired," as we have already explained. The word ויאמר (*lit.* and He said), occurring in the account of the creation, signifies "He wished," or "He desired." This has already been stated by other authors,[3] and is well known. A proof for this, namely, that all these references to speaking denote the Will, not the Speech, is found in the circumstance that a command can only be given to a being which exists and is capable of receiving the command.[4] Comp. "By the word of the Lord (בדבר יי) were the heavens made, and all the host of them by the breath of His mouth" (וברוח פיו) (Ps. xxxiii. 6). פיו, "His mouth," and רוח פיו, "the breath of His mouth," are undoubtedly figurative expressions, and the same is the case with "His word" and "His speech." The meaning of the verse is therefore that they [the heavens and all their host] exist through His will and desire. All our eminent authorities are cognisant of this; and I need not explain that in Hebrew אמר and דבר have the same meaning, as is proved by the passage, "For it has heard all the words (אמרי) of the Lord which He spake (דבר) unto us" (Jos. xxiv. 27).

---

[1] See ch. xlvi.
[2] Charizi adds here the words, או הוא בעצמו, "either he himself."
[3] According to Narboni, in his commentary, Saadia and Ibn Gannach are meant. Comp. Ibn Ezra, on Gen. i. 3.
[4] *Scil.*, and this could not have been the case in the Creation, in the report of which is likewise used the verb ויאמר, "and He said."

CHAPTER LXVI.

"*And the tables were the work of God*" (Exod. xxxii. 16).

והלחת מעשה אלהים המה, "And the tables were the work of God" (Exod. xxxii. 16), that is to say, they were the product of nature, not of art;[1] for all natural things are called "the work of the Lord," *e.g.*, "These see the works of the Lord" (מעשי יי, Ps. cvii. 24);[2] and the description of the several things in nature, as plants, animals, winds, rain, etc., is followed by the exclamation, "O Lord, how manifold are Thy works!" (מעשיך, Ps. civ. 24). Still more striking[3] is the relation between God and His creatures, as expressed in the phrase, "The cedars of Lebanon, which He hath planted" (*ib.* 16); the cedars being the product of nature, and not of art, are described as having been planted by the Lord. Similarly we explain, "And the writing was the writing of God" (מכתב אלהים, Exod. xxxii. 16); the relation in which the writing stood to God has already been defined in the words "written with the finger of God" (באצבע אלהים, *ib.* xxxi. 18), and the meaning of this phrase is the same as that of "the work of Thy fingers" (מעשה אצבעותיך, Ps.

---

[1] That is, of human work, as distinguished from the work of God or of nature. The tables of stone were left in their natural state in which they were found. Munk believes that Maimonides, in calling the tables a product of nature, expressed his opinion that they existed in the same form since the first days of creation. This is not probable; the phrase "product of nature" is used perhaps by the author in contradistinction to the "product of man's work;" and it implies simply that there is nothing more wonderful about the substance of the tables than is noticed in the whole of the creation. Ibn Ezra on Exod. xxxii. 16, says פי׳ מעשה אלהים שהיו ככה כמדה הראויה נבראים; "the meaning of the phrase 'work of God' is, they were thus, in the proper size, the direct product of the creation."

[2] This is said in reference to the natural changes of the sea.

[3] The application of the general term "the work of the Lord," to the Universe or to part of it, appears less remarkable than the use of phrases which ascribe to God a special action in reference to a single thing, as the planting of a tree, or the writing on the tables, if such action is not meant in a figurative sense, *viz.*, that it is the will of God that a certain thing should be done.

viii. 4), this being an allusion to the heavens; of the latter it has been stated distinctly that they were made by a word; comp. "By the word of the Lord (בדבר יי) were the heavens made" (*ib.* xxxiii. 6). Hence you learn that in the Bible, the creation of a thing is figuratively expressed by terms denoting "word" and "speech" (דבר and אמר). The same thing which according to one passage has been made by a word (בדבר), is represented in another passage as made by the "finger of God" (באצבע אלהים). The phrase "written by the finger of God" is therefore identical with "written by the word of God" (בדבר אלהים); and if the latter phrase had been used, it would have been equal to בחפץ אלהים, "written by the will and desire of God."[1] Onkelos adopted in this place a strange explanation,[2] and rendered it כתיבין באצבעא דיי, literally "written by the finger of the Lord"; he thought that אצבע, "the finger," was a certain thing[3] appertaining to God; so that אצבע יי "the finger of the Lord" is to be interpreted in the same way as "the mountain of God" (Exod. iii. 1), "the rod of God" (*ib.* iv. 20), that is, as being an instrument created by Him, which by His will engraved the writing on the tables. I cannot see why Onkelos preferred this explanation. It would have been more reasonable to say כתיבין במימרא דיי, "written by the word of the Lord," in imitation of the verse "By the word of the Lord the heavens were made." Or was the creation of the writing on the tables more difficult than the creation of

[1] That is, the writing which appeared on the tables was the product of a natural force which formed part of the creation. The "word" or "will" of God, the cause of that writing, does not imply a command addressed to Moses. Comp. Maim., Eight chapters, viii., and the Comm. of Ibn Ezra on Ex. xxxi. 18, באצבע אלהים על מנהג האדם כי כל חפץ השם בדבר פיו יקום, "'with the finger of God' is a figurative phrase, for the will of God is performed by the mere word of His mouth."

[2] Char., less strictly, סברא חדשה, "a new opinion." Probably Onkelos refrained from defining the miracle expressed in the figurative phrase "finger of God," and therefore retained the figure as in the original. See Berkowitz, Lechem ve-simlah *ad locum.*

[3] Charizi, כח, "a force."

the stars in the spheres? As the latter were made by the direct will of God, not by means of an instrument, the writing may also have been produced by His direct will, not by means of an instrument. You know what the Mishnah says, "Ten things were created on Friday in the twilight of the evening, and "the writing" is one of the ten things.[1] This shows how generally it was assumed by our forefathers that the writing of the tables was produced in the same manner as the rest of the creation, as we have shown in our Commentary on the Mishnah.[1]

CHAPTER LXVII.[2]

שבת
נוח } 1, To rest. 2, To discontinue. 3, To be firmly established.

SINCE the term אמר, "to say," has been figuratively used to express the will of the Creator, and the phrase ויאמר, "And He said," has repeatedly been employed in the account of all the things created in "the six days of the beginning," the expression שבת, "to rest," has likewise been figuratively

[1] See Mishnah, Abhoth, v. 6, and Maimonides, ad locum : "כתב, 'writing,' refers to the Law, which lay as it were written before Him; but we cannot know how this was. Comp. 'And I will give thee the tables of stone [and the Law, and the commandment which I have written to show them]' (Exod. xxiv. 12). והמכתב, 'and the writing,' refers to the writing on the tables ; comp. 'and the writing was the writing of God, engraved on the tables' " (ib. xxxii. 16).

[2] In accordance with the explanation given in the preceding chapters, that the verbs "He made," "He wrote," etc., meant "It was His will, that a certain thing be done, be written," etc., he shows in the present chapter that the verb "to rest" (שבת, נוח), used in reference to God, must not be understood in the ordinary sense, implying previous work, as if the Creation consisted in a material act. "God rested" means that it no longer was His will to create a new thing; the Universe, as it existed at the end of the sixth day, was complete; nothing followed, except the regular development of that which had been created.

applied to God in reference to the Sabbath-day, on which there was no creation; it is therefore said, וישבת ביום השביעי, "And He rested on the seventh day" (Gen. ii. 2). For "to leave off speaking" is, in Hebrew, likewise expressed by the verb שבת, as, *e.g.*, in וישברו שלשת האנשים האלה מענות את איוב, "So these three men ceased to answer Job" (Job xxxii. 1); also by נוח, as, *e.g.*, in וידבר אל נבל ככל הדברים האלה בשם דוד וינוחו, "They spake to Nabal according to all those words in the name of David, and ceased" (1 Sam. xxv. 9). In my opinion, וינוחו means "they ceased to speak," and waited for the answer; for no allusion to exertion whatever having previously been mentioned, the word וינוחו, "and they rested," in its primary signification, would have been entirely out of place in that narrative, even if the young men who spoke had really used some exertion. The author relates that having delivered that whole speech, which, as you find, consisted of gentle expressions, they were silent, that is to say, they did not add any word or act by which the reply of Nabal could be justified; it being the object of the entire passage to represent Nabal's conduct as extremely reprehensible. In that sense, [*viz.* "to cease," or "to leave off"] the verb נוח is used in the phrase וינח ביום השביעי, "And He left off on the seventh day."

Our Sages,[1] and some of the Commentators,[2] took, however, the word in its primary sense ("to rest"), but as a transitive verb,[3] explaining the phrase thus: "and He gave rest

---

[1] See Bereshith Rabba x.: "As long as the hands of their master were engaged with them, they were continually expanding, but as soon as the hands of the master ceased (כיון שנחו) to touch them, repose (נחת) was granted to them." In another part of the Midrash the following passage occurs: מה היה העולם חסר מנוחה בא שבת בא מנוחה וינח ביום השביעי, "What more did the Universe want? Rest; this came with the Sabbath, as it is said, 'And He gave rest on the seventh day.'"

[2] The idea of "rest" is by almost all commentators found in the word וינח, but none of the known authors explain וינח as the Hiphil of נוח; it can, therefore, not be determined who are meant by the phrase "and other commentators."

[3] This phrase is absent in Charizi's version.

PART I.—CHAPTER LXVII. 251

to the world on the seventh day " (וינח לעולמו ביום השביעי),[1] *i.e.*, no further act of creation took place on that day.[2]

It is possible that the word וינח is derived either from ינח, a verb פ"י, or נחח, a verb ל"ח, and has this meaning: "he established" or "he governed"[3] the Universe in accordance with the properties it possessed on the seventh day;" that is to say, while on each of the six days events took place contrary[4] to the natural laws now in operation throughout the Universe, on the seventh day the Universe was merely upheld and left in the condition in which it continues to exist. Our explanation[5] is not impaired by the fact that the form of the word (וַיָּנַח) deviates from the rules of verbs פ"י and ל"ח;[6] for there are frequent exceptions[7] to the rules of conjugations, and especially of the weak verbs; and any interpretation which removes such a source of error must not be abandoned in favour of certain grammatical rules. We know[8] that we are ignorant of the sacred language, and that grammatical rules only apply to the majority of cases.[9]—The

[1] That is, every new thing created on the six days produced a kind of revolution in the Universe; but when all was complete the Universe had stability and rest. See *supra*, page 249, note 2.

[2] This explanatory phrase seems to have been misplaced; its proper position being immediately after the quotation וינח ביום השביעי, for it refers to the author's own interpretation of the word ינח, "and he left off," and not to the explanation given by our Sages as signifying, "to cause rest."

[3] Ibn Tibbon adds והמשיך, "and prolonged;" Char. השקים את התמדת המציאות, "He firmly established the continuance of the Universe."

[4] Char. יוצאים מכח זה הטבע, "different from the force of nature in its present state." There is no reason why we should give a different meaning to the phrase יוצאים, employed both in Charizi's and Ibn Tibbon's versions. Munk wrongly states : " Al Harizi a fait un contre-sens en traduisant, qui *sortaient* ou émanaient de la faculté de cette nature."

[5] That וַיָּנַח signifies "he left firmly established."

[6] The ordinary future with Vau conversive of ינח would be וַיִּנַּח; of ויגח, נחה.

[7] Charizi זולת הסברא, "not according to what is expected."

[8] Charizi אע"פי שנודע, "although it is known."

[9] Arab. ואוקואנין כל לגה אכתריה. Tibb. ושדרכי כל לשון רבים. Char. וכן חקי תבונת כל לשון מוסכמות. Munk: " et que les règles de toute langue sont une chose de pluralité." The sense of the passage evidently is, that the rules admit of many exceptions in the several languages: lit., according to Tib-

same root is also found as a verb ע"י[1] in the sense "to place" and "to set," as *e.g.*, והוכן והניחה שם על מכונתה, "and it shall be established and placed there upon her own base" (Zec. v. 11), and לא נתנה עוף השמים לנוח עליהם, "and suffered neither the birds of the air to settle on them" (2 Sam. xxi. 10).[2] According to my opinion, the verb has the same signification in אשר אנוח ליום צרה, "that I might remain firm[3] in the day of trouble" (Hab. iii. 16).

The word וינפש is a verb derived from נפש, the homonymity of which we have already explained,[4] namely, that it has the signification of intention or will; וינפש accordingly means: "that which He desired was accomplished, and what He wished had come into existence."

CHAPTER LXVIII.

God includes in His Unity the intellectus (השכל), *the intelligens* (המשכיל), *and the intelligibile* (המושכל).[5]

You are acquainted with the well-known principle of the philosophers that God is the *intellectus*, the *ens intelligens*,

---

bon, "in every language the rules relate only to the majority" (רֻבִּים); or, according to Charizi, "the grammatical rules of every language only relate to those cases which agree."

[1] וְהֻנִּיחָה, as in our editions of the Bible, is a combination of Hophal and Hiphil of ינח.

[2] Maimonides perhaps objects to taking לנוח in the sense of "to rest," because the birds would not "rest" (in the literal sense of the word) upon the dead bodies, but eat them, and that was especially guarded against.

[3] Comp. Targ. Jon. דשבקני, "who left me."

[4] See chap. xli.

[5] See Ibn Ezra, Comm. on Exod. xxxiii. 23, and Dr. Friedlander, Ibn Ezra Literature, IV., pp. 23, 46. This proposition, that in God, the subject, action and object of His knowledge are identical, so frequently quoted and discussed by Jewish and Mahomedan philosophers, is traced to Aristotle's Metaphysics, xii. 9, αὑτὸν ἄρα νοεῖ, εἴπερ ἐστὶ τὸ κράτιστον, καὶ ἔστιν ἡ νόησις νοήσεως νόησις. Also in the last of the "Eight Chapters" Maimonides shows that God's knowledge is inseparable from His essence, and that both are identical.

and the *ens intelligibile*. These three things are in God one and the same, and do not in any way constitute a plurality. We have also mentioned it in our larger work, "Mishneh Thorah,"[1] and we have explained there that it is a fundamental principle of our religion, namely, that He is absolutely one, that nothing combines with Him; that is to say, there is no Eternal thing besides Him. On that account we say חַי יי, "the Lord liveth" (Ruth iii. 13), and not חֵי יי "the life of the Lord," for His life is not a thing distinct from His essence,[2] as we have explained in treating of the inadmissibility of the attributes.[3] There is no doubt that he who has not studied any works on mental philosophy, who has not comprehended the nature of the mind, who has no knowledge of its essence, and considers it in no other way than he would consider the nature of whiteness and of blackness, will find this subject extremely difficult, and to him our principle that the *intellectus*, the *intelligens*, and the *intelligibile*, are in God one and the same thing, will appear as unintelligible as if we said that the whiteness, the whitening substance, and the material which is whitened are one and the same thing.

[1] Comp.: "The Holy One, blessed be He, perceives His true essence, and knows it as it is in reality; for His knowledge is not like ours, separate from His essence; we and our knowledge are not identical, but the Creator with His knowledge and His life are one in every respect, in every way, and in every sense of the term unity; for, if He possessed life and knowledge as things separate from His essence, there would be several divine beings, God himself, His life, and His knowledge. This is not the case; He is One in every respect, in every way, and in every sense of the term unity; consequently He is the One who knows, the thing which is known, and also the knowledge itself; all these are One—a theory which cannot be clearly described in words, perceived by the ear, or understood by the heart of man. The phrase 'by the life of the Lord' (חֵי יי), is therefore not used in the Bible, but 'the Lord liveth' (חַי יי), although we find 'by the life of Pharaoh' (חֵי פרעה), 'by the life of thy soul' (חֵי נפשך)". (Yesode ha-torah, ii. 10.)

[2] חַי is an adjective, while חֵי is considered to be identical with חַיֵּי the construct state of חַיִּים. The phrase "the life of the Lord" would imply that He possesses life as something different from Himself. He may be called חֵי הָעוֹלָם, "the life of the world" (Dan. xii. 7), as being the cause of the life or the existence of the Universe.

[3] Chapter liii.; chap. lvii., etc.

And, indeed, many ignorant people refute at once our principle by using such comparisons. Even amongst those who imagine that they are wise, many find this subject difficult, and are of opinion that it is impossible for the mind to grasp the truth of this proposition,[1] although it is a demonstrated truth, as has been shown by Metaphysicians. I will tell you now what has been proved. Man, before comprehending a thing comprehends it in potentia (δυνάμει);[2] when, however, he comprehends a thing, e.g., the form of a certain tree which is pointed out to him, when he abstracts its form from its substance, and reproduces the abstract form, an act performed by the intellect, he comprehends in reality (ἐνεργείᾳ),[3] and the intellect which he has acquired in actuality, is the abstract form of the tree in man's mind. For in such a case the intellect is not a thing distinct from the thing

---

[1] Yesode ha-torah, ii. 10. See note 1, page 253.

[2] νοῦς παθητικὸς in the theory of Aristotle. The soul of man is like a *tabula rasa*, which is to be filled up by him, the τόπος εἰδῶν of Aristotle, a mere capacity of acquiring knowledge. Comp. Ibn Ezra Literature, IV. page 32. The writings on this tablet form the constituent elements of the intellect. The relation between the writing and the tablet, the νοῦς παθητικὸς and the νοῦς ποιητικὸς has been compared to the relation between matter and form, whence the former received the name hylic intellect (שכל הוליאני).

[3] νοῦς ποιητικὸς, שכל בפועל, "the intellect in action," the act by which that which has been a mere capacity, which has only existed as a possibility (δυνάμει), becomes a reality. Maimonides ascribes this act to the intellect itself (פועל השכל "the act of the intellect"); as, however, the intellect (שכל), is here defined by Maimonides to be nothing but the knowledge acquired, the question must naturally arise, whence comes that knowledge? What force gives the impulse to man's intellectual development? Some consider the active intellect (שכל הפועל) as the cause of all mental operations of man. See Moreh ha-moreh, pag. 141, והרביעי השכל הפועל והיא צורה שאינו בחומר והוא קרוב הדמות מהשכל הנאצל והוא הטשים אותו הדבר שיהיה (שהיה?) שכל בכח שכל בפעל, "the fourth; the active intellect, an immaterial form, similar to the abstract ideas; it causes that which is intellect in possibility (δυνάμει), to become intellect in action" (ἐνεργείᾳ). The same appears to be the opinion of Maimonides; see *infra*, pag. 256, note 2. The active intellect, being considered as the highest form which the soul by progressive development can attain (*ibid.*), is therefore not an original part of the soul, and the first impulse for mental operation is thus assumed to come from without. Comp. Arist., De gen. anim. II. ch. iii.

PART I.—CHAPTER LXVIII. 255

comprehended.[1] It is therefore clear to you[2] that the thing comprehended is the abstract form of the tree, and at the same time it is the intellect in action; and that the intellect and the abstract form of the tree are not two different things, for the intellect in action is nothing but the thing comprehended, and that agent by which the form of the tree has been turned into an intellectual and abstract object, namely, that which comprehends, is undoubtedly the intellect[3] in action. All intellect is identical with its action; the intellect in action is not a thing different from its action, for the true nature and essence of the intellect is comprehension, and you must not think that the intellect in action is a thing existing by itself, separate from comprehension, and that comprehension is a different thing connected with it; for the very essence of the intellect is comprehension.[4] In

[1] That is to say, the intellect (שכל) is nothing else but the sum of the notions or of the abstract ideas formed in the mind.

[2] That is, by assuming on the one hand that the notion formed (מושכל) is the substance of the intellect (שכל), and on the other hand that the action (שכל בפועל) by which the notion is formed, is likewise the intellect (שכל), we arrive at the conclusion that both are identical. In the same manner Maimonides asserts as a truth "which nobody doubts," that the *agens* (משכיל), or thing which acts in the formation of the notions, is identical with the action (שכל בפועל); he assumes that in fact that action is the essence of the intellect to which all mental operations are ascribed. Hence he concludes that the *agens*, the action and the object of the action are identical. It may appear a paradox to say that a certain notion which does not yet exist is the cause of its own existence. But the absurdity disappears when we consider that the three things distinguished by Maimonides as the subject, the action, and the object of the intellect, are nothing else but three different stages in the formation of notions, *viz.* the possibility of their being formed, their actual formation, and their existence in the mind as a basis for further operations. Although generally the impulse is ascribed to certain properties and capacities inherent in mind, the school to which Maimonides belonged considered mind as being passive, as receiving notions and ideas by impulses from without, and, to use the figure of the *tabula rasa*, being covered with self-acting inscriptions. In this sense the ideas may justly be considered as being at the same time the subject (משכיל), the action (שכל בפועל), and the object (מושכל).

[3] Charizi, השכל המושג בפועל, "the intellect that is obtained in reality."

[4] This sentence is a mere repetition of the preceding, and probably owes its origin to a revision of the work; for both the identity of the active intellect

assuming an intellect in action you assume the comprehension of the thing comprehended. This is quite clear to all who have made themselves familiar with the figurative language common to this discipline.[1] You therefore accept it as proved that the intellect consists in its action, which is its true nature and essence. Consequently the very thing by which the form of that tree has been made abstract and intelligible, viz., the intellect, is at the same time the *intelligens*, for the intellect is itself the *agens* which abstracts the form and comprehends it, and that is the action, on account of which it is called the *intelligens*; but itself and its action are identical; and that which is called intellect in action consists [in the abovementioned instance] of nothing else but of the form of the tree. It must now be obvious to you that whenever the intellect is found in action, the intellect and the thing comprehended are one and the same thing; and also that the function of all intellect, namely, the act of comprehending, is its essence. The intellect, that which comprehends and that which is comprehended, are therefore the same, whenever a real comprehension takes place. But,[2] when we speak of the power of comprehension, we necessarily distinguish two things: the power itself, and the thing which can be comprehended; *e.g.*, that hylic intellect[3] of Zaid[4] is the power of comprehension, and this tree is, in

---

and the action, as well as the definition have been stated in the preceding sentence as clearly as in this.

[1] Charizi, בעיונים כמו אלה. "in researches like these."

[2] Having shown that the intellect in action (שכל בפועל) includes in itself both subject and object, Maimonides proceeds now to show that the intellect in capacity (δυνάμει), is different both from subject and object. This intellect in capacity necessarily implies the absence of the object, the presence of which would transform it into the intellect in action. The intellect in capacity (שכל בכח) and its object (מושכל בכח) are thus two things separate from each other. A capacity cannot be imagined without a subject possessing that capacity; intellect itself does not yet exist in reality, and cannot be the subject, another subject (המשכיל) must be assumed; the three things, subject, action, and object are therefore different from each other.

[3] See page 254, note 2.

[4] In the Hebrew Versions: Reuben.

PART I.—CHAPTER LXVIII. 257

like manner, a thing which is capable of being comprehended; these, undoubtedly, are two different things. When, however, the potential is replaced by the actual, and when the form of the tree has really been comprehended, the form comprehended is the intellect, and it is by that same intellect,[1] by the intellect in action, that the tree has been converted into an abstract idea, and has been comprehended. For everything in which a real action takes place exists in reality.[2] On the other hand, the power of comprehension, and the object capable of comprehension are two things; but that which is only potential cannot be imagined otherwise than in connection with an object possessing that capacity, as, *e.g.*, man, and thus we have three things: the man who possesses the power, and is capable of comprehending; that power itself, namely, the power of comprehension, and the thing which presents itself as an object for comprehension, and is capable of being comprehended; to use the foregoing example, the man, the hylic intellect, and the abstract form of the tree, are three different things. They become one and the same thing when the intellect is in action, and you will never find the intellect different from the comprehensible object, unless the power of comprehending and the power of being comprehended be referred to. Now, it has been proved, that God is an intellect which always[3] is in action, and that—as has been stated,[4] and as will be proved hereafter[5]—there is in Him at no time a mere potentiality, that He does not comprehend at one time, and is without comprehension at another time, but He com-

---

[1] Some read וּבְדִלְךָ (Charizi וכן) instead of וּבְדִלְךָ (Tibbon ובשכל ההוא). See Munk, page 310, note 1.

[2] As *e.g.*, the intellect in action, שכל בפועל. The intellect performing some real action exists in reality, and therefore it can combine in itself the three elements, subject, action, and object: while to the intellect in capacity nothing but a possible action is ascribed: consequently it does not exist in reality, and those three elements cannot be combined in it. See *supra*, page 252, note 5.

[3] Omitted in Charizi and in some editions of Tibbon.

[4] See ch. lv., page 199, note 1.

[5] See Part II., i. *sqq.*

s

prehends constantly; consequently, He and the thing comprehended are one and the same thing, that is to say, His essence; and the act of comprehending because of which it is said that He comprehends, is the intellect itself, which is likewise His essence,[1] God is therefore always the *intellectus*, the *intelligens*, and the *intelligibile*.

We have thus shown that the identity of the intellect, the *intelligens* and the *intelligibile*, is not only a fact as regards the Creator, but as regards all intellect, and that the same is also the case with our intellect, when in action. There is, however, this difference,[2] that from time to time our intellect passes over from mere potentiality to reality, and that the pure intellect, *i.e.*, the active intellect, finds sometimes obstacles, though not in itself, but accidentally in some external cause.[3] It is not our present intention to explain this subject, but we will merely show that God alone, and none besides Him, is an intellect constantly in action, and there is, neither in Himself nor in anything beside Him, any obstacle whereby His comprehension would be hindered. Therefore He always includes the *intelligens*, the *intellectus*, and the *intelligibile*, and His essence is at the same time the *intelligens*, the *intelligibile*, and the *intellectus*, as is necessarily the case with all intellect in action.

We have reiterated this idea in the present chapter because it is exceedingly abstruse, and I do not apprehend that the reader will confound intellectual comprehension

---

[1] According to the definition of the intellect given above, *viz.*, that it is nothing but comprehension itself.

[2] Maimonides explains why man's intellect is not always in action. The transition of the passive intellect into that in action, is effected by the active intellect (שכל הפועל or שכל הנפרד), which might be assumed to be constantly active. Maimonides says that although in itself there can be no cause of interruption, yet by external agencies its action may be prevented; if, *e.g.*, the passive intellect is not capable of being influenced by the active intellect. The latter is uninterruptedly active, although its effect does not always manifest itself for the reason given. This is not the case in reference to God. See Part II., xii. and xviii.

[3] חרבה, Hebrew תנועה, Munk, "perturbation."

with the representative faculty—with the reproduction of the material image in our imagination;[1] since this work is designed only for those who have studied philosophy, and who know what has already been said on the soul and its faculties.

CHAPTER LXIX.

God is the Primal Cause.

THE philosophers, as you know, call God the First Cause[2] (העלה הראשונה and הסבה הראשונה): but those who are known by the name of Mutakallemim[3] are very much opposed to the use of that name, and call Him *Agens*, believing that there is a great difference whether we say that God is the Cause or that He is the *Agens*. They argue thus: If we were to say that God is the Cause, the co-existence of the Cause with that which was produced by that Cause would necessarily be implied; this again would involve the belief that the Universe was eternal, and that it was inseparable

---

[1] Charizi, שיסתפק עליך המחשבה השכלית עם המחשבה הדמיונית והנני מדבר על דמיון המורגש בכח העולה במחשבה: "that you will confound the intellectual notions with the imagination, I mean to say, with the image formed of a material object by means of the imaginative power." The word אחד in the original can be either the infinitive or first person future singular according to its being read أَخَذَ or آخَذَ.

[2] In Arabic and in Hebrew two terms are employed promiscuously to denote "cause," in Arabic علة and سبب, in Hebrew עלה and סבה.

[3] See pag. 4, note 1. Charizi: הנקראים בשם והמדברים. Palquera: המפורסמים והמדברים. The latter explains the term Mutakallemim as follows: Knowing the science of the words, which establishes, against the opponents of religion, proofs founded on scientific research; for there are some who have a knowledge of religion without science, and they are called Fakieh, lit., "judges": others examine the teaching of religion, and prove it by scientific research, these are called Mutakallemim. Moreh ha-moreh, page 152.

from God.[1] When, however, we say that God is the *Agens*, the co-existence of the *Agens* with its product is not implied; for the *agens* can exist anterior to its product; we cannot even imagine how an *agens* can be in action unless it existed before its own production. This is an argument advanced by persons who do not distinguish between the potential and the actual. You, however, should know that in this case there is no difference whether you employ the term "cause" or "*agens*"; for if you take the term "cause" in the sense of a mere potentiality, it precedes its effect; but if you mean the cause in action, then the effect must necessarily co-exist with the cause[2] in action. The same is the case with the *agens*; take it as an *agens* in reality, the work must necessarily co-exist with its *agens*. For the builder, before he builds the house, is not in reality a builder, but has the faculty for building a house[3]—in the same way as the materials for the house before it is being built are merely a house *in potentia*—but when the house has been built, he is the builder[4] in reality, and his product must likewise be in actual existence. Nothing is therefore gained by choosing the term "*agens*" and rejecting the term "cause." My object here is to show that these two terms are equal, and in the same manner as we call God an *Agens*, although the work does not yet exist, only because there is no hindrance or obstacle which might prevent Him from doing whenever He pleases, we may also call Him the Cause, although the effect may not yet be in existence.

The reason why the philosophers called God the Cause, and did not call Him the *Agens*, is not to be sought in their

---

[1] Arabic, אלעאלים לה; Tibbon, העולם מאתו; Charizi, וכי העולם עילה. The word עילה in Charizi is a mistake; it is to be read either עלול, "caused," or עליו, "in relation to him."

[2] Arabic, בוגודהא עלה; Charizi, במציאותה ותהיה עלה; Tibbon, במציאות העלה (Munk suggests במציאותה עלה), "on the existence of the cause."

[3] Ibn Tibbon adds here, "and when he builds, he is a builder in action." The allusion to the material for the building of a house is omitted in Charizi.

[4] Tibbon, נבנה, "it is built."

PART I.—CHAPTER LXIX.   261

belief that the universe is eternal, but in other motives, which I will briefly describe to you. It has been shown in the science of Physics that everything, except the Primal Cause, owes its origin to the following four causes:[1]—the substance, the form, the *agens*, the final cause.[2] These are sometimes direct, sometimes indirect;[3] but each by itself is called "a cause" (in Hebrew, עלה or סבה). They also believe—and I do not differ from their opinion—that God Himself is the *agens*, the form, and the end;[4] therefore they call God "the Cause," in order to express that He unites in Himself these three causes, *viz.*, that He is the *agens*, the form, and the final cause of the universe. In the present chapter I only wish to show you in what sense it may be said of God that He is the *agens*, the form, and also the final cause of the universe. You need not trouble yourself now with the question whether the universe has been created by God, or whether, as the philosophers have assumed, it is eternal, co-existing with Him. You will find [in the pages of this treatise] full and instructive information on this subject.[5] Here I wish to show that God is the "cause" of every event that takes place in the world, just as He is the Creator of the whole universe as it now exists.

[1] Lit., "that causes exist for everything that has a cause; and that they consist in the following four causes."

[2] Comp. Arist., Phys. ii. 7. The substance, *causa formalis*, *causa efficiens*, and *causa finalis*.

[3] Comp. Metaph., viii. 4.

[4] Although a fourth cause has been mentioned as being included in the term "cause," viz., "matter," the first cause of all existing beings includes, according to Aristotle and his followers, only the three causes named here; matter must be excluded; for the first cause is an immaterial being, and its relation to the Universe is similar to the relation of the soul to the body. The soul is likewise said to combine in itself the three causes: *causa efficiens*, *causa formalis*, and *causa finalis*. Comp. Arist. de Animâ, ii. 4; Phys., ii. 7, *sqq*. Maimonides says that he does not differ from the philosophers in that point, and for the present he leaves out of view the question as to the eternity of matter. He only points out that, contrary to the opinions of the Mutakallemim, he goes so far with Aristotle as to admit that in God, the first Cause, these three causes are comprised.

[5] See II., ch. i., *sqq*.

It has already been explained in the science of Physics, that a cause must again be sought for each of the four divisions of causes. When we have found for any existing thing those four causes which are in immediate connection with it, we find for them again causes, and for these again other causes, and so on until we arrive at the first causes. *E.g.*, a certain production has its *agens*, this *agens* again has its *agens*, and so on and on until at last we arrive at a first *agens*, which is the true *agens* throughout all the intervening links. If the letter *aleph* be moved by *beth*, *beth* by *gimel*, *gimel* by *daleth*, and *daleth* by *hé*—and as the series does not extend to infinity, let us stop at *hé*—there is no doubt that the *hé* moves the letters *aleph*, *beth*, *gimel*, and *daleth*, and we say correctly that the *aleph* is moved by *hé*. In that sense everything occurring in the universe, although directly produced by certain nearer causes, is ascribed to the Creator, as we shall explain. He is the *agens*, and He is therefore the ultimate cause. We shall also find, after careful examination, that every physical and transient form must be preceded by another such form, by which the substance has been fitted to receive the next form; the previous form again has been preceded by another, and we arrive at length at that form which is necessary for the existence of all intermediate forms, which are the causes of the present form. That form[1] to which the forms of all existence are traced is God. You must not imagine that when we say that God is the first[1] form of all forms existing in the Universe, we refer to that first[1] form which Aristotle, in the Book of Metaphysics, describes as being without beginning and without end,[2] for he treats of a form which is a physical, and not a

---

[1] Lit. "the last form."

[2] All bodies consist of matter and form; their production and destruction is nothing but the union and disunion of matter and a certain form. Matter and form separately are therefore not subject to production or destruction. Comp. Arist. Metaph., vi. 8, and xii. 3. What Maimonides calls צורה אחרונה, "the last form" is called by others "the first form"; it is the last, in so far as it is the most remote from the object which we examine; it is the first as being the origin from which all other forms arise. This form, however abstract, is

purely intellectual one. When we call God the form of the universe, we do not use this term in the sense of form connected with substance, namely, as the form of that substance, as though God were the form of a material being. It is not in this sense that we use it, but in the following: Everything existing and endowed with a form, is whatever it is through its form, and when that form is destroyed its whole existence terminates and is obliterated. The same is the case as regards the relation between God and all distant causes of existing beings; it is through the existence of God that all things exist, and it is He who maintains their existence by that process which is called emanation (in Hebrew שפע), as will be explained in one of the chapters of the present work.[1] If God did not exist, suppose this were possible, the universe would not exist, and there would be an end to the existence of the distant causes, the final effects, and the intermediate causes. Consequently God maintains the same relation to the world as the form has to a thing endowed with a form; through the form it is what it is, and on it the reality and essence of the thing depends. In this sense we may say that God is the first form, that He is the form of all forms; that is to say, the existence and continuance of all forms in the last instance depend on Him, the forms are maintained by Him, in the same way as all things endowed with forms retain their existence through their forms. On that account God is called, in the sacred language, חֵי הָעוֹלָמִים, "the life of the Universe,"[2] as will be explained.[3] The same argument holds good in reference to all final causes. If you assign to a thing a certain purpose, you can find for that purpose another purpose. We mention, e.g., a (wooden) throne; its substance is wood, the joiner is its *agens*, the

---

still related to matter; it is the form of a material object, and therefore Maimonides declares that it cannot be understood in the same sense, when God is to be regarded as the First Form.

[1] See II., xii.
[2] Comp. Hebrew Prayer-book, the portions beginning ברוך שאמר and ישתבח, and Daniel xii. 7.
[3] Ch. lxxii.

square its form, and its purpose is that one should sit upon it. You may then ask, For what purpose does one sit upon it? The answer will be that he who is sitting upon it desires to be high above the ground. If again you ask, For what purpose does he desire to be high above the ground, you will receive the answer that he wishes to appear high in the eyes of those who see him. For what purpose does he wish to appear higher in the eyes of those who see him? That the people may respect and fear him. What is the good of his being feared? His commands will be respected. For what purpose are his commands to be respected? That people shall refrain from injuring each other. What is the object of this precaution? To maintain order amongst the people. In this way one purpose necessitates the pre-existence of another, except the final purpose, which is the execution of the will of God, according to one of the opinions which have been propounded, as will be explained,[1] and the final answer will be "It is the will of God." According to the view of others, which will likewise be explained, the final purpose is the execution of the decree of His wisdom,[1] and the final answer will be, "It has been decreed by His wisdom." According to either opinion, the series of the successive purposes terminates, as has been shown, in God's will or wisdom, which, in our opinion,[2] are His essence, and not any thing separate from Himself or different from His essence. Consequently, God is the final purpose of everything. Again, it is the aim of everything[3] to become, according to its faculties, similar to God in perfection; this is meant by the expression "His will, which is identical with His essence,"[4] as will be shown below.[5] In this sense God is called the End of all ends (תכלית התכליות).

[1] See III., xiii. and xvii. [2] Ch. liii.

[3] Maimonides now shows, from another point of view, that God's will is the purpose of all purposes. According to the will of the Creator it is the purpose of everything to seek perfection, and to approach the perfection of the Creator.

[4] Comp. II. xiii., the explanation of למענהו (Prov. xvi. 4).

[5] See III. xiii., and I. liv.

I have thus explained to you in what sense God is said to be the *Agens*, the Form, and the End. This is the reason why the philosophers not only call Him "the Maker" but also "the Cause." Some of the scholars belonging to the Mutakallemim, went so far in their folly and in their vainglory as to say that the non-existence of the Creator, if that were possible, would not necessarily imply the non-existence of the things created by Him, *i.e.*, the Universe: for a production need not necessarily cease to exist when the producer, after having produced it, has ceased to exist. They would be right, if God were only the maker of the Universe, and if its permanent existence were not dependent on Him. The storehouse does not cease to exist at the death of the builder; for he does not give permanent existence to the building. God, however, is Himself the form of the Universe, as we have already shown, and it is He who causes its continuance and permanency. It is therefore wrong to say that a thing can remain durable and permanent, after the being that makes it durable and permanent has ceased to exist, while that thing can possess no more durability and permanency than it has received from that being. Now you understand the greatness of the error into which they have fallen through their assumption that God is only the *agens*, and not the end or the form.

CHAPTER LXX.

לרכב בערבות "*To Him that ruleth the Arabhoth.*" (Ps. lxviii. 4.)[1]

THE term רכב (*rakhabh*) "to ride" is a synonym. In its primary signification it is applied to man's riding on an

[1] Having shown that God is the First Cause and the First Form of the Universe, he explains in this chapter the term רכב בערבות as expressing the same idea.

animal, in the usual way;[1] comp. וְהוּא רוֹכֵב עַל אֲתֹנוֹ,
"Now he was riding upon his ass" (Numb. xxii. 22). It
has then been figuratively used to denote "dominion over
a thing;" because the rider governs and rules the animal
he rides upon. This sense the word has in יַרְכִּיבֵהוּ
עַל בָּמֳתֵי אֶרֶץ, "He made him ride on the high places of the
earth" (Deut. xxxii. 13); וְהִרְכַּבְתִּיךָ עַל בָּמֳתֵי אָרֶץ, "and I
will cause thee to ride upon the high places of the earth"
(Is. lviii. 14), that is, you shall have dominion over the
highest (people) on earth; אַרְכִּיב אֶפְרַיִם, "I will make
Ephraim to ride" (Hos. x. 11), *i.e.*, I shall give him rule
and dominion. In this same sense it is said of God רֹכֵב
שָׁמַיִם בְּעֶזְרֶךָ, "who rideth upon the heaven in thy help"
(Deut. xxxiii. 26), that is, who rules the heaven; and לָרֹכֵב
בָּעֲרָבוֹת, "Him that rideth upon the arabhoth" (Ps. lxviii. 4),
i.e., who rules the *arabhoth*, the uppermost, all-encompassing
sphere. It has also been repeatedly stated[2] by our Sages
that there are seven *rekiim*[3] (firmaments, heavens), and
that the uppermost of them, the all-surrounding, is called
arabhoth. Do not object to the number seven given by them,
although there are more *rekiim*, for there are spheres which
contain several circles (*gilgallim*),[4] and are counted as one;

---

[1] Charizi שֶׁהִרְגִּיל לִרְכּוֹב כְּמוֹ הֲלֹא אָנֹכִי אֲתוֹנְךָ אֲשֶׁר רָכַבְתָּ עָלַי which
he is accustomed to ride. Comp. "Am not I thine ass upon which thou hast
ridden." (Num. xxii. 30).

[2] וּבְדִבְרֵי חֲכָמִים ז״ל Tibbon, נָץ אל חכמים ז״ל אלמתכרר בכל מוצע.
דבר חז״ל (נגלגל) החוזר בכל מקום Charizi, הנכפלים בכל מקום. It is
strange that the phrase "which are repeated everywhere" has been added
here. The passage referred to is not repeated frequently, much less "everywhere." If instead of אלמתכרר we were to read אלמתקרר, "firmly established," the addition of "everywhere" would be intelligible, as Maimonides would then be understood to say, that the words of the Chachamim have
authority even in those scientific questions. הנכפלים in Tibbon's version may
be rendered "that have a double authority," although נכפל is mostly used in
the sense of "being repeated."

[3] Comp. Babyl. Talm. Chagigah 12b, where the following seven names are
mentioned by Resh Lakish וִילוֹן רָקִיעַ שְׁחָקִים זְבוּל מָעוֹן מָכוֹן עֲרָבוֹת.

[4] Munk: "On ne compte que pour un seul globe celui qui pourtant renferme

this is clear to those who have studied that subject, and I shall also explain it;[1] here I wish merely to point out that our Sages always assumed that *arabhoth* is the uppermost sphere. The *arabhoth* is also referred to in the words " who rideth upon the heaven (שמים) in thy help." Thus we read in Chagigah, "The high and exalted dwelleth on *arabhoth*,[2] as it is said, 'Extol Him that rideth upon *arabhoth*'" (Ps. lxviii. 4). How is it proved that "heaven" (שמים) and "*arabhoth*" (ערבות) are identical? The one passage has "who rideth on *arabhoth*," the other has "who rideth in heaven."[3] Hence it is clear that in all these passages reference is made to the same all-surrounding sphere, concerning which you will hereafter receive more information.[4] Consider well that the expression שוכן עליו, "dwelling over it," is used by them, and not שוכן בו, "dwelling in it." The latter expression would have implied that God occupies a place or is a power in the sphere, as was in fact believed by the Sabeans,[5] who held that God was the soul of the sphere. By saying שוכן עליו, "dwelling over it," they indicated, that God was separate from the sphere, and was

---

plusieurs sphères." The difference between "sphere" and "globe" is not clear. The Arabic אפלאך and the Hebrew גלגלים primarily denote "circles"; although the term is generally employed in the sense of "spheres," in passages like this, where it is distinguished from "sphere," it signifies "circles," or "the orbits" of certain celestial bodies, several of which may have been imagined to be in the same sphere.

[1] II. xxiv. Comp. II. iv. Ibn Ezra on Psalm viii. 3, in commenting on the words "Thy heavens, the work of Thy fingers," assumes ten spheres.

[2] Talm. Babyl., Chagigah xii. 6. The text in our editions of the Talmud is different, שוכן עליהם בערבות "dwells over them in the Arabhoth," the word עליו or עליהם is omitted in the version of Ibn Tibbon.

[3] This form of argument is frequently used in the Talmud, and is called גזרה שוה, "analogy;" or the assumption that the recurrence of the same term in two phrases is an indication of the identity of the two phrases, and that the one can be explained by the other. In the example cited above, the word רוכב occurring in both phrases indicates that רוכב שמים and רוכב בערבות are identical.

[4] II., chap. xxiv.

[5] Comp. chap. lxiii., pag. 236, note 2. In Charizi's version the explanation והם כשדים, "and these are the Chaldeans," is added.

not a power in it. Know also that the term רוכב שמים, "riding upon the heavens," has figuratively been applied to God in order to show the following excellent comparison. The rider is better than the animal upon which he rides—the comparative is only used for the sake of convenience, for the rider is not of the same class as the animal upon which he rides[1]—furthermore, the rider moves the animal and leads it as he likes; it is as it were his instrument, which he uses according to his will; he is separate from it, apart from it, not connected with it. In like manner the uppermost sphere, by the rotation of which everything moveable is set in motion, is moved by God, who is separate from the sphere, and is not a power in it. In Bereshith Rabba[2] we read that in commenting on the Divine words מעונה אלהי קדם, "The eternal God is a refuge" (lit., a dwelling, Deut. xxxiii. 27), our Sages said, "He is the dwelling of His world, the world is not His dwelling." This explanation is then followed by the remark, "The horse is secondary to the rider, the rider is not subservient to the horse; this is meant by כי תרכב על סוסיך, 'that Thou didst ride upon Thy horses'" (Hab. iii. 8). Consider and learn how they described the relation of God to the sphere, asserting that the latter is His instrument, by means of which He rules the universe. For whenever you find our Sages saying that in a certain heaven are certain things,[3] they do not mean to say that in the heavens there are any extraneous things, but that from a certain heaven the force emanates which is required for the production of certain things, and for their continuing in proper order. The proof for my statement you may find in the

[1] And therefore no comparison is admissible between God and His creatures, as has been stated above, chapter lvi.

[2] Chap. lxviii. on Gen. xxviii. 11. The phrase more frequently employed is הוא מקומו של עולם ואין העולם מקומו; it is likewise mentioned there, where in reference to the words ויפגע במקום the question is asked, why is God sometimes called "*makom*," and the answer is, because He is the place of the universe, but the universe is not His place.

[3] This refers to Babyl. Talm., Chagigah, 12 b, where to each of the seven heavens certain qualities are attributed.

following saying of our Sages—" The *arabhoth*, in which there are justice, charity, right, treasures of life, peace, treasures of blessing, the souls of the righteous, the souls and the spirits of those to be born, and the dew by which God will at some future time revive the dead, etc." It is clear that the things enumerated here are not material, and do not occupy a place—for "dew" is not to be taken in its literal sense.[1]—Consider also that here the phrase שבו, "in which," meaning "in the *arabhoth*," is used, and not שהם עליו, "over which they are," as if to say that all the things existing in the universe derive their existence from powers emanating from the *arabhoth*, which God made to be the origin and the place of these powers. They are said to include "the treasures of life;" a perfectly true and correct assertion! For all existing life originates in that treasure of life, as will be mentioned below.[2] Reflect on the fact that the souls of the righteous as well as the souls and the spirits of those to be born are named here! How sublime is this idea to him who understands it! for the soul that remains after the death of man, is not the soul that lives in man when he is born; the latter is a mere faculty, while that which has a separate existence after death, is a reality;[3] again, the soul (נשמה) and the spirit (רוח) of man[4] during his life are two different things; therefore the souls and the spirits are both named as existing in man; but separate from the body only one of them[5] exists. We have already explained the homonymity of רוח in this work,[6] and also at the end of Sefer ha-madda[7] we treated of the homonymity of these expres-

---

[1] According to Efodi and others, Maimonides finds in טל, "dew," an allusion to the "active intellect" which changes the passive intellect into the intellect in action (שכל בפועל).

[2] Ch. lxxii., and II. x.

[3] See above, pag. 254, notes 2 and 3; and also xli., pag. 143, note 1.

[4] רוח denotes the spirit of life, "vitality," which ceases to exist when life is extinct. By way of homonymy it is also used for "soul," the immortal element in man.

[5] Viz., the soul, נשמה.   [6] Chapter xl.

[7] Hilchoth Teshubhah, viii. 3 and 4. Comp. also Yesode ha-torah iv. 8 and 9.

sions.[1] Consider how these excellent and true ideas, comprehended only by the greatest philosophers, are found scattered in the Midrashim. When a student who disavows truth reads them, he will at first sight deride them, as being contrary to the real state of things. The cause of this is the circumstance, that our Sages spoke of these subjects in metaphors; they are too difficult for the common understanding of the people, as has been noticed by us several times.

I will now return to the subject which I commenced to explain, in order to bring it to a conclusion. Our Sages commenced to adduce proofs from Scriptures for their assertion that the things enumerated above are contained in the *arabhoth*. As to justice and right they refer to "justice and judgment are the habitation of Thy throne" (Ps. lxxxix. 18). In the same way they prove their assertion concerning all things enumerated by them, by showing that they are described as being related to God, as being near Him.[2] Note this.[3] In the Pirke Rabbi Eliezer[4] it is said: God created

---

[1] In Hilchoth Teshubhah, viii. 3, the use of נפש in the sense of נשמה is mentioned; in the next paragraph Maimonides enumerates the various names employed in describing the immortality of the soul, and its condition after its separation from the body. The homonymity of רוח and נשמה, mentioned here, is not found in the end of the Sefer ha-madda.

[2] According to Munk, the suffix in ענדה refers to "arabhoth," not to "God;" if this were the case Maimonides would have used בה (בו), as he constantly says בערבות. Ibn Tibbon has אצלו; Charizi אתו, "with him." The things being with God who rideth upon the arabhoth, are of course contained in the *arabhoth*.

[3] In the version of Ibn Tibbon this passage is repeated in a different form: וכן הביאו ראיה על השאר שהם בערבות מהיותם מיוחסים לשם ית' שהם אצלו והבן זה, "And thus they brought a proof for the other things, that they are in the arabhoth by the fact that they are related to God, and are with Him." It was originally a marginal note of the translator, who added the following remark which is found in the margin of some MSS: אמר שמואל בן תבון הלשון המונה מחוץ אינו יוצא מלשון הערבי אך הוא יוצא מגוף הענין מלשון חגיגה והוא האמת בעצמו והוא שהעיר עליו באמרו והבן זה: "Samuel Ibn Tibbon said, the form amended in the margin does not correspond to the Arabic, but to the subject contained in the passage of Chagigah; this is its true sense, and was indicated by Maimonides in his words 'and understand this.'"

[4] Ch. xviii. This passage is probably quoted in support of the inter-

PART I.—CHAPTER LXXI.

seven *rekiim* (heavens), and of all of them He selected the *arabhoth* for His royal throne; comp. "Exalt Him who rideth upon the araboth" (Ps. lxviii. 4). These are his words. Note them likewise.

You must know that in Hebrew the collective noun denoting animals used for riding is "mercabhah" (מרכבה). Instances of this noun are not rare. ויאסר יוסף מרכבתו, "And Joseph made ready his chariot" (Gen. xlvi. 29); במרכבת המשנה, "in the second chariot" (*ib.* xli. 43); מרכבות פרעה, "Pharaoh's chariots" (Ex. xv. 4). The following passage especially proves that this noun denotes a collection of animals: ותעלה ותצא מרכבה ממצרים בשש מאות וסוס בחמשים ומאה, "And a chariot came up and went out of Egypt for six hundred shekels of silver, and a horse for an hundred and fifty" (1 Kings x. 21). Hence we may learn that *mercabhah* denotes here four horses. Therefore I think that when it was stated,[1] according to the literal sense of the words,[2] that four *Chayoth* (beasts) carry the Throne of Glory, our Sages called this "*mercabhah*" on account of its similarity with the mercabhah consisting of four single animals. So far has the theme of this chapter carried us, and we shall be compelled to make many further remarks on this subject. Here, however, it is our object, and the aim of all we have said, to show that רוכב שמים, "who rideth upon heaven" (Deut. xxxiii. 26), means "who sets the all-surrounding sphere in motion, and turns it by His power and will." The same sense is contained in the conclusion of that verse: ובגאותו שחקים, "and in His excellency the spheres," *i.e.*, who in His excellency[3] moves the *shechakim*

---

pretation of the word רוכב as signifying "who governs"; for it contains the assertion that the arabboth are the seat of His government (למלכותו).

[1] Maimonides refers to the first chapter of Ezekiel.

[2] Arabic, בחשב מא קיל; Tibbon, לפי מא שנאמר; Charizi, לפי הראוי; Munk, "par la tradition (lit., selon ce qui a été dit)." The meaning of the phrase is "as far as it is said;" in truth, however, the throne is not borne by the chayoth, but all things are borne and moved by the throne.

[3] The commentators seem to be in doubt whether the pronoun in ובגאותו refers to God or to the heavens. Grammatically, it can only refer to God, שמים being a plural noun.

(spheres). In reference to the first sphere, the *arabhoth*, the verb רכב, "to ride," is used, in reference to the rest, the noun גאוה, "excellency," because through the motion of the uppermost sphere in its daily circuit, all the spheres move, participating as parts in the motion of the whole; and this being that great power that sets everything in motion, it is called גאוה, "excellency." Let this subject constantly remain in your memory when you study what I am going to say; for it—*i.e.*, the motion of the uppermost sphere—is the greatest proof for the existence of God, as I shall demonstrate. Note this.

CHAPTER LXXI.

The Origin of the Kalâm.

KNOW[1] that many branches of science relating to the correct solution of these problems,[2] were once cultivated by our

[1] Before discussing the theories of the Mutakallemim and the philosophers about the three fundamental principles of the Jewish faith, viz., the Existence of God, His Unity, and His Incorporeality, Maimonides describes in the present chapter the origin and development of the Kalâm. He apologizes, as it were, for having in these disquisitions frequent recourse to Christian and Mahomedan sources, and he begins with the statement that the philosophical theories of the Jewish wise men of former ages were not known, because owing to the dispersion and the oppression of the Jews their theories were not regularly transmitted from generation to generation. Comp. Mishnah, Sota ix. 15—משחרב בה״מ שרי חכימיא למהוי כספריא וגו׳, "Since the destruction of the Holy Temple, the Chachamim (wise men) began to be like the Soferim (elementary teachers) of former ages," etc. Midrash Rabba, Echa, Introd. § 22. "When the Israelites went into exile, not one of them could remember what he had learned." וחשכו הראות את סוצא כשנגלו ישראל לבין או״ה לא היה א׳ מהם יכול לזכור תלמודו, *et passim*, in Talmud and Midrash. Both Jewish and non-Jewish authors have repeatedly asserted that the Jews were the original cultivators of philosophy, and that other nations owed their progress in that study to the Jews. See Munk *ad locum*, also Arch. Israelites, March, 1848, p. 169 *sqq.*

[2] That is, problems treated of in Physics and Metaphysics, or, in the Talmudical terms, *Maaseh mercabhah* and *Maaseh bhereshith*.

forefathers, but were in the course of time neglected, especially in consequence of the tyranny which barbarous nations[1] exercised over us. Besides, speculative studies were not open to all men, as we have already stated;[2] only the subjects taught in the Scriptures were accessible to all. Even the traditional Law,[3] as you are well aware, was not originally committed to writing, in conformity with the rule to which our nation generally adhered,[4] "Things which I have communicated to you orally, you must not communicate to others in writing."[5] With reference to the Law, this rule was very opportune; for while it remained in force it averted the evils which happened subsequently, viz., great diversity of opinion, doubts as to the

[1] Lit., "the ignorant," who took no interest in science or study. Maimonides probably meant the Romans and Persians, who, in persecuting the Jews, used to interdict the study of the Law, which for the Jews included all wisdom and science. Comp. Zunz, Gottesdienstliche Vorträge, p. 40. The Arabic נאהיל is especially applied to the paganism before Mahomed.

[2] See Introd., p. 7 sqq., and ch. xxxi. sqq.

[3] "Talmud," (תלמוד) in both Hebrew versions, is not used here in its general acceptation, as the work consisting of the Mishnah and its interpretation, the Gemara, but in the sense of "doctrine, and system or code of laws," including both the Written Law and the Oral Law, and as in this passage the Oral Law only is to be understood, it is qualified by the adjective "traditional" (המקובל, in Arabic מקה מרויה). "Talmud," as a "system of laws," is contrasted to חכמת התורה על האמת, "the true science of religion," i.e., the philosophical treatment of religious principles. See Introd., p. 6, note 1.

[4] That is, it was not a rule laid down by authority: it was not understood as forming part of the Halacha, but was considered as a Midrashic interpretation without having any binding force.

[5] In the first instance this is an interpretation of the words addressed to Moses (Exod. xxxiv. 27), "Write thou these words," etc., viz., that Moses should write certain laws for the Israelites, and that he should orally impart to them additional laws. But it was assumed that the same rule applied to future teachers in Israel, who should not permit the Written Law to be récited by heart, or the Oral Law to be read from a book; also that the Oral Law should not be committed to writing. See Midrash Shemoth Rabba, c. xlvii.; Babyl. Talm., Gittin 60 b; Temurah, 14 b. Maimonides in the introduction to his Mishneh Torah asserts that since the time of Moses the chief authorities made copies of parts of the Oral Law for themselves, but did not use them in public.

T

meaning of written words, slips of the pen,[1] dissensions among the people, formation of new sects, and confused notions about practical subjects. The traditional teaching was in fact, according to the words of the Law,[2] entrusted to the Great Tribunal, as we have already stated in our works on the Talmud.[3]

Care having been taken, for the sake of obviating injurious influences, that the Oral Law should not be recorded in a form accessible to all, it was but natural that no portion of "the secrets of the Law," (*i.e.*, metaphysical problems) would be permitted to be written down or divulged for the use of all men. These secrets, as has been explained,[4] were orally communicated by a few able men to others who were equally distinguished. Hence the principle applied by our teachers, "The secrets of the Law can only be entrusted to him who is a councillor, a cunning artificer, etc." The natural effect of this practice was that our nation lost the knowledge of those important disciplines. Nothing but a few remarks and allusions are to be found in the Talmud and the Midrashim, like a few kernels[5] enveloped in such a quantity of husk, that the reader is generally occupied with the husk, and forgets that it encloses a kernel.

In addition you will find that in the few works composed[6]

---

[1] Lit., "and errors which are made in writing a book." Munk thinks that the Arabic סהו signifies an error in thought (une erreur de pensée), but it must not be forgotten that Maimonides enumerates the evils which result from the substitution of instruction by writing for oral instruction, and error in thought which equally occurs in both methods is here out of place.

[2] Deut. xvii. 8—12.

[3] Introduction to Mishnah Zeraim; and introduction to Mishneh Torah.

[4] Introduction p. 7 *sqq.*, ch. xxxiii and xxxiv.

[5] Ibn Tibbon, נרנרי לב מועטין; Charizi, שנים שלשה נרגרים שחם כמו לב.

[6] The Arabic כלאם means both "word," and "the system of the Mutakallemim" (comp. Logic from λόγος). The two Hebrew translators took it in the first signification, and render it מדברי, "of words"; Munk thinks that the *kalam*, that is the philosophy of the Mutakallemim, is here meant. But it is not likely that Maimonides meant to say, "that the few treatises which, in the writings of some Gaonim on those subjects, you find based on the principles of the kalām, are borrowed from the Mahomedan Mutakallemim." This

PART I.—CHAPTER LXXI.   275

by the Gaonim[1] and the Karaites[2] on the unity[3] of God and on such matter as is connected[4] with this doctrine, they followed the lead of the Mahometan Mutakallemim, and what they wrote is insignificant in comparison with the kindred works of the Mahometans. It also happened, that at the time when the Mahometans adopted this method of the Kalam, there arose among them a certain sect, called Mu'tazilah,[5] *i.e.*, Separatists. In certain things our

---

would imply that he regretted the absence of the *kalam* from the writings of the Jews, while in fact he is opposed to the *kalam*. It is by no means surprising that the Jewish thinkers of the time were not all adherents of the Aristotelian philosophy; some of them were in favour of the *Kalam*. See Munk *ad locum*; comp. Introd. pag. xlii.

[1] Gaon is the title of the spiritual heads of the Jews after the close of the Talmud, between the sixth and the eleventh centuries; the last Gaon was R. Hai. Maimonides probably alluded to Saadiah's Emunoth vedeoth. (See Commentary of Narboni *ad locum*.)

[2] The Karaites (from קרא, a reading, a Scriptural text) are the successors of the ancient Sadducees; they reject most of the traditional interpretations of the Law, and only recognise the authority of the written Law, and this according to their own interpretation. As to Karaite Mutakallemim, comp. Kuzri v. 15, חכמי שרש האמונה והם הנקראים אצל הקראים בעלי חכמת הדברים, "The interpreters of the fundamental principles of religion, called by the Karaites Logicians." Instead of קראים Charizi has המינין "dissenters." As to the origin of the name Karaites, whether it is to be derived directly from קרא, "the Scriptural text," or from the title or name Kara, of some distinguished scholar of that sect, see A. Neubauer, Beiträge und Dokumente zur Geschichte des Karäerthums, Leipzig, 1866, page 4. The history of the sect has been written in two volumes, "Geschichte des Karäerthums," by Prof. Dr. Julius Fürst, Leipzig, 1862–65. Valuable historical material has been contributed by S. Pinsker, Likute Kadmoniyoth, Wien, 1860.

[3] "The Unity of God" is here singled out of the several metaphysical problems as the centre of all theological and philosophical discussions of the age, both amongst the Jews and the Mahometans.

[4] The editions of Ibn Tibbon's version (except ed. pr.) have ומה שנתנלה מזה הענין probably a corruption of ומה שנתלה "and what is dependent on," or "connected with."

[5] The Mu'tazilah (from עזל "to separate") are the followers of Wâcil ibn-'Ata (born 699—700, and died 778—779), a disciple of Al-'Hasan al-Bassri (of Bassora). Wâcil separated himself (אעתזל) from the school of his master, and established a school of his own (אלמעתזלה). The sect had many subdivisions, but their common and principal characteristics were the following two propositions: 1, Man is perfectly free in his actions; he does good or evil on

scholars[1] followed the theory and the method of these Mu'tazilah. Although another sect, the Asha'ariyah,[2] with their own peculiar views, was subsequently established amongst the Mahometans, you will not find any of these views in the writings of our authors; not because these authors preferred the opinions of the first-named sect to those of the latter, but because they chanced first to become acquainted with the theory of the Mu'tazilah, which they adopted and treated as demonstrated truth. On the other hand our Andalusian[3] scholars followed the teachings of the philosophers, from whom they accepted those opinions which were not opposed to our own religious principles. You will find that they did not adopt any of the methods of the Mutakallemim; in many respects they approached the view expressed in the present treatise, as may be noticed in

---

his own account, and consequently has merits or faults; 2, God, absolutely one, possesses no attribute distinct from His essence. The sect is also called the partisans of Justice and Unity (אצחאב אלעדל ואלתוחיד). The historian Al-Masudi describes also the disciples of Anan as partisans of Justice and Unity, a proof that on the whole the Karaites followed the Mu'tazilah.— (Munk.)

[1] The Gaonim, to whom reference has been made above, are meant; perhaps also the Karaites.

[2] The Asha'ariyah are the disciples of Abu'l-hassan 'Ali ben Isma'il al-Ashari of Bassora (born about 880 and died 970), who after having followed the Mu'tazilah for some time, publicly declared in a mosque of Bassora, that he abandoned that doctrine, and recognised the pre-existence of the Koran, the attributes of God, and predestination as determining the acts of man (Munk). These doctrines were afterwards modified. Comp. li., pag. 176, note 3.

[3] Ibn Tibbon, הכפרדים האנדלוסים, probably a combination of two different renderings. It is difficult to say who were the philosophers to whose works Maimonides here refers. He himself appears to have seen only some of the writings of more recent philosophers. In a letter addressed to Samuel Ibn Tibbon, he says that he had not seen Joseph Ibn Tsaddik's Sefer ha-olam ha-katon (Book on the Mikrokosmos), but he appears to have known the character of that author's philosophy. (See Miscellany of Hebrew Lit., page 226.) The assertion that these philosophers adopted none of the methods of the Mutakallemim seems to be inaccurate, for Bachya Ibn Pakudah (in Chobhoth ha-lebhabhoth), and Joseph Ibn Tsaddik borrowed many arguments from the system of the Mutakallemim. See Munk *ad locum*, and Kaufman, Geschichte der Attributenlehre, Gotha, 1877, pages 280 and 336.

the few works which were recently written by authors of that school. You should also know that whatever the Mahomedans, that is, the Mu'tazilah and the Asha'ariyah, said on these subjects, consists in nothing but theories founded on propositions[1] which are taken from the works of those Greek and Syrian scholars[2] who attempted to oppose the systems of the philosophers, and to refute their arguments. The following was the cause of that opposition: At the time when the Christian Church brought the Greeks and the Syrians into its fold, and promulgated its well-known dogmas,[3] the opinions of the philosophers were current

[1] Ibn Tibbon renders the single word מקדמאה by והקדמות גזרות.

[2] The works of the Greek philosophers, especially of Aristotle, were first translated into Syriac, and then from the Syriac into Arabic for the Mahomedan scholars. When attacks were made on the Christian Church by followers of the Aristotelean philosophy, the Fathers or Ecclesiastical writers, the defenders of the Church, refuted the objections by arguments founded on Logic and Dialectics, and suggested by that very system of philosophy.

[3] Lit., "that which was already known." The force of the phrase "that which was already known" (מא קד עלם), is not apparent. If by this phrase Maimonides simply intended to avoid a description of the Christian dogmas, he would have said ודעו אלנצרי מא דעו (in Hebrew וטענו מה שטענו), "and they asserted their principles." Also the sentence "And kings arose who protected the religion" seems to be out of place, as it is not stated what share those kings had in the establishment of the new discipline. Again, the sentence "the wise men among the Greeks and the Syrians in those generations saw," etc., seems to imply that the educated portion of those nations were Christians, and tried to guard the religion against the philosophical views of the common people. We should perhaps read "the learned Christians in those generations," etc. Most probably the text has been corrupted by a fusion of two different readings: (a) וטענו הנצרים מה שכבר נודע שאלו טענות וגו' "the Christians set forth their dogma, which they knew as being very much exposed to great attacks emanating from those philosophical theories, etc. (b) והיו דעות הפילוסופים מתפשטות באומות ההם ומהם נולדה הפילוסופיא ונתחדשו מלכים שומרים הדת ראו חכמי הדורות ההם מן היונים והארמיים והולידו חכמת וגו'. "Philosophical ideas at the same time spread among the people, and while on the one hand philosophy was flourishing, kings on the other hand rose as defenders of the Christian faith, the Greek and Syrian scholars of those generations considered the state of things, and founded," etc. Narboni, *ad locum*, remarks: They did so in order to find favour in the eyes of the kings,

amongst those nations; and whilst philosophy[1] flourished, kings became defenders of the Christian faith. The learned Greek and Syrian Christians[2] of the age, seeing[3] that their dogmas were unquestionably exposed to severe attacks from the existing philosophical systems, laid the foundation for this science of Dogmatics; they commenced by putting forth such propositions as would support their doctrines, and be useful for the refutation of opinions opposed to the fundamental principles of the Christian religion.

When the Mahomedans caused Arabic translations of the writings of the Philosophers to be made, those criticisms were likewise translated. When the opinions of John the Grammarian,[4] of Ibn Adi,[5] and of kindred authors on those subjects were made accessible to them, they adopted them, and imagined that they had arrived at the solution of important problems. Moreover, they selected from the opinions of the ancient philosophers whatever seemed serviceable to their purposes, although later critics had proved that those theories were false[6]; as, *e.g.*, the theories of atoms and of a *vacuum*. They believed that the discussions of those authors were of a general character, and contained proposi-

---

the defenders of the Christian religion; "if a ruler hearken to lies, all his servants are wicked," Prov. xxix. 12.

[1] Br. Mus. MS., Or. 1423, has אלפלאספה, "the philosophers," and this corresponds better to "kings."

[2] "The scholars" (עלמא) are here contrasted with "the philosophers" (פלאספה); the Christian theologians are meant.

[3] Charizi, אשר ראו חכמי הדורות ההם וראו.

[4] John Philiponus, the grammarian, flourished at Alexandria in the sixth and the seventh centuries. The treatises of Philiponus, to which Maimonides seems to allude, are—Refutation of the work of Proclus on the eternity of the Universe, and Cosmogony of Moses.—(Munk.)

[5] Abu Zacariyya Yachya ibn Adi, a Christian Jacobite, of Mesopotamia, lived at Bagdad in the tenth century. He was a pupil of Al-farabi, and made himself known by his Arabic translations of the works of Aristotle and their Commentaries. Maimonides does not appear to have known when that author lived, otherwise he would not have said that the first Mahomedan Mutakallemim borrowed from his writings.—(Munk.)

[6] See Arist. Metaphys., I., i. and vii. Below, ch. lxxiii., Propos. 1 and 2.

PART I.—CHAPTER LXXI.   279

tions useful for the defence of positive religion.[1] At a subsequent period the same theories were more fully developed, and presented an aspect unknown[2] to those Theologians of the Greeks and other nations who were the immediate successors[3] of the Philosophers. At a later time, when the Mahomedans adopted certain peculiar theological theories, they were naturally obliged to defend them; and when their new theories again became the subject of controversy among them, each party laid down such propositions as suited their special doctrine.

Their arguments undoubtedly involved[4] certain principles[5] which concerned the three communities—Jews, Christians, and Mahomedans, such as the *creatio ex nihilo*, which afforded support to the belief in miracles and to various other doctrines. There are, however, other subjects of belief which the Christians and Mahomedans have undertaken to defend, such as the doctrine of the Trinity in the theological works of the former, and "the Word"[6] in the works of some

---

[1] This sentence is here out of place, and is but a different form of the one which begins "Their arguments undoubtedly," etc.

[2] The Arabic אלם denotes (according to Munk אלם, " to enter "), " to be troubled," Ibn Tibbon, נחלו (comp. Am. vi. 6); one MS. has ידעו instead of נחלו.—Charizi has נודעו. The original from which he translated had probably עלם instead of אלם; two Leyden MSS. have עלם.—(Munk.)

[3] This may be taken literally, that they lived a short time after the Philosophers, but also figuratively, that their opinions did not much differ from those of the Greek Philosophers.

[4] Lit., "There is no doubt that there are things," *scil.*, among those arguments. Ibn Tibbon adds here ביניהם, "among them," which is not, as Munk suggests, superfluous; for it is not necessary to say that there are things common to the three forms of religion, but that in those writings there are subjects which concern all the three communities.

[5] Although only one principle, the "creatio ex nihilo" is mentioned, the plural אשיא (Hebr. דברים) is here used, because that theory implies many questions. As regards the grammatical construction, the Hebrew deviates from the Arabic. The latter makes the pronoun והי agree with אששיא, while in the Hebrew the pronoun והוא agrees with מאמר which follows, and not with דברים, which precedes.

[6] *i.e.*, Whether the divine word addressed to Mahomed *is eternal as the Divine Being*, or a thing created, according to the opinion of the Mu'tazilah.

Mahomedan sects; with a view of proving the dogmas which they thus desired to establish, they were compelled to resort to certain hypotheses. It is not our object to criticise things which are peculiar to either creed, or books which were written exclusively in the interest of the one community or the other. We merely maintain that the earlier Theologians, both of the Greek Christians and of the Mahomedans, when they laid down their propositions, did not investigate the real properties of things; first of all they considered what must be the properties of the things which should yield proof for or against a certain creed; and when this was found they asserted that the thing must be endowed with those properties; then they employed the same assertion as a proof for the identical arguments which had led to the assertion,[1] and by which they either supported or refuted a certain opinion. This course was followed by able men[2] who originated this method, and adopted it in their writings. They professed to be free from preconceived opinions, and to have been led to a stated result by actual research. Therefore when philosophers of a subsequent date studied the same writings they did not perceive the true character of the arguments; on the contrary, they found in the ancient works, strong proofs and a valuable support for the acceptance or the rejection of certain opinions, and thus thought that, so far as religious principles were concerned, there was no necessity whatever to prove or refute any of their propositions, and that the first Mutakallemim had discussed those subjects with the sole object of defeating certain views of the philosophers, and demonstrating the insufficiency of their proofs.[3] Persons who hold this opinion, do not suspect how much they are mistaken; for the first Mutakallemim tried to prove a proposition when it was

[1] The words "which had led to its assertion" have no equivalent in Charizi's version.

[2] The term אלעקלא, Hebr. המשבילים is here used instead of האנשים ההם and חכמי הדורות ההם mentioned above.

[3] See page 277, note 2.

expedient to demonstrate its truth; and to disprove it, when its rejection was desirable, and when it was contrary to the opinion which they wished to uphold, although the contradiction might only become obvious after the application of a hundred successive propositions. In this manner the earlier Mutakallemim effected a radical cure of the malady! I tell you, however, as a general rule, that Themistius[1] was right in saying that the properties of things can not adapt themselves to our opinions, but our opinions must be adapted to the existing properties.[2]

Having studied the works of these Mutakallemim, as far as I had an opportunity,[3] just as I had studied the writings of the philosophers according to the best of my ability, I found that the method of all Mutakallemim was the same in its general characteristics, namely, they assume that the really existing form of things proves nothing at all, because it is

---

[1] An expounder of the Aristotelian philosophy. He lived in the fourth century.—Narboni expresses his surprise that Maimonides quoted Themistius, instead of citing the words of Aristotle himself, and finds, as the only solution of the difficulty, the fact that Maimonides, when writing this work, was not so much engaged in the study of the works of Aristotle as in the writings of later authors. The following passage of Aristotle's Metaph. (IV. 5) is quoted by Narboni: εἴτε γὰρ τὰ δοκοῦντα πάντα ἐστὶν ἀληθῆ καὶ τὰ φαινόμενα, ἀνάγκη πάντα ἅμα ἀληθῆ καὶ ψευδῆ εἶναι. πολλοὶ γὰρ τἀναντία ὑπολαμβάνουσιν ἀλλήλους, καὶ τοὺς μὴ ταὐτὰ δοξάζοντας ἑαυτοῖς διεψεῦσθαι νομίζουσιν· "If the thoughts and opinions of men were all true, then everything would at the same time be true and false; because frequently one man believes the opposite of another, and thinks that those who have not the same opinion as he himself are wrong." It may be true that Maimonides did not read the original works of Aristotle; but it cannot be denied that the words of Themistius convey the ideas which Maimonides expresses here more clearly than those of Aristotle.

[2] I.e., Our opinions concerning existing beings would not be correct, were we, like the first Mutakallemim, arbitrarily to assume certain axioms and principles, and thence deduct the properties which the things must have. The reverse is the correct method: to study first the properties of the things, and thence deduce general principles.

[3] Shemtob and others find in the two phrases "as far as opportunity was given to me" (lit., "when I had the chance,") and "as much as I could," used respectively in reference to the works of the Mutakallemim, and to those of the Philosophers, an indication that Maimonides studied the former only occasionally, while he devoted all his attention to the latter.

merely one of the various phases of the things,[1] the opposite of which is equally admissible to our minds. In many instances these Theologians were guided by their imagination,[2] and thought that they were following the dictates of the intellect. They set forth the propositions which I shall describe to you, and demonstrated by their peculiar mode of arguing that the Universe had a beginning. The theory of the *creatio ex nihilo* being thus established, they asserted, as a logical consequence, that undoubtedly there must be a Maker who created the Universe. Next they showed that this Maker is One, and from the Unity of the Creator they deduced His Incorporeality. This method was adopted by every Mahomedan Mutakallem in the discussion of this subject, and by those of our co-religionists who imitated them and walked in their footsteps. Although the Mutakallemim disagree in the methods of their proofs, and employ different propositions in demonstrating the act of creation or in rejecting the eternity of the Universe, they invariably begin with proving the *creatio ex nihilo*, and establish on that proof the existence of God. I have examined this method, and find it most objectionable. It must be rejected, because all the proofs for the creation have weak points, and cannot be considered as convincing except by those who do not know the difference between a proof, a dialectical argument, and a sophism.[3] Those who understand the force of the different methods will clearly see that all the proofs for the creation are questionable, because propositions have been employed

---

[1] Lit., "habit" (Munk: "habitude," Hebr. מנהג).

[2] Comp. ch. lxviii., pag. 259, and Eight Chapters, etc., ch. ii.

[3] Comp. ch. li., pp. 179 and 177. The difference between the three kinds of arguments is defined by Maimonides, in Milloth higgayon, ch. viii., as follows: "The conclusion made from two firmly established premises is called a demonstrative syllogism (הקש מופת), and the part of Logic treating of these inductions is called מלאכת המופת (syllogism): if both premises, or one of them, are probable, the conclusion is dialectical (הקש נצוח), and the part of Logic that treats of these is called מלאכת נצוח (dialectics); if one or both premises are false, the conclusion is a misleading conclusion, and the part of Logic that treats of them is called מלאכת ההטעאה (sophistry). Comp. Aristot. Metaph. IV. 2.: ἔστι δὲ ἡ διαλεκτικὴ πειραστικὴ περὶ ὧν ἡ φιλοσοφία γνωριστική· ἡ δὲ σοφιστικὴ φαινομένη, οὖσα δ'οὔ.

which have never been proved. I think that the utmost that can be effected by believers in the truth of Revelation is to expose the shortcomings in the proofs of philosophers who hold that the Universe is eternal, and if forsooth a man has effected this, he has accomplished a great deed! For it is well known to all clear and correct thinkers who do not wish to deceive themselves, that this question, namely, whether the Universe has been created or is eternal, cannot be answered with mathematical certainty; here human intellect must pause.[1] We shall have occasion to speak more fully on this subject,[2] but for the present it may suffice to state that the philosophers have for the last three thousand years[3] been continually divided on that question, as far as we can learn from their works and the records of their opinions.[4]

Such being the nature of this theory, how can we employ it as an axiom and establish on it the existence of the Creator? In that case the existence of God would be uncertain; if the universe had a beginning, God does exist; if it be eternal, God does not exist; the existence of God would therefore remain either an open question,[5] or we should have to declare that the creation had been proved, and compel others by mere force to accept this doctrine, in order thus to be enabled to declare that we have proved the existence of God. Such a process is utterly inadmissible. The true method, which is based on a logical and indubitable proof,[6]

[1] מוקף עקל, in Hebrew מעמד שכלי, a place where the intellect must stop, it being unable to pass that limit. Comp. ch. xxxi., pag. 107, "A boundary is undoubtedly set to the human mind, which it cannot pass."

[2] Part II., ch. i., seq.

[3] Maimonides seems to refer to the time of Abraham, who taught that the Universe was created by God, in opposition to His fellow-creatures, who had a different belief.

[4] In the editions of Ibn Tibbon's Version ודבריהם (Ar. ואכבאראהם), "and their records," is omitted.

[5] The words לנו בספק in Tibbon's Version are an addition, explaining the word כן, "so": in Charisi, על כל פנים או יהיה כן.

[6] Ibn Palquera says that a theory built upon a false, or at least a weak foundation, as, according to the opinion of Maimonides, the theory of the

consists, according to my opinion, in demonstrating the existence of God, His unity, and His incorporeality by such philosophical arguments as are founded on the theory of the eternity of the Universe. I do not propose this method as though I believed in the eternity of the Universe, for I do not follow the philosophers in this point, but because by the aid of this method these three principles, viz., the existence of God, His unity and His incorporeality can be fully proved and verified, irrespectively of the question whether the universe has had a beginning or not. After firmly establishing these three principles by an exact proof, we shall treat of the problem of creation and discuss it as fully as possible. You are at liberty to content yourself with the declaration of the Mutakallemim, and to believe that the act of creation has been demonstrated by proof; nor can there be any harm if you consider it unproven that the universe had a beginning, and if you accept this theory as supported by the authority of the Prophets. Before you learn our opinion on prophecy, which will be given in the present work,[1] do not ask, how could the belief in prophecy be justified, if it were assumed that the universe was eternal. We will not now expatiate on that subject. You should, however, know that some of the propositions, started and proved by the Radicals,[2] *i.e.*, the Mutakallemim, in order to

---

Eternity of the Universe is, could not be "perfectly correct" (האמת השלם). The argument of Maimonides is as follows: The Universe is either eternal or had a beginning; though he himself believes that it has been created, he cannot give a scientific proof. The principles of Faith must therefore be shown to be equally true according to both theories. It is easy to see (מושכל ראשון, without applying any logical demonstration) that a Creator must exist, if the *creatio ex nihilo* is assumed; he therefore thinks it more important to show that the three principles mentioned here can be demonstrated (בהכרח במופת "by a convincing proof") even according to the theory of those philosophers who believe that the Universe is eternal.

[1] Part II., ch. xxxii. *sqq*.

[2] The Radicals (אצוליון, Hebr. שרשיים) are philosophers who engage in examining and proving the fundamental principles of Religion as distinguished from the practice and the laws (פקה). Ibn Tibbon renders, in

prove the act of creation, imply an order of things contrary to that which really exists, and involve a complete change in the laws of nature; this fact will be pointed out to you,[1] for it will be necessary to mention their propositions and their argumentation. My method, as far as I now can explain it in general terms, is as follows. The universe is either eternal or has had a beginning; if it had a beginning, there must necessarily exist a being which caused the beginning; this is clear to common sense; for a thing that has had a beginning, cannot be the cause of its own beginning, another being must have caused it. The universe was, therefore, created by God. If on the other hand the universe were eternal, it could in various ways be proved that, apart from the things which constitute the universe, there exists a being which is neither body nor a force in a body, and which is one, eternal, not preceded by any cause, and immutable. That being is God. You see that the proofs for the Existence, the Unity and the Incorporeality of God must vary according to the propositions admitted by us. Only in this way we can succeed in obtaining a perfect proof, whether we assume the eternity or the creation of the universe. For this reason you will find in my works[2] on the Talmud, whenever I have to speak of the fundamental principles of our religion, or to prove the existence of God, that I employ arguments which imply the eternity of the universe. I do not believe in that eternity, but I wish to establish the principle of the existence of God by an indisputable proof, and should not like to see this most important principle founded on a basis which every one could shake or attempt to demolish, and which others might

---

ch. lxxiii., the term אלאצוליון by קדמוני המדברים שהיו עיקר חכמת המדברים.

[1] The phrases שנוי סדרי בראשית and הפוך העולם are given in Hebrew, also in the Arabic original, because these are terms occurring in Talmud and Midrash. Comp. Babyl. Talmud, Shabbath 53 b.

[2] There is no passage, either in his Mishneh Torah or in his Commentary on the Mishnah to which this remark would apply.

consider as not being established at all; especially when I see that the proofs of the philosophers are based on those visible properties of things, which can only be ignored by persons possessing certain preconceived notions,[1] while the Mutakallemim establish their arguments on propositions which are to such an extent contrary to the actual state of things as to compel these arguers to deny altogether the existence of the laws of nature. When I shall have to treat of the creation, I shall in a special chapter[2] prove my opinion to some extent, and shall attain the same end which every one of the Mutakallemim had in view, yet I shall not contradict the laws of nature, or reject any such part of the Aristotelean theory as has been proved to be correct. Even the most cogent of the proofs[3] offered by the Mutakallemim respecting the act of creation, has only been obtained by reversing the whole order of things and by rejecting everything fully demonstrated by the philosophers. I, however, shall be able to give a similar proof without ignoring the laws of nature and without being forced to contradict facts which have been clearly perceived. I find it necessary to mention to you the general propositions of the Mutakallemim, by which they prove the act of creation, the existence of God, His Unity and His Incorporeality. I intend to explain their method, and also to point out the inferences[4] which are to be drawn from each proposition. After this, I shall describe those theories of the philosophers which are closely connected with our subject, and I shall then explain their method.

Do not ask me to prove in this work the propositions of the philosophers, which I shall briefly mention to you; they

---

[1] Ibn Tibbon, קצת דעות; Charizi, סודות אחרות.
[2] Part II., ch. xix.
[3] This refers to the Fifth Proposition (ch. lxxiv.) according to which there must be a certain being that determines which, of all possible forms, accidents, etc., are to be connected with everything; for otherwise it would be inexplicable how it happened that one form came to be preferred to all other equally admissible forms.
[4] Charizi: מה שיתחייב מן התשובה, "to what objections that leads."

form the principal part of Physics and Metaphysics. Nor must you expect that I should repeat the arguments of the Mutakallemim in support of their propositions, with which they wasted their time, with which the time of future generations will likewise be wasted, and on which numerous books have been written. Their propositions, with few exceptions, are contradicted by the visible properties of things, and beset with numerous objections.[1] For this reason they were obliged to write many books and controversial works[2] in defence of their theories, for the refutation of objections, and for the reconciliation of all apparent contradictions, although in reality this object cannot be attained by any sophistical contrivance.[3] As to the propositions of the philosophers which I shall briefly explain, and which are indispensable for the demonstration of the three principles — the Existence, the Unity, and the Incorporeality of God, they will for the greater part be admitted by you as soon as you shall hear them and understand their meaning; whilst in the discussion of other parts reference must be made for their proofs to works on Physics and Metaphysics, and if you direct your attention to such passages as will be pointed out to you, you will find everything verified that requires verification.

I have already told you[4] that nothing exists except God and this universe, and that there is no other evidence for His Existence but this universe in its entirety and in its several parts. Consequently the universe must be examined as it is; the propositions must be derived from those properties of the universe which are clearly perceived, and hence you must know its visible form and its nature. Then only will you find in the universe evidence for the existence of a being not included therein. I have considered

---

[1] Ibn Tibbon: הספקות המתרגשות.

[2] Charizi: לרוב העניין, "on account of the great extent of the subject."

[3] Ibn Tibbon: ואם אי אפשר בזה תחבולה, "although no means can be found by which this could be done."

[4] Ch. xxxiv., pag. 119.

it, therefore, necessary to discuss first in a merely colloquial manner, in the next chapter, the totality of existing things, and to confine our remarks to such as have been fully proved and established beyond all doubt. In subsequent chapters I shall treat of the propositions of the Mutakallemim, and describe the method by which they explain the four[1] fundamental principles. In the chapters which will follow, I propose to expound the propositions of the philosophers and the methods applied by them in verifying those principles. In the last place, I shall explain to you the method applied by me in proving those four[1] principles, as I have stated to you.

CHAPTER LXXII.

A Parallel between the Universe and Man.

KNOW[2] that this Universe, in its entirety, is nothing else but one individual being;[3] that is to say, the outermost

---

[1] *I.e.*, The creation of the Universe, in addition to the three principles mentioned above.

[2] Of this chapter Shemtob says: זה הפרק יקר ונכבד מאד נקרא שיעור הקומה. "This chapter is most important and most interesting; it is called *Shiur hakkomah*" (lit. "the measure of the height"), alluding to a cabbalistic work of that title, which contains the most surprising mysteries concerning the Supreme Being.

[3] In this chapter the author treats of the principle that the whole universe is *one* organised body, every part of which has an individual function as a part of the whole. He further maintains that this organic body has the properties of a living being: it possesses life, it moves, and has a soul. The words "and nothing else" לא ניר, in Hebrew לא זולת זה Ibn Tibbon, בלבד Charizi,) are added, probably, for the sake of emphasis, in the sense of "doubtlessly" (בלא שך, Hebrew בלא ספק in the explanatory phrase which follows). Saadiah, in Emunoth ve-deoth I., says:—ואחר כן חקרתי ואמרתי שמא יש ארצות רבות ושמים רבים יקיפו כל שמים מהם הארץ שלהם ויהיו עולמים שאין להם הכלית וראיתי זה נמנע מצר הטבע. The theory that the universe is to be considered as one finite system, being in all its parts regulated by one and the same idea, was held by the greatest representatives of ancient

PART I.—CHAPTER LXXII.   289

heavenly sphere,[1] together with all included therein, is as regards individuality beyond all question a single being like Said and Omar.[2] The variety of its substances—I mean the substances of that sphere and all its component parts—is like the variety of the substances of a human being:[3] just as, e.g., Said[2] is one individual, consisting of various solid substances, such as flesh, bones, sinews, of various humours,[4] and of various spiritual elements;[5] in like manner this

---

philosophy, by Plato and Aristotle, and continued to be maintained by the philosophers of the Middle Ages. Comp. Plato, Timæus :—οὕτως οὖν δὴ κατὰ λόγον τὸν εἰκότα δεῖ λέγειν, τόνδε τὸν κόσμον, ζῶον ἔμψυχον ἔννουν τε τῇ ἀληθείᾳ διὰ τὴν τοῦ θεοῦ γενέσθαι πρόνοιαν . . . . τῷ γὰρ τῶν νοουμένων καλλίστῳ καὶ κατὰ πάντα τελίῳ μάλιστ' αὐτὸν θεὸς ὁμοιῶσαι βουληθεὶς ζῶον ἓν ὁρατόν, πάνθ' ὅσα κατὰ φύσιν αὐτοῦ συγγενῆ ζῶα ἐντὸς ἔχον ἑαυτοῦ, ξυνέστησε· πότερον οὖ ὀρθῶς ἕνα οὐρανὸν προςειρήκαμεν, ἢ πολλοὺς καὶ ἀπείρους λέγειν ἦν ὀρθότερον, ἕνα. τὸ γὰρ περιέχον πάντα ὁπόσα νοητὰ ζῶα, μεθ' ἑτέρου δευτέρου οὐκ ἂν ποτ'εἴη. Similarly, Aristotle, in De Cœlo I., c. 7, 8.

[1] The Universe was believed to consist of a sphere, including several spheres within itself, and having the earth in its centre. The outermost sphere is the all-encompassing sphere (גלגל המקיף כל), or from another point of view, called by Charizi גלגל העליון, the uppermost sphere. Of that sphere Ibn Ezra says in his Commentaries, כי אין גוף למעלה מגלגל המזלות (on Gen. i. 16); and איך יהיו מים למעלה מן מקיף הכל (ibid. i. 6, second recension).

[2] The Hebrew translations substitute for these Arabic names the Hebrew Reuben and Shimeon.

[3] Charizi: והשתנות כחות זה העגול כהשתנות כחות איברי אדם; "the variety of the forces of that sphere corresponds to the variety which is noticed in the forces of the various portions of the human body."

[4] The ancients assumed four kinds of humour which constituted the temperament of man; the latter varied according to the relative proportion of the different humours. Man was held to be of a sanguine, phlegmatic, bilious, or melancholic temperament, according to a supposed predominance of the red, white, green, or black humour in his system.

[5] The spirits here mentioned are material; as compared with the aforementioned humours they are more rarefied; they seem to be a species of gas pervading the body, and having different functions according as it comes into contact with the different organic parts. Although these "spiritual elements" or "spirits" determine to some extent the disposition, the emotion, and even the mental operations of man, they are different from his soul and his intellect.

The following is a translation of what Maimonides, in a letter to al-Malek al-Afdal, son of Saladin, had to say of these spirits (the Arabic, with a

U

sphere in its totality is composed of the celestial orbs, the four elements and their combinations; there is no vacuum whatever therein, but the whole space is filled up with matter. Its centre[1] is occupied by the earth, earth is surrounded by water, air encompasses the water, fire envelopes the air, and this again is enveloped by the fifth substance (quintessence). These substances form numerous spheres, one being enclosed within another so that no intermediate empty space, no vacuum, is left.[2] One sphere surrounds and closely joins the

---

French translation, is given by Munk in a note *ad locum*; the Hebrew version is printed in Kerem Chemed, Vol. IV., pag. 24): "What the medical men call spirits (רוחות) are vapours which exist in the bodies of animals. The air which the animals breathe is the origin and the principal substance of these spirits. The vapours in the blood of the liver and the veins which issue from it are called the physical spirit (רוח טבעית, πνεῦμα φυσικὸν); in the heart and the arteries they are called the vital spirit (רוח חיונית, πνεῦμα ζωτικόν); in the inner part of the brains and in the canals of the nerves they are called animal spirit (רוח נפשית, πνεῦμα ψυχικόν). The origin and the substance of all these spirits being the air which the animal breathes, they change, and their action produces an effect which is contrary to their proper function if the air is damp or vitiated or impure. Galenus advises that the air to be breathed should be of the utmost uniformity and purity. The more the spirit is rarefied the more it is affected by the changes of the atmosphere. The physical spirit is denser than the vital spirit; the latter denser than the animal spirit; so that the smallest change in the condition of the atmosphere produces a noticeable change in the condition of the animal spirit. Hence you find people whose mental operations suffer from the deteriorated condition of the atmosphere; I mean to say, they are confused, deficient in reasoning and in memory, although no change can be noticed in the physical and vital functions of the body." Charizi renders ומן ארואה by ומבחות ומרוחות; Palquera omits the phrase altogether, and seems to use here the term לחות in the sense of רוחות, for he explains it by החיוני הרוח, והנפשי, הטבעי; it is possible that the word has been omitted by the neglect of the copyist, or by a typographical error. In the Commentary of Mosheh b. Shelomoh, of Salerno (MS. of the London Beth-ha-midrash Library), the word כחות is explained: כבר באר הרב רבינו כי חלקי הנפש הם חמשה הזן הסרניש והסרמה והסתעורר והשכלי ולכל חלק וחלק יש כחות רבות לחלק הזן יש שבעה כחות ולחלק המרניש יש ה׳ כחות וכן לכולן

[1] In Ibn Tibbon's Version the Hebrew for "centre" is מרכז, like the Arabic, or נקודת מרכז. Charizi uses instead of it עמוד "that which stands still," in contradistinction to all other parts which move around it.

[2] The substance filling space, though immutable (II. 11, לא ישתנה הנושא

PART I.—CHAPTER LXXII.

other. All the spheres[1] revolve with constant uniformity, without acceleration or retardation;[2] that is to say, each sphere retains its individual nature as regards its velocity

───────────────

וההוא בעצמו), must at least be of an elastic nature, contracting and expanding according to necessity. The Universe, consisting of a sphere with the earth in its centre, contains, according to the statement of our author, eccentric spheres, whose centres rotate round the centre of the whole system, and which, therefore, continually change their position with regard to the fixed centre. On that account, Ibn Caspi wholly denies the existence of the eccentric spheres. The various heavenly phenomena are the results of the apparent diurnal rotation of the whole celestial sphere with sun, moon, and stars, and of the course of sun, moon, and planets, through the constellations of the Zodiac. Their deviations from an imaginary middle course, apparent irregularities, the number of which increases with the progress of science and the improvement of the means of observations, phenomena which, according to the present state of science, are all explained by the Law of Gravitation, were in the time of Maimonides, according to the theory of Ptolemy, considered to be the result of the combined action of several eccentric spheres appertaining to each of the planets and moving in different directions. Instead of eccentric spheres some preferred epicycles; others combined the two. The number of spheres and epicycles was gradually increased to 55, (their number was considered to be 38 in the time of Ibn Roshd, see Moreh ha-moreh *ad locum*). Although Maimonides speaks here with an apparent conviction of the theory of the spheres, and with still greater positiveness in Mishneh Torah (Madda', I. iii. 27), he is by no means satisfied with the Ptolemean system. His view is that both the eccentricity of the spheres (Mishneh Torah, *l.c.*, "the spheres appear to be concentric"), and the existence of epicycles are systems which have not been proved; they are mere hypotheses assumed for the sake of explaining certain phenomena, and introducing system into the apparent disorder and confusion. (Comp. Part II. xi. and xix.)

[1] Maimonides seems to use the two terms כדור (Hebr. כדור, lit. "sphere" or "globe,") and פלך (Hebr. גלגל, lit. "circle" or "orbit,") indiscriminately in the sense of sphere; *e.g.*, speaking of the relative velocity of the spheres (אלאכר, Hebr. כדורים), he describes the velocity of the all-encompassing sphere (פלך, Hebr. גלגל) as the greatest. Comp. "The stars contained in those spheres (אלאכר) are part of their respective orbits (פלך)." In the translation, the variation of the original has here been retained, but the two terms denote evidently one and the same thing.

[2] Maimonides only speaks of the regular retrocession of the equinoctial nodes; the precession is not recognised by him. Ptolemy knows only of the motion of the Zodiac in one direction; others after him, but long before Maimonides, also noticed the periodical motion of the Zodiac in the opposite direction. See Yesod Olam, by Isaac Israeli (ed. by B. Goldberg and L. Rosenkranz; Berlin, 1848), II. 6.

and the peculiarity of its motion; it does not move at one time quicker, at another slower. Compared with each other, however, some of the spheres move with less, others with greater velocity. The outermost, all-encompassing sphere, revolves with the greatest speed; it completes its revolution in one day, and causes every thing to participate in its motion, just as every particle of a thing moves when the entire body is in motion; for all existing beings stand in the same relation to that sphere as a part of a thing stands to the whole. These spheres have not a common centre; the centres of some of them are identical with the centre of the Universe, while those of the rest are different from it.[1] Some of the spheres have a motion independent of that of the whole Universe, constantly revolving from East to West, while other spheres move from West to East. The stars contained in those spheres are part of their respective orbits; they are fixed in them, and have no motion of their own, but participating in the motion of the sphere of which they are a part, they themselves appear to move. The entire substance of this revolving fifth element is unlike the substance of those bodies which consist of the other four elements, and are enclosed by the fifth element.

The number of these spheres encompassing the Universe cannot possibly be less than eighteen;[2] it may even be larger; but this is a matter for further investigation. It also remains an open question whether there are spheres which, without moving round the centre of the Universe, have nevertheless a circular motion.[3] Within that sphere

---

[1] See page 290, note 2.

[2] The number eighteen mentioned here as a minimum is in Mishneh Torah, *l.c.*, given without any reserve. The eighteen spheres are, according to Shem-tob and Efodi, distributed in the following way: the Moon has three, Venus three, each of the remaining five planets two, the fixed stars one, the *arabhoth* one. A different account occurs in the Perush Mishneh Torah, *l.c.*: Sun and Venus, each three; the other planets, each two, etc.

[3] See page 290, note 2. Ibn Caspi, and after him Efodi, Shem-tob, and Narboni, contend that this is impossible, because only three kinds of motion are admissible; the circular motion round the permanent centre, the linear

which is nearest to us,[1] a substance is contained which is different from the substance of the fifth element; it first received four primary forms,[2] and then became in those four forms, four kinds of matter: earth, water, air, fire. Each of the four elements occupies a certain position of its own assigned to it by nature; it is not found in another place, so long as no other but its own natural force acts upon it; it is a dead body; it has no life, no perception, no spontaneous motion,[3] and remains at rest in its natural place. When moved from its place by some external force, it returns towards its natural place as soon as that force ceases to operate. For the elements have the property of moving back to their place[4] in a straight line, but they have no properties which would cause them to remain where[5] they are, or to move otherwise than in a straight line. The rectilinear motions of these four elements when returning to their original place are of two kinds, either centrifugal, *viz.*, the motion of the air and the fire; or centripetal, *viz.*, the motion of the earth, and the water; and when the elements have reached their original place, they remain at rest.

The spherical bodies,[6] on the other hand, have life, possess

---

motion in a straight line towards the centre, and that in the opposite direction; that of the epicycles is different from all these three. Maimonides expresses the same opinion in the second part of this work.

[1] That is, the sphere included within the sphere of the Moon. Comp. Mishneh Torah, Madda', III.

[2] The original uniform, or rather formless, substance received—it is here not stated how—four different forms, by which it changed into the four elements.

[3] This is said in order to distinguish the elements from the spheres and from the bodies contained in the spheres, which were stated to be living and moving on their own accord. According to Palaquera, this remark has been made in opposition to those who attribute life to water and to air.

[4] Charizi has here the addition אם לא ימנענו סונע, "if not prevented by some other force."

[5] *I.e.*, In the place to which some power forced it, away from its own place. Munk unnecessarily adds in the translation "toujours."

[6] *I.e.*, The spheres and the heavenly bodies contained in them. Comp. Sefer ha-madda': Yesode ha-torah, iii. 9, כל הכוכבים והגלגלים, וגו, "All the stars and the spheres," etc.

a soul by which they move spontaneously; they have no properties by which they could at any time come to a state of rest; in their perpetual rotations they are not subject to any change, except that of position.[1] The question[2] whether they are endowed with an intellect, enabling them to comprehend, cannot be solved without deep research. Through the constant revolution of the fifth element, with all contained therein, the four elements are forced to move and to change their respective positions,[3] so that fire and air[4] are driven into the water, and again these three elements enter the depth of the earth. Thus are the elements mixed together; and when they return to their respective places, parts

---

[1] In Hebrew, בהנחה (Ibn Tibbon); בתשומה or בתכונה (Charizi).

[2] The question is answered by Maimonides in the affirmative. Comp. II. iv., *et seqq.*, and Sefer ha-madda', Yesode ha-torah, iii. 9.

[3] Maimonides does not tell us how in his opinion the fifth substance affects the four elements by its circular motion. He says that they are forced out of their original and natural place. The four elements being placed in the centre of the whole system, one above or around the other, remain at rest so long as their natural order is not disturbed. The fifth element, that of the spheres, being in close contact with the nearest of the four elements, sets parts of it in motion, and this motion is gradually communicated to the other elements. The tendency of the particles of the elements to move in a straight line towards the centre or away from it, while the motion of the spheres forces them in a circular path round the centre, together with the specific weight which gives to one element a greater, to the other a smaller velocity, appear, according to the ancient philosophers, to effect a mixture of the four elements. Ibn Sina (quoted in Moreh ha-moreh, page 45) describes the change in the following words: מהגלגלים יפלו כחות ביסודות וינועו אותם ויערבו אותם ויתהוו מהם נמצאים רבים ואלו היסודות הארבעה יראה שאינם על פשיטותם כי כחות הגופים הגלגלים יפלשו בהם ויתחדשו בגופים התחתונים הקרים חמימות יתערבו בהן ויתחדשו מפני זה אידים עשניים יתערבו בהם מימות ואידות ויעלו למעלה כמו כן אידים סימיים ועשניים ארציים ויתערבו בהם וגו׳, "The spheres influence the elements in such a manner, that the latter are moved, mixed and changed into the forms of existing things. These four elements do not appear to be simple; for the influence of the bodies of the spheres penetrates into them, and in the lower cold bodies a certain heat is created, causing vapours to rise and to mix with the elements; all kinds of vapours then rise," etc.

[4] Char.: האש והאויר, "the fire and the air," as subject to the verb יצאו, "they go out"; Ibn Tibbon, באש ובאויר in apposition to ביסודות.

of the earth, in quitting their places, move together with the water, the air and the fire. In this whole process the elements act and react upon each other. The elements intermixed, are then combined,[1] and form at first various kinds of vapours; afterwards the several kinds of minerals, every species of plants, and many species of living beings,[2] according to the relative proportion of the constituent parts. All transient beings have their origin in the elements, into which again they resolve when their existence comes to an end. The elements themselves are subject to being transformed from one into another; for although one substance is common to all, substance without form is in reality impossible,[3] just as the physical form of these transient beings cannot exist without substance. The formation and the dissolution of the elements, together with the things composed of them, and resolving into them, follow each other in rotation.[4] The changes of the finite substance,[5] in successively receiving one form after the other, may therefore be compared to

[1] That is to say, they do not form a mechanical mixture of the elements but rather a compound, in which each of the elements loses its essential properties.

[2] Maimonides probably follows the Biblical account of the Creation, according to which, the vapours and the atmosphere (rakia) were formed first (on the second day), then followed the formation of the dry land (yabbashah) with the minerals, the creation of the vegetable world (on the third day), and of the animals (on the fifth and sixth days).

[3] That is to say, the elements are not resolved into the original infinite ὕλη, for it has no form (i.e., no specific properties), and cannot have a real existence. If the elements were resolved into the hylic substance, and again into one of the elements, this change would be equal to destruction and a new creation. In a previous passage, when explaining the act of Creation, Maimonides assumed an infinite, formless substance, which subsequently received the four different forms. But here he explains the changes which take place in the existing, material world; he therefore denies the existence of formless matter, and of forms without matter. Destruction and origination are described as transitions from one form of existence into another. These forms being of a finite number, their changes are compared to the motion of a circle revolving round its centre, and to the periodical reappearance of every point of the circle in the same place.

[4] Comp. ch. xi., pag. 59, note 3.

[5] Lit., "substance possessing the form."

the revolution of the sphere in space,[1] when each part of the sphere periodically[2] reappears in the same position.[3]

As the human body consists both of principal organs and of other members which depend on them and cannot exist without the control of those organs, so does the universe consist both of principal parts, *viz.*, the quintessence,[4] which encompasses the four elements and of other parts which are subordinated and require a leader, *viz.*, the four elements and the things composed of them.

Again, the principal part in the human body, namely, the heart,[5] is in constant motion, and is the source of every motion noticed in the body; it rules over the other members, and communicates to them through its own pulsations the force required for their functions. The outermost sphere by its motion rules in a similar way over all other parts of the universe, and supplies all things with their special properties. Every motion in the universe has thus its origin in the motion of that sphere; and the soul[6] of every animated being derives its origin from the soul of that same sphere.

[1] Lit., "as regards 'where'"; Hebrew, באנה. While the abstract terms of quantity and quality are expressed in Hebrew by nouns derived from the interrogative particles כמה and איך to which the suffix ות (כמות, איכות) is added, no such abstract term has been derived from אנה, "where;" this word is therefore employed in the sense of "space" or "position."

[2] The Arabic בתכרר has been rendered בהחזרת by Charizi and Palquera, בהשתנות by Ibn Tibbon. The latter word generally means "in changing;" but here it seems to be employed in the sense of "in repeating," like הִשָּׁנוֹת (Gen. xli. 32).

[3] The fem. termination in the Arabic, בעינהא, agreeing with the plural, אלאוצאע, has been erroneously retained by Ibn Tibbon and Charizi in the Hebrew בעצמה, where the suffix should be ן, agreeing with הנחות (Tibbon), or תשומות (Charizi).

[4] The editions of Ibn Tibbon's version have והמקיף, "and the sphere which encompasses," as if the outermost sphere consisted of a substance different from that of the other spheres.   [5] *I.e.*, The blood in the heart.

[6] נפס (Hebr. נפש), "soul," appears to correspond to קואהא (Hebr. כחתיו), "forces," mentioned before. In the next passage, however, the "forces" are divided into four classes, one of which is "the soul." We must either assume that the term has in this place a wider meaning, and is identical with "force," or we must say that the sentence is here out of place. In the Moreh ha-moreh (page 48) it is omitted.

The forces which according to this explanation are communicated by the spheres [1] to this sublunary world are four in number, viz., (a) the force which effects the mixture and the composition of the elements, and which undoubtedly suffices to form the minerals; (b) the force which supplies every growing thing with its vegetative functions; (c) the force which gives to each living being its vitality, and (d) the force which endows rational beings with intellect. All this is effected through the action of light and darkness, which are regulated by the position [2] and the motion of the spheres round the earth.

When for one instant the beating of the heart is interrupted, man dies, and all his motions and powers come to an end. In a like manner would the whole universe perish, and everything therein cease to exist if the spheres were to come to a standstill.[3]

The living being as such is one through the action of its heart, although some parts of the body are devoid of motion and sensation, as, e.g., the bones, the cartilage,[4] and similar

---

[1] Although in Arabic the singular is used, אלפלך, it includes all the spheres, since all that is said about the principal and leading portion of the universe applies equally to the "fifth element," which includes the all-surrounding sphere as well as the other spheres. Ibn Tibbon, in rendering the word by the plural, translated correctly, according to the sense, the plural suffix in אורם and הקפם (Arab. נורהא and דורתהא), agreeing with this noun.

[2] יושרם, which occurs instead of אורם in most of the printed editions of Ibn Tibbon's Version, seems to be a mistake. Efodi and others explain it "their vertical position straight above the earth," (כשהשמש ביושר על הארץ); but the word "straight" is still superfluous and unintelligible. אורם, "their lustre," i.e., their stars, refers to the stars contained in the several spheres; the stars as well as the motion of the spheres are the causes of the constant changes of darkness and light. Crescas and other commentators appear to have found the reading אורם in the Version of Ibn Tibbon.

[3] Caspi finds it necessary to observe that the miracle by which the sun and the moon stood still at the bidding of Joshua does not contradict this statement, miracles being an exception to the ordinary course of nature.

[4] Charizi and Palquera: עצמות הרבים, "cartilage." נצאריף in the Arabic text has been translated by והאלל. (Comp. Talm. Babyl., Zebhachim, 109; Mishnah Taharoth, i. 4); explained by some to signify בשר המת; by others, גיד הצואר. By the Talmudical אלל such portions of the flesh must

parts. The same is the case with the entire universe; although it includes many beings without motion and without life, it is a single living being through the motion of the sphere, which may be compared to the heart of an animated being.[1] You must therefore consider the entire globe as one individual being which is endowed with life, motion, and a soul. This mode of considering the universe is, as will be explained,[2] indispensable, that is to say, it is very useful[3] for demonstrating the unity of God; it also helps to elucidate the principle that He who is One has created only *one* being.

Again, it is impossible that any of the members of a human body should exist by themselves, not connected with the body, and at the same time should actually be organic parts of that body, that is to say, that the liver should exist by itself, the heart by itself, or the flesh by itself. In like manner, it is impossible that one part of the Universe should exist independently of the other parts in the existing order of things as here considered,[4] *viz.*, that the fire should exist without the co-existence of the earth, or the earth without the heaven, or the heaven without the earth.

In man there is a certain force which unites the members of the body, controls them, and gives to each of them what

---

be understood as are attached to the skin when it is being removed from the body. (See Aruch., *sub voce*, אלל.)

[1] Lit., "of those possessing a heart."

[2] In Part II., ch. i., our author again lays stress on the fact that the universe is one organic system.

[3] The word הכרחי, "necessary," is modified by the phrase מועיל מאוד במופת, "very useful for the proof," etc. כלומר, "that is to say," in the Version of Ibn Tibbon, has here the same meaning as או, "or," in that of Charizi.

[4] The *ed. princeps* of Ibn Tibbon's Version, and the MSS. have the reading כן א"א שימצאו חלקי העולם קצתם מבלתי קצתם בזה המציאות המיושב אשר דברנו בו.—Munk. The last words, "in the existing order of things of which we speak," are added, in order to make it clear that he does not deny the successive creations which are recorded in the first chapter of Genesis. Maimonides does not treat here of the Creation, but of the condition of the universe after it had been created.

it requires for the conservation of its condition, and for the repulsion of injury—the physicians distinctly call it the leading force in the body [1] of the living being; sometimes they call it "nature." The Universe likewise possesses a force which unites the several parts with each other, protects the species from destruction, maintains the individuals of each species as long as possible, and endows some individual beings [2] with permanent existence. Whether this force operates through the medium of the sphere or otherwise remains an open question.[3]

Again, in the body of each individual there are parts which are intended for a certain purpose, as the organs of nutrition for the preservation of the individual, the organs of generation for the preservation of the species, the hands and eyes for administering to certain wants, as to food, etc.; there are [4] also parts which, in themselves, are not intended for any purpose, but are mere accessories and adjuncts to the constitution of the other parts. The peculiar constitution of the organs, indispensable for the conservation of their

[1] Ibn Tibbon, הכח המנהיג; Charizi, הכח השומר. This force is more fully described in Part II., ch. x.: "Nature, which is represented as wise, as ruling and regulating the existence of the living," etc. Comp. Shahrastani, "On Religious Sects and Philosophical Schools," translated by Haarbrücker, II., pag. 147, "Sayings of Hippocrates."

[2] Namely, the spheres and stars, which, according to Aristotle and his followers, are imperishable.

[3] That is, whether the ideals or universalia (שכלים הנפרדים) have a direct influence on the material world, or affect directly the spheres, and through them indirectly all things in nature. In the Second Part, ch. x., Maimonides appears to assume the indirect influence of the ideals. Although the question refers to the nature of the spheres themselves, the expression "by means of the spheres" (במצוע הגלגל), is used, because of their relation to the perpetuation of the species and to the temporary preservation of the individua on this earth. According to Narboni, the term refers to the "ideal sphere" (צורת הגלגל), in which the properties and forces of the spheres take their origin.

[4] Arabic, ופה, "and in it," that is, in the body of man; Ibn Tibbon, בהם, "in them," that is, in those parts of the body which perform certain functions; Charizi: ויש מהם, "some of them"; according to Munk, the reading פיהא, "in them," instead of פה, is found in one of the MSS.

particular forms and for the performance of their primary functions, produces, whilst it serves its special purpose,[1] according to the nature of the substance, other things, such as the hair and the complexion of the body. Being mere accessories, they are not formed according to a fixed rule; some are altogether absent in many individuals; and vary considerably in others. This is not the case with the organs of the body. You never find that the liver[2] of one person is ten times larger than that of another person, but you may find a person without a beard, or without hair on certain parts of his body, or with a beard ten times longer than that of another man. Instances of this phenomenon, viz., great variation as regards hair and colour, are not rare. The same differences occur in the constitution of the Universe. Some species exist as an integral part of the whole system; these are constant and follow a fixed law; though they vary[3] as far as their nature permits, this variation is insignificant in quantity and quality.[4] Other species do not serve any purpose;[5] they are the mere result of the general nature of transient things, as, e.g., the various insects which are generated in dunghills, the animals generated in rotten fruit, or in fetid liquids, and worms generated in the intestines, etc. In short, everything devoid of the power of generation belongs to this class. You will, therefore, find that these things do not follow a fixed law, although their entire absence is just as impossible as the absence of different complexions and of different kinds of hair amongst human beings.

In man there are substances the individual existence of which is permanent,[6] and there are other substances which

[1] Lit., "and according to the requirements of the substance, other things, such as the hair and the colour of the body, are formed as accessories of the existence of the body."
[2] Charizi: כבדות, "weight."
[3] That is, in the various individuals of each species.
[4] Arabic, ערץ; Charizi, מקרה; Tibbon, רוחב. See ch. lvii., pag. 206, note 3, "in accordance with the limits set for that class."
[5] Comp. R. Gershon, Sha'ar ha-shamayim, iv. 1.
[6] That is, "during the whole life of an individual."

are only constant in the species, not in the individuals, as, *e.g.*, the four humours.[1] The same is the case in the Universe; there are substances which are constant in individuals, such as the fifth element, which is constant in all its formations, and other substances which are constant in the species, as, *e.g.*, the four elements[2] and all that is composed of them.

The same forces which operate in the birth and the temporal existence of the human being operate also in his destruction and death. This truth holds good with regard to this whole transient world. The causes of production are at the same time the causes of destruction. This may be illustrated by the following example. If the four forces which are present in every being sustained by food, *viz.*, attraction, retention, digestion, and secretion,[3] were, like intelligent forces, able to confine themselves to what is necessary, and to act at the proper time and within the proper limits, man would be exempt from those great sufferings and the numerous diseases [to which he is exposed]. Since, however, such is not the case,[4] and since the forces

[1] The four humours, the red, the white, the green, the black, constitute, according to ancient philosophers, the temperament of man. They are never found separately, but are always combined in proportions which vary constantly, so that the humours existing in man at one time are not the same which existed at another time, while the heart, the head, etc., although changeable in dimension, seem always to be the same parts as at the beginning.

[2] That is to say, the elements themselves, in the dissolution of bodies change their forms, and, *e.g.*, that which now is water, has previously been another element; but none of the elements disappear entirely; the things in nature always remain compounds of these four elements.

[3] Not only the digestive organs of an animal, but all parts of the body which through food, undergo a change of matter, include these four forces:— the force of attraction or absorption, retention, assimilation, and secretion. עכל in Ibn Tibbon's Version signifies to digest, to assimilate the nutritive elements of the food to the various parts of the body. Charizi has instead, המוחנת, "the grinding" or "dissolving" process. It is remarkable that Ibn Tibbon here uses כח as a masculine noun, while in Charizi it is joined with the feminine form of the adjectives.

[4] Maimonides does not explain the reason of this phenomenon: he probably is of opinion that, without reason and intellect, a systematic and regular process is impossible. Nature, though described by our author as "a wise manager,"

perform their natural functions without thought and intelligence, without any consciousness of their action, they necessarily cause dangerous maladies and great pains, although they are the direct causes of the birth and the temporal existence of the human being.[1] This fact is to be explained as follows: if the attractive force would absorb nothing but that which is absolutely beneficial, and nothing but the quantity which is required, man would be free from many such sufferings and disorders. But such is not the case; the attractive force absorbs any humour[2] that comes within the range of its action,[3] although such humour be ill-adapted in quality or in quantity. It is, therefore, natural that sometimes a humour is absorbed which is too warm, too cold, too thick, or too thin, or that too much humour is absorbed, and thus the veins are choked, obstruction and decay ensue, the quality of the humour is deteriorated, its quantities altered, diseases are originated, such as scurvy, leprosy, abscess,[4] or a dangerous illness, such as cancer,[5] elephantiasis, gangrene,[6] and at last the organ or organs are destroyed. The same is the case with every one of the[7] four forces, and with all existing beings. The same force that originates all things, and causes them to exist for

---

etc., (comp. pag. 299, note 1,) does not work with intelligence in all these forces of the body, and irregularities are therefore unavoidable. (Comp. Narboni.)

[1] Charizi: חי, "living being."

[2] מאדה; Hebr., לחה. Although the literal translation would be חומר or גוף, the Hebrew translators preferred לחה, "fluid," because they thought that the substance before assimilation, is reduced to the state of לחות, "moisture."

[3] Lit., "of the class of its absorption." Each of the several parts of the body has its own limited power of absorption; what is not within these limits cannot be absorbed.

[4] Ibn Tibbon, היבלות; Charizi, המחורים.

[5] Ibn Tibbon, מורסא; in the editions we find the explanatory remark, שקורים גרנק בלעז, which is called in the vernacular "crania,"; Charizi, סרטן (cancer).

[6] והאיכל, Ibn Tibbon; והנגע האוכל הבשר, Char.

[7] Lit., "with the rest of the four forces."

a certain time, namely, the combination of the elements which are moved and penetrated[1] by the forces of the heavenly spheres, that same cause becomes throughout the world a source of calamities, such as devastating rain, showers, snow-storms, hail, hurricanes, thunder, lightning, malaria, or other terrible catastrophes by which a place or many places[2] or an entire country may be laid waste, such as landslips, earthquakes, meteoric showers[3] and floods issuing forth from the seas and from the interior of the earth.

Bear in mind, however, that in all that we have noticed about the similarity between the Universe and the human being, nothing would warrant us to assert that man is a microcosm; for although the comparison in all its parts applies to the Universe and any living being in its normal state, we never heard that any ancient author called the ass or the horse a microcosm.[4] This attribute has been given to man alone on account of his peculiar faculty of thinking, I mean the intellect, *i.e.*, the hylic intellect[5] which appertains to no other living being. This may be explained as follows. An animal does not require for its sustenance any plan, thought or scheme; each animal moves and acts by its nature, eats as much as it can find of suitable

---

[1] The passive אלמבתּוֹתה (II. Conjug.) is perhaps a misreading for the active אלמבתּתה, "which disperse" the elements, that is to say, force them beyond their natural boundaries, and thus cause their mixture.

[2] Arabic, בלאד, "city," has been rendered by Ibn Tibbon ארץ, and by Charisi אנשי מדינה.

[3] Arabic, צואעק. Charisi: אבני אלנביש; the same term is rendered by ואבני הרעמים היורדים מן השמים "thunderbolts," or "meteoric showers." Also זועות, the rendering of Ibn Tibbon, and זיקות וזועות of Palquera, have the same signification. Comp. Sha'ar ha-shamayim of R. Gershon I., ch. 3. on (רעם ברק זיעה). Munk: "les violents orages."

[4] Narboni: "I see that Aristotle mentioned the horse as an illustration; and so also Ibn Roshd." Palquera quotes from Ibn Gabirol, that, of all living creatures, man alone, by his structure, by the arrangements and proportions of his constituent parts, can be considered as a likeness of the universe, as a microcosmos.

[5] *i.e.*, The capacity innate in man to acquire the faculty of reasoning. See c. lxviii., pag. 254, note 2.

things, it makes its resting-place wherever it happens to be, cohabits with any mate it meets while in heat in the periods of its sexual excitement. In this manner each individual conserves itself for a certain time, and perpetuates the existence of its species without requiring for its maintenance the assistance or support of any of its fellow creatures; for all the things to which it has to attend it performs by itself. With man it is different; if an individual had a solitary existence, and were, like an animal, left without guidance, he would soon perish, he would not endure even one day, unless it were by mere chance, unless he happened to find something upon which he might feed. For the food which man requires for his subsistence demands much work and preparation, which can only be accomplished by reflection and by plan; many vessels must be used, and many individuals, each in his peculiar work, must be employed. It is therefore necessary that one person should organise the work and direct men in such a manner that they should properly co-operate, and that they should assist each other. The protection from heat in summer and from cold in winter, and shelter from rain, snow, and wind, require in the same manner the preparation of many things, none of which can properly be done without design and thought. For this reason man has been endowed with intellectual faculties, which enable him to think, consider, and act, and by various labours to prepare and procure for himself food, dwelling and clothing, and to control every organ of his body, causing both the principal and the secondary organs to perform their respective functions. Consequently, if a man, being[1] deprived of his intellectual faculties, only possessed vitality, he would in a short time be lost. The intellect is the highest of all faculties of living creatures; it is very difficult to comprehend, and its true character cannot be understood as easily[2] as man's other faculties.

[1] Lit., "If you imagined that."
[2] Lit., "by the beginning of common reasoning," *i.e.*, "at first sight" or "easily."

PART I.—CHAPTER LXXII.   305

There also exists in the Universe a certain force which controls the whole, which sets in motion the chief and principal parts,[1] and gives them the motive power for governing the rest. Without[2] that force, the existence of this sphere, with its principal and secondary parts, would be impossible. It is the source of the existence of the Universe in all its parts. That force is God; blessed be His name! It is on account of this force that man is called microcosm; for he likewise possesses a certain principle which governs all the forces of the body, and on account of this comparison God is called "the life of the Universe";[3] comp. "and he swore by the life of the Universe"[4] (Deut. xii. 7).

You must understand that in the parallel which we have drawn between the whole universe, on the one hand, and the individual man, on the other, there is a complete harmony in all the points which we mentioned above; only in the following three points a discrepancy may be noticed.

First, the principal organ of any living being which has a heart,[5] derives a benefit from the organs under the control of the heart, and the benefits of the organs thus become the benefits of the heart. This is not the case in the constitution of the universe. That part which bestows authority or distributes power, does not receive in return any benefit from the things under its control; whatever it grants, is granted in the manner of a generous benefactor, not from any selfish motive,[6] but from a natural generosity and

---

[1] Arabic עָצֻוָה sing., Ibn Tibbon אברין plur., probably meant for אברו; so also Charizi has the sing. אבר; it is explained by the words which follow הראש הראשון, "the principal, the first." He means the highest sphere, המקיף כל, "the all-surrounding one," which moves the whole system by its own motion.   [2] Lit., "If man were to imagine the absence of."

[3] Comp. lxviii., pag. 253, note 1. Charizi: חי העולמים כי הוא חי העולם.

[4] A.V., "By Him that liveth for ever."

[5] Charizi: והוא הלב vis., "the heart."

[6] Arabic: כרם מבאט ופצילה סניה לא לתרג; Charizi: בעבור טבע; נכבד שיש בו ויתרון נפש לא לתקח similarly but more exactly Palquera: לנדיבות טבע למעלה יתירה לא לתוחלת גמול. Ibn Tibbon (according to

x

kindliness; only for the sake of imitating the ways of the Most High.

Secondly, living creatures endowed with a heart have it within the body and in the midst thereof; there it is surrounded by organs which it governs. Thus it derives a benefit from them, for they guard and protect it, and they do not allow that any injury from without should approach it. The reverse occurs in the case of the Universe. The superior part encompasses the inferior parts,[1] it being certain that it cannot be affected by the action[2] of any other being; and even if it could be affected,[3] there is nobody without it that could affect it. While it influences all that is contained within, it is not influenced by any act or force of any material being. There is, however, some similarity[4] [between the universe and man] in this point. In the body of animals, the organs more distant from the principal organ, are of less importance than those nearer to it. Also in the universe, the nearer the parts are to the centre, the

---

לתועלתם.—לנדיבות טבעים ולמעלתם לא לתוחלת (MSS.) in the editions seems to be a mistake; the suffix plur. ם does not agree with the subject המטיב החונן to which it refers.

[1] Charizi: היקר מקיף בזולל והנכבד בנקלה (Jer. xv. 19; Is. iii. 5).

[2] Arab. מלקבל מעשה; Ibn Tibbon: מן קבול אלאתר טמא סואה; Palquera: מזולתו (impression) מקבול הרשום; Charizi: זולתו (action); מזולתו (harm) מלקבל הזק. Charizi is not consistent in his rendering of אתר; in the next sentence he translates it שנוי "change," and in other passages אותות.

[3] That is to say, it does not possess that property which would enable it to receive the influence of others, but even if it possessed that property there is nothing in existence that could exercise that influence.

[4] Although there is a discrepancy between the Universe and the Microkosmos in the relative position of their several parts, some similarity (שבה Hebr., דמיון Ibn Tibbon, ססס Charizi) is nevertheless perceptible—namely, that the greater the distance of the several parts is from the principal member, the less important these parts are in the entire system of the human body. Palquera and Caspi criticise this dictum, and point out that the brains though at a great distance from the heart are of the greatest importance to the existence of man. Perhaps the ססס in Charizi's version, which gives no sense, is part of a marginal note which began ויש ססס; but there is a doubt about this comparison, for it does not apply to the brains of man.

greater is their turbidness, their solidity, their inertness, their dimness and darkness, because they are further away from the loftiest element, from the source of light and brightness, which moves by itself and the substance of which is the most rarefied and simplest: from the outermost sphere. At the same ratio at which a body is near this sphere, it derives properties from it, and rises above the spheres behind it.

Thirdly. The faculty of thinking is a force inherent in the body, and is not separated from it,[1] but God is not a force inherent in the body of the universe, but is separate from all its parts. How God rules the universe and provides for it is a complete mystery; man is unable to solve it. For, on the one hand, it can be proved that God is separate from the universe, and in no contact whatever with it; but, on the other hand, His rule and providence can be proved to exist in all parts of the universe, even in the smallest.[2] Praised be He whose perfection is above our comprehension.

It is true, we might have compared the relation between God and the universe, to the relation between the absolute acquired intellect[3] and man; it is not a power inherent in the

---

[1] Shemtob is surprised at this assertion, and says, "no philosopher except the author ever said such a thing."—Palquera in Moreh ha-moreh explains the words of Maimonides as follows: Man's rational capacities are not as independent of the body as the Causa Prima is of the material world. Comp. ch. lxviii., pag. 255, note 2.

[2] Char. במלאכה נמבזה ונמס. (1 Sam. xv. 9.)

[3] Comp. Ibn Ezra Literature IV., page 44, sqq. and notes. Maimonides distinguishes the faculty of speaking and thinking from the intellect which is the sum total of acquired abstract knowledge; it is called שכל הנקנה in so far as it is the result of man's efforts; שכל הנאצל because it is abstract and not connected with matter, or because it is an emanation from the universal active intellect (שכל הפועל). Comp. Scheyer, Psych. Syst. des Maim., page 45. Wolff, Muse ben-Maimon's Acht Cap., page 87, note 10. The Arabic אלמוסתפאד has been rendered by Charizi השכל הקנוי, by Palquera השכל הנאצל. Ibn Tibbon uses both words השכל הנקנה הנאצל. Although, according to this translator, the intellect may be described by both these epithets (see פי׳ מלות זרות of Ibn Tibbon, and Munk ad loeum), it is more probable that two readings have here been fused into one.

body, but a power which is absolutely separate from the body, and is from without brought into contact with the body. The rational faculty of man may be further compared to the intelligence of the spheres, which are, as it were, material bodies. But the intelligences of the spheres, purely spiritual beings, as well as man's absolute and acquired intellect, are subjects of deep study and research; the proof of their existence, though correct, is abstruse, and includes arguments which present doubts, are exposed to criticism, and can be easily attacked by objectors.[1] We have, therefore, preferred to illustrate the relation of God to the universe by a simile which is clear, and which will not be contradicted in any of the points which have been laid down by us without any qualification.[2] The opposition can only emanate either from an ignorant man, who contradicts truths even if they are perfectly obvious, just as a person unacquainted with geometry rejects elementary propositions which have been clearly demonstrated, or from the prejudiced[3] man who deceives himself. Those, however, who wish to study the subject must persevere in their studies until they are convinced that all our observations are true, and until they understand that our account of this universe unquestionably[4] agrees with the existing order of things.[5] If a man is willing to accept this theory from one who understands how to prove things

[1] Charizi less accurately: ויש לטעון בהן מענות לרוצה לשבש שבוש.

[2] Arab. מרסלא; Ibn Tibbon סתם. This term generally signifies "anonymously" or "generally," here it is used in the sense "without any qualification," "unqualified"; Charizi expresses this by פשוט (simple), and Palquera by מוחלם (decided).

[3] Lit., "he who chooses to adhere to an opinion already formed," בראי סא סאבק; Ibn Tibbon: בדעת אחת קודם (the word קודם is as an adverb to be joined with יבחר in the beginning of the sentence), "he who has already chosen to defend a certain view;" Charizi: בעצת הקדמונים, "the advice founded on preconceived ideas."

[4] Arabic ולא ריב, "and without suspicion;" Charizi ולא כזב, "and without falsehood." Ibn Tibbon and Palquera omit the phrase altogether.

[5] Maimonides seems to have added this phrase in order that no inference should be drawn from this about his view of the Creation. He speaks here only of the existing order of things. Comp. page 295, note 3.

which can be proved,[1] let him accept it, and let him establish on it his arguments and proofs. If, on the other hand, he refuses to accept without proof even the foregoing principles, let him enquire for himself, and ultimately he will find that they are correct. "Lo this, we have searched it, so it is; hear it, and know thou it for thy good."[2]

After these preliminary remarks, we will treat of the subject which we promised to introduce and to explain.[3]

CHAPTER LXXIII.

Twelve Propositions of the Mutakallemim.[4]

THERE are twelve propositions common to all Mutakallemim, however[5] different their individual opinions and methods may be; the Mutakallemim require them in order to establish their views on the four questions.[6] I shall first enumerate these propositions, and then discuss each separately, together with the inferences which may be drawn from it.

[1] In Charisi's version ואם ירצה לקבל עליו זה ממי אשר בא עליו המופת, the phrase אשר בא עליו המופת (generally, "for which a proof has been given") is used in the unusual sense of "to whom a proof has come," "who has accepted a proof as conclusive."

[2] Comp. Job v. 27.

[3] That is, to discuss the views of the Mutakallemim on the four fundamental problems mentioned in the conclusion of the preceding chapter.

[4] According to Palquera, in Moreh ha-moreh, the system of the kalām is discussed by Maimonides in this and the following chapters, in accordance with the request made by his pupil and mentioned in the dedicatory letter in the beginning of this work, "to teach you the system of the Mutakallemim, to tell you whether their arguments were based on logical proof, and if not what was their method" (page 3).

[5] Munk justly points out the inaccuracy of the Hebrew translators in rendering the Arabic, עלי, "with," "in spite of" (malgré), by לפי and כמי, "in accordance with." Maimonides proceeds now to enumerate and discuss the principles adopted by all Mutakallemim in spite of the differences in their views on many other points. The correct Hebrew rendering is עם.

[6] *I.e.*, the *creatio ex nihilo*, the Existence of God, His Unity, and His Incorporeality.

PROPOSITION I. All things are composed of atoms.[1]

PROPOSITION II. There is a vacuum.

PROPOSITION III. Time is composed of time-atoms.[2]

PROPOSITION IV. Substance cannot exist without numerous accidents.

PROPOSITION V. Each atom is completely furnished with the accidents[3] (which I will describe), and cannot exist without them.

PROPOSITION VI. Accidents do not continue in existence during two time-atoms.

PROPOSITION VII. Both positive and negative properties have a real existence, and are accidents which owe their existence to some *causa efficiens*.[4]

PROPOSITION VIII. All existing things, i.e., all creatures,[5] consist of substance and of accidents, and the physical form[6] of a thing is likewise an accident.

PROPOSITION IX. No accident can form the substratum for another accident.

[1] Lit., "to establish the [theory of] atom." Arabic אלנוהר אלפרד; Ibn Tibbon עצם פרדי; Charizi עצם הנפרד. All bodies are supposed to consist of a number of small particles or molecules, each of which, when considered as separated from the rest, is עצם פרדי, "a substance in separation," "a solitary substance," i.e., "an atom."

[2] Arabic אלאנאת; Ibn Tibbon, adhering to the original, has עתות (the plural form of עתה "now," like אנאת, plural of אן "now"). Charizi has עתים. The present moment has the same relation to time, as an infinitely small molecule has to a substance or to material bodies; both, the moment and the molecule, are considered as indivisible.

[3] Arabic בה; Ibn Tibbon תקום בה; Charizi תשלם מציאותו ועמידתו. Ibn Tibbon seems to have found a different reading in the original text. The same variation is noticed further on where the author discusses this proposition. Palquera, criticising Ibn Tibbon's rendering, suggests the following translation יקוימו בו אותם המקרים, and says that the author describes the accidents as having no such independent existence as the substance has, but as existing in these molecules. This cannot be the meaning of the phrase: the principal object of the fifth proposition is to establish the fact that the accidents exist completely in each of the atoms.

[4] Lit., "the law of their presence is the same as of their absence; they all are accidents in real existence, and require an agent."

[5] This qualification has been added, because God, though an existing being, does not consist of substance and of properties.

[6] See page 29, note 3.

PROPOSITION X. The test for the possibility of an imagined object does not consist in its conformity with the existing laws of nature.[1]

PROPOSITION XI. The idea of the infinite is equally inadmissible, whether the infinite be actual, potential, or accidental,[2] i.e., there is no difference whether the infinite be formed by a number of co-existing things, or by a series of things, of which one part comes into existence when another has ceased to exist,[3] in which case it is called accidental infinite; in both cases the infinite is rejected by the Mutakallemim as fallacious.

PROPOSITION XII. The senses mislead, and are in many cases inefficient; their perceptions, therefore, cannot form the basis of any law, or yield data for any proof.

FIRST PROPOSITION.

"The Universe, that is, everything contained in it, is composed of very small parts [atoms] which are indivisible on account of their smallness; such an atom has no magnitude;[4] but when several atoms combine, the sum has

[1] Lit., "The possibility [of a thing] does not depend on the agreement of man's conception [of the thing] with actual nature." Charizi : במה שיאות זה המציאות אל המחשבה ההיא "as far as this actual world agrees with the idea."

[2] In the editions of Ibn Tibbon's Version the order is inverted או מקרה או בכח. The potential infinite is explained below as referring to the divisibility of a thing ad infinitum; it cannot be actually carried out, but is possible in theory.

[3] Ibn Tibbon, משוערים מן המציאות וטמה שכבר נעדר; Charizi, מוסכמות; מוסכמות באלו הם ממה שהוא נמצא ומה שהוא אפס is here used in the sense of "added together;" comp. סכום "number."—It is noteworthy that the potential infinite is not described here.

[4] The Mutakallemim appear to differ essentially from their Greek teachers Democritus and Epicurus. Lucretius in describing their theory of atoms describes the *primordia rerum* as *minima*, indivisible and indestructible, but at the same time as consisting of parts and having size, shape and weight. Comp. Lucretius, " De Rerum Natura," I. 601 *sqq.* :—

Id (extremum cacumen) nimirum sine partibus extat
Et minima constat natura nec fuit unquam

a magnitude, and thus forms a body." If, therefore, two atoms were joined together, each atom would become a body, and they would thus form two bodies, a theory which in fact has been proposed by some Mutakallemim. All these atoms are perfectly alike;[1] they do not differ from each other in any point. The Mutakallemim further assert, that it is impossible to find a body that is not composed of such equal atoms which are placed side by side.[2] According to this view *genesis* and combination are identical; destruction is the same as decomposition. They do not use the term "destruction," for they hold that "genesis"[3] implies composition and decomposition, motion and rest. These atoms, they believe, are not, as was supposed by Epicurus and other Atomists numerically constant in the order of things;[4] but

> Per se secretum neque posthac esse valebit,
> Alterius quoniam ipsum pars, primaque et una.
> Inde aliae atque aliae similes ex ordine partes
> Agmine condenso naturam corporis explent,
> Quae quoniam per se nequeunt constare, necessest
> Haerere unde queunt nulla ratione revelli.

The indivisibility of atoms, according to this theory, does not involve an absence of dimension, but is caused by their great solidity and by the absence of a vacuum within each of them; they are divisible *in potentia*, not in reality. The objection of Maimonides to the atomic theory concerns only the modification it received in the schools of the Mutakallemim, who described the atoms as being without weight, shape and dimensions; the atom can therefore not be called a body, and still the combination or juxtaposition of the atoms forms bodies with dimensions and with other properties of material bodies.

[1] Lit., "similar, alike."

[2] Ibn Tibbon, הרכבת שכנות composition by juxtaposition; Charisi, קרבת מקום. The indestructibility and the indivisibility of the atoms make a chemical combination impossible.

[3] Arabic אכואן (from כון) "the generations" (probably the plural is used because the term is referred to both generation and destruction). Ibn Tibbon renders it הויה (sing.); Charisi (who read אלואן instead of אכואן) יקראו שמם אחים, call them (*i.e.*, generation and destruction) brothers, that is to say, cognate states of existing beings.

[4] ליסת מחצורה פי אלמוגוד "is not limited in the existing things"; Ibn Tibbon (reading probably מחצורה instead of מחצורה), אינם נמצאם מאן, "are not in existence from eternity"; Charisi, אינם נכללים במציאות, "are not comprised among the existing things." In opposition to the ancient

are created anew whenever it pleases the Creator; their annihilation is therefore not impossible. Now I will explain to you their opinion concerning the vacuum.[1]

SECOND PROPOSITION.

On the vacuum. The Radicals [2] also believe that there is a vacuum, *i.e.*, one space, or several spaces [3] which contain nothing, which are not occupied by anything whatsoever, and which are devoid of all substance.[4] This proposition is to them an indispensable sequel to the first. For, if the Universe were full of such atoms, how could any of them move?[5] For it is impossible to conceive that one atom should move into another. And yet the composition, as well as the decomposition of things, can only be effected by the motion of atoms! Thus the Mutakallemim are compelled to assume a vacuum, in order that the atoms may combine, separate, and move in that vacuum which does not contain any thing or any atom.

---

atomists, who held the atoms to be eternal, neither increasing nor decreasing in quantity, the Mutakallemim assumed that the number of the atoms is not constant, the Creator being able at any time to destroy part of them as well as to create new ones.

[1] Arabic, ‏וסאסמעך אראיהם פי עדם אלנוהר‎; Munk, "je vais te faire connaître leurs opinions concernant la privation de la substance." Here ‏עדם‎ (Hebrew ‏העדר‎) is not used in the same sense as in the preceding sentence. Charizi, ‏ועוד אשמיעך סברותם באפיסת העצם‎, "I will again inform you on their opinion concerning the total absence of substance."

[2] Arabic, ‏אלאצוליון‎; Charizi, ‏בעלי העקרים‎; Ibn Tibbon has the explanatory phrase ‏קדמוני המדברים שהיו עיקר חכמת המדברים‎, "the first Mutakallemim who established the doctrine of the Kalām." The simple translation ‏השרשיים‎ seems to have been replaced by the phrase ‏קדמוני וגו'‎ which was originally intended as an explanation. Comp. lxxi., page 284, note 2.

[3] ‏רוחק אחד‎ one distance, a continuous space, space in general, including all existing things; ‏רחקים‎ "spaces," that is, the vacuum between, and the pores within the bodies. The phrase "which contain nothing," etc., applies only to the plural "spaces."

[4] The vacuum is not only without bodies, but contains no indivisible atoms.

[5] Comp. Lucr. *l.c.*—
        Nec tamen undique corpora stipata tenentur
        Omnia natura; namque est in rebus inane.

Third Proposition.

"Time is composed of time-atoms," *i.e.*, of many parts, which on account of their short duration cannot be divided. This proposition also is a logical consequence of the first.[1] The Mutakallemim undoubtedly saw how Aristotle proved that space, time, and locomotion are of the same nature, that is to say, can be divided into parts which stand in the same proportion to each other: if one of them is divided, the other is divided in the same proportion. They, therefore, knew that if time were continuous and divisible *ad infinitum*, their assumed atom of space would of necessity likewise be divisible. Similarly, if it were supposed that space be continuous, it would necessarily follow, that the time-element, which they considered to be indivisible, could also be divided. This has been shown by Aristotle in the treatise called *Acroasis*.[2] Hence they concluded that space was not continuous, but was composed of elements that could not be divided; and that time could likewise be reduced to time-elements, which were indivisible. An hour is, *e.g.*, divided

> Quod si non esset, nulla ratione moveri
> Res possent, namque officium quod corporis extat
> Officere atque obstare, id eis omni tempore adesset
> Omnibus; haud igitur quicquam procedere posset,
> Principium quoniam cedendi nulla daret res.

[1] The admission of atoms—elements that cannot be divided any further—involves the extension of the atomic theory to space, time, and motion, although atoms are described as being without magnitude. For when a body, that is, a system of atoms, moves, each atom changes its position; it leaves the whole space it has occupied, and occupies another space. The way through which each atom moves, therefore, consists of atoms; and time, the measure of motion, is therefore likewise divisible into atoms. It can easily be understood that material bodies may be considered as discrete, so that the atoms of matter are separated from each other by atoms of vacuity, also that motion is discrete, and atoms of motion are separated from each other by atoms of rest; but it is impossible to understand the discontinuity of time and space, or the connection of their discontinuity with their atomicity.

[2] φυσικὴ ἀκρόασις, Arabic אלסמאע אלטביעי; Hebrew, השמע הטבעי. Comp. Arist. Phys. VI., ch. i. *seqq.*

into sixty minutes, the minute into sixty seconds, the second again into sixty parts, and so on; at last after ten or more successive divisions by sixty, time-elements are obtained, which are not subjected to division, and in fact are indivisible, just as is the case with space. Time would thus be an object of position and order.[1]

The Mutakallemim did not at all understand the nature of time. This is a matter of course; for if the greatest philosophers became embarrassed when they investigated the nature of time, if some of them were altogether unable to comprehend what time really is, and even if Galenus declared time to be something divine and incomprehensible, what can be expected of those who do not examine the nature of things?

Now, mark what conclusions were drawn from these three propositions, and were accepted by the Mutakallemim as true. They held that locomotion consisted in the translation of each atom of a body from one point to the next one; accordingly the velocity of one body in motion cannot be greater than that of another body.[2] When, nevertheless, two bodies are observed to move during the same time through different spaces, the cause of this difference is not

---

[1] That is, if time were composed of indivisible particles, it would be like an aggregate of things which can be arranged one by the side of the other. This seems to be the principal argument of Maimonides against the discontinuity of time; and as he does not apply it to space, he appears to hold that discontinuity as regards space is less objectionable than that of time. The reason of this is perhaps the following: the division of a thing into parts, even if it were only in theory, requires that the thing to be divided be present, and its parts co-existing; such a division as regards time is impossible, the chief characteristic of time being succession, and consequently the reverse of co-existence. As time can be represented by dimensions in space, it is not more objectionable to assume atoms of time, than it is to assume atoms of space.

[2] Since every motion is to be resolved into a series of successive motions of single atoms of substance through one atom of space, and as these atoms are supposed to be equal, the velocity of all moving bodies must be the same. In reality different velocities are observed in the moving bodies, and, therefore, the author argues, the atomic theory is to be rejected. The reply given by the atomists is, that the difference is caused by the inequality of the pauses which separate the motion-atoms from each other.

attributed by them to the fact that the body which has moved through a larger distance had a greater velocity, but to the circumstance that motion, which in ordinary language is called slow, has been interrupted by more moments of rest, while the motion which ordinarily is called quick has been interrupted by fewer moments of rest.[1] When it is shown that the motion of an arrow, which is shot from a powerful bow, is in contradiction to their theory, they declare that in this case too the motion is interrupted by moments of rest. They believe that it is the fault of man's senses if it is believed that the arrow moves continuously, for there are many things which cannot be perceived by the senses, as they assert in the twelfth proposition. But we ask them: "Have you observed a complete revolution of a millstone? Each point in the extreme circumference of the stone describes a large circle in the very same time in which a point nearer the centre describes a small circle; the velocity of the outer circle is therefore greater than that of the inner circle. You cannot say that the motion of the latter was interrupted by more moments of rest; for the whole moving body, i.e., the millstone, is one coherent body." They reply, "During the circular motion, the parts of the millstone separate from each other, and the moments of rest interrupting the motion of the portions nearer the centre are more than those which interrupt the motion of the outer portions." We ask again, "How is it that the millstone, which we perceive as one body, and which cannot be easily broken, even with a hammer, resolves into its atoms when it moves, and becomes again one coherent body, returning to its previous state as soon as it comes to rest, while no one is able to notice the

[1] According to the theory of the Mutakallemim, that all motion is to be resolved into atoms, a pause naturally takes place after each atom. The difference could, therefore, not consist in the number of pauses, but in their duration. Either (יותר) אבתר and (מעט) אקל must be understood in the sense of "longer" and "shorter," or the "moments of rest" mentioned here include other interruptions besides those which ordinarily intervene between the motion-atoms.

breaking up [of the stone]?" Again their reply is based on the twelfth proposition, which is to the effect that the perception of the senses cannot be trusted, and thus only the evidence of the intellect is admissible. Do not imagine that you have seen in the foregoing example the most absurd[1] of the inferences which may be drawn from these three propositions: the proposition relating to the existence of a vacuum leads to more preposterous and extravagant conclusions. Nor must you suppose that the aforegoing theory concerning motion is less irrational than the proposition resulting from this theory, that the diagonal of a square is equal to the side of the square,[2] and some of the Mutakallemim go so far as to declare that the square is not a thing of real existence.[3] In short, the adoption of the first proposition would be tantamount to the rejection of all that has been proved in Geometry.[4] The propositions in Geometry would, in this respect, be divided into two classes: some would be absolutely rejected; *e.g.*, those which relate to properties of the incommensurability and the commensurability of lines and planes, to rational[5] and to irrational lines, and all other propositions contained in the tenth book of Euclid, and in similar works. Other propositions would appear to be only partially true; *e.g.*, the solution of the problem to

[1] Ibn Tibbon, סגונה; Charizi, חידוש.

[2] That is, the diagonal of the square contains as many atoms as the side; the space between one atom and the other, measured in the direction of the diagonal, being larger than that in the direction of the sides. If, however, the vacuities and the atoms be added together, the diagonal would of course, be found to be larger than the sides of the square, and the absurdity of the theory would at once be removed.

[3] The sense of this can only be, that the sum of atoms contained in the diagonal of a square is not larger than the sum of atoms in each of its sides, and the diagonal may therefore be considered as equal to a side of the square.

[4] Because all propositions in Geometry are founded upon the continuity of lines and surfaces in space.

[5] מדובקים, in the editions of Ibn Tibbon's version, is a mistake, and should be מדוברים, "rational," as in the MSS., and in the editio princeps. (Munk.) As to the use of דבר in the sense of reason or thought, comp. ch. lxv., pag. 245. MS. Brit. Mus. Add. 14764, has מדוברים, on the margin לא מאוזרים. Charizi has likewise מאוזרים.

divide a line into two equal parts, if the line consists of an odd number of atoms; according to the theory of the Mutakallemim such a line cannot be bisected. Furthermore, in the well-known book of problems by the sons of Shakir [1] are contained more than a hundred problems, all solved and practically demonstrated; but if there really were a vacuum, not one of these problems could be solved, and many of the waterworks [described in that book] could not have been constructed. The refutation of such propositions is a mere waste of time. I will now proceed to treat of the other propositions mentioned above.

Fourth Proposition.

"The accidents of things have real existence; they are elements superadded to the substance itself, and no material thing can be without them."[2] Had this proposition been left by the Mutakallemim in this form it would have been

---

[1] The three sons of Musa Ibn Shakir, called Mo'hammed, A'hmed and al-Hasan, flourished in the ninth century. They favoured the study of Greek literature among the Arabs, and distinguished themselves in mathematics. The book known by the title حِيَل , Artifices (תחבולות), included ingenious inventions, especially concerning hydraulic and pneumatic machines, based on the principle of *horror vacui*.—Munk.

[2] Munk, "Et qu'il n'y a aucun corps qui en soit entièrement exempt; and in a note: c'est à dire que dans chaque corps la substance doit être accompagnée d'un accident quelconque." This cannot be correct, as is apparent from the form which the proposition has in the beginning of this chapter, viz., substance cannot exist without numerous accidents. Also, from the criticism which follows, the Mutakallemim appear to have maintained that none of the properties could be absent from any object, and this would in fact be the sense of the proposition taken literally: "a body cannot be free of one (or of either) of them" (אחדהא, Hebr. מאחד מהם), that is to say, a body cannot be without substance and accidents; and in this form Maimonides would approve of the proposition. (Comp. lxxii., pag. 295, note 3.) But according to the theory of the Mutakallemim, every object has all the properties either positively or negatively, or, considering a property and its opposite as two modifications of the same property, the theory can also be expressed thus: a body must necessarily have all properties either in one or in the other modification. That the absence of a certain property is considered a real property, is the subject of the seventh proposition.

correct, simple, clear, and indisputable.[1] They have, however, gone further, asserting that a substance which has not the attribute of life, must necessarily have that of death; for it must always have one of two contrasting properties. According to their opinion, colour, taste, motion or rest, combination or separation, etc., can be predicated of all substances, and, if a substance have the attribute of life, it must at the same time possess such other kinds of accidents,[2] as wisdom or folly, freewill or the reverse, power or weakness, perception or any of its opposites, and, in short, the substance must have the one or the other of all correlative accidents appertaining to a living being.

Fifth Proposition.

"The atom is fully provided with all these foregoing accidents,[3] and cannot exist if any be wanting."[4] The meaning of this proposition is this: The Mutakallemim say that each of the atoms created by God must have accidents, such as colour, smell, motion, or rest, except the accident of quantity: for according to their opinion[5] an atom has no magnitude;[6] and they do not designate quantity as an accident,[7] nor do they apply to it the laws of accidents. In accordance with this proposition, they do not say, when an accident is noticed in a body, that it is peculiar to the body as such, but that it exists in each of the atoms which

[1] Charizi adds ולא דמיון, "nor a mere imagination." The proposition in its entirety is rejected by the author as a mere fiction.
[2] Charizi has simply מקרים אחרים, "some other accidents."
[3] See *supra*, page 310, note 3.
[4] That is, no change takes place in the properties of the atom when they combine to form a body; hence all the properties noticed in the aggregate of atoms exist also in each of them individually. There is no property in a body which is solely due to the constitution of the whole body.
[5] אצלם in the Hebrew version before לא יקראהו, is superfluous; it has no equivalent in the Arabic text.
[6] See *supra*, page 311, note 4.
[7] Quantity is only a form of thought, not a real property possessed by the object.

form the constituent elements of that body. *E.g.*, take a quantity of snow; the whiteness does not exist in that quantity as a whole, but each atom of the snow is white, and therefore the aggregate of those atoms is likewise white. Similarly they say that when a body moves, each atom of it moves, and thus the whole body is in motion.[1] Life likewise exists, according to their view, in each atom of a living body. The same is the case according to their opinion with the senses; in each atom of the aggregate they notice the faculty of perception. Life, sensation, intellect, and wisdom are considered by them as accidents, like blackness and whiteness, as will be shown in the further discussion of their theory.[2]

Concerning the soul, they do not agree. The view most predominant[3] among them is the following:—The soul is an accident existing in one of the atoms of which, *e.g.*, man is composed; the aggregate is called a being endowed with a soul, in so far as it includes that atom. Others are of opinion that the soul[4] is composed of ethereal atoms,[5] which have a peculiar faculty by virtue of which they constitute the soul, and that these atoms are mixed with the atoms of the body. Consequently they[6] maintain that the soul is an accident.[7]

As to the intellect, I found that all of them agreed in

---

[1] See *supra*, page 315, note 2. 　　　[2] See Proposition VIII.

[3] Arab. אנלב אקואלהם. Ibn Tibbon, החזק שבדבריהם; Charizi, וכלל דבריהם.

[4] The word נסם, found in most of the MSS., has been omitted by Charizi and Ibn Tibbon. (Munk.)

[5] Charizi, כחות; and כחות ועצמים below.

[6] *I.e.*, the Mutakallemim, both those who adhere to the first, and those who follow the second opinion concerning the soul.

[7] That is, even according to the second theory, according to which the soul consists of atoms, different from the atoms of the body, the substance of the soul is a certain property of those atoms. The soul, therefore, or the essence of the soul (Hebr. ענין הנפש), is a property. "All agree that the soul is a property; some of them hold that it is a property in all the atoms of the body, while others assume that it is a property only in one atom, or in some of the atoms."—Caspi.

considering it to be an accident joined to one of the atoms which constitute the whole of the intelligent being. But there is a confusion among them about knowledge; they are uncertain whether it is an accident to each of the atoms which form the knowing aggregate, or whether it belongs only to one atom. Both views can be disproved by a *reductio ad absurdum*, when the following facts are pointed out to them. Generally metals and stones have a special colour, which is strongly pronounced, but disappears when they are pulverised. Vitriol, which is intensely green, becomes white dust when pounded;[1] this shows that that accident exists only in the aggregate, not in the atoms. This is more striking in the following instance: when parts of a living being are cut off they cease to live, a proof that the accident [of life] belongs to the aggregate of the living being, not to each atom. In order to meet this objection they say that the accident is of no duration, but is constantly renewed. In discussing the next proposition I shall explain their view on this subject.

Sixth Proposition.

"The accidents do not exist during two time-atoms."—The sense of this proposition is this: They believe that God creates a substance, and simultaneously its accidents; that the Creator is incapable of creating a substance devoid of an accident, for that is impossible;[2] that the essential characteristic of an accident is its incapability of enduring for two periods, for two time-atoms; that immediately after its creation it is utterly destroyed,[3] and another accident of the same kind is created; this again is destroyed and a third

---

[1] Charizi, במצאנו המחצבים והאבנים כי רובם היו בעלי צבע ירוק מאד ונעשה אבק לבן כשנשחק; this corresponds with the Arabic in Cod. Oxf. (Sheyer, *ad locum*).

[2] That is to say, man cannot imagine substance without accidents, and, therefore, it cannot exist in reality. See Proposition X.

[3] Lit., "it is lost and does not remain."

accident of the same kind is created, and so on, so long as God is pleased to preserve [in that substance] this kind of accident; but He can at His will create in the same substance an accident of a different kind, and if He were to discontinue the creation and not produce a new accident, that substance would at once cease to exist. This is one of the opinions held by the Mutakallemim; it has been accepted by most of them, and it is the so-called "theory[1] of the creation of the accidents." Some of them, however, and they belong to the sect of the Mu'tazilah, say, that there are accidents which endure for a certain period, and other accidents which do not endure for two atoms of time; they do not follow a fixed principle in deciding which class of accidents has and which class has not a certain duration. The object of this proposition is to oppose the theory that there exists a natural force[2] from which each body derives its peculiar properties. They prefer to assume that God himself creates these properties without the intervention of a natural force or of any other agency: a theory which implies that no accident can have any duration. For suppose that certain accidents could endure for a certain period and then cease to exist, the question would naturally be asked, What is the cause of that non-existence?[3] They would

---

[1] Arabic, בֹּלק אלאעראץ אלתי יקלונהא. Ibn Tibbon, בריאת המקרים אשר יאמרו אותה. The fem. suffix הא in the Arabic, agrees with אלאעראץ; according to the sense, a suffix agreeing with בלק is required; so in Hebrew אותה agrees with בריאת (Charizi omits the suffix altogether). It is possible that Maimonides had a form בֹלקה similar to the Hebrew בריאה.

[2] See lxxi., page 281 and page 284.

[3] That is to say, the creation of an accident, a momentary act, causes the accident to exist an atom, that is as an indefinite portion, of time; its existence in the next moment depends on the repetition of that act; if the act is not repeated, the accident is *eo ipso* not in existence. If a thing were supposed to continue for some time, as the result of *one* creative act, the cause of its non-continuance after that time, could not be supposed to be only the non-repetition of the creative act, but would result either from some positive act of destruction—and this according to the view of the Mutakallemim is inadmissible in the Creator, who is constantly creating—or from some natural property of

not be satisfied with the reply that God by His will brought about this non-existence, because an *agens* does not cause non-existence, and non-existence does not at all require any *agens* whatever; for as soon as the *agens* leaves off acting, the product of the *agens* ceases likewise to exist. This is true to some extent. Having thus chosen [1] to establish the theory that there does not exist any natural force upon which the existence or non-existence of a thing depends, they were compelled to assume that the properties of things were successively renewed. When God desires to deprive a thing of its existence, He, according to some of the Mutakallemim, discontinues the creation of its accidents, and *eo ipso* the body ceases to exist.[2] Others, however, say, that if it pleased the Almighty to destroy the world, He would create the accident of des-

---

the thing, which contingency is equally denied by them. The state of non-possession of a certain property (העדר), which according to Proposition VII. requires the action of the Creator for its existence, is considered by that school as a real property; here the author speaks of the disappearance of a property, and this requires no positive act of the Creator. This distinction between the act of destroying a property (Proposition VI.), and the creation of a negative property (Proposition VII.), appears to have been misunderstood by Caspi, and other commentators who followed him; for he says "they (who accept this proposition) do not accept Proposition VII." This cannot be right, as Maimonides introduces these Propositions as having been accepted by all the Mutakallemim, however different their views might have been on other points. Comp. Munk *ad locum.*

[1] That is, the successive creation of the accidents has not been accepted on account of its own intrinsic truth, but as a consequence of the principle accepted arbitrarily without proof (ברצונם), viz. that everything is done directly by the Creator, without the agency of natural forces.

[2] This sentence can only have the following meaning: as soon as God discontinues the creation of the accidents of the Universe, the Universe ceases to exist. The non-existence of the Universe according to the first-mentioned opinion is not a state that requires the action of the Creator for its continuance, because there is no substance; according to the second opinion it is subject to the same law as other negative properties, and must be continually renewed. Compare the objection of the author to the theory of the repeated creation of "death" in Proposition VII. It need scarcely be added that this view is most absurd, as has been shown by Ibn Roshd in his "Destruction of Destruction," second question. See Munk, *ad locum.*

truction, which would be without any substratum. The destruction of the Universe would be the correlative accident to that of existence.—In accordance with this [sixth] proposition they say, that the cloth which according to our belief we dyed red, has not been dyed by us at all, but God created that colour in the cloth when it came into contact with the red pigment; we believe that colour to have penetrated into the cloth, but they assert that this is not the case. They[1] say that God generally acts in such a way,[2] that, e.g., the black colour[3] is not created unless the cloth is brought into contact with indigo; but this blackness, which God creates in the instant when the cloth touches the black pigment is of no duration, and another creation of blackness then takes place; they further say that after the blackness is gone, He does not create a red or green colour, but again a black colour.

According to this principle, the knowledge which we have of certain things to-day, is not the same which we had of them yesterday; that knowledge is gone, and another like it has been created. They positively believe

[1] Ibn Tibbon here adds the words ולא זו בלבד אמרו אבל אמרו גם כן "and not only this they said, but they also asserted." The corresponding words in Arabic ולים הדא קאלוא פקט בל קאלוא are found in the text of a Leyden MS. (Munk.)

[2] The following objection was made to their theory: If God created the accident every moment independently of any natural law, why is a certain means required to produce that colour? Does this not prove that a certain colour is produced by properties which are contained in the materials employed for that purpose? The answer to this objection is simply that God does it regularly in this way (without being forced by any law or property); He could do it otherwise, but it is His will to do it always in this particular way. עאדה (Heb. מנהג) is here not used in the sense of custom or habit, a property acquired by repeating frequently the same thing, but merely in the sense of "an act regularly repeated." Too much stress has been laid on the literal meaning of this term by Ibn Roshd (quoted by Palquera, Caspi and others) in his objections to the theory of the Mutakallemim.

[3] נילוג (Ibn Tibbon איסטיס, in the version of Charizi explained by בל״ע אינדי) is "indigo," and its colour is blue; it is called "black," because the Mutakallemim only counted five colours: black, white, red, yellow, and green, and considered blue as a modification of black. See Munk.

that this does take place,[1] knowledge being an accident. In like manner it would follow that the soul, according to those who believe that it is an accident, is renewed each moment in every animated being, say a hundred thousand times; for, as you know, time is composed of time-atoms. In accordance with this principle they assert that when man is perceived to move a pen, it is not he who has really moved it; the motion produced in the pen, is an accident which God has created in the pen; the apparent motion of the hand which moves the pen is likewise an accident which God has created in the moving[2] hand; but the creative act of God is performed in such a manner that the motion of the hand and the motion of the pen follow each other closely; but the hand does not act,[3] and is not the cause of the pen's motion; for, as they say, an accident cannot pass from one thing to another.[4] Some of the Mutakallemim accordingly contend that this white cloth, which is coloured when put into the vessel filled with indigo, has not been blackened by the indigo; for blackness being an attribute of indigo, does not pass from one object to another. There does not exist any thing to which an action could be ascribed; the real[5] *agens* is God, and He has [in the foregoing instance] created the blackness in the substance of the cloth when it came into contact with the indigo, for this is the method adopted by Him. In short, most of the Mutakallemim believe that it must never be said that one thing is the cause of another; some of them who assumed causality were blamed for doing so. As regards, however, the acts of man their opinions are divided. Most of them, especially the sect of the Asha'ariyah, assume that when the pen is set in motion God has created four accidents, none of which is the

[1] Charizi omits this phrase.
[2] Ibn Tibbon המניע, "that moves" (trans.)
[3] Ibn Tibbon מעשה; Charizi יתרון.
[4] Charizi מקומו. The accident "of motion" possessed by the hand is not of a transitive character, and has no part in the motion of the pen.
[5] Lit., "the last." The expression, however, is inexact after the assertion that there does not exist anything to which an action could be ascribed.

cause of any of the rest, they are only related to each other as regards the time of their co-existence, and have no other relation to each other. The first accident is man's[1] will to move the pen, the second is man's power[1] to do so,[2] the third is the bodily motion itself, *i.e.*, the motion of the hand, and the fourth is the motion of the pen. They believe that when a man has the will to do a thing and, as he believes, does it, the will has been created for him, then the power to conform to the will, and lastly the act itself. The act is not accomplished by the power created in man; for, in reality, no act can be ascribed to that power. The Mu'tazilah contend that man acts by virtue of the power which has been created in him.[3] Some of the Asha'ariyah assert that the power created in man participates in the act, and is connected with it,[4] an opinion which has been rejected by the majority. The will and the power created in man, according to the concurrent belief of the Mutakallemim, together with the act created in him, according to some of them, are accidents without duration. In the instance of the pen, God continually creates one motion after the other so long as the pen is in motion; it only then ceases to move when God has created in it the accident of rest; and so long as the pen is at rest, God continually renews in it that accident. Consequently in every one of these moments, *i.e.*, of the time-atoms, God creates some accident in every existing individual, *e.g.*, in the angels, in the spheres and in other things; this creation takes place continually and without interruption. Such is, according to their opinion, the right interpretation of the creed that God is the *causa efficiens*. But I, together with all rational

[1] In the Arabic, 'אראדתי, קדרתי, "my will," "my power." Ibn Tibbon and Charizi have the third person (יכלתו רצונו) instead of the first.

[2] It is difficult to see why "the power to do so" is introduced; according to the theory under consideration, it can never be ascertained whether man possesses the power, the ultimate action being independent of that power.

[3] They hold that man has a free will. See lxxi., page 275, note 5.

[4] This is perhaps the same view as expressed above, ch. li., page 176, by the words "man has no freedom at all, but has acquirement" (קנין).

persons, apply to those theories the words, "Will you mock at Him, as you mock at man?" for they are indeed nothing but mockery.

Seventh Proposition.

"The absence of a property is itself a property that exists in the body,[1] a something superadded to its substance, an actual accident, which is constantly renewed; as soon as it is destroyed it is reproduced." The reason why they hold this opinion is this: they do not understand that rest is the absence of motion; death the absence of life; that blindness is the absence of sight, and that all similar negative properties are the absence of the positive correlatives. The relation between motion and rest is, according to their theory, the same as the relation between heat and cold, namely, as heat and cold are two accidents found in two objects which have the properties of heat and cold, so motion is an accident created in the thing which moves, and rest an accident created in the thing which rests; it does not remain in existence during two consecutive time-atoms, as we have stated in treating of the previous proposition. Accordingly, when a body is at rest, God has created the rest in each atom of that body, and so long as the body remains at rest, God continually renews that property. The same, they believe, is the case with a man's wisdom and ignorance; the latter is considered by them as an actual accident, which is subject to the constant changes of destruction and creation, so long as there remains a thing of which such a man is ignorant. Death and life are likewise accidents, and as the Mutakallemim distinctly state, life is constantly destroyed and renewed during the whole existence of a living being; when God decrees its death, He creates in it the accident of death after the accident of life, which does not continue during two time-atoms, has ceased to exist. All this they state clearly.

[1] Comp. Propos. IV.

The logical consequence of this proposition is that the accident of death created by God instantly ceases to exist, and is replaced by another death which again is created by God; otherwise death could not continue. Death is thus continually created in the same manner as life is renewed every moment. But I should wish to know how long God continues to create death in a dead body. Does He do so whilst the form remains, or whilst one of the atoms exists? For in each of the atoms of the body the accident of death which God creates is produced, and there are to be found teeth of persons who died thousands of years ago; we see that those teeth have not been deprived of existence, and therefore the accident of death has during all these thousands of years been renewed, and according to the opinion prevailing amongst those theorists, death was continually replaced by death. Some of the Mu'tazilah hold that there are cases in which the absence of a physical property[1] is not a real property, that weariness is the absence of strength, and ignorance the absence of knowledge; but this cannot be said in every case of negative[2] properties: it cannot be said that darkness is the mere absence of light, or that rest is the absence of motion. Some negative properties are thus considered by them as having a real existence, while other negative properties are considered as non-existing, just as suits their belief. Here they proceed in the same manner as they proceed respecting the duration of accidents, and they contend that some accidents exist a long time, and other accidents do not last two time-atoms. Their sole object is to fashion the Universe according to their peculiar opinions and beliefs.

[1] הענינים הטבעיים in the editions of Ibn Tibbon's version is a mistake: the MSS. have הקנינים. (Munk.)

[2] That is, according to the general belief; the Mutakallemim would not consider them as negative, but as positive properties.

Eighth Proposition.

"There exists nothing but substance and accident, and the physical forms of things belong to the class of accidents."[1] It is the object of this proposition to show that all bodies are composed of similar atoms, as we have pointed out in explaining the first proposition. The difference of bodies from each other is caused by the accidents, and by nothing else. Animality, humanity, sensibility, and speech, are denoted as accidents like blackness, whiteness, bitterness, and sweetness, and the difference between two individuals of two classes is the same as the difference of two individuals of the same class. Also the body of the heaven,[2] the body of the angels, the body of the Divine Throne—such as it is assumed to be[3]—the body of anything creeping on the earth, and the body of any plant, have one and the same substance; they only differ in the peculiarity of the accidents, and in nothing else; the substance of all things is made up of equal atoms.

Ninth Proposition.

"None of the accidents form the substratum of another accident; it cannot be said, This is an accident to a thing which is itself an accident to a substance. All accidents are directly connected with the substance." The Mutakallemim deny the indirect relation of the accident to the substance, because if such a relation were assumed it would follow that the second accident could only exist in the substance after another accident had preceded it, a conclusion

---

[1] Comp. pag. 310, note 5.

[2] Charisi renders בל wrongly by אבל instead of גם or אף.

[3] That is, as the הכבוד כסא is generally conceived to be, not as it is in reality. Charisi wrongly: ונוף מי שיעלה על לב.

to which they would object even with regard to some special accidents;[1] they prefer to show that these accidents[2] can exist in every possible substance, although such substance is not determined by any other accident; for they hold that all the accidents collectively determine the thing. They advance also another proof [in support of this proposition], namely: The substratum which is the bearer of certain attributes must continue to exist for a certain time; how, then, could the accident, which—according to their opinion—does not remain in existence for two moments, become the substratum of something else?

Tenth Proposition.

This proposition concerns the theory of "admissibility,"[3] which is mentioned by the Mutakallemim, and forms the principal support of their doctrine. Mark its purport: they observe that everything conceived by the imagination is admitted by the intellect as possible; e.g., that the terrestrial globe should become the all-encompassing sphere, or that this sphere should become the terrestrial globe; reason does not find here an impossibility; or that the sphere of fire should move towards the centre, and the sphere of earth towards the circumference.[4] Human intellect does not perceive any reason why a body should be in a certain place

---

[1] Lit., "they deny this (to be the case) in some of the accidents," that is, in those concerning which the philosophers believe that they have other accidents for their substratum, e.g., time an accident of motion, which is an accident of the thing that moves.

[2] Lit., "some accidents," that is, the accidents in question; for, in reality, the Mutakallemim endeavour to show that *all* accidents unite with every substance.

[3] The Arabic אלתגויז (Hebr. העברה) is derived from גוז, "to let pass," "to declare as admissible," and signifies the theory of the Mutakallemim, according to which reason must accept as admissible everything which can be imagined, so that the only test to find out whether a thing is possible or not, is man's imagination. The nature and the properties of things (צורה טבעית) are altogether ignored by them.

[4] See ch. lxxii., pag. 290.

PART I.—CHAPTER LXXIII. 331

instead of being in another. In the same manner they say[1] that reason admits the possibility that an existing being should be larger or smaller than it really is, or that it should be different in form and position from what it really is; e.g., a man might have the height of a mountain, might have several heads, and fly[2] in the air; or an elephant might be as small as an insect, or an insect as huge as an elephant. This method of admitting possibilities is applied to the whole Universe. Whenever they affirm that a thing belongs to this class of admitted possibilities, they say that it can have this form, and that it is also possible that it be found differently, and that the one form is not more possible than the other; but they do not ask whether the reality confirms their assumption.[3] They say that the thing which exists with[4] certain constant and permanent forms, dimensions, and properties, only follows the direction of habit,[5] just as[6] the king generally[5] rides on horseback through the streets of the city, and is never found departing from this habit; but reason does not find it impossible that he should walk on foot through the place; there is no doubt that he may do so, and this possibility is fully admitted by the intellect. Similarly, the earth moves towards the centre, the fire turns away from the centre; the fire causes heat, the water causes cold, in accordance with a certain habit; but it is logically not impossible that a deviation from this habit should occur, namely, that fire should cause cold, move downward, and still be fire; that the water should cause heat, move up-

[1] קאלוא without any conjunction (Ibn Tibbon, אמרו) appears to be quite superfluous. It has been omitted by Charizi.

[2] יטפו and טף'; Ibn Tibbon, יפרח, "to fly;" Charizi, ישום, "to swim."

[3] Charizi, מה שיאות וגו', "what part of their assertions harmonises with the existing order of things;" Ibn Tibbon, שווי המציאות, "to the equality between the existing things and their own assertions."

[4] Charizi, יש לו, "has"; the relative in the Arabic and in the Version of Ibn Tibbon makes the construction of the sentence irregular.

[5] See supra, pag. 324, note 2.

[6] Charizi, כי כן; Ibn Tibbon, אמנם היותה כך הוא כפי המשך המנהג כמו ש...

ward, and still be water. On this foundation their whole fabric was constructed. They admit, however, the impossibility of two opposite properties coexisting at the same time in one substance.[1] This is impossible; reason would not admit this possibility. Again, reason does not admit the possibility of a substance existing without an accident, or an accident existing without a substance, a possibility admitted by some of the Mutakallemim.[2] It is also impossible that a substance should become an accident, that an accident should become a substance, or that one substance should penetrate another. They admit that reason rejects all these things as impossible. It is perfectly true that no notion whatever can be formed of those things which they describe as impossible; whilst a notion can be formed of those things which they consider as possible. The philosophers object to this method, and say, You call a thing impossible because it cannot be imagined, or possible because it can be imagined; and thus you consider as possible that which is found possible by imagination, not by the intellect, consequently you determine that a thing is necessary, possible, or impossible in some instances, by the aid of the imagination—not by the intellect—and in other instances by the ordinary common sense,[3] as Abu Nasr[4] says in speaking of that which the Mutakallemim call intellect. It is clear that they describe as possible that which can be imagined, whether the reality correspond to it or not,[5] and as impossible that which cannot be imagined. This proposition can only be established by the nine aforementioned propositions, and no doubt these were exclusively required for the support of this proposition. This you will see clearly when I

[1] That is, they reject all logical impossibilities.
[2] See *supra*, pag. 323, note 2.
[3] Charizi adds ופעם בשכל, "and sometimes by reason." This is a mistake, for the author repeatedly declares that they do not test the possibility of a thing by a process based on logical truths.
[4] See Munk, "Mélanges de Philosophie Juive et Arabe," pag. 341 *sqq*., and below, end of ch. lxxiv.
[5] See lxxi., pag. 282, and end of ch. lxviii.

shall show and explain to you some important[1] parts of this theory, which I shall now introduce in the form of a discussion supposed to have taken place between a Mutakallem and a philosopher.

The Mutakallem said to the philosopher: What is the reason that we find the substance of iron extremely hard and strong, with a dark colour; the substance of cream, on the other hand, extremely soft and white? The philosopher replied as follows: All physical bodies have two kinds of accidents: those which concern their substance, as, *e. g.*, the health and the illness of a man; and those which concern their form, as, *e.g.*, the astonishment and laughter of a man.[2] The substances of compound bodies differ very much in their ultimate form,[3] according to the difference of the forms peculiar to each component substance. Hence the substance of iron has become in its properties the opposite of the substance of cream, and this difference is attended by the difference of accidents. You notice, therefore, hardness in the one, and softness in the other: two accidents, whose difference results from the difference which exists in the forms of the substances; while the darkness and the whiteness are accidents whose divergence corresponds to that of the two substances in their ultimate condition. The Mutakallem refuted this reply by means of his propositions, as I am now going to state:—There does not exist a form which, as you believe, modifies the substance, and thus causes substances to be different from each other; this difference is exclusively effected by the accidents—according to the theory of the Kalām, which we mentioned in explaining the eighth proposition. He then continued thus: There is no difference between the substance of iron and that of cream; all things are composed of the same kind of atoms.—We explained

[1] Charizi, מסתרי "the secrets;" Shem-tob, מצפוני.

[2] Health and disease concern the body of man; while surprise and laughter concern that element which is the characteristic (צורה) of man, his soul.

[3] The "ultimate form" of a thing is the form and the condition in which the thing is noticed by man; and the substance of that composition (חומר האחרון) is the same as החומר הקרוב. See page 18, note 1.

the view of the Mutakallemim on this point in treating of the first proposition, the logical consequences of which are, as we have shown, the second and the third propositions; they further require the twelfth proposition, in order to establish the theory of atoms. Nor do they admit that any accidents determine the nature of a substance, or predispose it to receive certain other accidents; for, according to their opinion, an accident cannot be the substratum of another accident, as we have shown in explaining the ninth proposition; nor can it have any duration, according to the sixth proposition. When the Mutakallemim have established all that they wish to infer from these propositions, they arrive at the conclusion[1] that the component atoms of cream and of iron are alike.—The relation of each atom to each of the accidents is the same; one atom is not more adapted than another to receive a certain accident; and as a certain atom is not more fitted to move than to rest, so[2] one atom is not more apt than another to receive the accident of life, of reason, of sensation. It is here of no moment whether a thing contains a larger or smaller quantity of atoms, for, according to the view of the Mutakallemim, which we explained in treating of the fifth proposition, every accident [of a thing] exists in each of its atoms. All these propositions lead to the conclusion that a human being is not better constituted to become wise than the bat,[3] and establish the theory of admissibility expressed in this [tenth] proposition. Every effort was made to demonstrate this proposition, because it is the best means for proving anything they like, as will be explained.

NOTE.—Mark, O reader, that if you know the nature of the soul and its properties, and if you have a correct notion of everything which concerns the soul, you will observe that most animals possess imagination. As to the higher

[1] Charizi, והיה המתברר לנו.
[2] Ibn Tibbon, כי, "for."
[3] Arabic, אלכנפס; Ibn Tibbon, העטלף; Charizi and Palquera, השרץ. Palquera suggests that Ibn Tibbon perhaps had the reading עטלף = אלבמאש.

PART I.—CHAPTER LXXIII.

class of animals, that is, those which have a heart, it is obvious that they have imagination.[1] Man's distinction does not consist in the possession of imagination, and the action of imagination is not the same as the action of the intellect, but the reverse of it.[2] For the intellect analyses and divides the component parts of things, it forms abstract ideas of them, represents them in their true form as well as in their causal relations, derives from one object a great many facts, which—for this intellect—totally differ from each other, just as two human individuals appear different to the imagination; it distinguishes that which is the property of the *genus* from that which is peculiar to the individual,—and no proof is correct, unless founded on the former;[3] the intellect further determines whether certain qualities of a thing are essential or non-essential. Imagination has none of these functions. It only perceives the individual, the compound in that aggregate condition in which it presents itself to the senses; or it combines things which exist[4] separately, joins some of them together, and represents them all as one body or as a force of the body. Hence it is that some imagine a man with a horse's head, with wings, etc. This is called a fiction, a phantasm; it is

---

[1] Comp. Maimon. Eight Chapters, i.; Aristotle, Περί ψυχῆς. chap. iii., τῶν δὲ θηρίων ἐνίοις φαντασία μὲν ὑπάρχει, λόγος δ' οὔ.—ibid. ii. 3. οἷς δ' ἐκείνων ἕκαστον, οὐ πᾶσι λογισμός, ἀλλὰ τοῖς μὲν οὐδὲ φαντασία, τὰ δὲ ταύτῃ μόνῃ ζῶσιν. Essays on Ibn Ezra, by M. Friedländer, pag. 27, note 2.

[2] Three characteristic actions of the intellect, as distinguished from imagination, are here mentioned:—1. Analysis of the things perceived by the senses; 2. Abstraction and Generalisation; 3. Classification of the Attributes of things as essential and non-essential. Imagination reproduces the things as they represent themselves to the senses of man, in their individuality and totality, either each by itself, or several things combined.

[3] A proof, being a purely intellectual operation, requires for its *data* purely intellectual notions; such are conveyed by generic terms, or abstract expressions which denote the sum of the properties common to all individuals of the same class.

[4] The words פ' אלונוד (Hebr. במציאות) have no equivalent in the translation of Munk; they have been omitted by Shemtob, Efodi, etc., in their paraphrases of this passage. Charizi, בעת עבור המחשבה במציאות.

a thing to which nothing in the actual world corresponds. Nor can imagination in any way[1] obtain a purely immaterial image of an object, however abstract the form of the image may be.[2] Imagination yields therefore no test for the reality of a thing.

Hear what profit we derive from the preliminary disciplines, and how excellent the propositions are which we learn through them. Know that there are certain things, which would appear impossible, if tested by man's imagination, being as inconceivable as the co-existence of two opposite properties in one object; yet the existence of those same things, which cannot be represented by imagination, is nevertheless established by proof, and attested by their reality. *E.g.*, Imagine a large globe, of any magnitude you like, even as large as the all-encompassing sphere; further an axis passing through the centre, and two persons standing on the two extremities of the axis in such a manner that their feet are in the same straight line with the axis, which may be either parallel to the equator or not; in the first case both persons would fall, in the second case one, namely the one who stands on the lower extremity would fall, the other would remain standing, as far as our imagination can perceive. It has, however, already been proved that the earth has the form of a globe, that[3] it is inhabited on both extremities of a certain diameter, that both the inhabitants have their heads towards the heaven, and their legs towards each other, and yet neither of them falls nor do we ever suppose[4] that they fall; for it is incorrect to say that the one

[1] The words להשיג הדבר הכללי "to perceive that which belongs to the *genus*," which are found in the several editions of Ibn Tibbon, are superfluous; they are not found in the *ed. princeps* nor in the MSS. (Munk.)

[2] That is, the most abstract form that can be produced by man's imagination.

[3] ושמוה in Ibn Tibbon's version is a corruption of ושמן. (Munk.)

[4] That is to say, we are so familiar with the fact that there are antipodes on this earth, and that their relative position to the sky is exactly the same as of those beings who exist on the opposite side of the globe, that we cannot even conceive the idea (לא יצוייר) how a thing can fall *down* from the earth

extremity is above, the other below; but the terms "above" and "below" apply to both of them as regards their relative position to each other. Similarly it has been proved in the second chapter of the book on Conic Sections,[1] that two lines, which at first are at a certain distance from each other, may approach each other[2] in the same proportion as they are produced further, and yet would never meet, even if they were produced to infinity, although they are observed to be constantly converging. This is a fact which cannot easily be conceived, and which does not come within the scope of imagination. Of these two lines the one is straight, the other curved,[3] as stated in the aforementioned book. It has consequently been proved that things which cannot be perceived or imagined, and which would be found impossible if tested solely by imagination, are nevertheless in real existence. The non-existence of things which are represented by imagination as possible has likewise been established by proof, *e.g.*, the corporeality of God, and His existence as a force residing in a body. Imagination perceives nothing except bodies, or properties inherent in bodies.

It has thus been clearly shown that in man exists a certain faculty which is entirely distinct from imagination, and by which the necessary, the possible, and the impossible can be distinguished from each other. This inquiry is most useful. It is of the greatest profit to him who desires to guard himself against the errors of men guided by imagination!

---

towards the sky, although in reference to other globes it could not be imagined (לא יציירם כלל) how two objects placed on the two extremities of a diameter could both remain in their positions.—Ibn Caspi explains the phrase לא יצויר בשכל and distinguishes it from לא יציירם בדמיון.

[1] Κωνικὰ στοιχεῖα (Conic Sections) of Apollonius; in Arabic Kitab al-mahrutāt (Book II. Theorem 13). (Munk.) Ibn Tibbon, חרוטים; Charizi, מצוקים חרוחים.

[2] Lit., "Their distance becomes smaller and they approach each other."

[3] The author alludes to the asymptotes of the hyperbola; they approach nearer the curve the more they are produced, but they can never touch it.—This sentence should follow immediately after the words "to be constantly converging."

Do not think that the Mutakallemim ignore this altogether; to some extent they do take it into consideration; they know it, and call that which can be imagined without having reality—as, *e.g.*, the corporeality of God—a phantom and a fancy;[1] they state frequently that such phantoms are not real. It is for this reason that they advance the first nine propositions and establish on them the proof of the tenth, according to which all those imaginable things which they wish to admit as possible are really possible, because of the similarity of all atoms and the equality of all accidents as regards their accidentality, as we have explained.

Consider, O reader, and bear in mind that this requires deep research. For there are certain notions which some believe to be founded on reason, while others regard them as mere fictions. In such cases it would be necessary to find something that could show the difference between conceptions of the intellect and mere imaginary fancies. When the philosopher, in his way of expressing himself, contends, "Reality is my evidence; by its guidance I examine whether a thing is necessary, possible, or impossible," the religionist replies, "This is exactly the difference between us; that which actually exists, has, according to my view, been produced by the will of the Creator, not by necessity; just as it has been created with that special property, it might have been created with any other property, unless the impossibility which you postulate be proved by a logical demonstration."

About this admissibility (of imaginable things) I shall have to say more, and I shall return to it in various parts

---

[1] The Arabic text has והמא וכיאלא; Charizi, שקר, "falsehood;" Ibn Tibbon, לא דמיון. The words עולה על רוח מחשבה לא דמיון, "but not an image," have probably been added to make it clearer that the Mutakallemim meant something different from "imagination," although the term כיאלא is used, which is generally translated by דמיון. Munk suggests that דמיון is a variation of מחשבה and that לא = ליא = אחר, לשון, as is found in several manuscripts. As to the use of מחשבה in the sense of דמיון, see pag. 111, notes 1 and 2.

PART I.—CHAPTER LXXIII.   339

of this treatise; for it is not a subject which should be rejected in haste[1] and on the spur of the moment.

ELEVENTH PROPOSITION.

"The existence of the infinite is in every respect impossible." The following is an explanation of this proposition. The impossibility of the existence of an infinite body has been clearly demonstrated; the same can be said of an infinite number of bodies, though each of them be finite, if these beings, infinite in number, exist at the same time;[2] equally impossible is the existence of an infinite series of causes, namely, that a certain thing should be the cause of another thing, but itself the effect of another cause, which again is the result of another cause, and so on to infinity, or that things in an infinite series, either bodies or ideals, should be in actual[3] existence, and in causal relation to each other. This causal relation is the essential order of nature, in which, as has been fully proved, the infinite is impossible. As regards the virtual and the accidental[4] existence of the infinite, it has been established in some cases; it has been proved, *e.g.* that a body can virtually be divided *ad infinitum*, also that time can be divided *ad infinitum*; in other cases it is still an open question, as *e.g.* the existence of the infinite[5] in succession, which is called the accidental infinite, *i.e.*, a series of things in which one thing comes forth when the other is gone, and this again in its turn succeeded a thing

---

[1] The word פתאום in the editions of Ibn Tibbon's Version is superfluous; it is not found in the MSS. (Munk.)

[2] See Part II., Introd., Propositions i., ii. and iii.

[3] That is to say, that all these causes really coexist.

[4] אלא in Charizi's Version is superfluous. The division of any magnitude or of time *ad infinitum* is said to be infinite *in potentia*, בכח, because the actual division arrives at last at a point where it cannot be continued, though, theoretically, the continued division is possible. The successive repetition of a magnitude *ad infinitum* is said to be infinite by accident, במקרה, because the repetition is not *necessarily* included in the nature of the magnitude.

[5] אלא במקרה in Ibn Tibbon's Version is superfluous.

which had ceased to exist, and so on *ad infinitum*. This subject requires deep research.

Those who boast that they have proved the eternity of the Universe say that time is infinite ; an assertion which is not necessarily erroneous; for only when one atom has ceased to exist, the other follows. Nor is it absolutely wrong, when they assert, that the accidents of the substance succeed each other in an infinite series, for these accidents do not co-exist, but come in succession one after the other, and the impossibility of the infinite in that case has not been proved.[1] The Mutakallemim, however, make no difference between the existence of an infinite body and the divisibility of a body or of time *ad infinitum*, between the co-existence of an infinite number of things, as *e.g.* the individual human beings who exist at present, and the infinite number of beings successively existing, as, *e.g.*, Reuben the son of Jacob, and Jacob the son of Isaac, and Isaac the son of Abraham,[2] and so on to infinity. This is according to their opinion as inadmissible as the first case; they believe these four forms of the infinite[3] to be quite equal. Some of the Mutakallemim endeavour to establish their proposition concerning the last named form of the infinite, and to demonstrate its impossibility by a method which I shall explain in this treatise;[4] others say that this impossibility is a self-evident axiom and requires no further proof. But if it were undoubtedly wrong to assume that an infinite number of things can exist in succession, although that link of the series which exists at present is finite, the inadmissibility of the eternity of the Universe would be equally self-evident, and would not require for its proof any other proposition. This, however, is not the place for investigating the subject.

[1] See Introd. to Part II. Propos. xxvi.

[2] Arabic: Zeid is the son of Amr, Amr the son of Khaled, Khaled the son of Beir.

[3] Viz., 1. The infinite dimensions of a body ; 2. The division of a body continued *ad infinitum* ; 3. The infinite number of co-existing things ; 4. The infinite number of things existing one after the other.

[4] See ch. lxxiv., Second Argument.

PART I.—CHAPTER LXXIII.

TWELFTH PROPOSITION.

"The senses are not always to be trusted." For two reasons the Mutakallemim find fault[1] with the perception of the senses. First, the senses are precluded from perceiving many objects, either on account of the smallness of the objects—this is the case with the atoms, and with other things intimately connected with the atoms,[2] as we have already stated—or on account of the remoteness of the objects from the person who desires to perceive them; e.g., we cannot see, hear, or smell at a distance of many miles; nor do we perceive the motion of the heavens. Secondly, the senses misapprehend the objects of their perception: a large object appears small from a distance; a small object immersed in water appears larger; a crooked thing appears straight when partly placed in water, and partly out of it;[3] things appear yellow to a person suffering from jaundice; sweet things are bitter[4] to him whose tongue has imbibed[5] red gall; and they mention many other things of this kind. Therefore they say, we cannot trust our senses so far as to establish any proof on their perceptions. You must not believe that the Mutakallemin had no purpose in agreeing upon this proposition, or as most of the later adherents

---

[1] חשבו in the several editions of Ibn Tibbon's Version is the corrupt reading of חשרו, "they suspected," found in some MSS. and in the *editio princeps*.

[2] That is, the motion of the atoms. Comp. Proposition iii. (page 314).

[3] More frequently a straight object, half immersed in water, appears to be bent.

[4] Comp. Shaar ha-shamayim of R. Gershon b. Shelomo (ed. Heidenheim), page 52b, כשתנבר הלחה הירוקה תטעם כל דברים מרים. Ibn Tibbon and Charizi render the word by אדומה. According to Munk מרה אדומה was included in the several kinds of מרה ירוקה. Charizi (MS.), ואשר נברה על טבעו המרה הירוקה ונשתקעה בלשונו.—(Munk.)

[5] Instead of ואשר בלשונו in the editions of Ibn Tibbon's Version, the MSS. and the *editio princeps* has ואשר שוקה לשונו, "and whose tongue has absorbed."—(Munk.)

of that school affirm, that the first Mutakallemim had no ulterior object in endeavouring to prove the existence of atoms. On the contrary, every proposition here mentioned is indispensable; if one of these be rejected, the whole theory falls to the ground.[1] The last-mentioned proposition is of particular importance; for when our senses perceive things by which any of the foregoing propositions are confuted, the Mutakallemim say that no notice should be taken of the perception of the senses so long as the proposition is supported by the testimony[2] of the intellect, and established (as they believe) by proof. Thus they say that the continuous motion is interrupted by moments of rest; that the millstone in its motion is broken into atoms; that the white colour of a garment ceases to exist, and another whiteness comes in its stead.[3] All these theories are contrary to what the eye perceives, and many inferences are drawn from the assumed existence of a vacuum, all of which are contradicted by the senses. The Mutakallemim, however, meet these objections by saying, whenever they can do so, that the perception of these things is withheld from the senses; in other instances they maintain that the contradiction has its source in the deceptive character of the senses. You know that this theory is very ancient, and was the pride of the sophists, who asserted[4] that they themselves were its authors; this is stated by Galenus[5] in his treatise on natural forces; and you know well what he says of those who will not admit the evidence of the senses.

Having discussed these propositions, I now proceed to explain the theory of the Mutakallemim concerning the above-mentioned four problems.

[1] See lxxi., pag. 281, note 2.

[2] The feminine form תורה in both the Hebrew Versions is inaccurate, or עד must be altered into ערות.

[3] See lxxiii., pages 315 and 320.

[4] היו מתפארים בהם ואמרו שהם אמרום תחלה appears to be a fusion of two different renderings of the Arabic כאנה תנתחלהא.

See Gal., περὶ δυνάμεων φυσικῶν, I., 2.

CHAPTER LXXIV.

In this chapter will be given an outline of the proofs by which the Mutakallemim attempt to demonstrate that the universe is not eternal. You must of course not expect that I shall quote their lengthy[1] arguments *verbatim*; I only intend to give an abstract of each proof,[2] to show in what way it helps to establish the theory of the *creatio ex nihilo* or to confute the eternity of the universe, and briefly to notice the propositions they employed in support of their theory. If you were to read their well-known and voluminous writings, you would not discover any argument with which they support their view left unnoticed in the present outline, but you might find there greater copiousness of words combined with more grace and elegance of style; frequently[3] they employ rhyme, rhythm,[4] and poetical diction, and sometimes mysterious phrases which perhaps are intended to startle persons listening to their discourses, and to deter those who might otherwise criticise them. You would also find many repetitions; questions propounded and, as they believe, answered, and frequent attacks on those who differ from their opinions.[5]

---

[1] Lit., "in their language and in their prolixity," that is, he does not pretend to reproduce the elegance or the prolixity of their writings, which is described below.

[2] Maimonides does not promise an enumeration of all Mutakallemim (בל אחד מהם) and their arguments, but to reproduce those arguments and methods which include the opinions of all of them.

[3] Arabic, וקד; Munk, *Quelquefois*. The Hebrew translators rendered it inaccurately by אולי (Tibbon), and אשר (Charizi), thus making it doubtful whether Maimonides had seen the books of the Mutakallemim here referred to.

[4] In a letter addressed to R. Samuel Ibn Tibbon (Bodl. Libr. 74 Poc.), Maimonides explains these terms as follows:—By סנאעה the rhyme is to be understood; the Hebrew equivalent for it is חרוז; אלפקרה consists in the formation of one line according to the metre of another; it is called in Hebrew מלות שקולות.

[5] See ch. li., pag. 176 and 177.

The First Argument.

Some of the Mutakallemim thought that by proving the creation of one thing, they demonstrated the *creatio ex nihilo* in reference to the entire universe. *E.g.*, Zaid, who from a small molecule has gradually been brought to a state of perfection, has undoubtedly not effected this change and development by his own efforts, but owes it to an external agency. It is therefore clear that an agent is required for such organisation and successive transmutation. A palm-tree or any other object might equally be selected to illustrate this idea. The whole universe, they argue, is analogous to these instances. Thus you see how they believe that a law discovered in one thing, may equally be applied to everything.[1]

The Second Argument.

This argument is likewise based on the belief that the proof by which the creation of one thing is demonstrated, holds good for the *creatio ex nihilo* in reference to the whole universe. *E.g.*, a certain individual, called Zaid,[2] who one time was not yet in existence, subsequently came into existence; and if it be assumed that Amr, his father, was the cause of his existence, Amr himself must likewise have passed from non-existence into existence; suppose then that Zaid's father unquestionably owed his origin to Khaled, Zaid's grandfather,[3] it would be found that Khaled himself did not exist from eternity,[4] and the series of causes could thus be carried back to infinity. But such an[5] infinite

---

[1] In criticising this method, Maimonides shows the weakness of this proof, which is based on analogy, *i.e.*, on the assumption that the law discovered in one thing is applicable to all things. Efodi adds that this proof is not supported by any of the afore-mentioned propositions.

[2] See pag. 289, note 2.

[3] In the editions of Ibn Tibbon's Version, ואם אי אפשר היות אביו אלא מאברהם, "and if his (*i.e.*, Jacob's) father is necessarily the descendant of Abraham."

[4] This sentence is omitted in Ibn Tibbon's Version.

[5] That is, the infinite in a series of things following each other, called the infinite by accident (במקרה). See pag. 339, note 4.

series of beings is inadmissible according to the theory of the Mutakallemim, as we have shown in our discussion of their eleventh proposition. In continuing this species of reasoning, you come to a first man, who had no parent, *viz.*, to Adam. Then you will of course ask, whence came this first man? If, *e.g.*, the reply be given that he was made out of earth, you will again inquire, " Whence came that earth ?" " Out of water." " Whence came the water ?" The inquiry would be carried on, either *ad infinitum*, which is absurd, or until you meet with a something that came into existence from absolute non-existence; in this latter case you would arrive at the real truth;[1] here the series of inquiries ends. This result of the questions proves, according to the opinion of the Mutakallemim, that the whole universe came into existence from absolute non-existence.

The Third Argument.

The atoms of things are necessarily either joined together or separate, and even the same atoms may at one time be united at another disunited. It is therefore evident that the nature of the atoms does not necessitate either their combination or their separation; for if they were separate by virtue of their nature they would never join, and if they were joined by virtue of their nature, they could never again be separated. Thus there is no stronger reason why atoms should be combined than separate, or *vice versâ*, why rather in a state of separation than of combination. Seeing that some atoms are joined, others separate, and again others subject to change, they being combined at one time and separated at another, the fact may therefore be taken as a

---

[1] Lit., " And that is the truth." This phrase corresponds to " which is absurd." The theory of a Primal Cause is accepted by the Mutakallemim, while that of an infinite number of causes is rejected. Instead of אלחק, one Leyden MSS. has אלחד, " the limit " (Munk); but the idea of " limit " is expressed already twice in this sentence, *viz.*, " till " (בסוף, " at last "), and " here the series of inquiries ends."

proof that the atoms cannot combine or separate without an agent. This argument, according to the opinion of the Mutakallemim, establishes the theory that the universe has been created from nothing. You have already been told, that those who employ this argument, rely on the first proposition of the Mutakallemim with its corollaries.

The Fourth Argument.

The whole Universe is composed of substance and accidents; every substance must possess one accident or more, and since the accidents are not eternal, the substance, the substratum of the accidents, cannot be eternal; for that which is joined to transient things and cannot exist without them is itself transient.[1] Therefore the whole Universe has had a beginning. To the objection, that the substance may possibly be eternal while the accidents, though in themselves transient, succeed each other in an infinite series, they reply that, in this case, an infinite number of transient things would be in existence, an eventuality which, according to their theory, is impossible. This argument is considered by them the best and safest, and has been accepted by many of them as a strict proof. Its acceptance implies the admission of the following three propositions, the object of which is well understood by philosophers.[2] 1. An infinite series of things, of which the one succeeds when the other has ceased to exist, is impossible. 2. All accidents have a beginning.—Our opponent, who defends the theory of the eternity of the universe, can refute this proposition by pointing to one[3] particular accident, namely to the

[1] Because no substance can be without accidents, which are admitted to have had a beginning, the substance must have a beginning.

[2] That is to say, the thinker sees easily that these propositions were not accepted because of their intrinsic value, but because of their utility for disproving the eternity of the universe.

[3] The phrase עֹרֶץ מִן אלאעראץ׳ (Hebr. מקרה מן המקרים) signifies here "a certain particular accident" (מקרה אחד מן המקרים), while similar phrases are generally employed in an indefinite sense (any accident).

circular motion of the sphere; for it is held by Aristotle that this circular motion is eternal,[1] and, therefore, the spheres which perform this motion are, according to his opinion, likewise eternal. It is of no use to prove that all other accidents have a beginning; for our opponent does not deny this; he says that accidents may supervene an object which has existed from eternity, and may follow each other in rotation. He contents himself with maintaining that this particular accident, viz., circular motion, the motion of the heavenly sphere, is eternal, and does not belong to the class of transient accidents.[2] It is, therefore necessary to examine this accident by itself and to prove that it is not eternal. 3. The next proposition which the author of this argument accepts, is as follows: Every material object consists of substance and accidents, that is to say, of atoms and accidents in the sense in which the Mutakallemim use the term. But if a material object were held to be a combination of matter and form, as has been proved by our opponent,[3] it would be necessary to demonstrate that the primal matter and the primal form are transient, and only then the proof of the *creatio ex nihilo* would be complete.

[1] Comp. Arist. Metaph., xii. 7: καὶ ἔστι τι ἀεὶ κινούμενον κίνησιν ἄπαυστον. αὕτη δ' ἡ κύκλῳ, καὶ τοῦτο οὐ λόγῳ μόνον ἀλλ' ἔργῳ.

[2] According to Ibn Tibbon (in a marginal note in some MSS. of his translation) the words ו האדרת גיר (Hebr. ו מחודשת בלתי) "without beginning and" are superfluous, because the same has already been stated before. The remark, however, is not quite correct; for Maimonides first mentioned the opinion of Aristotle on which the objections are founded, and then he quotes the objections themselves which have been made to Propositions vi. and xi. (ch. lxiii.), and which are supported in the first place by the periodical recurrence of each element in a finite series of accidents, which, though limited, may still recur an infinite number of times; and in the second place, by the circular motion of the heavenly spheres, which is likewise believed by the objector to be infinite as regards the number of circuits accomplished.

[3] That is, it does not suffice for the proof of the *creatio ex nihilo* to show that such atoms as have been assumed by the Mutakallemim are finite; but it must also be proved that matter and form in the most general sense of the term are finite, since an authority like Aristotle taught that everything is a combination of matter and form.

The Fifth Argument.

This argument is based on the theory of Determination,[1] and is made much of by the Mutakallemim. It is the same as the theory which I explained in discussing the tenth proposition. Namely, when they treat either of the Universe in general, or of any of its parts, they assume that it can have such properties and such dimensions as it actually has; that it may receive such accidents as in reality are noticed in it, and that it may exist in such a place and at such a time as in fact is the case; but it may be larger or smaller, may receive other properties and accidents, and come to existence at an earlier or a later period, or in a different place. Consequently, the fact that a thing has been determined in its composition, size, place, accident and time—a variation in all these points being possible—is a proof that a being exists which freely chooses and determines these divers relations; and the circumstance that the Universe or a part of it requires a being able to make this selection, proves that the Universe has been created *ex nihilo*. For there is no difference which of the following expressions is used: to determine, to make, to create, to produce, to originate, or to intend; these verbs have all one and the same meaning. The Mutakallemim give a great many examples, both of a general and a special character. They say, it is not more natural for earth to be under water than to be above water;[2] who[3] then determined its actual position? Or, it is not more natural that the sun is round than that it should be square or triangular; for all qualities have the same relation to a body capable of possessing them. Who[3] then determined one particular quality? In a similar way they treat of every individual being; when, *e.g.*, they notice flowers of different

---

[1] Arab. אלתכציץ; Ibn Tibbon התיחד; Charizi המיוחדת, and also הגבלה; Palquera סגול. All mean the same thing, namely, the act of determining by free will, which of the many possible forms is to unite with a certain substance. [2] See ch. lxx., page 290.

[3] מייחד in Ibn Tibbon's Version is to be read מי יחד.

colours, they are unable to explain the phenomenon, and they take it as a strong proof in favour of their theory; they say, "Behold, the earth is everywhere alike, the water is alike; why then is this flower red and that one yellow? Some being must have determined the colour of each, and that being is God. A being must therefore exist which determines everything, both as regards the Universe generally, and each of its parts individually."[1] All this is the logical consequence of the tenth proposition. The theory of determination is moreover[2] adopted by some of those who assume the eternity of the Universe, as will be explained below. In conclusion, I consider this to be the best argument; and in another part[3] I shall more fully acquaint you with the opinion I have formed concerning the theory of Determination.

The Sixth Argument.

One of the modern Mutakallemim thought that he had found a very good argument, much better than any advanced hitherto, namely, the argument based on the triumph of existence over non-existence. He says that, according to the common belief, the existence of the Universe is merely possible; for if it were necessary, the Universe would be God,[4]—but he seems to forget that we are at issue with those who, whilst they believe in the existence of God, admit at the same time the eternity of the Universe.—The expression " A thing is possible " denotes that the thing may either

---

[1] Arab. באחד אלנואיאת; in some MSS. באחד אלנואיאת, " by one of the admissible properties." The Hebrew באחד מן הפרטים agrees with the former reading.—(Munk.)

[2] Maimonides finds two weak points in this method. First, it is based on the tenth proposition, the weakness of which was exhibited above (ch. lxxiii. page 330 *sqq.*). Secondly, it is not conclusive, because there are some philosophers who adopt the theory of determination and still believe in the eternity of the Universe. [3] Part II., ch. xix.

[4] Comp. Ibn Gabirol; והנמצא יסודר על מעלות והם המחויב והאפשר והנמצע והמחויב הוא האחד הפועל ית׳ (quoted by Palquera, Moreh ha-moreh, page 63). " As regards existence things may be either necessary, or possible or impossible. The Creator alone is necessary."

be in existence or not in existence, and that there is not more reason why it should exist than why it should not exist. The fact that a thing, the existence of which is possible, actually does exist—although it bears the same relation to the state of existence as to that of non-existence —proves that there is a Being which gave the preference to existence over non-existence. This argument is very forcible;[1] it is a modified form of the foregoing argument which is based on the theory of determination. He only chose the term "preference" instead of "determination," and instead of applying it to the properties of the existing being he applies it to "the existence of the being itself." He either had the intention to mislead, or he misunderstood the proposition, that the existence of the Universe is possible. Our opponent who assumes the eternity of the Universe, employs the term "possible," and says, "the existence of the Universe is possible" in a sense different from that in which the Mutakallem applies it, as will be explained below.[2] Moreover it may be doubted whether the conclusion, that the Universe owes its origin to a being which is able to give preference to existence over non-existence, is correct. For we may apply the terms "preference" and "determination" to anything capable of receiving either of two properties which are contrary or opposed to each other; and when we find that the thing actually possesses one property and not the other, we are convinced that there exists a determining agent. *E.g.*, you say that a piece of copper could just as well be formed into a kettle as into a lamp; when we find that it

---

[1] That is to say, for the author of this method; not in the opinion of Maimonides. Crescas: this Maimonides said satirically (כמלעיג עליהם).

[2] See Introduction to Part II., Proposition xix. *sqq.* "Possible" in the sense of the philosophers (δυνάμει) is that which requires some *causa efficiens* to become real (ἐνεργείᾳ), while the Mutakallemim understood by "possible" that which may become real by the free will of some external agent. But the Mutakallemim who do not admit causality, and who refer everything to the direct interference of the Creator, are consistent in making no difference between the two kinds of "possibilities."

is a lamp or a kettle, we have no doubt that a deciding and determining agent has advisedly chosen one of the two possible forms; for it is clear that the substance of copper existed, and that before the determination took place it had neither of the two possible forms which have just been mentioned. When, however, it is the question whether a certain existing object is eternal, or whether it has passed from non-existence into existence, this argument is inadmissible; for it cannot be asked who decided in favour of the existence of a thing, and rejected its non-existence, except when it has been admitted that it has passed from non-existence into existence; in the present case this is just the point under discussion. If we were to take the existence and the non-existence of a thing as mere objects of imagination, we should have to apply the tenth proposition, which gives prominence to imagination and fiction, and ignores the things which exist in reality, or are conceived by the intellect. Our opponent, however, who believes in the eternity of the Universe, will show that we can imagine the non-existence of the Universe as well as we can imagine any other impossibility. It is not my intention[1] to refute their doctrine of the *creatio ex nihilo*: I only wish to show the incorrectness of their belief that this argument differs from the one which precedes; since in fact the two arguments are identical, and are founded[2] on the well-known principle of determination.

[1] According to Shem-tob: I need not disprove this, because the premises have been proved to be wrong. Crescas adds "now" (עתה). This addition does not appear to be correct; for, in fact, Maimonides does not entirely reject this proof advanced by the Mutakallemim in demonstrating the *creatio ex nihilo*. From the fact that a thing could be different from what it is, he likewise infers that a Being must exist, on whose decision the actual forms of things depend. The only difference is that according to the Mutakallemim each individual case is considered as the direct result of that decision, while Maimonides assumes a series of natural causes between the Primal Cause (the determining power), and the individual beings. Comp. Part II., ch. xix.

[2] Instead of מְשֻׁעָר some MSS. and *ed. princeps* have מְיָשָּׁב; these two renderings correspond with the two readings in the original: תקדיר and תקריר. —(Munk.)

The Seventh Argument.

One of the modern Mutakallemim says that he is able to prove the creation of the Universe from the theory put forth by the philosophers concerning the immortality of the soul. He argues thus: If the world were eternal, the number of the dead would necessarily be infinite, and consequently an infinite number of souls would coexist, but, it has long since been shown that the coexistence of an infinite number of things, is positively impossible. This is indeed a strange argument! One difficulty is explained by another which is still greater! Here the saying, well known among the Arameans, may be applied: "Your guarantee wants another guarantee."[1] He rests his argument on the immortality of the soul, as though he understood this immortality, in what respect the soul is immortal, or what the thing is which is immortal! If, however, he only meant to controvert the opinion of his opponent, who believed in the eternity of the Universe, and also in the immortality of the soul, he accomplished his task, provided the opponent admitted the correctness of the idea which that Mutakallem formed of the philosopher's view on the immortality of the soul. Some of the later philosophers[2] explained this difficulty as follows: the immortal souls are not substances which occupy a locality or a space, and their existence in an infinite number is therefore not impossible. You must bear in mind that those abstract beings which are neither bodies nor forces dwelling in bodies, and which in fact are ideals—are altogether incapable of being represented as a plurality[3] unless some ideals be the cause

---

[1] A proverb, which also is quoted in the Babyl. Talm. Succah, 26a; Maimonides probably only knew it from the Talmud. According to Munk ערבײם "Arabs" in the editions of Ibn Tibbon's Version is a misprint for ארמײם.

[2] Maimonides probably alludes here to the theory of Ibn Sina. Comp. Shahrastani (transl. by Haarbrücker) II., page 318.

[3] See Introduction to Part II., Proposition xvi. Albertus Magnus wrote against this theory: Libellus contra eos qui dicunt quod post separationem ex omnibus animalibus non remanet nisi intellectus unus et anima una. See Alb. M., Opera V., page 218 *sqq.*, ed. de Jamroy.—(Munk.)

of the existence of others, and can be distinguished from each other by the specific difference that some are the efficient cause and others the effect; but that which remains of Zaid [after his death] is neither the cause nor the effect of that which is left of Amr, and therefore the souls of all the departed form only one being as has been explained by Ibn Bekr Ibn Al-saig,[1] and others who ventured to speak on these profound subjects. In short, such intricate disciplines, which our mind can scarcely comprehend, cannot furnish any principles for the explanation of other subjects.—It should be noted that whoever endeavours to prove or to disprove the eternity of the Universe by these arguments of the Mutakallemim, must necessarily rely on one of the two following propositions, or on both of them; namely on the tenth proposition, according to which the actual form of a thing is merely one of many equally possible forms, and which implies that there must be a being capable of making the special selection; or on the eleventh proposition which rejects the existence of an infinite series of things coming successively into existence. The last-named proposition is demonstrated in various ways, e.g.,[2] they advert to a class of transient individuals, and to a certain particular date. From the theory which asserts the eternity of the Universe, it would follow that the individuals of that class up to that particular date are infinite[3] in number; a thousand years later the individuals of that class are likewise infinite in number; the last number must exceed the previous one by the number of the individuals born in those thousand years, and consequently one infinite number would be larger than another. The same[2] argument is applied to the revolutions of the heavenly sphere, and in like manner it is shown that one

---

[1] He is also called Ibn Badja; his view on the subject is found in his Risalat alvidaa (אגרת הפטירה). Comp. Munk Mélange, pag. 386, note 2.

[2] Lit. "either"; Hebrew אם; Munk "d'abord": instead of the corresponding או, "or," the phrase וכיוצא בזה) והכדא), "similarly," is used.

[3] The plural אין תכלית להם (Arab. מתנאהית) agrees with the plural sense in כל איש (Arab. כל שכץ); it is *constructio ad sensum*.

infinite number of revolutions would be larger than another; the same result is obtained when revolutions of one sphere are compared with those of another moving more slowly; the revolutions of both spheres [though unequal] would be infinite in number. Similarly they proceed with all those accidents which are subject to destruction and production; the individual accidents that have passed into non-existence are counted and represented as though they were still in existence, and as though they were things with a definite beginning;[1] this imaginary number is then either increased or reduced. Yet all these things have no reality and are mere fictions. Abunazar Alfarabi[2] in criticising[3] this proposition, has exposed all its weak points, as you will clearly perceive, when you study his book on the changeable beings[4] earnestly and dispassionately.[5] These are the principal arguments of the Mutakallemim in seeking to establish the *creatio ex nihilo*. Having thus proved that the Universe is not eternal, they necessarily infer that there is an *Agens* who created it in accordance with His intention, desire and will. They then proceed to prove the unity of that *Agens* as I am going to point out in the next chapter.

[1] The Arabic דאת בראת denotes "things that have a beginning." Maimonides explains its meaning in a letter addressed to R. Samuel Ibn Tibbon as אמורא להא אבתדא מחדוד "things that have a marked beginning"; and adds "for everything limited in its totality on both extremities is called דאת אלבדאה; it can be increased and diminished. But things that come gradually into existence, and have therefore no definite beginning—as *e.g.*, the revolutions of the heavenly spheres—do not admit of any increase or diminution.—The translation of Ibn Tibbon: דברים שיש להם התחלה מסוימת has been suggested by the author himself.—(Munk.)

[2] See page 332, note 4.

[3] The Arabic רמג has been explained by the author in the letter addressed to R. Samuel Ibn Tibbon as follows: "רמג (אדמג, as in some copies, is wrong) denotes to strike on the head, similar to the phrase met with in the Talmud, מחו ליה אמוחא, 'they struck him on the head.' I meant to say that Alfarabi has proved the absurdity of this proposition, which the Mutakallemim accepted as an important principle."

[4] Narboni: זה המאמר לא הגיע אלינו "This work is not extant."

[5] Comp. ch. xxxiv., page 123, and note 1.

CHAPTER LXXV.

On the arguments of the Mutakallemim to prove the Unity of God.

In this chapter I shall explain to you how the Mutakallemim prove the Unity of God. They contend that the Maker and Creator of the Universe, the existence of whom is testified by all nature, is One. Two propositions are employed by them in demonstrating the Unity of God, *viz.*, two deities or more would neutralise each other, and if several deities existed they would be distinguished from each other by a specific difference.[1]

First Argument.

The first argument is that of mutual neutralisation, and is employed by the majority of the Mutakallemim. It is to the following effect:—If the Universe had two Gods, it would necessarily occur that the atom—subject to a combination with one of two opposite qualities—either remained without either of them, and that is impossible, or, though being only one atom, included both qualities at the same time, and that is likewise impossible.[2] *E.g.*, whilst one of

---

[1] Arabic: אלתמאנע ואלתנאיר. Ibn Tibbon, דרך ההמנעות ודרך ההשתנות (in the editions the word והחלוק, probably another reading for ההשתנות, has been added), Charizi: דרך הנמנע ודרך השני. The verb תמאנע signifies "to hinder each other;" אלתמאנע "the mutual obstruction" or "the neutralisation." As the Niphal in Hebrew expresses "reciprocity" the Inf. Niphal הסנעות and the participle נמנע employed respectively by Ibn Tibbon and Charizi may both be taken in the same sense as the Arabic תמאנע. תנאיר denotes the condition of things which differed from each other; in Hebrew this is expressed by השתנות, חלוף, שנוי or חלוק. Reciprocity need not be expressed in this case by a separate form, because it is implied in the meaning of the word itself.

[2] A third case which is likewise possible—namely, that both forces act in the same direction—has been entirely ignored either by the Mutakallemim or by Maimonides who quoted them. The possibility of this third case would lead to the admission of two Gods acting in the same direction towards each

the two deities determined that one atom or more should be warm, the other deity might determine that the same should be cold; the consequence of the mutual neutralisation of the two divine beings would thus be that the atoms would be neither warm nor cold—a contingency which is impossible, because all bodies must combine with one of two opposites; or they would be at the same time both warm and cold. Similarly, it might occur that whilst one of the deities desired that a body be in motion, the other might desire that it be at rest; the body would then be either without motion and rest, or would both move and rest at the same time. Proofs of this kind[1] are founded on the atomic theory contained in the first proposition of the Mutakallemim, on the proposition which refers to the creation of the accidents, and on the proposition that negatives are properties of actual existence and require for their production an *agens*.[2] For if it were assumed that the substance of this world which, according to the philosophers is subject to successive production and destruction, is different from the substance of the world above, *viz.*, from the substance of the spheres—a fact established by proof[3]—and that as the

---

thing, and that would be the same as assuming only one God. Maimonides here contents himself with naming the propositions which form the basis of this proof; their insufficiency having been discussed by him in ch. lxxiii.

[1] By employing the term "proofs of this kind," instead of "this proof," Maimonides indicates that the proof which he mentioned is merely one instance of a number of proofs which were founded on the principle and the method described.

[2] Prop. i., vi. and vii., see pag. 310.—If Prop. i., *viz.*, that all things consist of equal constituent atoms, were not admitted, two Creators or more might be assumed for the different classes of things, as *e.g.*, for the sublunar world and for the heavenly spheres. Without Prop. vi., *viz.*, that the accidents are constantly renewed, it could not be shown that the existence of two Gods would lead to mutual neutralisation in the creation of accidents. In the same manner Prop. vii., *viz.*, that the negative property is not merely absence of the positive, but a real property requiring an *agens*, is indispensable; for without it, the negative property would only require non-creation; and two Gods being assumed, they would not neutralise each other, even if one desired an object to have a positive quality, the other a negative; the positive would then be created.   [3] Comp. ch. lxxii., page 292, *sqq.*

Dualists assert, there are two divine beings, one of whom rules this world without influencing the spheres, whilst the other governs the world above without interfering with this world [1]—such a theory would not involve the mutual neutralisation of the two deities. If it were then objected, that the existence of two deities would necessitate an imperfection in both of them, in so far as one deity would be unable to influence the province of the other, the objection would be met by the reply, that this inability need not be considered a defect in either of them; for that which is not included within the sphere of action of a being can of course not be performed by that being, and an *agens* is not deficient in power, if it is unable to perform what is intrinsically impossible. Thus we, Monotheists, do not consider it a defect in God, that He does not combine two opposites in one object, nor do we test His omnipotence by the accomplishment of any sinister impossibility. When the Mutakallemim noticed the weakness of their argument,[2] for which they had some apparent support, they had recourse to another argument.

Second Argument.

If there were two Gods, there would necessarily be some element common to both, whilst some element present in the one would be absent in the other, and constitute the specific difference between them.[3] This is a philosophic

---

[1] Lit., ὕλη—See *Ibid*.

[2] The weak point of the proof consists in its being inapplicable to the theory of the philosophers, according to which there exist two different substances, one of the sublunary beings, another of the heavenly spheres. The difference of the substances would suggest two distinct creative and managing powers, for the collision of which there is no chance. The proof, however, holds good for the Mutakallemim, who believe that the spheres above and the things below consist of the same kind of atoms, and that, therefore, there is no reason to assume two Creators.

[3] The conclusion can easily be supplied, namely, that neither of the two Gods could be the Primal Cause, because each of them is a combination of several forces or properties, and thus requires again a cause for that combination

and sound argument for those who are able to examine it, and to obtain a clear insight into its premises, which will be further explained, in our exposition of the view of the philosophers on this point.² But³ it cannot be accepted by those who admit the existence of divine attributes. For according to their opinion, the Primal Cause⁴ includes many different elements.⁵ They represent its wisdom and its omnipotence as two different things, and again the omnipotence as different from the will. Consequently it would not be impossible that either of the two divine beings possessed several properties, some of which would be common to both, and some peculiar to only one of them.

Third Argument.

This argument is likewise based on one of the Propositions of the Kalām.⁶ For some of the Mutakallemim belonging to the old school, assume, that when the Creator *wills* a thing, the will is not an element superadded to the essence of God: it is a will without a substratum.⁷ In accordance with the

¹ Lit., "to follow." Some MSS. have תחבת "to establish" instead of תחבע.

² Comp. Part II. ch. i., and Part II. Introd. Propos. xix. and xxi.

³ That is, the Mutakallemim who reject the propositions of the philosophers (Part II. Propos. xix. and xxi.) have no demonstrative proof; and besides, those who admit that God possesses attributes, cannot apply this proof at all, because they do not hold that the possession of properties is contrary to the theory of God's unity.

⁴ In the Arabic text the usual ית׳ follows the word ענדה, so also in the Version of Charizi, while Ibn Tibbon inverted it אצלו ית׳ שהקדמון.—Maimonides added ית׳ before alluding to the notion that there are various elements in God—an idea which, according to his view, amounts to blasphemy.

⁵ מתנאירה and מתנאהיה (in a Leyden MSS.) have the same meaning, viz., things which differ from each other, or things which are limited and can be distinguished from each other.

⁶ Instead of אלו הדברים in the editions of Ibn Tibbon's Version, the MSS. have אלו הדרכים.

⁷ Comp. "the accident of destruction without a substratum," ch. lxxiii., Proposition vi., page 323.

propositions which we have mentioned, and of which, as you will see, it is difficult to form a true conception, they say that *one* will, which is independent of any substratum, cannot be ascribed to *two* beings; for, as they assert, *one* cause cannot be the source of two laws for two essences. This is, as I told you, the method of explaining one difficulty by means of another and still greater difficulty. For as they define the Will, it is inconceivable, and some have, therefore, considered it to be a mere non-entity; others who admit its existence, meet with many insuperable[1] difficulties. The Mutakallemim, nevertheless, establish on its existence one of the proofs for the unity of God.

Fourth Argument.

The existence of an action is necessarily positive evidence of the existence of an *agens*, but does not prove the existence of more than one *agens*. There is no difference whether the existence of one God be assumed or the existence of two, or three, or twenty, or any number. This is plain and clear. But the argument does not seem to prove the non-existence of a multitude of deities; it only shows that their number is unknown; the deity may be one sole being, but may also include several divine beings. The following supplemental argument has therefore been advanced: possibility is inapplicable to the existence of God, which is absolute; the possibility of the existence of more than one God must therefore be denied. This is the whole essence of the proof, and its fallacy is self-evident; for although the notion of possibility cannot be applied to the existence of God, it can be applied to our knowledge of God: for an alternative in our knowledge of a thing does not involve an alternative in the actual existence of the thing, and perhaps there is neither[2] a tripartite deity

---

[1] Munk, "innombrables"; Charizi, לא יספרו; Ibn Tibbon, אי אפשר לדחותם. The Arabic לא תנחצר admits of both interpretations.

[2] The words ואינו כן have been omitted in the editions of Ibn Tibbon's Version.

as the Christians believe, nor an undivided Unity as we believe. This is clear to those who have been taught to notice the conclusions implied in given premises.

Fifth Argument.

One of the modern Mutakallemim thought that he found a proof of the Unity of God in the idea of requisiteness. Suppose there were two divine beings; if one of them were able to create the universe, the second God would be superfluous, and there would be no need for his existence. If, on the other hand, the entire universe could not be created or governed except by both of them, each of them would be imperfect in so far as he would require the co-operation of another being, and would thus be limited in power. This argument is, in fact, only a variation of "the mutual neutralisation of two deities." There is this difficulty in such proofs, that a certain degree of imperfection is ascribed to a Being which does not accomplish tasks beyond its sphere.[1] We do not call a person weak because he cannot move a thousand hundredweights, and we do not say that God is imperfect because He cannot transform Himself into a body, or cannot create another being like Himself, or make a square whose diagonal should be equal to its side. In the same manner we should not consider it an imperfection in God, if he were not the only Creator, and if it were absolutely necessary, that there should be two Creators; not because the one God required the assistance of the other, but because the existence of both of them was equally necessary, and because it was impossible that it should be otherwise. Further we do not say that the Almighty is imperfect, because He does not, according to the opinion of the Mutakallemim, produce a body otherwise than by the creation of atoms, and by their combination with accidents created

---

[1] In Ets Chayim, ch. lxiv., a distinction is made between that which is logically impossible, and that which is impossible because of the limited power of the efficient cause.

in them. That inability is not called want or imperfection, since another process is impossible. In like manner the Dualist might say, that it is impossible for one Being to act alone, and that this circumstance constitutes no imperfection in either of the deities, because the absolute existence of one Deity necessitates the coëxistence of the other. Some of the Mutakallemim, weary of these arguments, declared that the Unity of God is a doctrine which must be received as a matter of faith, but most of them rejected this theory, and reviled its authors. I, however, hold, that those who accept this theory are right-minded, and shrink from admitting an erroneous opinion; when they do not perceive any cogency in the arguments, and find that the proofs advanced in favour of the doctrine are inconclusive, they prefer to assume that it could only be received as a matter of faith. For the Mutakallemim do not hold that the Universe has any defined properties on which a true proof could be founded, or that man's intellect is endowed with any such faculty[1] as would enable him to form correct conclusions. It is, however, not without a motive that they defend this theory; they wish to assume such a form of the Universe, as could be employed to support a doctrine for which otherwise no proof could be found, and would lead us to neglect the investigation of that which in fact can be proved. We can only appeal to the Almighty[2] and to those intelligent persons who confess their error when they discover it.

[1] Arabic: פטרה מסתקימה, "right beginning" or "right disposition;" Ibn Tibbon: ידיעה טוטבעת ישרה; Char.: תכונה; Munk: justesse innée (Lit., disposition naturelle droite).

לאלו למודים, in the editions of Ibn Tibbon's Version, is a corruption of לאל שיעשה :—follows as Shemtob by explained is which ,לאל ולמודים נקמה בהם, למודים על האמת שיראו כמה כזבים שקריות וגנויות ותועבות אמרו אלו המדברים.

CHAPTER LXXVI.

On the arguments of the Mutakallemim for the Incorporeality of God.

THE reasonings and arguments of the Mutakallemim to demonstrate the Incorporeality of God are very weak, and indeed inferior to their arguments for the Unity of God. They treat the doctrine of the Incorporeality of God as if it were the logical sequence of the theory of His Unity, and they say that the attribute "one" cannot be applied to a corporeal object. Those who maintain that God is incorporeal because a corporeal object consists of substance and form—a combination known[1] to be impossible in the Divine Being, are not in my opinion Mutakallemim, and such an argument is not founded on the propositions of the Kalām; on the contrary it is a logical proof based on the theory of substance and form, and on a right conception of their properties. It has the character of a philosophical argument, and I shall fully explain it when treating of the arguments of the philosophers.[2] Here we only propose to discuss the arguments by which the Mutakallemim desire to prove the Incorporeality of God in accordance with their propositions and the method of their reasoning.

First Argument.

If God were corporeal, His true essence would necessarily either exist entirely[3] in every part of the body,

[1] Lit., "this is a combination, and a combination is known." וזאת ההרכבה תבאר in the editions of Ibn Tibbon's Version is a corruption of וזאת היא ההרכבה והתבאר; Similarly Charizi: וזאת הרכבה ויבאר.

[2] Part II., ch. i.

[3] In the Version of Ibn Tibbon two renderings appear to have been fused into one; for either יתוקן or שתשלם מציאות would have sufficed. Some MSS. have in fact שיתוקן בו כלל, and on the margin as another reading שתשלם מציאותו (בכלל) (Munk).—Charizi renders the passage rather inaccurately as follows:—שיתחברו בו כל עצמי הגוף ר״ל כל עצם נפרד מהם או שיהיה בו עצם א׳ וגו׳.

that is to say, in each of its atoms, or would be confined to one of the atoms. In the latter alternative the other atoms would be superfluous, and the existence of the corporeal being [with the exception of the one atom] would be of no purpose. If, on the other hand, each atom fully represented the Divine Being, the whole body would not be *one* deity, but a complex of deities, and this would be contrary to the doctrine adopted by the *kalâm* that God is one. An examination of this argument shows that it is based on the first and the fifth propositions.[1] But there[2] is room for the following objection: "God does not consist of atoms, that is to say, He is not as you assert composed of a number of elements created by Himself, but is one continuous body, and indivisible except in man's imagination,[3] which affords no test; for in man's imagination the substance of the heavens may be torn or rent asunder.[2] The philosopher holds that such a possibility results from assuming a similarity and an analogy between the visible, *i.e.*, the bodies which exist among us, and the invisible."

Second Argument.

This argument, they believe, is of great importance. Its main support is the impossibility of comparison, *i.e.*, the belief that God cannot be compared to any of His creatures; and that He would be comparable to other corporeal objects if He were corporeal. They put great stress on this argument, and say as follows: "If it were asserted that God is corporeal, but that His substance is not like that of other corporeal beings, it would be self-contradictory; for all bodies are alike as regards their substance, and are distinguished from each other by other things, *viz.*, the accidents."

[1] *Viz.*, that all things consist of atoms, and that the properties of the things are united with the atoms.

[2] Lit. "If one said unto them." The principal sentence: "They could not give a satisfactory answer," must be supplied.

[3] Arab. אוהאם "ideas" or "imaginations;" Hebrew מחשבה and דמיון; Munk "fausses idées." Comp. lxxiii., Propos. x., page 334 *sqq.*

They also argue that if God were corporeal it would follow that He has created another being like Himself.[1] This argument is refuted in two ways. First, the objector does not admit the impossibility of comparison; he asks how it could be proved that God can not be compared to any of His creatures. No doubt[2] that, in support of their view, that a comparison between the Almighty and any other being is inadmissible, they would have to cite the words of the Prophets, and thus accept this doctrine by the authority of tradition, not by the authority of reason. The argument, that God, if comparable to any of His creatures, would be found to have created beings like Himself, is refuted by the objector in the following way: "The created things are not like Him in every respect; for I do not deny that God has many properties and peculiarities." For he who admits the corporeality of God does not deny the existence of properties in the divine Being. Another and more forcible[3] argument is this: All who have studied philosophy, and have made themselves thoroughly acquainted with philosophical theories, assume as demonstrated facts, first that the term substance, when applied to the spheres above and to the corporeal objects here on earth is a perfect homonym, for the substance of the one is not the substance of the other;[4] and secondly[5] that the forms of the things on this earth are different from the forms of the spheres; the terms substance and form when applied both to things below and to the spheres above are homonyms;

[1] Namely, things which have corporeality in common with Him.

[2] The adj. האלחיים in the ed. of Ibn Tibbon's Version is a mistake, and should be האלהים "by God" as in *ed. princeps*. Charizi omits the word altogether.

[3] Arab. אשכל rendered by Ibn Tibbon יותר נאותים "more appropriate." Charizi יותר משובש "more absurd," he probably wrote יוֹתֵר מְשַׁפֵּשׁ "better proving the absurdity of."

[4] See ch. lxxii., page 292.

[5] That is to say, not only the term "body" but also the terms "substance" and "form" are homonymously applied to the things below and the spheres above. Munk omits to translate the word איצא; Charizi likewise ignores it.

although there is no doubt that the spheres have [like the things below, three] dimensions, they are corporeal because they consist of substance and form, not because they have dimensions. If this explanation is admitted with reference to the spheres, how much more is he who believes that God is corporeal justified in saying that God is a corporeal being which has dimensions, but which in its substance, its true nature and properties is very different from all created bodies, and that the term "substance" is applied to Him and to His creatures homonymously, in the same manner as the true believers, who have a correct conception of the divine idea, apply the term "existence" homonymously to Him and to His creatures. The Corporealists do not admit that all bodies consist of similar atoms; they believe that God created all things, and that these differ from each other both in their substances and in their constituent properties; and just as the substance of dung[1] differs from the substance of the sun, so does, according to this theory, the substance of the spheres and the stars differ from the substance of the created light, *i.e.*, the Divine Glory (*Shechinah*), and again the substance of the Divine Glory, or the pillar of cloud created [for the purpose],[2] differ from the substance of the Most High; for the substance of the latter is sublime, perfect, simple, constant and immutable. His absolute existence remains always the same, and He creates all things according to His will and desire. How could this argument, though it be weak, be refuted by these strange methods of the Mutakallemim, which I pointed out to you?

[1] In Arabic אלארואת, in some MSS. אלארואת or אלארואת; one MS. (Uri, No. 359) has אלנוריאת. Ibn Tibbon הצואות which, in the editions of his Versions, has been altered into נצוצות "sparks;" in some MSS. גשם הצמחים "the substance of the plants" is found instead.—(Munk.) Charizi renders the expression by העצבים (? העשבים).

[2] See ch. x., page 57, note 4.

Third Argument.

If God were corporeal, He would be finite, and so far this argument is correct; if He were finite, He would have certain dimensions and a certain form; this is also a correct conclusion. But they continue thus: Attribute to God any magnitude or form whatever: He might be either larger or smaller, and might also have a different form. The fact that He has one special magnitude and one special form presupposes the existence of a determining *agens*. I have heard that they attach great importance to this argument, but in truth it is the weakest of all the arguments mentioned above. It is founded on the tenth proposition, the feebleness of which, in ignoring the actual properties of things, we have clearly shown in regard to ordinary beings, and must be much more evident in regard to the Creator. There is no difference between this argument and their assertion that the fact of the existence of the Universe having been preferred to its non-existence proves the existence of an *agens* that preferred the existence of the Universe to its non-existence at a time when both [1] were equally possible. If it were asked, why this argument should not be applied to God,—*viz.*, that His mere existence proved the existence of an *agens* which determined His existence and rejected His non-existence—they would undoubtedly answer that this admission would only lead to a repetition of the same argument until at length a being be found whose existence is not merely potential but necessary, and which does not require a *causa efficiens*. But this same answer can also be applied to dimensions and to form. It can only be said in reference to all other forms and magnitudes, the existence of which is *possible*, that is to say which came into existence after a state of non-existence, that they might have been

---

[1] ועדמה "and its non-existence" has no equivalent in the Hebrew translations; it is also absent in one Leyden MS.—(Munk.)

larger or smaller than they actually are, or that they might have had a form different from that which they actually possess, and require for this reason some determining *agens*. But the forms and dimensions of God (who is above all imperfection and similitude!) did not come into existence according to the opinion of the Corporealist after a state of non-existence, and therefore no determining *agens* was necessary; His substance with its dimensions and forms has a necessary existence; no *agens* was required to decide upon His existence, and to reject[1] His non-existence, since non-existence is altogether inadmissible in God. In like manner there was no force required to determine His magnitude and form, they were absolutely inseparable from His existence.

If you wish to go in search of truth, to cast aside your passions, your tradition, and your fondness of things you have been accustomed to cherish, if you wish to guard yourself against error: then consider the fate of these speculators and the result of their labours; observe how they[2] rushed, as it were, from the ashes into the fire. They denied the nature of the existing things, misrepresented the properties of heaven and earth, and thought that they were able, by their propositions, to prove the creation of the world, but in fact they were far from proving the *creatio ex nihilo*, and have weakened the arguments for the existence, the unity, and the incorporeality of God. The proofs of all these doctrines must be based on the well-known nature of the existing things, as perceived by the senses and the intellect.

Having thus discussed the arguments of the Mutakallemim, we shall now proceed to consider the propositions of the

[1] Lit., "to determine or to prefer the existence to the non-existence." The words ולא למרנֹח absent from most MS., and only found in Oxf. MS., Uri 359, appear to have formed part of the original text, and to have been omitted, as may be inferred from the negation לא before מבצץ.—(Munk.)

[2] שהוא in the editions of Ibn Tibbon's Version is a mistake; the MSS. have שהם.—(Munk.)

philosophers and their arguments for the existence of God, His Unity and His Incorporeality, and we shall for the present assume the Eternity of the Universe without finally accepting it. Next to this we shall develop our own method, which is the result of deep study, in demonstrating these three principles, and we shall then examine the theory of the Eternity of the Universe as assumed by the philosophers.[1]

[1] MS. Uri 359 (written 1275) has a marginal note, the translation of which is as follows:—"I intend to refute them; I do not, however, pretend to be the only one who has taken the trouble to refute them. On the contrary, other persons have done it before me, as, *e.g.*, Rabbenu Hai, Ahron ben Serdjado, Ibn Ganach, Ibn al-Akuli, Ben Hofni ha-kohen, Rabbi Dosa and his father Rabbenu Saadiah Gaon. With the support of the Almighty, I also will endeavour to refute them in the Second Part, the first chapter of which commences The Propositions, etc." Comp. Wissenschaftliche Zeitschrift für jüdische Theologie, IV., pages 389 and 390.—(Munk.)

ADDENDA ET CORRIGENDA.

Page ix., note 1.—Tales about the birth, youth, learning, fame and skill of Maimonides are found in *Shalsheleth ha-kabbalah* of Ibn Yachyah; also in *Sippurim* of Pascheles (Vol. I.); some will be published by A. Neubauer, in Dr. Roest's Letterbode, from MSS. of the London Beth ha-Midrash, and of the Bodl. Library.

Page xiv.—It cannot be stated with certainty when Maimon and his family left Cordova, whether they were in Cordova when that place was taken by the Almohades, or where they lived between 1148 and 1158. About 1158 Maimonides was probably in Spain; he commenced in that year his Commentary on the Mishnah, in which Spanish words are employed to illustrate his explanations. It may, however, be fairly assumed, unless the contrary be proved, that those who preferred exile and privations to conversion between 1158 and 1168, had adopted a similar course during the previous ten years.

Pages xviii. and xxix.—Ibn Osaibiah appears to have sought to damage the fame of Maimonides. He says that Maimonides had never practised as a physician, while the contrary is repeatedly stated by Maimonides himself.

Page xxiv.—It is noteworthy that Maimonides, on several occasions when enumerating the sources for his decisions in the Mishneh Thorah, omits the *Mechilta*. He mentions only works which, according to his opinion, supplement or explain the Mishnah; the *Mechiltoth* of R. Yishmael and R. Akibah, who lived before Rabbi, were superseded by the Mishnah.

Page xxxii.—Two Latin translations of the Guide are extant: those of Aug. Justinianus (1520) and of Buxtorf (1629); the former is based on the Hebrew Version of Charizi, and is a mere copy of an older Latin translation (comp. J. Perles in Monatschrift, 1875, Jan., p. 399); the latter on that of Ibn Tibbon. Thomas Hyde, chief librarian of the Bodl. Library, proposed (1690, Dec. 10), to publish the original text, with a Latin translation and notes; he prepared a specimen of three pages, but the delegates refused to be at the charge of printing this work.

Page xxxvii., note 8.—Maimon, in his address (*Iggereth ha-nechamah*), comforts his brethren, and exhorts them to seek refuge in the Law and in prayer. The forced outward conversion is not mentioned by Maimon; he only speaks of persecution and oppression. If he had been addressing a community of forced converts he would certainly have given them some advice how to act in order to remain faithful to the Holy Law. It is dated 1476 Sel.=1165 (not 1457 Sel., as in the Hebr. transl. in Lebanon, Vol. VIII.).

ADDENDA ET CORRIGENDA.

Page 1, line 2, Aknin, *loco* Aknim ; page 4, line 23, words, *loco* word ; page 5, note 2, page 202, note 1, *loco* c. lvi., note 5 ; page 7, *et passim*, Mishneh thorah *loco* Mishnah torah.

The quotation, "It is impossible," etc. (page 12), I could not find in any of the printed Midrashim ; it occurs, however, in a Yemen Midrash on Gen. i. 1 (Brit. Mus. MS., Or. 2213 ; and Bodl. Libr. MS. Opp. Add. 124a) ; it runs thus : להגיד כח סוד מעשה בראשית לבשר ודם אי אפשר לפיכך סתם הכת׳ ואמר בראשית ברא אל׳. It may be that the quotations, p. xxii. (ברוך המחזיר אבדה לבעלה), and p. xxxii. (שמרא עביד דבטיל), for which I was unable to give any reference, are found in this or similar Midrashim.

Page 15, line 19, xxv. 11, *loco* xi. 25 ; page 38, note 1, in פניו, *loco* פניו ; page 42, note 2, xliv., *loco* liv. ; page 47, note 3, explanations, *loco* explanation ; page 48, line 22, and ideas, and of, *loco* and of ideas, and ; page 51, note 1, page 52, note 1, *loco* note 3 ; page 52, note 1, page 54, *loco* page 55 ; page 56, line 14, will[2] . . . earth, *loco* will . . . earth[3] ; page 56, note 3, The expression כפי רצונו הקדום, " in accordance with his will," lit., *loco* The expression ; page 61, line 22, servant, *loco* servants ; page 62, line 12, is also, *loco* also ; page 70, note 2, which deserve, *loco* deserve ; page 71, note 1, i., *loco* iv. ; page 77, note 2, " figuratively" always, *loco* "it was figuratively applied " ; page 78, note 4, choisissant, *loco* choisissent ; page 83, line 19, Ez., *loco* Ex.; 100, note 2, II. xix., *loco* xlvii. ; page 101, line 1, not, *loco* is not ; page 140, line 21, והיו, *loco* והיה : page 145, line 7, חיים, *loco* חים ; page 151, line 17, sense. Remarks,[2] *loco* sense.[2] Remarks ; page 168, note 7, xxxii., *loco* xvi. ; page 176, note 2, lxxiii., *loco* lxxii. ; page 186, note 2, " I mean psychical, *loco* I mean " psychical ; page 187, note 1, and, *loco* and nature ; page 189, note 4, הֹרה, *loco* הֹרה ; page 211, note 1. liii., p. 190, *loco* lii. p. 178 ; page 222, note 1, 202, *loco* 201 ; page 257, note 4, 199, *loco* 199, note 1 ; page 264, note 4, III., *loco* II. ; page 267, note 5, 237, *loco* 236 ; page 277, note 2, Mahometan, *loco* Mahomeddan ; page 279, note 6, as according, *loco*, according ; page 282, note 3, pp. 176, *loco* pp. 179 ; page 286, note 3, Method, *loco* Proposition ; page 289, note 3, (contin. from p. 288) ὁμοιῶσαι, συγγενῆ, οὖν, *loco* ὁμοιῶσαι, συγγενῇ. οὔ ; page 290, note 5, הרוח החיוני, *loco*, הרוח חחיוני ; page 306, note 4, ויש " but. . . man," *loco* ויש but . . . man : page 307, note 2, בטלאכה, *loco* הטלאכה ; page 322, note 2, 287, *loco* 284 ; page 331, note 2, In Arabic יסֹפוּ, *loco* יסֹפוּ ; page 347, note 1, ἄπαυστον, *loco* ἄπουστον ; page 348, note 1, אלתכציץ, *loco* אלתכציץ ; page 368, note 1, Comp. Geiger *loco* Comp.

CPSIA information can be obtained
at www.ICGtesting.com
Printed in the USA
BVHW04*0820170818
524832BV00005B/14/P